W9-AFS-879

10.00
B & T

BLACK ACTIVISM

BLACK

ACTIVISM

RACIAL REVOLUTION
IN THE UNITED STATES 1954–1970

Robert H. Brisbane

WINGATE COLLEGE LIBRARY
WINGATE, N. C.

JUDSON PRESS, VALLEY FORGE

BLACK ACTIVISM

Copyright © 1974
Judson Press, Valley Forge, PA 19481

All rights reserved. No part of this publication may be reproduced, stored in a retrieval system, or transmitted in any form or by any means, electronic, mechanical, photocopying, recording, or otherwise, without the prior permission of the copyright owner, except for brief quotations included in a review of the book.

Library of Congress Cataloging in Publication Data

Brisbane, Robert H.
  Black activism. Valley Forge: Judson Press, 1974.

  Bibliography: p. 332 p.
  1. Negroes—History—1964- 2. Negroes—Politics
and suffrage. I. Title.
E185.615.B72   322.4'4'0973   74-2492
ISBN 0-8170-0619-2

E
185
615
B72

Printed in the U.S.A.

Table of Contents

62426

Acknowledgments

More than a decade ago I committed myself to the study of black activist and protest movements in the United States. *The Black Vanguard: Origins of the Negro Social Revolution, 1900–1960*, published in 1970, was the first fruit of this research. The present volume is, in fact, a second installment in the study. I hope to continue the work as least into a third publication. Meanwhile, however, I would like to give thanks to all of those who assisted me in the preparation of this volume. My special appreciation to Mrs. Minnie H. Clayton, archivist in the Martin Luther King, Jr., Center for Social Change; to Mrs. Lillian Lewis and Mr. Julio J. Hernandez of the Trevor Arnett Library of Atlanta University; to the staff of the Lyndon Baines Johnson Library in Austin, Texas; and to those who assisted me in the Mugar Collection in the Library of Boston University.

My thanks also to Professors Gloria Gayles and Rashid Halloway who read the manuscript and offered suggestions for improvement and to Professor Tobe Johnson who made valuable criticism of data going into the book. Nor can I overlook Mrs. Elfa Halloway who laboriously translated my script into type and Miss Nora McNiven who worked up the index. Again also I acknowledge my indebtedness to the Danforth Foundation who through a grant to Morehouse College made it possible for me and others of the faculty to engage in meaningful research, and finally to my wife Kathryn who in this, as in all of my endeavors, has given me unfailing encouragement and inspiration.

FOREWORD

The most eventful and exciting period in the history of black Americans has been the decade and a half following the successful Montgomery bus boycott led by Dr. Martin Luther King, Jr., in 1955. This period has included the height of drama—daring displays of courage, the confrontation of nonviolent warriors and angry mobs, the unleashing of the demands and the deepest desires of a people long shackled by the chains of exploitation and physical repression.

It was in the heart of the Deep South, where oppression by whites was at its worst, that the civil rights movement was born. The Montgomery boycott signaled the beginning of a revolution where black people would rise up and thrust the black movement into world prominence as a liberation struggle. Within a year, forty-two local movements had been organized throughout the South and were waging effective combat with racial segregation.

Young blacks, primarily students, joined the movement in large numbers in 1960, putting their bodies and their lives on the front lines in the sit-in demonstrations against segregated public accommodations facilities. Utilizing the philosophy and techniques of creative, nonviolent direct action, the walls of segregated facilities were destroyed in cities and towns across the South.

These were the events which ushered in the decade and a half of struggle, change, hope, and movement. In small towns, on the farms of sharecroppers, in the urban centers, ordinary people, by exercising their commitment to the human struggle, were transformed into movement leaders and folk heroes. It was an infectious period—one in which it was difficult to remain on the sidelines. An old folk song, born in the labor struggle of Kentucky, was adapted for use in the civil rights movement, and Americans, black and white, were forced to answer its poignant question, "Which side are you on?"

Looking back on the period, we can see that black Americans came

7

a long way, but they still have far to go before reaching the distant goals which were verbalized at the March on Washington, during the bloody struggle for the right to vote in Selma, and in the devastating period of frustration which led to the burning of cities in the latter years of the 1960s. Civil rights laws were passed; the Congress of the United States was forced to take a stand; black people became involved in the political process; and opportunities were created in education, employment, housing, and public accommodations.

Not only an eventful period for blacks, the civil rights movement had an unequaled impact on the nation as a whole. The legitimate aspirations which were voiced, the civil disobedience in the face of immoral laws and regulations, the organizing of a movement for change, the tactics of public demonstrations, the utilization of the mass media to voice demands—all these factors were later incorporated and duplicated by the liberation struggles of women, Chicanos, Puerto Ricans, Indians, youth, farm workers, gay communities, and in the massive organizational efforts of the anti-war movement. Civil rights activists and theorists pioneered the way which led to questioning many a sacred cow in American life, and that questioning led to struggle and change.

Looking back, it is disturbing and even frightening to realize that people today take for granted the conditions and opportunities which they experience and enjoy. Too many people enjoy the fruits of sacrifice and struggle, either not aware of or forgetting the pain which made the present moment possible.

But, more, this lack of awareness is a departure from the sense of urgency which has characterized the civil rights movement. As one movement veteran recently stated, "Those who don't see how far we've come are not likely to care about how far we have to go."

As Executive Director of the Voter Education Project, Inc. (VEP), I have traveled throughout the South and the nation, speaking on black college campuses, in high school gyms, in the urban ghettos, and in the cotton fields. Coming through a period of "black awareness," we find a flood of publications on black history and have witnessed the establishment of Black Studies programs throughout the nation. Young people today are acquiring a knowledge of Benjamin Banneker, Frederick Douglass, W.E.B. Du Bois, Toussaint L'Ouverture, Sojourner Truth, and Denmark Vesey. This education is yet another direct benefit of the civil rights movement, but there is a woeful gap of awareness of contemporary individuals and movements.

How many Americans know the names of contemporary civil rights martyrs, such as Gus Courts, George Lee, Medgar Evers, James Reeb, Vernon Dahmer, Jimmie Lee Jackson, Viola Liuzzo, Lamar Smith, William Moore, Herbert Lee, or James Chaney? How many Americans know of black activists like Ella Baker, Charlie Cobb, Marion Barry, Diane Nash. Slater King, E.D. Nixon, or Rosa Parks?

Dr. Brisbane's comprehensive writings are a major contribution to the black struggle itself. The events which he so carefully chronicles should be firmly embedded in the consciousness of all Americans, and particularly those who would play a role in helping to shape the future. More than a cold, historic narrative, Robert Brisbane's book brings to life the tensions and emotions which charged the air in times of crisis. He retains editorial objectivity while piecing together a view of events which he observed and with which he was closely associated.

In facing the future, I am filled with a sense of hope. As a people, black Americans have come through some stormy periods. In the revolutionary social and political movements which Dr. Brisbane illuminates, there is a message of hope. Perhaps the greatest lesson we have learned is that of the necessity for common struggle. This great truth was best spoken by Frederick Douglass in 1857:

> If there is no struggle, there is no progress. Those who profess to favor freedom and yet deprecate agitation are men who want crops without plowing up the land. They want rain without thunder and lightning. They want the ocean without the roar of its many waters. The struggle may be a moral one, or it may be a physical one, or it may be both moral and physical, but it must be a struggle.
>
> Power concedes nothing without a demand. It never did, and it never will. Men may not get all they pay for in this world, but they must certainly pay for all they get.

The black activism of which Dr. Brisbane writes is not a closed book, an event of the past. Though many would counsel us that the civil rights movement is dead, we have to understand the natural process of evolution and change. We may change battlegrounds; we may abandon organizational structures; we may have lost some of our finest and most creative leaders and spokesmen; but black people continue to be very much involved in that same movement for liberation.

It is my sincere hope that Dr. Brisbane's work will inspire others to become involved and give of themselves to continue the struggle—not for just a month, a season, or a year, but for a lifetime. The goal of black activists is not merely a self-seeking one, but should be a quest for the Beloved Community—an all-encompassing, all-inclusive community of justice, compassion, brotherhood, and peace. By uniting our human resources, through militant and determined struggle, and with the creative use of our talents, I am confident that, one day, we will be able to complete the building of that new world— that Beloved Community which we seek.

JOHN LEWIS
Atlanta, Georgia

September, 1973

CHAPTER 1

Introduction

Protests and protest movements among black people in the United States against the varying forms and degrees of white racism are as old as the nation itself. As a matter of record, these movements first began among free blacks toward the end of the eighteenth century and have continued to ebb and flow for almost two hundred years. Changes in the social and political status of blacks have been reflected in the shifting goals and priorities of these movements, but they are to be regarded nevertheless as recurring phenomena within the American social order.

Between 1795 and 1930 there were four major protest movements among black people in the United States. A fifth period began in 1955 and was clearly coming to an end by 1970. Each of these periods lasted from about fifteen to twenty years with about an equal period of time separating them. The periods were as follows:

The Post-Revolutionary Protest. 1795–1815
The Militant Anti-Slavery Movement. 1831–1850
Post-Reconstruction Separatism and Emigrationism. 1876–1896
The Era of Marcus Garvey. 1916–1930
The Black Revolution. 1955–1970

The Post-Revolutionary Protest. In 1791 the first decennial census of the United States reported a total of 59,000 free blacks in the country. Concentrated largely in the eastern seaboard cities, these people were in the words of one historian "a well-organized, militant and highly-articulate group."[1] For them as well as for the three-quarters of a million blacks in bondage, the period between 1783 and 1790 had been one of rising expectations. They had been aroused and encouraged by the egalitarian ideology of the American Revolution and by the anti-slavery activities in the Northern colonies. They had enlisted by the thousands in the Continental armies, and they had fought in every major engagement in the war.

For a time it appeared that the new nation would respond favorably to the hopes of the free black populace. After the adoption of the Federal Constitution, however, white racism began to reassert itself throughout the land. Far from easing the bonds of chattels as some optimistic freedmen had hoped, this document, to the contrary, made slavery more secure than it had ever been before. Between 1795 and 1810 the condition of freedmen declined precipitously. North or South, no state regarded them as suitable members of the general community. Almost every state barred them from marrying whites, from voting, and from giving evidence in court; no state would make them citizens by legislative act or allow them to join the military. And by its so-called Black Laws of 1804 and 1807 Ohio compelled blacks to leave its jurisdiction. Other Northern states were soon to follow.[2]

In their anguish and shock the free blacks began to mount a protest that was to continue intermittently for two decades. Among the first to be heard was the famed Benjamin Banneker. Banneker bitterly chided his friend and patron Thomas Jefferson as representative of the new white establishment which by 1790 had so quickly forgotten its pious professions of liberty and justice for all. Indeed, almost before the ink was dry on the Federal Constitution and only a few blocks from the hall in which it was written, blacks were to be the victims of a brazen violation of its spirit. In November, 1787, Richard Allen and a number of other blacks were expelled from a white church that had long accepted them as regular worshipers. Allen went on to establish the African Methodist Episcopal Church and to become one of the handful of black leaders during the period.

In 1787 Allen and his friend Absalom Jones organized the Free African Society of Philadelphia. Within a few years, with branches set up in Boston, Newport, Rhode Island, and New York, the Free African Society became in effect the first black protest organization in the nation's history. In petition after petition to state legislatures and even to the Federal Congress blacks protested against excessive and discriminatory poll taxes and against the denial of equal educational opportunities for black children. They complained also against the brutality and assaults and even the murder of blacks on the public thoroughfares.

In sheer desperation some of the more militant blacks began to consider emigration to Africa. Thus, in 1787, eighty blacks in Boston requested sufficient funds from the Massachusetts legislature to enable them to leave this "very disagreeable and disadvantageous land" and return to Africa. Two years later, the Free African Society of Newport suggested to the Free African Society of Philadelphia that an emigration movement to Africa be initiated so that blacks could escape from conditions in the United States.

The leading emigrationist of the period was Paul Cuffe, a wealthy black shipowner of New England. In 1811 Cuffe made an exploratory trip to Sierra Leone and became so enamored of the idea of colonization that in 1815 mostly at his own expense he transported thirty-eight blacks to the African West Coast colony. Later Cuffe remarked that he had received so many applications for the trip that he could have colonized the greater part of Boston. Generally, however, the free blacks were not interested in setting up shop in a distant land. As conditions in the country eased for them with the coming of national prosperity after 1816, their faith in the future was revived. Indeed in 1817, free blacks from all over the eastern seaboard met in a convention in Philadelphia to protest against the "back-to-Africa" plans of the new American Colonization Society.[3]

The Militant Anti-Slavery Movement. If the protest activities of the free blacks during the post-Revolutionary period were rather sporadic and unorganized in nature, the period after 1830 presents a startlingly new picture. For one thing, there were now some 200,000 free blacks in the cities of the Atlantic seaboard. Group consciousness among them had been mounting and black leaders of national stature had emerged. The new modes of protest were to be the mass demonstration and the national convention, both to be characterized by a rising feeling of black nationalism and militancy. Between 1830 and 1835 six great black national conventions or caucuses were held in Philadelphia.[4] Others were held intermittently until 1860. The basic functions of the black convention were the organizing and the channelizing of the black protest. Resolutions were adopted urging the free blacks to boycott all products of slave labor and slave plantations, to ignore the Fourth of July and to fast and pray on the fifth instead, and to collect funds for the support of their brothers who had been forced by Ohio's Black Laws to flee to Canada.

However, the main interest of the black conventions was in the slavery question. Initially the free blacks had been of the belief that "moral suasion" or nonviolent agitation was the best means for bringing about abolition. In this connection they were following the leadership of the predominantly white Anti-Slavery Society. The appeal of David Walker and others for the use of violence was ignored.

WINGATE COLLEGE LIBRARY
WINGATE, N. C.

As the economic and political power of the slave South mounted, however, the blacks became progressively disenchanted with the nonviolent program of William Lloyd Garrison. The so-called "moral suasionists" had stood by, wringing their hands, while free blacks were being kidnapped and sold into slavery and while agents of the slaveholders had seized, chained, and dragged runaways off the streets. Young black militants began demanding an immediate and violent attack on slavery by all blacks, free and slave alike. The young Henry Highland Garnet suggested, for instance, that slaves go to their masters and demand their freedom immediately, then refuse to work if that were denied.[5]

Aside from the mounting evil of slavery, the condition of the 300,000 free blacks was rapidly deteriorating in the North and the South. Not only were an increasing number of them being kidnapped, but also the hostility of the Northern white population toward them was rising. Blacks were being daily insulted, assaulted, and murdered in the towns and cities. With agitation and protest getting them nowhere, black leaders began to despair of any future for black people in the United States. Robert Purvis, a wealthy light-skinned alumnus of Amherst College, spoke for many blacks when he said that to support the government of the United States and the Constitution upon which it is based was to endorse "one of the basest, meanest, most atrocious despotisms that ever saw the face of the sun." Any self-respecting man would look upon this "piebald and rotten Democracy" with "contempt, loathing, and unutterable abhorrence.[6]

By 1850 black nationalism was clearly in the ascendancy among the nation's free blacks. Such black leaders as James T. Holly, James M. Whitfield, H. Ford Douglass, and Samuel Ringgold Ward were becoming separatists or emigrationists or both. Henry Highland Garnet, who once opposed emigrationism, was now one of its staunchest advocates. The leading black nationalist of the period, however, was Dr. Martin Delaney. Delaney was perhaps the first member of the race to refer to black people in America as being "a nation within a nation." In 1852, Delaney privately published a book entitled *The Condition, Elevation, Emigration and Destiny of Colored People in the United States*. The book was designed to promote the founding of a new black nation on the eastern coast of Africa which would be settled by black people from the United States and other parts of the world. Largely through Delaney's efforts a national emigrationist convention was held in Cleveland, Ohio, in

1854. Other such conventions were held in Canada in 1856 and in 1858. In 1859 Delaney traveled for about a year in Africa during which time he concluded treaties with several tribal kings for grants of land upon which to establish a nation for American blacks. They later disowned the treaties.[7]

In spite of the clamor and rhetoric of the militants and nationalists, however, the vast majority of the 500,000 free blacks in the country in 1860 entertained no notion of leaving. Frederick Douglass spoke for them when he said: "The truth is we are here and *here* we are likely to remain. . . . We have grown up with this republic, and I see nothing in her character or even the character of the American people, as yet, which compels the belief that we must leave the United States."[8] The guns at Fort Sumter stopped all talk of separatism and emigration. Before the Civil War was over, almost 200,000 blacks had "rallied to the flag." Among the blacks to be found serving as officers in the Union Army were such former militants and black nationalists as Major Martin Delaney and Captain H. Ford Douglass.

Post-Reconstruction Separatism and Emigrationism. During the early morning of March 11, 1879, a group of 280 weary black migrants stopped briefly in the cold and wintry city of St. Louis, Missouri, on their way to Kansas.[9] During the ensuing weeks some 20,000 additional blacks in torn and tattered raiment with their meager belongings on their backs poured through the St. Louis gateway into the promised land of Kansas. As is the case with most social movements of this kind, both "push" and "pull" influences were at work in the background. The pull influence was principally the highly advertised cheap new land available in Kansas. The push was provided by the terror and the bloodshed of the "counter revolution" in the South.

In 1866, just as after the conclusion of the American Revolution, blacks discovered that rising expectations are seldom realized—for blacks. The great hopes and promises of the Civil War were evaporating in the aftermath of Appomattox, and worse yet, the white South was attempting to reinstitute slavery in everything but name. However, the assertion by historians that the blacks were docile and submissive during this period is a libel on the race. As early as 1865 they began to battle against what to many of them must have seemed a lost cause. Indeed the blacks fought against intimidation and terrorism and for the right to serve on juries and to testify in court, for

scale of the exodus of blacks from the South that had occurred some thirty or forty years earlier. The basic causes of both migrations were the same, with one exception. The shortage of skilled labor in the North brought about by the outbreak of World War I was of decisive importance as a catalyst in the later migration. The prospects of ready employment, better living conditions—freedom—were collectively irresistible. The North was almost universally being depicted as a promised land for blacks. The *Christian Recorder* commented in 1917: "If a million Negroes leave the South for the North and West during the next year, it will be the greatest thing since the Emancipation Proclamation." [14]

For a time—a very short time—the North seemed to live up to the expectations of the migrants. But with the end of World War I the bottom fell out for all. When the defense industries shut down in 1919, tens of thousands of semiliterate, rural-oriented blacks found themselves jobless in the promised land. Economically they were far worse off than they had ever been in Dixie. In terms of living they had merely managed to establish beachheads for future black ghettos in the Northern metropolises. Beyond this the postwar competition with whites for jobs and living space led to the first race riots of this century. The "long bloody summer" of 1919 saw interracial conflicts flare up in a half dozen urban areas at the cost of some four hundred killed and more than one thousand injured.

By 1920 black communities all over the North were seething. Militancy everywhere was on the rise. A new black press that had sprung up during the migration contributed greatly to the unrest. The postwar black protest reached the point where the conventional approaches of organizations such as the NAACP were being rejected as too timid and ineffective. Blacks were now ready for a new flirtation with black nationalism. All that was needed was a demagogue with a program.

When Marcus Garvey came to the United States from the West Indies in 1916, he brought with him the rudimentary plans for the building of a great new black nation on the African continent. To get it launched, he was determined to build black nationalism in the United States into a mighty force. He would teach American blacks to pride themselves in the black identity and to glorify the black experience. Above all, he would get them to cease their futile beating against the solid walls of American white racism and look homeward to Mother Africa. His watchword was to become: "Africa for the

Africans at home and abroad." In 1917, Garvey established his Universal Negro Improvement Association. Within three years there were chapters of the organization in thirty-eight states and six foreign countries. Memberships totaled approximately 300,000, and Garvey counted his personal following at more than two million. His weekly *Negro World* had become the most widely read publication in the nation, if not in the world.

In the end, however, Garvey's brand of black nationalism was to know no more success than that of Dr. Martin Delaney or Bishop Henry McNeal Turner. For one thing, Garvey's schemes were too grandiose and too impractical to have any chance of realization. For another, Garvey managed to stir the ire of the black middle class as had no other black nationalist before him. Finally, black nationalism, no matter how intense or pervasive it may seem to be, is never more than a temporary obsession with black people. The business of day-to-day survival among them has forever been too demanding to allow for more than brief excursions into the realm of fantasy.

For various reasons, with the fadeout of the Garvey movement by 1930, there was to be no major black protest movement in the nation for a quarter of a century. During the decade of the 1930s, the American Communist Party made an all-out attempt to organize blacks and to convert them to its ideology. Given the historic oppression and exploitation of American blacks, the Party considered them to be prime subjects for revolutionary propaganda. But the Communists grievously misjudged the Afro-American. They did not understand that blacks considered their chief problem to be white racism and not American capitalism, and that blacks were interested in joining the system rather than overthrowing it. Moreover, except for periodic flirtations with black nationalism, blacks were among the least ideology-oriented people in the world.

At the other end of the ideological spectrum the NAACP was redoubling its efforts to gain support in the black communities. However, the organization was interested in gaining mass support rather than in building a black mass movement. In its long battle for the rights of the race its chosen arena was the court and not the streets. With its leadership drawn principally from the middle class the organization was dependably system-oriented. It stood four square for orderly, controlled progress, and as such it constituted a main bastion against radicalism within the race.

Blacks during the decade of the 1930s, the years of the Great Depression, were far more interested in economic welfare and jobs than in political and civil rights. The Jobs-for-Negroes Campaign, for instance, gained a good deal of support in the Northern urban areas. Beginning in Detroit in 1933, the movement spread quickly to other midwestern cities and finally to those on the Atlantic seaboard. The basic tactic was the boycott of white businesses, large and small, that operated in black communities while refusing or failing to employ black help on any appreciable scale. The campaign was enthusiastically supported in black communities; and before it petered out in 1936, it managed to put thousands of black employees in retail shops, department stores, public utilities, and public transportation.

On the eve of World War II, the nation's blacks found themselves in a particularly exasperating and unfortunate position. In spite of the acknowledged and widely publicized shortage of labor, defense industries and war contractors adamantly refused to hire either skilled or unskilled blacks or to upgrade the meager number they had taken on. In desperation, blacks in the spring of 1941 decided to resort to direct action. Under the leadership of the redoubtable A. Philip Randolph, blacks were organized into the March-on-Washington campaign, the first black mass protest in some twenty years. The March-on-Washington was short-lived, but it resulted directly in the promulgation by President Franklin D. Roosevelt of Executive Order 8802 which established the Fair Employment Practices Committee. The FEPC did not, of course, end all discrimination against blacks; but before the war had run its course, a greater number of blacks were enjoying a greater measure of economic well-being than ever before in the nation's history.

The need for workers to meet wartime production quotas during World War II opened many new jobs to black people. The war brought about an unprecedented rise in the standard of living for them throughout the country. Many of the gains made during wartime employment were retained after 1945. Tens of thousands of blacks were holding down jobs in the aircraft, electronics, automotive, and chemical industries. In the retail trade blacks were being employed on an increasing scale as salesmen, clerks, bookkeepers, and buyers. The promotion and upgrading of black workers and the recognition of their seniority rights opened the way for them to move into job classifications hitherto closed to nonwhites.

CHAPTER 2

The Impact of the __Brown__ Decision

The period between 1945 and 1955 was a buoyant one for black people in the United States. Indeed, in terms of the optimism, confidence in the future, and sheer excitement among them this was an incomparable decade. The nation as a whole was, of course, involved in the Cold War and was later to be afflicted with the witch-hunt of Senator Joseph McCarthy, but black people were not unduly concerned with these matters. Many areas of employment had opened up to them during World War II, and they looked ahead with great anticipation.

To protect and to improve these gains, the President's Committee on Civil Rights in 1947 recommended the enactment of fair employment legislation at both the federal and the state levels. And while no congressional action was immediately forthcoming, some sixteen states and thirty-six major cities ultimately established fair employment commissions. Of critical importance to black aspirations during this period was the G. I. Bill of Rights. The educational provisions of this legislation made it possible for almost an entire generation of young blacks to obtain education or training that they could not possibly have otherwise afforded. This was of especial importance in view of the fact that education has always been the main vehicle of social mobility among blacks. Another factor contributing to the new mood among black people were the gains that the race was making in the areas of politics and political rights. By the mid-1940s the Northern black vote had become a potential balance of power in national elections.

His appreciation of this fact impelled President Harry Truman to force the Democratic Convention in 1948 to adopt a strong civil rights position which resulted in the alienation and defection of the Southern bloc. Truman continued his pursuit of the black vote during the campaign of 1948 with the issuance of two executive orders. With one of these he ordered segregation and discrimination abolished in the armed services, and with the other he desegregated all departments and agencies in the federal government. The payoff for Truman came with the more than 80 percent of the black vote he received during the election of 1948. In the South, blacks looked confidently to a future of expanded and broadened activity in the political life of the region. The *Smith* v. *Allwright* decision of 1944, in abolishing the white primary laws of the South, had restored the ballot to the blacks after a disfranchisement of almost a half century. Blacks began to use their new power almost immediately to effectuate changes in their social, political, and economic positions.

In the area of civil rights, however, blacks made the great leap forward during this decade. For one thing, the NAACP was winning its fight to invalidate the odious separate-but-equal doctrine which was the legal foundation of apartheid in the United States. In 1947, the major hotels in Washington, D.C., began to operate on a desegregated basis with motion-picture houses, theaters, and other places of public entertainment following suit. In 1953 the United States Supreme Court, basing its decision on an 1872 statute, ordered all restaurants in the nation's capital to serve all patrons regardless of race, creed, or color. As of 1948 the Court had ruled that restrictive covenants could not be enforced in the courts of the land, and in 1950 it ruled that segregation of blacks in dining cars on interstate railroads was an undue burden on interstate commerce. Five years later, the Interstate Commerce Commission ruled that *all* racial segregation on interstate trains and buses, waiting rooms, and terminals must end by January, 1956.

In the meanwhile, the NAACP was conducting a successful campaign to compel Southern states to drop their barriers against the admission of black students to their institutions of higher learning. Between 1948 and 1952 state universities and professional schools in Delaware, Kentucky, Tennessee, Oklahoma, Missouri, North Carolina, and Louisiana were ordered by the federal courts to admit blacks on a nonsegregated basis. By far the most important of these cases was the one involving Texas. In its ruling in *Sweatt* v. *Texas,* the Court virtually killed the separate-but-equal doctrine. All that now remained was its interment and this, in due course, would be accomplished by *Brown* v. *Board of Education* of Topeka. By mid-1953 more than fifteen hundred blacks were attending graduate and professional schools in the deep South and border states.

Of crucial importance to racial progress during the decade was the existence òf a sympathetic and supportive social milieu. This was one of the few periods in American history clearly exhibiting a low racist profile. White civic and social organizations for the first time ever interested themselves in the improvement and betterment of race relations in their communities. Major groups, such as the American Friends Service Committee and the Anti-Defamation League of B'Nai B'rith, published reports and studies dealing with race relations and set up programs to improve intergroup relations. And perhaps under directions from the Vatican, Roman Catholic prelates called for the elimination of discrimination and segregation from American life.

It is probable that at no time in the history of the country did black people have greater faith in the promise, the viability, and the efficacy of American democracy. Walter F. White, then executive director of the NAACP, noted what he considered to be the final "disappearance from the American scene of 'nationalist' movements among Negroes such as the Marcus Garvey Universal Negro Improvement Association." White felt that the black American rejected such movements because of an awareness that "he was not a hyphenated American, but more truly than most, one whose roots were inextricably planted in American soil." "As the American Negro sees it," said White, "American democracy is going forward." [1] These observations were made in 1955 and White was to pass from the scene during the same year. He was never to know, therefore, that he was in effect pronouncing the benediction on an era and that not for more than a full generation would any black leader in the United States publicly extol the virtues of American democracy.

The *Brown* case marked the end of the era. In its decision in the case the United States Supreme Court invalidated statutes in seventeen states that compelled school segregation by law and those in four other states and the District of Columbia that permitted it. Specifically, the decision was concerned only with the type of segregation complained against in the five cases before it. The principle and practice of separate-but-equal was invalidated only so far as it extended to tax-supported educational facilities, and nothing else. An overwhelming number of black people in the country, however, were oblivious to the limitations and specifications of the decision. To many it was a second Emancipation Proclamation—a second deliverance. After almost a century of struggle against the evils of segregation, discrimination, and racism in general, freedom had been handed down by a benign and merciful high court of justice. Black people wept and prayed and shouted hallelujah in innumerable Southern towns and cities.

To be sure, the victorious lawyers of the NAACP warned against excessive and unjustified exuberance. This advice, however, was to go largely unheeded. The black *Chicago Defender* euphorically declared on May 29:

> Neither the atom bomb nor the hydrogen bomb will ever be as meaningful to our democracy as the unanimous decision of the Supreme Court that racial segregation violates the spirit and the letter of our Constitution. This means the beginning of the end of the dual society in American life and the system of segregation which supported it.

And so it went for almost a year following that fateful day, May 17, 1954. Indeed, in spite of the quickly mounting Southern white opposition to the *Brown* decision, blacks did not really begin to sober up until the full meaning of the Court's second *Brown* decision began to dawn upon them.

In the second decision (May 31, 1955) the Court modified its 1954 decree with the concession that local situations required locally devised programs to comply with the law. It directed Federal District Courts to enforce the decision with "all deliberate speed." Blacks then began to realize that there would not be instant desegregation of the schools nor of anything else and that the white South intended to use the command "all deliberate speed" to postpone and delay compliance as long as humanly possible.

The truth of the matter was that the country was about to witness a revival of white racism in the deep South reminiscent of the worst days of Reconstruction. Segregation was an ancient and hallowed institution in the region and the *Brown* decision was viewed as an unwarranted almost immoral attack upon it by a clique of high-handed "Nigger-loving" Northerners. It would be opposed by all of the resources at the command of the white South. As one Southern newspaper put it: "There are only two sides in the Southern fight— those who want to maintain the Southern way of life and those who want to mix the races."[2] On June 14, just two weeks after the first *Brown* decision was handed down, a group of fourteen white men met in Indianola, Mississippi, to discuss their response to the Supreme Court decision. This was the initial meeting of the group that subsequently adopted the name White Citizens' Council.

The idea was to spread like wildfire among segregationists. Dozens of chapters of the Council sprang up in all deep South and border states. By 1957 there was a sufficient number of them to merit the formation of an Association of Citizens' Councils. In addition to the Councils, a number of other segregationist associations appeared. Among these were the States Rights Councils, the National Association for the Advancement of White People, Southern Gentlemen, Inc., the Pro-Southerners, and the Tennessee Society to Maintain Segregation. On December 29, 1955, Senator James O. Eastland of Mississippi brought all of these organizations into an interstate group known as the Federation for Constitutional Government. Its avowed purpose was the creation of a "united movement for the preservation of America under a constitutional form of government."[3] The advisory and executive committees of the new organization listed some forty politicians who were holding either state or federal offices. Many of these same people had been leaders in the so-called Dixiecrat party of 1948.

In keeping with its determination to mount a massive resistance against the *Brown* decision, the Federation promulgated a document commonly known as the *Southern Manifesto* which it presented to the U.S. Congress on March 12, 1956. Among other things, the Manifesto declared that "Without regard to the consent of the governed, outside agitators are threatening immediate and revolutionary changes in our public-school systems." It commended the "motives of those States which have declared the intention to resist forced integration by any lawful means."[4] The Manifesto required no congressional action, and as such it had no legal standing. It was signed by 101 Southern members of Congress, among whom some of the more prominent were: William Fulbright, Richard B. Russell, Strom Thurmond, Allen J. Ellender, Harry F. Byrd, Sam J. Ervin, and John L. McClellan. Not all of the congressmen from the South could be persuaded or browbeaten into signing the Manifesto. However, of three North Carolina congressmen who refused to sign it, two were defeated in the Democratic primary in the following May.

Beyond the Manifesto the Southern states began devising more effective means of scuttling desegregation. These were to include the following:

1. Interposition: state legislative action nullifying the *Brown* decision and any federal action to implement it.
2. Threat of or the actual mass closure of public school systems.

3. Economic pressure upon black and white advocates of desegregation.
4. The substitution of private schools in place of the public school system.
5. Protracted litigation to stall and delay court orders to desegregate.
6. The use of violence and intimidation to bar blacks from actually attending white schools.

The doctrine of interposition was a revival of the theories of Thomas Jefferson and James Madison as put forward in their "Kentucky and Virginia Resolutions" of 1798. The doctrine claimed for the states, individually or collectively, the right to reject or to nullify any federal law, ruling, or action which they may deem not to be in keeping with either the letter or the spirit of the Constitution. As a possible weapon against desegregation, the use of interposition was first suggested by an elderly Virginia country lawyer by the name of William Olds. Olds was later rewarded for his contribution by being appointed a circuit court judge. The *Richmond News Leader* quickly seized the idea and gave it tremendous promotion.[5] The result was that early in February, 1956, the Virginia General Assembly solemnly adopted the historic doctrine of interposition. During the next eighteen months seven other Southern states—Alabama, Georgia, South Carolina, Florida, Louisiana, Mississippi, and Arkansas—followed suit. This was the end of such actions. None of the states followed up, as South Carolina had done in 1832, with machinery to enforce its declarations. The interposition resolutions were forwarded to each member of the U. S. Supreme Court and the Congress and, thereafter, languished in the neglected files.

Along with their interposition resolutions, the Southern state legislatures were also laying the groundwork for the closing of the school systems if this appeared to be the only alternative to desegregation. The proposals put forward in the several states differed in detail, but in general they all included the following fundamentals:

1. The withholding of state funds from schools which accepted students of both races because of court orders or otherwise.
2. Plenary powers to be given local school boards and administrators with regard to the assignment and transfer of students.
3. The use of the "police powers" of the state in enforcing racial

separation on the grounds of protecting the health, morals, peace, and order of individual communities.

In every case legislative proposals to close the schools were put before the state electorate in the form of a referendum, and in every case the white community by its vote indicated a determination to resist desegregation even to the point of abolishing public education.

By 1956 some seven Southern states had thus gone on record, but only in one of these was the tragedy of school closure to be carried to the bitter end. Beginning in 1958 the public school systems in four Virginia counties and metropolitan areas were closed down to prevent desegregation, the most widely known of these being that of Prince Edward County.[6] However, the private school and scholarship plans sponsored by the state as substitutes proved so costly, chaotic, and shoddy that Virginia was on the way to abandoning them even before the state and federal courts ordered her to restore the public school system. The meaning of the Virginia experience was not lost to the other Southern states. In Georgia, Governor Ellis Arnall announced that he would not close the schools to prevent integration. Other Georgia politicians hurriedly endorsed Arnall's pronouncement. In Florida the state legislature called off a runaway session, thereby abandoning thirty-two pieces of anti-integration legislation. By 1960 virtually all Southern states had discarded plans to close the schools as a means of preventing desegregation. However, the battle was to be continued by other means.

In a large number of areas throughout the South the White Citizens' Councils began to subject local black and white advocates of desegregation to severe and sometimes disastrous economic reprisals. In July, 1954, the Councils in Mississippi thus explained the policy: "We can accomplish our purposes largely with economic pressure in dealing with members of the Negro race who are not co-operating, and with members of the white race who fail to co-operate we can apply social and political pressure."[7] In due time blacks were fired or laid off from their jobs, bank loans were refused, and ordinary credit was denied. In addition, automobile insurance policies were canceled and black tenant farmers were forbidden by their employers to use the services of black professionals and businessmen who were known to advocate integration.[8]

Whites who were known to "think wrong" on segregation were driven into bankruptcy if not out of town. In a number of instances blacks retaliated by mounting counter boycotts and by organizing

self-help programs in black communities. The NAACP was instrumental in a number of instances in raising funds for loans to
blacks who had become financially distressed by the normal credit. In
Memphis, Tennessee, the NAACP, along with several Northern labor
unions, deposited more than $200,000 in the Tri-State Bank for loans
to black victims of economic reprisals. This move, of course, was one
more strike against the NAACP in the eyes of its opponents. The
White Citizens' Councils had long identified the Association as the
white South's number one enemy. Thus a leading Alabama politician
spoke for many a white Southerner when he charged that the main
goal of the NAACP was "to open the bedroom doors of our white
women to the Negro men."[9] Even before the *Brown* decision
individual Southern states had begun to harass the Association with
an unending series of legislative, administrative, and judicial
entanglements.

The South Carolina legislature in 1956 forbade the employment of
any member of the NAACP by any agency of the state or its political
subdivisions including school districts. Some forty pages of evidence
purporting to show that the Association was subversive were entered
into the *Congressional Record* by a congressman from Arkansas.
Officials in Texas charged the NAACP with lobbying, barratry, and
failure to pay taxes as a profit-making organization. Both Alabama
and Louisiana enjoined the NAACP from operating within their
jurisdictions as a penalty for refusing to make public its membership
list. Ultimately, all of the penalties imposed on the organization were
reversed in the federal courts, but the campaign to put it out of
business in the Southern states was to continue until its activities were
overshadowed by the far more radical black organizations of the
1960s.

A few months after the *Brown* decision was handed down, Senator
James Eastland made the comment: "I predict this decision will bring
on a century of litigation."[10] During the next several years it appeared
that Eastland knew whereof he spoke. The Southern states were
successfully involving black desegregationists in endless administrative red tape supplemented by long and costly litigation in
the state and federal courts. The device they were employing to such
effect was the so-called pupil-placement plan. The concept was first
put forward in the Mississippi legislature in 1954, just prior to the
Brown decision. It was quickly adopted by eight other Southern
states. Under the plan, school officials were authorized to designate

the school that each pupil was to attend, the assignment being based upon such conditions as the health and welfare of the student in question and of the other students, the type of curriculum offered, availability of transportation, and other relevant factors. Segregationists were, of course, invoking the time-honored power of school boards to assign pupils under their jurisdictions. They were relying also upon the rule which requires petitioners to exhaust administrative remedies before relief can be granted by the courts.

There was also the conviction among the segregationists that differences between black and white children were great enough to justify considerable separation or segregation if they were classified along strict sociological, psychological, educational, and aptitudinal lines. This assumption was one of the reasons that none of the pupil-placement laws mentioned race. Another was the attitude of the federal courts. A federal court invalidated the Virginia pupil-placement plan because race was one of the factors to be considered in pupil assignments. On the other hand, a North Carolina plan was approved because race was not a factor. On the whole, the pupil-placement plan had the result intended by its originators. Black parents' objections to the assignments of their children were hamstrung and tied up in school-board red tape for months and even years. After this, if justice had still been denied, there were the courts, with the process still likely to be interminable. Thus in 1960 NAACP officials complained:

> Negro children denied their rights are indeed injured parties, but to require them to bear the whole burden of seeking redress of their injury through costly and prolonged litigation, to compete against the massive weight of official state opposition, is to deny justice.[11]

During the five-year period following the *Brown* decision some 226 suits were filed in state and federal courts involving pupil-placement plans and other desegregation issues. Every state in the South was involved in some of this litigation.

For more than a century prior to the *Brown* decision, the country listened to the racist rhetoric and demagoguery of white Southern politicians and public officials. Much of this had been dismissed as a legacy of Reconstruction or a ritualistic requirement of Southern politics. After 1954, however, the new threats of violence against blacks and meddling Yankees could no longer be taken lightly. In their passion to rally and stiffen the opposition to desegregation, the White Citizens' Councils and other segregationist groups were in fact encouraging the employment of any means necessary to do the job. They were proceeding consciously and deliberately to establish a climate of lynch law and repression in the South. Of course, desegregation was the main target, but once the ancient hatreds of the region were rekindled, any transgression, real or imagined, brought on an assault on or even the murder of a black man or woman.

Thus, in Belzoni, Mississippi, on May 7, 1955, the Reverend George W. Lee was shot and killed in his car for refusing under pressure to take his name off the voter registration list. And on August 13, a sixty-three-year-old election campaign worker, Lamar Smith of Brookhaven, Mississippi, was gunned down in broad daylight in front of the courthouse after having worked to get the black vote out for an impending primary election. The most shocking of all such incidents, however, was the wanton murder of a fourteen-year-old black boy in Money, Mississippi. On the morning of August 28, 1955, the badly mutilated body of Emmett L. Till was fished out of a local river. The boy had come from Chicago to visit with relatives in Mississippi. Two white men, J. W. Milam and Roy Bryant, admitted assaulting Till for allegedly having whistled at Bryant's wife. The murder drew national and even international attention.

In other Southern states the campaign of violence against blacks was centered more directly on keeping them from physically desegregating the public schools, colleges, and universities. In October, 1955, the United States Supreme Court ordered the University of Alabama to admit two black students, Autherine Lucy and Mrs. Polly Ann Myers Hudson, for the term beginning February, 1956. Mrs. Hudson was subsequently refused admission because of her marital status, but Miss Lucy successfully completed registration on February 1. On February 3 and 4 she attended classes without molestation and with but minor harassment. Over the weekend, however, the situation underwent a drastic change. Pro-segregationists and other extremists had come into Tuscaloosa from as far away as Birmingham and Mississippi to support the local racists. On Monday, February 6, Miss Lucy was able to evade a mob on the campus and step into her first class unnoticed. By mid-morning, however, the mob had swelled to about three hundred, and as Miss Lucy was being escorted to her second class by the dean and an assistant to the president, the mob screamed epithets and smashed the windshield and rear window of the dean's car.

By noon the crowd, then consisting of far more outsiders than students, had grown to more than one thousand. With her life clearly in jeopardy Miss Lucy remained in Groves Hall on the campus until 1:15 P.M. when the state police hustled her to an automobile where she lay on the floor as the vehicle sped off the campus. The board of trustees of the university met later that night and voted to exclude Miss Lucy until further notice to prevent a recurrence of violence on the campus. On March 5, Miss Lucy was permanently expelled by the board for having charged university officials with complicity in the ugly events of February 6. This was the end of the matter. But whether the university was or was not guilty as alleged by Miss Lucy, there was no question but that the mob action had been planned. The Alabama Council on Human Relations reported sometime later that the demonstrations were "the result of approximately two weeks of preparation." The segregationists were leaving nothing to chance. By the beginning of 1957 it became clearly apparent that no attempt at desegregation anywhere in the South stood much of a chance without the assistance of local and state police, the National Guard, and possibly the United States Army.

In fact, in Arkansas the state police and the National Guard were used to *prevent* desegregation rather than to assist it. When a federal court ordered Little Rock's Central High School to admit nine black pupils, Governor Orval Faubus declared that he could not and would not comply and that if an attempt at desegregation was made over his objections, blood would run in the city's streets. On the first day of school in September, 1957, however, eight of the nine black students showed up at Central High School. They were unceremoniously turned back by the Arkansas National Guard. The ninth black student, a girl, who came alone because of a mix-up in plans, was almost lynched by a frenzied mob of white women screaming taunts. When the troopers made no effort to block the mob as it moved in on the young black girl, she was finally helped onto a bus by a *New York Times* reporter. After the girl had safely boarded the bus, one of the women urged the mob to attack the reporter. A couple of days later a federal court issued an injunction ordering Faubus not to interfere with desegregation. The governor responded by withdrawing the National Guard from Little Rock entirely. This was a willful and deliberate exposure of the city to the pleasure of the mob.

On the morning of September 23 another attempt at integrating Central High School was made. This time the nine black children were spirited into the school through a side door and registered.

Within minutes the mob which had been maintaining a vigilance on the school grounds discovered that the black children were inside. Pandemonium broke loose. Shortly before noon all classes were suspended and the black children were sent home. The integration attempt had lasted all of three hours and thirteen minutes. The mob, now numbering more than a thousand, turned its fury on the city, beating up any blacks whom they could corner. In answer to a request of the mayor of Little Rock for assistance, President Eisenhower later that day federalized the entire ten-thousand-man Arkansas National Guard. And on September 24 with federal troops as escorts, the nine black children went unmolested through the main entrance of Central High School. For several weeks thereafter they continued to be escorted to and from school by the military. They were harassed, kicked, threatened, and insulted, but they steadfastly obeyed the admonition of the school authorities that they not retaliate verbally or physically to any provocation.

The sorry events in Little Rock were later duplicated, if on a smaller scale, in such other Southern towns as Clinton and Nashville, Tennessee; Charlotte, North Carolina; and Dallas, Texas. In each place there was the shameful, shoddy spectacle of little black children having to face the insults, taunts, obscenities, and physical violence of hysterical white women, bigots, and local hoodlums, all in the name of white supremacy. But there was to be no turning back on the part of the blacks. In their supreme courage and fortitude they constituted the vanguard of an unprecedented black challenge to the status quo— a challenge that was as truly revolutionary as any mass confrontation with privilege, repression, and injustice. What has come to be known as the Black Revolution, therefore, had its beginnings on the public school grounds of the towns and cities of the deep South and border states—places where the first black skulls were cracked and where the first black blood was spilled. Its first heroes were spartan little black children and their intrepid parents, many of whom could never be sure that they would live to witness the next sunrise.

Toward the end of 1955, the spirit of rebellion and resistance was spreading among black people in every corner of the South. The movement, however, was unorganized, without focus and utterly devoid of effective, recognized leadership. There was the growing determination on the part of the younger blacks to meet violence with violence, to retaliate in kind against the white racists and pro-segregationists. All over the black community blacks were oiling their pistols, sharpening their switchblades, and building up an arsenal of pipes, baseball bats, and spiked sticks. This was the direction in which the blacks were heading until Martin Luther King was catapulted into the position of leadership in Montgomery in December, 1955. King thereafter pointed the incipient black rebellion in a new direction; he equipped it with a moral armament which confounded the bigots; and he converted it ultimately into a full-blown black revolt against any and all forms of racism in the United States.

Martin Luther King, Jr., was born in Atlanta, Georgia, on January 15, 1929. He was both the son and the grandson of Baptist preachers, and he was destined to follow the same calling. In 1944 King enrolled at Morehouse College in Atlanta and during his junior year he was ordained as a Baptist minister. After graduating from Morehouse in 1948, King entered Crozer Theological Seminary to work toward his Bachelor of Divinity degree. His scholastic record at the seminary was outstanding. In addition to his selection as valedictorian of his class, he was awarded two prizes, one carrying a stipend of $1,200. In June, 1953, King married Coretta Scott of Perry County, Alabama, in a ceremony performed by his father, the Reverend Martin Luther King, Sr. King was then pursuing his doctoral degree at Boston University. At the beginning of 1954, with a brilliant academic record behind him, there were a number of career options open to King. He could have been dean of one college, a professor in another, or a pastor in one of two churches—all in the North. In the end, however, it was the South that exerted the strongest pull on the young preacher. He had been inculcated by his father and his colleagues with a sense of mission to blacks in the region. Thus, in January, 1954, he answered the call to take up the pastorate in the Dexter Avenue Baptist Church in Montgomery, Alabama.

The arrest of Mrs. Rosa Parks on December 1, 1955, for refusing to yield her seat to a white passenger was simply the latest in a long line of ugly transgressions committed by the Montgomery City Line bus drivers against black passengers. Earlier during the year a fifteen-year-old black girl was handcuffed and jailed for refusing to give up her seat to a white passenger. The black community appointed a committee, which included Rev. Martin Luther King, to lodge a complaint against the driver. Infractions of segregation requirements in public accommodations were criminal offenses and were treated as such. During 1955 five women and two children were jailed for such offenses and one man was shot to death for ignoring a bus driver's orders. The arrest of Mrs. Parks finally exhausted the patience of the black community. On the night of her arrest a friend of Mrs. Parks, E. D. Nixon, casually suggested to his wife that "every Negro in town should stay off the buses for one day in protest for Mrs. Parks' arrest." [12] During the next morning Nixon discussed his idea over the telephone with the Reverend Ralph D. Abernathy, pastor of the First Baptist Church. Abernathy was in full agreement. Nixon then phoned the Reverend Mr. King who also concurred in the idea. A meeting of these three plus several other local blacks was held at the Dexter Avenue Church that evening. After an animated discussion by the group present, it was agreed that a one-day boycott of all city buses should be observed by blacks on Monday, December 5.

Leaflets to this effect were distributed throughout the black community. At a planning and strategy session among the leaders on Monday afternoon, Abernathy proposed the name of Montgomery Improvement Association (MIA) for the new movement. Martin Luther King was declared president by acclamation. The one-day boycott in the meanwhile had been almost 100 percent successful. Carl Rowan reports that "some three hundred Negro-owned automobiles—old clunks fresh from used-car lots and new family chariots'" were kept at the task of transporting blacks about the city.[13] Later Monday night a mass meeting was held at the Holt Street Baptist Church to give the black community a progress report on the boycott and to hear from the young leader of the new movement. In his talk at the meeting King unveiled the fundamentals of a philosophy that would guide him unswervingly for the rest of his career:

> Our actions must be guided by the deepest principles of our Christian faith. Love must be our regulating ideal. Once again we must hear the words of Jesus echoing across the centuries: "Love your enemies, bless them that curse you, and pray for them that despitefully use you." If we fail to do this our protest will end up as a meaningless drama on the stage of history, and its memory will be shrouded with the ugly garments of shame.[14]

It was voted at the meeting to extend the boycott until such time as the city and the bus line agreed to the following conditions: more courteous treatment of black passengers; seating on a first come, first served basis with blacks continuing to fill the bus from the rear and whites from the front; and employment of black bus drivers on runs in the predominantly black neighborhoods.

A few days later the Montgomery Improvement Association took out a paid advertisement in the daily press which read in part as follows:

> At no time have the participants of this movement advocated or anticipated violence. We stand willing and ready to report and give any assistance in exposing persons who resort to violence. This is a movement of passive resistance, depending on moral and spiritual forces. We, the oppressed, have no hate in our hearts for the oppressors, but we are, nevertheless, determined to resist until the cause of justice triumphs.[15]

This message was a direct reflection of King's emerging philosophy. He said: "I had come to see early that the Christian doctrine of love operating through the Gandhian method of nonviolence was one of the most potent weapons available to the Negro in his struggle for freedom."[16] For almost a decade nonviolence was to be the watchword of the black protest as it spread throughout the United States. In the South with its tradition of swift and terrible retaliation upon blacks nonviolence appeared to be the soundest tactic to pursue.

At the end of the first week of the boycott, negotiations were begun between the leaders of the MIA on the one hand and the officials of the city and spokesmen for the bus company on the other. These were to continue for several weeks; but as time passed, it became increasingly clear that they were a waste of time. The black leaders could not call off the boycott without concessions, no matter how small. For their part, the city and the bus company officials were standing firm in an anticipation of an early collapse of the boycott. Toward the end of December the negotiations were called off by common agreement. As the boycott continued, even becoming more effective, the city administration decided to adopt a "get-tough policy." Black vehicle operators were arrested on vague charges, and blacks standing on corners waiting for rides were arrested for vagrancy or hitchhiking. King himself was jailed for speeding—going 30 miles an hour in a 25-mile-an-hour zone. He paid the fine. In time, many drivers began dropping out of the car pool, fearing loss of their operator's licenses and insurance. The result was that more and more of the 17,500 blacks who were staying off the buses were daily walking to and from their places of employment.

On January 30, while he was attending a meeting at the Reverend Ralph Abernathy's church, a bomb was thrown on the porch of King's home. The missile did minimal damage. When Mrs. King answered the telephone, amid smoke and splintered glass, a female voice said: "Yes, I did it. And I'm just sorry I didn't kill all you bastards."[17] Such incidents, however, did not have the effects intended either upon King or upon the movement as a whole. As a matter of fact, they merely increased the determination of the black community to carry on. As the boycott moved into its third month, the White Citizens' Councils worked to rally the white community. Thus some twelve thousand whites were gathered at a meeting on February 10 to listen to the anti-Negro tirades of Senator James Eastland. A leaflet circulated among the crowd read in part:

> In every stage of the bus boycott we have been oppressed and degraded because of black, slimy, juicy, unbearably stinking niggers. The conduct should not be dwelt upon because behind them they have an ancestral background of Pygmies, Head hunters and snot suckers. . . .
> If we don't stop helping those African flesh eaters, we will soon wake up and find Reverend King in the white house.[18]

By the early spring of 1956 the boycott was beginning to have a punishing effect on the city's economy. During the first three months alone the downtown stores suffered a loss of more than three million dollars in sales. The boycott of the buses had in effect become a boycott of the city's retail establishments. Worried businessmen met with officials of the MIA on two separate occasions seeking to find a way out of the impasse. With a loss of more than seven thousand dollars a day the officials of the near-bankrupt bus line were making it clear that they were ready to grant the demands of the black community. But city and county officials remained adamant. On February 13 Circuit Judge Eugene Carter ordered a grand jury to investigate the MIA, the boycott, and all related matters in order to determine what, if any, state or local laws were being violated. Some ten days later, the grand jury returned indictments against 115 people, 20 of whom were members of the clergy. They were all charged with violating a 1921 law making it a misdemeanor to conspire without a just cause or legal excuse to hinder any company in its conduct of business. Some 90 of the defendants, including the Reverend Martin Luther King, were rounded up, fingerprinted, and released upon $300 bail.

At court on March 19 the defendants demanded and were granted separate trials. King's case was the first to be heard. He was accused of having organized the MIA for the purpose of unjustly boycotting the bus company and forcing upon it the illegal demands of the black community. Represented by eight attorneys, King pled that the protest (he disclaimed boycott) was spontaneous and arose from a just cause. At the end of four days of testimony and legal fencing Judge Carter announced that he was ruling King guilty, but that he was imposing only half the possible penalty because of King's insistence that his followers observe a policy of nonviolence. However, the fine and the court costs of $500 were converted into 386 days in jail when King announced that he was going to appeal. He was released on a bond of $1,000, and the cases of the 89 others were continued pending appeal.

National as well as international attention was now being focused on the Montgomery boycott and the sterling leadership of Martin Luther King. Often overlooked in all of the excitement, however, was the fact that the basic issue involved was segregation in intrastate commerce and, secondly, that the fight against this injustice had been initiated (though less dramatically) some two years prior to Montgomery. Indeed, in 1953 the NAACP went to court on behalf of Mrs. Sarah Mae Fleming who was suing the South Carolina Gas and Electric Company for $25,000 in damages for having been forced off a bus owned and operated by that company. On July 1, 1955, exactly five months before Mrs. Parks' arrest in Montgomery, a United States Circuit Court ruled in the Fleming case that segregation on intrastate buses violated the Constitution of the United States. When the decision was affirmed by the United States Supreme Court on April 23, 1956, bus companies throughout the South moved to comply. The Montgomery City Line, seeing a chance of "getting off the hook," made ready to desegregate.

The officials of the city of Montgomery, however, had other thoughts on the matter. They flatly refused to recognize the decision as applying in their case and peremptorily ordered the bus company to hold the line on segregation. When the company refused, the city turned to Judge Walter B. Jones who ruled that the decision did not apply and that the bus company would have to stay in line. As the cradle of the Old Confederacy, Montgomery was apparently determined to fight to the bitter end. Mayor W. A. Gayle thus spoke for the city:

> Negro leaders have forced the bus boycott into a campaign between whether the social fabric of our community will continue to exist or will be destroyed by a group of Negro radicals. . . . This is not a matter of a bus boycott. It is a matter of a community relationship.[19]

It was also a state matter, for on June 5, when a three-judge federal court ruled that segregation on the bus lines of Montgomery was unconstitutional, Alabama state attorneys made ready to carry the issue all the way back to the United States Supreme Court.

In the meanwhile King was emerging from the struggle as a figure of national and international prominence. At the age of twenty-seven he was already being included in Afro-American hagiology alongside such legendary figures as Frederick Douglass, Booker T. Washington, and William E. B. Du Bois. As a black Baptist preacher King was not devoid of the messianic touch. His voice was rich and his delivery was paced with the cadence so characteristic of great black speakers. Beyond all of this, King was a proud, patient, intelligent, and supremely courageous man. His rise to fame was not an accident, but his presence in Montgomery in December, 1955, was fortuitous. He happened to be the right black man in the right place at the right time. By the summer of 1956 he was being literally worshiped by the black rank and file in both North and South. And if the traditional black leadership was somewhat less enthusiastic about him, it was, nonetheless, receptive. During the month of June, King addressed the annual convention of the NAACP telling of the trials and tribulations of the boycott.

By the midsummer of 1956 the Montgomery bus boycott had become the most popular cause in the United States. In New York City a gigantic freedom rally was held for the benefit of the MIA. In attendance were such personalities as Eleanor Roosevelt, Sammy Davis, Congressman Adam Clayton Powell, A. Philip Randolph, and Tallulah Bankhead. The money from this affair, plus the other thousands of dollars which were pouring into the headquarters of the MIA, was a source of worry as well as of elation for some of the leaders of the movement, for, although the organization, at least for the time being, was financially secure, it had never adopted orthodox bookkeeping procedures. The fact was that the MIA was plainly becoming vulnerable to charges of waste and excessive and un-warranted expenditure of the contributions made to it. On June 11 such a charge was made by the Reverend U. J. Fields, pastor of the Bell Street Baptist Church. Fields said he was resigning from his post as recording secretary of MIA because its officials were "misusing money sent from all over the nation" and were using it "for their own purposes." He complained further that the members of the executive board were "egotistical and interested in perpetuating themselves." [20] Almost immediately Fields' charges were being sent over the wires by the nation's news media.

Contacted in California where he was on a brief vacation with his wife, King caught the next plane back to Montgomery. In the meanwhile, people in the community were already denouncing Fields and calling him a "Black Judas." The congregation of the Bell Street Baptist Church met and unceremoniously voted him out as pastor. Upon King's return, Fields called him and set up a meeting with him in the offices of the Dexter Avenue Church. Fields was repentant and ashamed. He told King: "I want you to know that I was not referring to you in my accusations. I have always had the greatest respect for your integrity, and I still do. But there are some members of the MIA board that I don't care for at all. We never could get along." [21] As the conversation between the two continued, it developed that Fields had become vindictive because of his failure to be reelected to the executive board of the organization. Satisfied that this was all there was to the matter, King brought Fields before a mass meeting that same evening and asked the crowd to forgive him. "Will we be like the unforgiving elder brother, or will we, in the spirit of Christ, follow the example of the loving and forgiving father?" [22] Fields himself asked for forgiveness assuring the crowd that he had no evidence of any wrongdoing by MIA officials. When he turned to leave, in obvious contrition, the crowd burst into applause.

Montgomery city officials had been gleefully watching the Fields incident in anticipation of the long-hoped-for collapse of the movement. When the matter was so quickly and decisively cleared up, they began to resort to last ditch stratagems. White insurance companies began canceling liability insurance on the MIA's station wagons with the result that the organization had to go all the way to Lloyds of London and pay higher premiums for the coverage. The MIA had previously placed its collision insurance with black companies in Atlanta, and to avoid seizure of its funds, it had placed them out of the state in the black Citizens Trust Company of Atlanta. In desperation the city now moved to obtain an injunction against the further operation of the MIA's car pool. Subpoenas were served on King and other members of his organization. In Judge Carter's court on November 13 the city asked that compensation be granted for damages resulting from the operation of a car pool by the MIA, several churches, and individuals. The city's petition charged further that the car pool was a "public nuisance" and a "private enterprise" operating without a license fee or franchise. [23] Attorneys for the MIA argued that the car pool was simply a community share-the-ride plan being temporarily operated to protest segregation in the city's bus transportation.

As the arguments moved back and forth in the court, an Associated Press reporter moved over to King and handed him a short sheet of teletype. It read:

> The United States Supreme Court today affirmed a decision of a special three-judge U.S. District Court in declaring Alabama's state and local laws requiring segregation on buses unconstitutional. The Supreme Court acted without listening to any argument; it simply said "the motion to affirm is granted and the Judgment is affirmed."[24]

King later recalls this moment: "The darkest hour of our struggle had indeed proved to be the first hour of victory."[25] The night before the hearing he had gone before a mass meeting and warned the people that the car pool would very probably be enjoined. Now on the day of the hearing deliverance had come. Indeed, when word of the Supreme Court decision reached the crowd of black spectators in the back of the court, one voice boomed aloud: "God Almighty has spoken from Washington, D.C."[26]

In spite of the Supreme Court's decision Judge Carter proceeded to grant the injunction against the operation of the car pool. And since some time would elapse before the court order to end segregation would be delivered to city officials, the MIA decided to end the car pool but not the boycott. Everyone would simply have to walk. In the meanwhile the Fellowship of Reconciliation represented by the Reverend Glenn E. Smiley, Bayard Rustin, and others set up a program to indoctrinate the black community in the techniques of nonviolence. Lectures, skits, and demonstrations were held nightly in various churches. A circular was distributed indicating conduct that blacks should exemplify when the actual desegregation of the buses began. The order to desegregate was received in Mongomery on December 21. On the morning of the next day King, accompanied by E. D. Nixon, the Reverend Ralph Abernathy, and the Reverend Glenn Smiley, prepared to go through the ritual of desegregating the first bus in the city of Montgomery. The bus arrived at the bus stop at approximately 5:55 A.M. When King boarded, the driver greeted him with a cordial smile, "I believe you are Reverend King, aren't you?" King answered, "Yes, I am." And the driver, with newsmen and TV reporters looking on, replied, "We are glad to have you this morning."[27] With this the Montgomery bus boycott became a chapter in American history. Later that month the Southern Regional

Council announced that twenty-five Southern cities had ended bus segregation, some as a result of boycotts and some voluntarily. In most cases, black clergymen, largely in emulation of King, had led in the movements.

In February, 1957, black preachers from ten states of the deep South assembled in New Orleans and established a new organization to be known as the Southern Christian Leadership Conference. Martin Luther King, Jr., was elected president and his nonviolence formula was adopted as a basic blueprint for the future work of the SCLC. Had nonviolence failed in Montgomery, it would have been buried there along with King's future. But King had gambled and won. He had been perceptive enough to detect the emergence of a changed social milieu in the nation. If blacks had attempted to mount a protest, nonviolent or otherwise, in the decade of the 1920s, 1930s, or even the 1940s, they would have been given short shrift by the lynch mobs and hooded racists. No more than passing interest or a yawn would have characterized the reaction of the average Northern white. By mid-century, however, the national level of tolerance for violence against black people had lowered considerably. The murder of Emmett Till in Mississippi in 1955 brought on a tidal wave of abhorrence, indignation, and protest throughout the nation. Among the reasons for the new concern was America's new international status. She was now recognized as a great world power and was eager to promote her image as a paradigm of democracy, justice, and human rights. As such, her internal affairs were no longer her private business. Any deceit, any fraud, any cheating on this image was mercilessly spotlighted and unsparingly condemned. The world kept watch. Thus, when King went into court in Montgomery, he was accompanied by representatives of the foreign press from as distant a land as India. Much of the success of the Montgomery movement can be attributed to this new state of affairs. Under any circumstances nonviolence was to be the hallmark of the black protest for the next ten years, and the leader, the new black messiah, was to be Martin Luther King, Jr.

CHAPTER 3

Martin Luther King, Jr., and the High Tide of Nonviolence

As might be expected, the great crusade in Montgomery inspired black leaders throughout the South to attempt to project the style and charisma of Martin Luther King. But while no one quite managed to walk in the footsteps of the master, his movement was fittingly apotheosized in the sit-in crusade which was launched by black students early in 1960. To young black people in the South the Montgomery boycott was the only important social action ever brought off by blacks in the nation's history. To them, King became an instant hero—something of a black superman. At the very least, he was for them a new father figure—a welcome substitute for the obsequious, ingratiating, and cowardly image historically portrayed by adult black males in the region. In short, King was a new "ego-ideal" of action with dignity, and in 1960 black students would be acting upon the internal dictates of this new ego-ideal, carrying out the creed of nonviolence in a movement of their own.

In less than twenty months, January, 1960, to August, 1961, they brought about the desegregation of places of public accommodation in 110 cities and towns in Southern and border states. They involved some seventy thousand people both black and white in picketing, marching, protesting, and some violence. Upwards of four thousand of them willingly suffered imprisonment for the cause.[1] The movement managed to shake the foundations of Southern white society as it had not been shaken since Reconstruction, and in the process it presented America with its first truly "new Negro" since 1619. Historians of the sit-in movement invariably charge the black middle class with timidity and even outright opposition to the student movement. They imply, on the other hand, that the black rank and file was enthusiastic and receptive. None of this squares entirely with the facts. For in the matter of race relations almost the entire population in the South subscribed to a pragmatic gradualism.

Even after Montgomery and several federal court decisions outlawing segregation, blacks in the region continued to sit in the Negro waiting rooms of railroad and bus terminals, eat in filthy segregated lunchrooms invariably located adjacent to toilets, and drink from "Negro" water fountains in department stores. The fact is that the sit-ins shook up everybody in the South, rich and poor, black and white alike. This was a social movement of revolutionary proportions and no one save the black students was ready for it.

While the student crusade derived its philosophy and main motivation from King's movement, the stratagems, tactics, and techniques of nonviolence were borrowed in the main from sources which anticipated Montgomery. A main organization in this area had been the Congress of Racial Equality, created in 1942 by the Fellowship of Reconciliation. Between 1943 and 1959, CORE had employed the sit-in technique to desegregate public accommodations in Chicago, St. Louis, and Baltimore. In 1947, CORE and FOR sent some sixteen persons, black and white, on the "Journey of Reconciliation," the first freedom ride challenging racial segregation in interstate commerce.[2] In 1958, FOR opened a regional branch in Nashville, Tennessee. From this office it sent out a team of three young ministers, James M. Lawson, Glenn Smiley, and Ralph Abernathy, which for more than two months traveled in the South, directing workshops and seminars in nonviolence in black colleges and churches. FOR also prepared and distributed some 200,000 copies of a comic book entitled *King and the Montgomery Story*, a leaflet on *How to Practice Nonviolence*, and a new edition of Richard B. Gregg's *The Power of Nonviolence*. All of this literature was thoroughly disseminated among the black colleges and universities in the South.

One of the many thousands of black students to read the comic book on Martin Luther King was Ezell Blair, a freshman enrolled in North Carolina Agricultural and Technical College in Greensboro, North Carolina. On January 31, 1960, Blair and his roommate, Joseph McNeill, had been rebuffed when they attempted to eat at the white lunch counter in the city's bus terminal. Back in their room on the campus the two students decided to take a leaf from the comic book on King and stage some kind of protest.[3]

Shortly after 4 P.M. on the next day, February 1, Blair and McNeill accompanied by two others went down to the local Woolworth store and leisurely shopped around for toothpaste, combs, and other articles. At 4:30 P.M. the four of them took seats at the lunch counter in the section reserved for whites only. When Blair, the smallest of the group, asked for a cup of coffee, the waitress responded: "I'm sorry. We don't serve Negroes here." After several moments of a heated exchange between Blair and the white waitress, a black woman from the steam table lashed out at the boys: "You're acting stupid, ignorant! That's why we can't get anywhere today. You know you're supposed to eat at the other end."[4] With it all, however, the boys remained seated where they were. They were four who were making a revolution. That afternoon the students decided to continue the activity on a day-to-day basis. On February 4 they were joined by three white students from the Women's College of the University of North Carolina who demanded, unavailingly, that the blacks be served. With the story going out over the local media it was not long before students from other institutions joined the activity. In Durham, North Carolina, on February 8, students from black North Carolina College joined with whites from Duke to initiate the sit-in at a local establishment. In Winston-Salem there was a joint activity by black students from Teachers College and whites from Wake Forest. Within two weeks the sit-in movement had spilled over into Virginia, Tennessee, and South Carolina.

For the first couple of months the sit-in movement consisted essentially of a series of uncoordinated activities taking place in black college communities. The decision to stage a sit-in was invariably initiated by a handful of student activists who were able to pull in a larger number of their colleagues after the initial thrust. Each campus movement was autonomous and there was little if any communication among them. In most cases the mantle of leadership was assumed by the student who initiated the activity; in others it was delegated to the president of the student body. Significantly the ugly head of authoritarianism never reared itself anywhere and at any time in the movement. Participatory democracy was the rule. Despite its spontaneity, however, the movement did observe one common and binding principle—strict adherence to the practice of nonviolence. This could be attributable in part to the FOR and CORE people who went to work among the students as early as Greensboro. The dominant influence, however, was that of Martin Luther King. The students' commitment to nonviolence was to receive its acid test in Nashville, Tennessee, during the first month of the movement.

Nashville rather than Atlanta was pivotal during the early period of the sit-ins. As early as 1958 James Lawson, a divinity student at Vanderbilt University and a field representative of FOR, began conducting workshops on nonviolence under the sponsorship of the Nashville Christian Leadership Conference. These workshops provided the basic training for such future leaders of the movement as John Lewis, Diane Nash, James Bevel, and Marion Barry. In December, 1959, two months before the sit-in began in Greensboro, Lawson decided to "test-run" a sit-in in two of Nashville's largest department stores. As John Lewis put it:

> Jim Lawson had this whole idea saying if we really wanted to put some of what we'd been studying and learning all those months into action and try to make it real, why didn't we go down to the two stores and try to establish whether they really practiced segregation.[5]

In mid-December, Lawson led about twenty-five of his trainees into the department stores where they made mild attempts to desegregate the lunch counters. The Christmas vacation intervened. And before they could make a more serious attempt, Blair and McNeill had made their fateful move.

When news of the sit-in at Greensboro reached Nashville, the reaction was immediate. On February 7 some five hundred students from Fisk, Tennessee State University, Meharry Medical College, and the American Baptist Seminary met on the Fisk campus. With John Lewis, James Lawson, and Marion Barry in the leadership the decision was made to begin the sit-ins in Nashville. Thus, on February 10, some forty-five black students dressed in their "Sunday best" with books under their arms were divided into three groups of fifteen each, with one group going to the Woolworth store, another to McClellan's and a third to the Kress store. The students occupied seats at the lunch counters and, as white patrons got up and left, students filled the vacant seats. They of course were not served, but there was no disorder and no arrests were made. The Nashville city officials were studiously avoiding confrontations and incidents. However, by the end of the month whites in the city were clearly succumbing to a Klan and White Citizens Councils' mentality. When the students sat in at the lunch counters on February 27, they were met with violence. They were beaten with fists and clubs, knocked down repeatedly, and stomped. Lighted cigarettes were pushed into the backs of black girls. Several scores of students were jailed. Through it all the students held firmly to the practice of nonviolence.

In Orangeburg, South Carolina, a similar pattern of events was unfolding. Early in February students from the black Claflin and South Carolina State Colleges began training in the techniques of nonviolence. Their teacher and director was the Reverend Matthew McCullum, a friend of King and one of the founding members of SCLC. McCullum insisted upon strict obedience to nonviolence. An example of the instructions was:

> You may choose to face physical assault without protecting yourself, hands at the sides, unclinched; or you may choose to protect yourself making plain you do not intend to hit back. If you choose to protect yourself, you practice positions such as these:
>
> To protect the skull, fold hands over the head.
>
> To prevent disfigurement of the face, bring the elbows together in front of the eyes.
>
> For girls, to prevent internal injury from kicks, lie on the side and bring the knees upward to the chin; for boys, kneel down and arch over with skull and face protected.[6]

The exact number of seats in Kress's lunch counter was noted, and the time it took to walk from the campus to the store was calculated to the second. Students were formed into small groups and dispatched by different routes, all timed to reach the store at the same time. This was done to prevent arrest for staging an unauthorized march. When the first attempt at a sit-in was made on February 14, the lunch counter was promptly closed down. Three weeks later, however, the situation had changed considerably. When upwards of a thousand students staged a march to town, the police met them with clubs, tear gas, and fire hoses. Better than 500 were arrested. Of these, 150 were booked and lodged in cells; the other 350, drenched and shivering from the bitter cold, were confined in an open stockade.

Atlanta was the last of the major Southern cities to become involved in the sit-in movement.[7] The city had long prided itself in its reputation of good race relations, and this image acted initially as a restraint upon the potential activists on the black campuses. On February 5, just four days after the sit-ins had begun in Greensboro, three Morehouse College students, Lonnie King, Julian Bond, and Joe Pierce, met and resolved to involve Atlanta's black students in the movement. The initial decision of the three was to kick off the movement on Lincoln's birthday, February 12, but somebody suggested that it would be wiser to defer the date until students of Atlanta's other black colleges had been contacted. As a result a steering committee of three students from each of the institutions was established with Lonnie King of Morehouse serving as chairman. On February 17, King and several members of the new committee met with Dr. Benjamin E. Mays, then president of Morehouse College, to apprise him of their plans. Mays gave his full blessing to the students though he suggested that "Each student should make up his own mind about participating in the sit-ins, should be coerced by no one, and once he had made up his mind to demonstrate, he should be prepared to take the consequences for violating the law, however unjust it surely was."[8]

In the meanwhile, the lawmakers of the state of Georgia were closely watching the events in Greensboro in anticipation of their repetition in Atlanta and other Georgia cities. On February 18, 1960, the Georgia General Assembly enacted the first of the so-called anti-trespass laws which made it a misdemeanor for persons to fail to leave a premise when ordered to do so. The students, however, remained undaunted. In preparing for action, they named themselves the Committee on Appeal for Human Rights, and with the backing of the presidents of the six black institutions they drew up a manifesto entitled "An Appeal for Human Rights."[9] The document was carried as a paid advertisement in the local press; it read in part as follows:

> We, the students of the six affiliated institutions forming the Atlanta University Center . . . have joined our hearts, minds and bodies in the cause of gaining those rights which are inherently ours as members of the human race and as citizens of these United States. . . . We, therefore, call upon all people in authority—State, County and City officials, all leaders in civic life—ministers, teachers and businessmen; and all people of good will to assert themselves and abolish these injustices. We must say in all candor that we plan to use every legal and nonviolent means at our disposal to secure full citizen rights as members of this great democracy of ours.

For several days the students attended workshops and seminars on the techniques of nonviolence, picketing, and sit-ins. At 11 A.M. on March 15, more than two hundred of them left the campuses and proceeded downtown where they staged sit-ins in cafeterias, lunch counters of state, county, and city buildings, two federal complexes, two railroad and two bus terminals. All of these were places which were either federally tax supported or subject directly or indirectly to the interstate commerce provision of the United States Constitution. There was violence, but seventy-seven students were arrested for violation of the state's month old anti-trespass law. As the weeks moved on, the sit-ins were extended to five-and-dime, variety, and department stores. The entire black community was now drawn into the movement. On May 17, the sixth anniversary of the *Brown* decision, some three thousand protesters marched through town to a mass meeting at one of the city's largest black Baptist churches.

In a few Southern cities the mere threat of a sit-in movement was sufficient to bring about desegregation. Thus, in Houston and San Antonio, Texas, variety-store owners met with local black leaders after which they voluntarily desegregated their lunch counters. Everywhere, however, the dignity and courage of the students won commendation and acclaim. The *Richmond News Leader* thus commented:

> Here were the colored students, in coats, white shirts, ties, and one of them was reading Goethe and one was taking notes from a biology text. And here, on the sidewalk outside, was a gang of white boys come to heckle, a ragtail rabble, slack-jawed, black-jacketed, grinning fit to kill, and some of them, God save the mark, were waving the proud and honored flag of the Southern States in the last war fought by gentlemen. Eheu! It gives one pause.[10]

In the North on the predominantly white campuses, students were responding with sympathetic sit-ins, fund raising, and the picketing of five-and-dime chains which continued to maintain segregated lunch counters in the South. At Yale University some two hundred Divinity School students marched in silent protest against the treatment of sit-in activists in the South. And in New York City, on April 4, union leaders, liberals, and CORE members picketed one hundred Woolworth stores so effectively that, in the words of one participant, "In some stores there weren't a dozen customers all afternoon."[11]

By the middle of April, after more than ten weeks of rather haphazard, hectic, and uncoordinated activity all over the South, pressure began to mount among the students to coordinate their activities, to establish a clearinghouse or headquarters, and to select at least a nominal director. Many suggestions had been made in this connection, but nothing material was done until Miss Ella Baker of the SCLC stepped into the picture. Long a friend of King, Miss Baker in 1958 had set up the SCLC headquarters in Atlanta. In February, 1960, she prevailed upon the officials of SCLC to underwrite a general conference on student sit-in activity. She was successful also in getting her alma mater, Shaw University in Raleigh, North Carolina, to host the conference. Years later John Lewis, one of the founders of the movement, was to say of her: "Ella Baker, in the real sense of the word, was our personal Gandhi. The spiritual mother, I would guess you would call her, of S.N.C.C."[12]

The opening session of the three-day conclave came on Good Friday, April 15. The 212 delegates in attendance included 145 students from some sixty communities in twelve states. Others were present from such groups as the SCLC, CORE, and FOR. The two keynote speakers were the Reverend James Lawson and the Reverend Martin Luther King. Lawson had recently been expelled from Vanderbilt's Divinity School for his participation in the Nashville sit-ins. As the conference's first speaker Lawson opened with a blast against the leadership of the NAACP. He was following a trend. It had become almost standard procedure for young black radicals to pillory the NAACP and other so-called black middle-class or "Tom" organizations. Lawson thus denounced the NAACP's *Crisis* as a magazine for a "black bourgeoisie club" and insisted that the organization was a legal agency which had failed to mobilize the black rank and file in the fight for freedom and justice.[13] In his speech King continued the theme. He characterized the sit-in movement as "a revolt against those Negroes in the middle class who have indulged themselves in big cars and ranch-style homes rather than in joining a movement for freedom." King then listed prerequisites for the continued success of the student movement. The first was a "continuous organization" to promote the work of the movement; second, a nationwide campaign of selective buying; third, a willingness to go to jail rather than pay bail or fines; fourth, a challenge to take the freedom struggle into every community in the South, and finally, rigid adherence to the philosophy of nonviolence.[14]

Toward the end of the conference fifteen students were selected to constitute the "continuous organization" advised by King. Perhaps the most significant decision made at the conference was the resolve of the students not to affiliate with the SCLC but to remain independent. Even at this early date some of the young blacks were adjudging King's group to be too conservative and too doctrinaire in the matter of nonviolence. An increasing number of them did not want to close out any options in view of the mounting white violence besetting the movement. In Atlanta at the first monthly meeting following the Raleigh conference, the students chose the name Temporary Student Nonviolent Coordinating Committee. And with the decision to establish temporary headquarters in Atlanta, they accepted the offer of Martin Luther King to share office space with the SCLC. Marion Barry, of the Nashville movement, was designated as chairman, and a young white girl from Virginia agreed to serve as the first secretary. Julian Bond busied himself getting out a newsletter later to be known as the *Student Voice.* (See chapter 6.)

The sit-ins continued throughout the South all through the hot and sultry summer of 1960. On August 10, the United States Attorney General, William P. Rogers, announced that discrimination had been abolished by chain-store branches in sixty-nine communities in the South. But with the battle far from won, the students during the early fall decided to establish their organization on a permanent basis. At an October conference the permanent name, Student Non-Violent Coordinating Committee, was adopted. The terms "coordinating" and "committee" were reflective of the students' firm decision not to attempt to build a membership organization or a mass movement. Structurally SNCC was to consist of one delegate from each of sixteen Southern states and the District of Columbia, plus a few voting members and observers from such groups as SCLC, CORE, and the National Student Association. There was to be only a minimal staff at the headquarters in Atlanta which would exercise only minimal control over the activities of SNCC groups in other communities.

The sit-in movement in Atlanta did not really get off the ground until mid-October when Dr. King led some students into Rich's department store to desegregate its lunch counters and plush restaurants.[15] The police promptly arrested King and thirty-six students on the charge of trespassing. When they refused to post bond, they were jailed. King spoke for them all when he declared that he would stay in jail a year or ten years if it took that long to end segregation at Rich's. Atlanta's white power structure, however, had no intention of allowing King to be made a martyr at the city's expense. Thus Mayor William B. Hartsfield hastily arranged a two-months' truce during which the issue was to be negotiated. Dr. King and the students were released on their recognizance for future trial. Dr. King, however, was still subject to the terms of a probationary sentence imposed upon him in an adjacent county some months before. Because of his participation in the sit-in at Rich's, his probation was revoked by a county judge and he was sentenced to four months at hard labor.

Despite the tireless efforts of his attorney, Donald Hallowell, King in leg irons and handcuffs was transferred on October 25 to Georgia's notorious Reidsville State Prison. Within minutes the news of King's transfer was broadcast to the nation. This was an election year and the advisers of Vice-President Richard Nixon, who was the Republican candidate for president, thought that it would be smart politics to issue the following statement:

> It seems to be fundamentally unjust that a man who has peacefully attempted to establish his right to equal treatment, free from racial discrimination, should be imprisoned on an unrelated charge, in itself insignificant. Accordingly, I have asked the Attorney General to take proper steps to join with Dr. Martin Luther King in an appropriate application for his release.[16]

Fearful of alienating the white South and not expecting any black support in any event, Nixon vetoed publishing the statement. Democratic candidate John F. Kennedy, however, was to rush to King's assistance. On the next day after King's transfer he telephoned King's wife in Atlanta, and on that same afternoon his brother, Robert Kennedy, phoned the county judge to inquire why King was being denied bail.[17] The phone call had almost immediate effect. Dr. King was released from Reidsville on October 27, and on the following Sunday his father, "Daddy" King, told his congregation that he would do all that he could to work for the election of John Kennedy.[18]

In establishing itself on a permanent basis in the fall of 1960, one of the intentions of the SNCC's leaders was to limit the participation in their affairs of such well-meaning but "pushy" groups as CORE, FOR, and SCLC. This was, after all, a students' movement and SNCC meant to keep it under student control as much as possible. To the leaders of the SCLC this decision was not of great concern. Dr. King was still the patron saint of the student movement and his influence among them remained undiminished. With CORE, however, it was a different situation. The exclusionary tendencies of SNCC were discomforting to CORE activists. After all, CORE had been in the nonviolence and sit-in business since 1943, and it had written what amounted to manuals for both these types of social action. Since February, 1960, CORE's lieutenants had acted as advisers and coaches for student activists, and many of them had been on the firing line in hostile Southern cities. All of this, however, was no substitute for the broad and deep involvement that James Farmer and other CORE activists so ardently desired. Indeed, Farmer insisted that CORE, too, would have to operate on a national scale formulating policies and organizing projects that would make it competitive on the national scene with SNCC and SCLC.[19]

An opportunity to do this was presented to CORE with the U.S.

Supreme Court decision in the case of *Boynton* v. *Virginia*. In 1958, Bruce Boynton had gone to court to compel Virginia to obey the ICC decree of 1955 abolishing segregation in waiting rooms and other accommodations in railway and bus terminals. In the 1960 decision the Supreme Court upheld the decree. Among the black population of the South, however, the decision caused hardly more than a stir. Everyone knew that it would not be obeyed unless direct action of some kind were employed.[20] After discussing the matter among themselves for some time, CORE officials announced on March 13, 1961, that they would conduct "Freedom Rides" throughout the South to challenge segregation in interstate depots and terminals. On April 28, CORE dispatched a message to President Kennedy advising him of the proposed Freedom Rides and providing him with an itinerary of the projected routes. It then set up a crash program of indoctrination and simulation for the thirteen people who were to begin the rides on May 4.[21] CORE was thus readying itself for what it considered to be a rendezvous with destiny.

As a matter of fact, there were two Freedom Rides; the first extended from May 4 through May 15, and the second, from May 17 to May 25. The thirteen people who went out on the first ride included six whites and seven blacks, ranging in age from eighteen to sixty-one. Leaving Washington, D.C., on May 4 they split up and boarded separate buses, one a Greyhound and the other a Trailways. They traveled through Richmond and Danville, Virginia, and thence through Charlotte, North Carolina, without encountering much difficulty. Up to this point the Freedom Ride did not differ very greatly from CORE's 1947 Journey of Reconciliation through the upper South. On May 9 at Rock Hill, South Carolina, however, two of the riders were set upon and beaten. John Lewis recounts the incident:

> Albert Bigelow [white] and myself got off the bus and started walking into the white waiting room. These hoodlums met us at the door. They just knocked us down and started beating us. We got up and the local police came up and asked us if we wanted to press charges against the guys. We said, "No!"[22]

The Georgia leg of the ride was surprisingly uneventful. The riders were served at the ʻwhite lunch counters in Augusta, Athens, and Atlanta.

On May 14, after recounting their experiences to the staff of SCLC in Atlanta, the riders set out for the no-man's-land of Alabama. The U.S. Department of Justice in the meanwhile had advised the Birmingham, Alabama, police that it had received warnings of planned violence when the buses reached their city. Some six miles outside of Anniston, Alabama, the first bus was met by a mob of whites who halted it and proceeded to slash its tires. An incendiary device was pitched into the vehicle setting it afire and completely destroying it. Several of the riders were taken to a local hospital where they were treated for smoke inhalation. They were later transported to Birmingham in automobiles sent up by Rev. Fred Shuttlesworth. When the second bus, the Trailways, arrived in Anniston, several white hoodlums rushed aboard and began assaulting the Freedom Riders. One of those injured was James Peck of New York's Peck and Peck. Two hours later the bus arrived in Birmingham. A mob of angry, half-hysterical whites armed with pipes and iron bars met them at the depot and moved in to attack. As one of the first to leave the bus, young Peck was seized and dragged into a nearby alley. The beating he received about the head and face later required more than fifty stitches. On Monday, May 15, the entire group of Freedom Riders assembled and made ready to continue their journey to Montgomery. However, no bus driver could be found who would be willing to take them on as passengers. The decision was now made to fly on to New Orleans in time to participate in a Freedom Rally marking the anniversary of the *Brown* decision. At the airport, however, the group was met by another ugly mob. When a bomb threat caused cancellation of the flight, the group was forced to wait six interminable hours for another. In New Orleans on May 17, these first Freedom Riders participated in a rally at a black church and quietly disbanded.[23]

The second Freedom Ride began virtually as an act of defiance. The youthful members of SNCC had been close observers of the first Freedom Ride and they regarded the disruption of the journey in Birmingham as a defeat for the "movement." Thus, they themselves would man the next Freedom Ride—they would ride to Jackson, Mississippi, regardless of consequences to themselves. The Nashville SNCC group was the first to take to the road. On May 17, ten students—eight black and two white—boarded a bus for Birmingham after which they planned to proceed to Jackson. On the outskirts of Birmingham, however, the police came aboard the bus and arrested the students upon reaching the city. Police Chief Bull Connor kept them locked up overnight, and on the next day they were driven 120 miles to the Tennessee border where they were released and warned to keep moving northward. Back in Nashville that same evening the students decided to disregard Bull Connor's admonition. As John Lewis described it: "We got together; Diane Nash, Bevel, C. T. Vivian, Jim Lawson. We just started talking that this ride has got to continue. It must not stop. We cannot let it stop."[24] With their numbers swelled by seven additional students, John Lewis and his intrepid colleagues boarded a bus and headed directly back to Birmingham and bloodshed.

In the meanwhile, President Kennedy was attempting somewhat unsuccessfully to communicate with Alabama's Governor John Patterson. Later on that night Patterson in his own good time advised an aide to Attorney General Robert Kennedy: "We are going to do all we can to enforce the laws of the state on the highways and everywhere else, but we are not going to escort these agitators. We stand firm on that position."[25] Once in Birmingham, the students had to wait some eighteen hours in the bus terminal before U.S. Justice Department officials could secure a bus and a driver to get them on their way. Montgomery was the next stop and it would prove to be a harrowing experience. One of the young Freedom Riders commented upon their approach to the city: "There were police cars all around the bus, and helicopters flying overhead. But when we got inside the Montgomery city limits, it all disappeared."[26] Instead, the group was greeted by a mob of surly young white hoodlums and screeching white women. The first Freedom Rider to get off the bus was James Zwerg, a clean-shaven white student from Wisconsin. An hysterical white woman in the mob screamed, "Kill the nigger-lover son-of-a bitch." Zwerg was quickly beaten into a pulp. Before leaving him for dead, one of the mob, for good measure, paused to kick Zwerg's front teeth out. John Lewis was a special target. Like Zwerg he was beaten into unconsciousness. Still on the pavement when he came to, Lewis reports: "While I was there bleeding and all, the Attorney General of the State of Alabama . . . walked up and served me with an injunction. . . ."[27] Other Freedom Riders, fleeing the scene, were run down and whipped with clubs and baseball bats.

When news of the bloodshed reached Washington, Robert Kennedy ordered U.S. attorneys to go into federal district courts in Montgomery and secure injunctions against the Ku Klux Klan, the National States Rights party, and any other individuals interfering with peaceful interstate travel by bus. He then sent a contingency of federal marshals into the city. The next day, Sunday, May 21, the Freedom Riders with bandaged heads, assorted bruises, and lacerations assembled in Rev. Ralph Abernathy's church to be part of a mass rally. There were more than 1,200 people in attendance. Dr. King had broken off a speaking engagement in Chicago to be present. While the meeting was going on, a new situation was building up outside. A mob of angry whites bent upon invading the church was restrained only with the utmost efforts of U.S. marshals, local and state police. The city was finally placed under martial law and eight hundred National Guardsmen were given the task of maintaining order. During the next three days the Freedom Riders remained in seclusion nursing their injuries and husbanding their strength for the final leg of their journey. Federal marshals along with state police from Alabama and Mississippi were cooperating to expedite the trip. At exactly 7 A.M. on May 24, the first bus of Freedom Riders moved out of the Montgomery bus depot. It was convoyed by twenty-two highway patrol vehicles, two complete battalions of Alabama National Guardsmen, three U.S. Army reconnaissance planes, and two helicopters. Seventeen newspaper reporters went along. Upon reaching the Mississippi state line, the bus was picked up by Mississippi National Guardsmen and escorted to the bus terminal in Jackson. The second bus went through the same routine. At the bus terminal in Jackson all of the Freedom Riders were arrested for attempting to desegregate the lunch counter. All of them were found guilty, given two months' suspended sentences, and fined $200. They were remanded to Parchman Prison when they refused to pay the fine.

All through the summer of 1961, miscellaneous self-appointed Freedom Riders, both black and white and largely from the North, kept showing up in Jackson. All of them kept trying to desegregate the lunch counter and all of them were arrested by the Jackson police. Sometime later in recounting the events of the spring and summer of 1961, James Farmer declared: "The hundreds of people who rode Freedom buses into the South and the thousands who cheered them on created a thunder-and-lightning storm which even we professional rain-makers had not intended."[28] But intended or not, the bloody self-sacrificing assaults by black and white youth upon Southern white racism caused more misgivings and doubts about the wisdom of the Freedom Rides than had ever been raised by the sit-ins. In the nation's capital the Kennedy administration, while refraining from openly criticizing the demonstrations, called for a cooling-off period. In Atlanta, a Freedom Rides Coordinating Committee composed of representatives of SCLC, CORE, SNCC, and others was put together.

As spokesman for this group Dr. King promised instead a "temporary lull." In defense of the Freedom Rides he insisted that "creative tension" was necessary for the birth of a new order. "If we can get through this, I think it will mean breaking the backbone of massive resistance and discrimination."[29]

On the other hand, King himself was beginning to experience some difficulty. There was a growing feeling among the students that he was ambivalent—that he secretly harbored reservations about what many people called undue provocation of the white South. They were disturbed also by King's failure to accompany the Freedom Riders from Montgomery to Jackson. Indeed, one extremist, Robert Williams, wired King during the bloodshed in Montgomery:

> The cause of human decency and black liberation demands that you physically ride the buses with our gallant freedom riders. No sincere leader asks his followers to make sacrifices that he himself will not endure. You are a phony. Gandhi was always in the forefront, suffering with his people. If you are the leader of this nonviolent movement, lead the way by example.[30]

Whatever may have been the reason for Dr. King's failure to go on the second Freedom Ride, lack of courage was out of the question. His record during and after the bus boycott bore ample testimony to his fearlessness. One of the things that undoubtedly did disturb King was the new type of people being recruited or volunteering for temporary duty in the nonviolence movement. Many of the white and black adults who got themselves locked up for a few days in the Alabama and Mississippi jails did so merely to earn "badges of honor" of which they could boast among their colleagues back home in the North. And there were those among the new recruits of SNCC who had read nothing on the philosophy of nonviolence and did not subscribe to it. The best that CORE could do under the circumstances was to funnel these inexperienced people through checkpoints in Chicago and New Orleans.

For its part, the Kennedy administration wanted an end to the Freedom Rides. It was interested, on the other hand, in diverting the efforts of the black students to tasks it considered more effective in the solution of the black man's problems in the South. The Freedom Rides dramatized Southern white racism, if that were needed, but they were otherwise of limited value, and they were definitely counterproductive. In the calculations of John and Robert Kennedy, what was needed was an alteration in the political balance of the deep South, and this could be brought about only by a significant increase in the black vote. Of course, this task would call for hard, dangerous, and protracted labor in hostile territory, and not many blacks could be expected to volunteer for it. However, the Kennedy administration was convinced that it must be done. "Accordingly," writes Arthur Schlesinger, "in a behind-the-scenes effort reminiscent of the campaign to save the Bay of Pigs prisoners, the administration, with helpful assistance from the Taconic Foundation and collaboration from the Southern Regional Council," [31] went to work to persuade the leading black organizations to ·undertake a drive to increase the Southern black vote. The Field Foundation entered the picture at this point with a $100,000 grant for black voter education in the South.

To sell its program directly to the students, the administration designated Burke Marshall, Assistant Attorney General, in charge of civil rights and Harris Wofford, FOR member and the president's Special Assistant on Minority Problems. In the late spring of 1961, Tim Jenkins, the black vice-president of the National Student Association, met with Marshall and Wofford as well as with the representatives of the Taconic and Field foundations. Convinced of the need of black voter education, Jenkins championed its adoption at the June meeting of SNCC in Louisville, Kentucky. No effort was needed to convince Dr. King of the value of voter education. Since 1958, this project had been high on the SCLC list of priorities. On the other hand, some $40,000 of the $100,000 grant from the Field Foundation for voter education was to go to the SCLC in addition to the fact that one of Dr. King's aides, the Reverend Andrew Young, was to head up the whole Field project. [32] At their August meeting at the Highlander Folks School in Tennessee, the majority of the members of SNCC remained opposed to the voter-education project. Some of them charged that the "establishment" was attempting to divert them, and to the extent that the Kennedy administration and Dr. King were using their influence for the voter project, the charge was true. Nevertheless, Tim Jenkins, Charles Jones, and others persisted in their efforts at the meeting for a switch to voter education. The result was that for the first time in its year and a half of existence SNCC was threatened with fragmentation. As the crisis worsened, Ella Baker stepped into the breach. She suggested that SNCC set up two divisions: one to remain with direct action and one to move into voter education and registration. [33] This compromise left no one in SNCC entirely satisfied. For some of the more militant students Highlander was a "sellout." At any rate, SNCC would never again be the same.

In the fall of 1961 the Southern Regional Council reported that between February, 1960, and September, 1961, the sit-ins had brought about the desegregation of public accommodation in more than one hundred Southern towns and cities. This was an accomplishment of which SNCC could justly be proud, but it was not the whole story. There were still some Southern cities, little ones as well as big ones, that had thumbed their noses at the sit-ins and the Freedom Riders. Their white leaderships were resolute on the question of separation of the races, and they were bent upon fighting to the bitter end. One such town was Albany, Georgia, and before it was all over, this little bastion of racism would outmaneuver and defeat both SNCC and Martin Luther King. In 1961 Albany was a thriving middle-sized town located deep in southwest, "woolhat" Georgia. It had known better days. Before the Civil War it had been the cotton capital of the region. In more recent times, with cotton being abandoned, Albany became the so-called peanut capital of the United States. It was, in 1961, known also as the capital of white racism in southwest Georgia. Of the city's population of 56,000 the one-third of it that was black was seemingly immune to the virus of the black social revolution. This situation, however, was soon to change.

During the early fall of 1961, SNCC headquarters in Atlanta assigned a field secretary and two staff members to Albany. These men, Charles Jones, Robert Sherrod, and Cordell Reagan, set up a SNCC office in a run-down building in the black community. They began to recruit young blacks for instruction in the philosophy and tactics of nonviolence. On September 22, the Interstate Commerce Commission had issued a ruling banning segregation on buses and terminal facilities. The order was to go into effect on November 1. On that date Sherrod and Reagan, who had been in Atlanta conferring with SNCC leaders, rode back on a Trailways bus with Charles Jones and James Forman. The police in Atlanta had alerted Albany officials. When the bus arrived in Albany, a squad of policemen was ready and waiting. The SNCC people quickly decided to hold off a confrontation and go into town for reenforcements. Later that day, they returned to the bus depot with nine black students and proceeded to occupy seats at the white lunch counter. Disregarding the ICC order which was posted all around the terminal, the police proceeded to chase the black youths out to the streets.

The SNCC strategists, however, had their needed "incident." The timid, hesitant black establishment of the city decided to take some action. On Monday, November 17, Dr. William C. Anderson, an osteopath, called together several local black organizations to form the so-called "Albany Movement." The group included the Negro Voters' League, the local NAACP, the Federation of Women's Clubs, and the Youth Council. SNCC was included but not without some misgiving. One of the black leaders told Louis Lomax: "I wouldn't say we didn't want the students here. I would say, however, that they found us not too receptive to them."[34] Leaders of the new movement dispatched a message to city officials demanding the establishment of a biracial commission to consider and deal with the many grievances of the black citizens. The white officials turned thumbs down on the suggestion. The die was cast. During the next few weeks SNCC organizers began activating the students at the black Albany State College, and plans were made to assault the city with Freedom Riders, sit-ins, and boycotts. The police now began a get-tough policy. On December 10, they jailed nine Freedom Riders attempting to desegregate the bus terminal lunch counter, and two days later they arrested more than four hundred black high school and college students who were staging a march on the city hall. On December 15, with more than five hundred black protesters in jail or out on bond the city officials decided to establish the biracial commission and hear out the black complaints. As a conciliatory gesture the police released 118 juvenile prisoners. On December 15, the biracial negotiations between three blacks and three whites broke down almost as soon as they got started, and city officials hurriedly put in a call to the governor to dispatch units of the National Guard to the city.

The black leadership now called for Dr. King to come to Albany. The decision was not unanimous. Some of the leaders did not resent Dr. King as much as they did his arrogant, self-confident top lieutenants. The Reverend Wyatt T. Walker was a main target. As one of Albany's black leaders put it: "After all, we did the spadework for this thing. Why didn't Walker stay the hell in Atlanta, send us more money, let us have Martin to speak and walk with the marchers!"[35] In short, what the Albany black leaders wanted was King, not his movement—they already had their own movement. Said one of them: "We can bake our own cake. All we need from the Atlanta boys is some more flour and sugar."[36] In Albany on December 16, Dr. King spoke to a capacity audience at the Shiloh Baptist Church. On the next day Dr. King, in a familiar role, led a freedom march of some 250 blacks through the streets toward the city hall. Before they reached their destination, however, they were intercepted by Police Chief Laurie Pritchett and more than a hundred policemen. After warning them repeatedly to disperse, the police arrested Dr. King, Dr. Anderson, Rev. Ralph Abernathy, and several hundred marchers. The mass media immediately picked up the story, and in a few hours Albany had become an unwilling host to several hundred newsmen.

From his jail cell Dr. King announced: "If convicted, I will refuse to pay the fine. I expect to spend Christmas in jail. I hope the thousands will join me."[37] The city was now in a turmoil with the black leadership definitely holding the psychological edge. However, on the very next day, Monday, December 18, it was announced out of the clear blue that a truce had been arrived at between the black and white leadership. All demonstrations, protests, and the like were to cease until January 23. The blacks in jail were to be freed on bail pending trial to be set at a later date. Most important of all Dr. King, in violation of his public "jail no bail" vow, was posting bond and departing from the county jail. He had been there less than twenty-four hours. People in the city of Albany as well as the nation at large were astounded. One city official gave this explanation: "We killed them with kindness. Apparently, it was a condition M. L. King and the other outsiders had never encountered before."[38] In truth, Albany had not repeated the mistakes of Birmingham and Montgomery of a year earlier. There were no hoses, no dogs, no brutality, and no obscenity as there had been in the two Alabama cities. King and the others arrested with him had been housed in a model prison and handled with the utmost in restraint and civility. Police Chief Pritchett boasted that "we . . . met 'nonviolence' with 'nonviolence' and we are, indeed, proud of the outcome."[39]

When a young SNCC leader was asked his view of the "outcome," he remarked, "You curse first, then I will." The question persisted as to whether this was a truce or a capitulation by black leaders, or worse yet, an agreement between the black and white leadership to ease King and his lieutenants out of Albany. At any rate Dr. King was apparently not party to the real conditions of the so-called truce. By his own admission he had been duped. As he later explained it: "I'm sorry I was bailed out. I didn't understand at the time what was happening. We thought that the victory had been won. When we got out, we discovered it was all a hoax."[40] Late in January, 1962, and without the assistance of Dr. King the black leadership renewed its demands upon the city. But the white leadership now held the upper hand. It would grant no demands. Instead, the black leaders would have to "earn acceptance for their people by encouraging the improvement of their moral standards."[41] The truth was that the Albany movement was dead even if the black leadership did not know it. King was to return to the city several times in 1962 even spending several days in jail that summer. But insofar as Albany was concerned, King's mystique had been shattered by the events of December, 1961. The major blame could perhaps be laid at the feet of Albany's black leadership but King himself was not without fault. As one of his biographers summed it up: "King allowed himself to be pushed into action, without adequate preparation, on a battlefield he did not choose with a faction-ridden army he never completely commanded."[42]

By the summer of 1962, the black social revolution in the United States was beginning to achieve a life of its own. It could no longer be considered any one man's personal movement, nor could it any longer be dominated by any one black organization. The SCLC, which had led in the struggle up to 1960, was politely but firmly shouldered aside by the uninhibited young revolutionaries of SNCC. And in 1961, both the SCLC and SNCC were forced to share the national spotlight with James Farmer's CORE and its intrepid Freedom Riders. Spawned in the South the movement was thus becoming national in scope. Indeed, by 1962, almost every sizable black community in the nation could boast of its local black freedom movement, committee, or conference. Nonviolence was still pretty much the rule throughout. But the demand for at least a retaliatory violence was being heard in the Northern black ghettos in response to the exhortations of Malcolm X. With it all, however, the most powerful voice among American blacks was still that of Martin Luther King. His enemies were legion and his detractors were multiplying, but in charisma he still outmatched any living black man anywhere. Indeed, there were legions of black people in the United States who would have followed King in an assault upon the gates of hell itself.

In 1963, hell was located in Birmingham, Alabama. King once described the city as "a community in which human rights had been trampled for so long that fear and oppression were as thick in its atmosphere as the smog from its factories."[43] The traditional black leadership of the city was as fear-ridden as the rank and file for whom it presumed to speak. But there were others—those who could not be intimidated. Since 1956, Dr. King's friend and associate, the Reverend Fred Lee Shuttlesworth, and his Alabama Christian Movement for Human Rights (ACHR) had been skirmishing with Police Chief "Bull" Connor and the city's racist administration. But the halfhearted protests and petitions had been brushed aside, and in obvious retaliation Shuttlesworth's home and church were set to dynamite. Weary and drained of patience, Shuttlesworth finally turned to Dr. King for assistance. The response was favorable. During its board meeting in May, 1962, the SCLC voted to support Shuttlesworth with what King described as a "massive direct-action campaign" to end segregation in Birmingham. At an earlier meeting the SCLC had selected Birmingham as the site for its annual September conclave. Hearing of these plans, Birmingham officials took precautions to keep down bad publicity for the city. They asked black leaders for a moratorium on protests. Wary and expecting duplicity, Shuttlesworth nevertheless agreed to a truce which called for a suspension of demonstrations in return for the removal of white and Negro signs from water fountains and rest rooms. It was a short-lived truce and Shuttlesworth's instincts proved correct. The last of the SCLC convention delegates had hardly left the city before the segregation signs were restored.

King and the SCLC leadership now got down to the serious consideration of the proposed massive direct action. At the three-day conference in Dorchester, Georgia, a plan of attack, to be known as Project C (Confrontation), was worked out in detail. The commencement of the campaign was set for March 6, 1963, with the initial target being the Birmingham business district. Early in January, SCLC temporary headquarters were set up in Birmingham's black-owned Gaston Motel. King, Walker, and Abernathy held lengthy, soul-searching meetings with the local black leadership in order to prevent a recurrence of the Albany fiasco. King then set out on a speaking tour, making twenty-eight speeches in sixteen cities. His purpose was to line up volunteers for Birmingham and to secure pledges for cash bonds for the arrests expected from the demonstrations. On the New York end of the trip Harry Bélafonte and a group of nationally known personages pledged their support to the campaign. King returned South with promises of almost a half-million dollars.

On March 5, the day before Project C was scheduled to begin, the Birmingham city elections took place. The mayoralty candidates were Albert Boutwell, Tom King, and the infamous Eugene "Bull"

Connor. None of them won a majority of the ballots; thus a runoff election was set for April 2, between the top two contenders, Boutwell and Connor. The strategists of the SCLC now decided to move up the date of Project C to April 3. In the interim Wyatt T. Walker was detailed to begin on-the-spot planning in Birmingham. He conferred with lawyers about the city's code on picketing and demonstrations; he surveyed downtown eating facilities noting entrances and exits and even counting stools, tables, and chairs that might accommodate demonstrators; and he recruited some 250 volunteers to assist in training the city's blacks in the techniques of nonviolence. April 2 came with Boutwell winning the runoff election. Blacks were not ecstatic. To them, Boutwell was simply a dignified Bull Connor. Under any circumstances, the road was now open for Project C to begin.

On April 3, Shuttlesworth's ACHR issued a manifesto setting forth the grievances of the black community with painstaking detail. On the same day, the first contingent of black demonstrators set out for the business district to commence the picketing and sit-ins. For the next few days as the demonstrations continued, Bull Connor seemed to be following the Albany formula for dealing with black demonstrations. The blacks were first warned politely; then without brutality or obscenity they were escorted to waiting police vans. King and his aides in the meanwhile moved from meeting to meeting throughout the black community explaining the nature and requirements of nonviolence and boosting the morale of the new recruits. On April 10, Bull Connor decided to change his tactics or, more accurately, to revert back to type. He secured a sweeping injunction barring almost every conceivable kind of demonstration, march, sit-in, and boycott. The writ named the SCLC, the ACHR, Dr. King, and the Reverends Fred Shuttlesworth and Ralph Abernathy. As for himself Dr. King had from the outset resolved to go to jail when the opportunity presented itself so as to obtain the maximum publicity and dramatization for the campaign. So, when the court order was delivered to him at 1:30 A.M. Thursday, April 11, King was literally waiting for it.

On the next day, Good Friday, King and Abernathy, dressed in blue denims and gray work shirts, set out on a march at the head of fifty other blacks. As they neared the downtown area, Bull Connor intercepted them. Then, as Dr. King described it: "Ralph and I were hauled off by two muscular policemen, clutching the backs of our shirts in handfuls. All the others were promptly arrested."⁴⁴ King had spent time in the lockup many times since the Montgomery boycott, but his experience in the Birmingham jail was to prove the most trying of his career. No brutality or force was used against him, but upon reaching the prison, he was separated from Abernathy and placed in solitary confinement. Dr. King's wife, Coretta, spent an entire Easter weekend futilely attempting to reach President Kennedy via telephone. She did succeed in talking to Attorney General Robert Kennedy, and finally on Monday morning the president, who had been out of Washington visiting his ailing father, returned her call:

> I want you to know we are doing everything we can. I have just talked to Birmingham, and your husband will be calling you shortly. If you have any further worries about your husband or about Birmingham in the next few days, I want you to feel free to call me.⁴⁵

With conditions eased for him in confinement as a result of Kennedy's intercession, King got down to the business of replying to eight white Alabama pastors who in January had published a statement entitled "An Appeal for Law and Order and Common Sense."⁴⁶ While sympathizing with the cause of the blacks in Birmingham, the pastors were of the view that the demonstrations, "led in part by outsiders," were "unwise and untimely." They insisted that "when rights are consistently denied, a cause should be pressed in the courts and in negotiations among local leaders and not in the streets." They concluded with a plea to the black community to "withdraw support from these demonstrations" and to work "peacefully" for a better Birmingham.

King replied to the ministers in a statement entitled "Letter from Birmingham Jail."⁴⁷ The letter was a bill of indictment against the white South for its cruel and dehumanizing treatment of black people. King insisted that whenever blacks had quietly petitioned for a redress of their grievances they had been told to "wait." But beyond this, King argued that the blacks were protesting laws which were unjust in light of the moral law of God. Even so, they were willing to accept the penalty of disobedience in order to sensitize the community to the injustice of the existing law. In so doing, they were actually expressing the highest respect for true law.

On Saturday, April 20, King and Abernathy decided to post bond and leave the jail. News had reached them that, in their absence, the movement was showing signs of weakening and was in danger of collapsing. After an evening of lengthy discussions at the Gaston

Motel, the decision was made to use children in the next massive demonstration. This stratagem had previously been employed in Statesville and Durham, North Carolina. Staff of the SCLC were sent out to the public schools to recruit the black children. They were urged to come to the black churches to see the films—*Walk to Freedom* and *The Nashville Story*. May 2 came to be known as "D" Day. Shortly after 1 P.M. almost a thousand black children were sent out wave after wave from the Sixteenth Street Baptist Church. Cheered on by black spectators they headed for town, some singing, some shouting, and some dancing. A few of them broke ranks as the police approached, while others knelt and prayed. Older youths sought to keep order by means of walkie-talkies. In arresting them, the police soon ran out of vans and began using school buses. In all, 959 children were jailed on this first day of the "Children's Crusade."

On the next day with five hundred more children on the march, Bull Connor made his move. High-powered hoses were turned on the children, knocking them down like tenpins. Police then waded into the youngsters with nightsticks, fists, feet, and snarling dogs. The German shepherds, being used to attack rather than to contain the demonstrators, slashed and bit at least five people. On Monday and Tuesday, May 6 and 7, the demonstrations and the violence reached a peak. Crowds of black adults were beginning to defy the police. Rev. James Bevel had seen pistols and knives in the hands of black adults and was fearful of a riot. In the meantime photographs of police dogs biting women and children were sent around the world. In the nation's capital Senator Wayne Morse declared in the United States Senate that what was happening in Birmingham "would disgrace a Union of South Africa or a Portuguese Angola." [48] President Kennedy told a group of White House visitors that the pictures made him sick. He said: "I can well understand why the Negroes of Birmingham are tired of being asked to be patient." [49]

Blacks in Birmingham were demanding that the city agree to a fourfold program: (1) desegregation of lunch counters, rest rooms, fitting rooms, and drinking fountains, (2) placement of blacks through upgrading and hiring in previously all-white clerical and sales positions in stores, (3) release of prisoners, and (4) firm establishment of permanent communications between black and white leaders. Using these demands as a starting point, Burke Marshall, under orders from President Kennedy, struggled to bring about negotiations between the black and white leadership. In the meanwhile, the president, along with members of his cabinet, went to work to persuade national business and corporate leaders with contacts and branches in Birmingham to use their influence toward mediation. As a result of these combined efforts the impasse was broken, and on Wednesday, May 8, King, Abernathy, and Shuttlesworth announced at a press conference that progress was being made in negotiations and that a twenty-four-hour truce would be observed.

That same evening, however, King and Abernathy were arrested and returned to jail. On April 26, they had been convicted for the Good Friday offenses, and since then they had been free pending appeal. Bull Connor was obviously acting out his anger over the imminence of a black victory. Shuttlesworth countered by ordering some 1,200 black demonstrators to be ready to march into the heart of the city. The Kennedy administration again got busy and by Thursday morning, King and Abernathy were back on the streets and what could have been a bloody riot had been averted. On Friday afternoon, Dr. King announced that the city had accepted the basic demands of the black community. Amendments to these demands included a ninety-day time limit for desegregating such public accommodations as lunchrooms, rest rooms, etc. A sixty-day period was set for implementation of fair-employment practices. However, the city refused to dismiss charges against the more than two thousand blacks who were still in jail. Bail for their release, some $237,000, was put up by the United Auto Workers and the National Maritime Unions. On May 20, the United States Supreme Court put an end to the whole business when it declared Alabama's laws on segregation to be unconstitutional. The black community was elated over the outcome of the crusade.

However, a mood of bitterness settled over much of the white community. At 11:45 P.M. on the Saturday of that hectic week two time bombs demolished the home of A. D. King, the brother of Martin Luther King. Within minutes, the black community had picked up the news and had proceeded to act upon it. For more than five hours mobs of angry blacks stormed about the city breaking windows, setting fires, and stoning firemen who sought to put them out. Policemen were beaten and knifed. To many of the blacks this was deferred payment for the brutality that they had suffered at the hands of the police during the past week. The community was finally brought under control by the local police and the state highway patrol. Federal troops remained on standby alert some distance away. Fomented by blacks instead of whites, this was the first such riot in the history of the modern South. Of even greater significance, it ignited the first of the long hot summers. For beginning with Birmingham in 1963, American cities North, South, East, and West were to be wracked with violence and disorder for five consecutive years.

Perhaps no two white men in the United States were more deeply involved emotionally and otherwise in the Birmingham crusade than John and Robert Kennedy. The president and his brother did not always agree with what Dr. King and his supporters were doing, but they invariably rendered their support. The Kennedys wanted to identify with the black social revolution. On May 25, Robert Kennedy invited a group of black writers, show people, and others to meet with him in his New York apartment. Those in attendance included James Baldwin, Lena Horne, Harry Belafonte, and Dr. Kenneth B. Clark. In the group also was a young man, Jerome Smith, who as a Freedom Rider had been brutally assaulted in the deep South. With discussion centering on the government's role in the civil rights crusade, Smith averred that he felt like vomiting for having to plead before the attorney general for rights to which he was entitled as an American citizen. Baldwin added that the only reason the government had sent federal troops to Alabama was because white people had been assaulted. The other blacks present applauded these sentiments. Shocked and angered, Kennedy could hardly believe his ears. Later he was to assert:

> They didn't know anything. They don't know what the laws are. . . . You couldn't talk to them as you can to Roy Wilkins or Martin Luther King. . . . It was all emotion, hysteria. They stood up and orated. They cursed. Some of them wept and walked out of the room.[50]

At the conclusion of the meeting one of Dr. King's representatives drew Kennedy aside and confided: "I just want to say that Dr. King appreciates the way you handled the Birmingham affair." His Irish temper bristling, Kennedy barked: "You watched these people attack me over Birmingham for forty minutes, and you didn't say a word. There's no point in your saying this to me now."[51]

With it all, however, the Kennedy commitment to the cause of the blacks was to continue undiminished. Arthur Schlesinger suggests that the president's interest in the black revolution had reached the point that he was seeking to "assume its leadership." This kind of interest seems to be reflected in the president's June 11 speech on civil rights. He said:

> We face, therefore, a moral crisis as a country and a people. It cannot be met by
> repressive police action. It cannot be left to increased demonstrations in the streets. It
> cannot be quieted by token moves or talk. . . .
> A great change is at hand, and our task, our obligation is to make that revolution,
> that change peaceful and constructive for all.[52]

Within a few hours after this speech was delivered to the nation, however, an event transpired that was to jeopardize seriously any possibility that the revolution would be peaceful. Medgar Evers, state executive secretary of the Mississippi NAACP, was killed by a sniper's bullet in Greenwood, Mississippi. The cry from the black communities across the nation was instantaneous.

The assassination sparked demonstrations that would number more than seven hundred during the ensuing weeks. Some 200,000 blacks in Los Angeles almost staged a dress rehearsal of the Watts riot. In New York City, blacks staged a sit-in in the offices of Mayor Robert Wagner and Governor Nelson Rockefeller. And in Danville, Virginia, some fifty blacks were hospitalized after policemen armed with submachine guns and moving in armored vehicles broke up a demonstration. Dismayed and thoroughly exasperated over Evers' killing, President Kennedy thus confided to an aide: "I don't understand the South. I'm coming to believe that Thaddeus Stevens was right. I had always been taught to regard him as a man of vicious bias. But, when I see this sort of thing, I begin to wonder how else you can treat them."[53] On the same day as Evers was buried in Arlington National Cemetery, the president submitted to Congress a bill that would rival Stevens' best efforts to protect the rights of black Americans. Kennedy's bill later became the Public Accommodation Act of 1964.

If the Birmingham victory was not all that some black leaders proclaimed it to be, it was unquestionably another milestone in the racial history of the deep South. Dr. King considered it sufficient to merit a coast-to-coast speaking trip or what was more accurate, a triumphal tour of some of the nation's largest black communities. Thus, in mid-June, King recounted the Birmingham ordeal to more than 25,000 listeners in Los Angeles. Later in Chicago he addressed an eager audience of 10,000. His appearance in Detroit on June 23 helped mark the twentieth anniversary of the city's bloody race riot of 1943. King led 125,000 people on a freedom walk through town after which he delivered an address which included a phrase which would later become the title of his greatest speech—"I Have a Dream." While there can be no doubt about the great enthusiasm with which the Northern blacks greeted Dr. King, the point must be made that this enthusiasm was for the man and not his methods. Every Northern black community that King visited during the summer of 1963 was a veritable tinderbox. The white flight to the suburbs was in full swing and the socioeconomic condition of the center-city blacks was rapidly deteriorating. In this milieu King's nonviolence philosophy was incongruous.

Besides, the Northern blacks were already beginning to rally to their own "indigenous" leader—Malcolm X. It was Malcolm's disciples who splattered Dr. King's car with rotten eggs as it moved through Harlem during the last week in June. During that same week, A. D. King also got the message. A meeting he was addressing in Harlem was almost broken up by a group of young militants yelling: "We want Malcolm. We want Malcolm." Malcolm X had indeed made no secret of his antipathy and contempt for Martin Luther King. In an interview with Dr. Kenneth Clark, Malcolm insisted that the Birmingham movement was a failure and that nonviolence was, in effect, cowardice. He was convinced that the "masses of black people" did not support Dr. King.

> King is the best weapon that the white man, who wants to brutalize Negroes, has ever gotten in this country, because he is setting up a situation where, when the white man wants to attack Negroes, they can't defend themselves, because King has put this foolish philosophy out—you're not supposed to fight or you're not supposed to defend yourself.[54]

Perhaps no activity during the summer of 1963 was more intense and touchy than what might be described as the politics of the "March-on-Washington." After somewhat hesitantly identifying itself with the black revolution, the Kennedy administration turned its efforts toward keeping the revolution peaceful and off the streets. The president was somewhat dismayed, therefore, when he learned that the black leaders were planning a massive demonstration in Washington during the late summer. Fearful lest such a demonstration might lead to violence, Kennedy called upon top black spokesmen to meet with him at the White House on June 23. The president took the approach that the proposed march could seriously jeopardize the passage of his public accommodation bill through Congress. He insisted that the wrong kind of demonstration at the wrong time would give the enemies of the bill all the arguments they needed. Moreover, the prestige of the administration was involved. "We're in this up to our neck," he said.

A national poll had just indicated a drop from 60 percent to 47 percent in the country's support for the administration. A. Philip Randolph warned the president that "Negroes are already in the streets. It is very likely impossible to get them off."[55] Randolph knew as did the others that no black leader would risk going on record as opposing the march. The administration did not succeed in calling off the march, but it made its point about violence. A few weeks later the black leaders organized themselves into the so-called Council of United Civil Rights Leadership. With financial assistance coming from a consortium of sixty-five corporations and foundations, the Council proceeded to plan and promote a peaceful demonstration for the District of Columbia.[56]

With its galaxy of dignitaries and celebrities on the raised platform and some 200,000 people assembled before them at the Lincoln Memorial, the March-on-Washington was easily the greatest demonstration ever to be held in the nation's capital. Organizations with every conceivable excuse for being were represented. More than one man in the vast throng had spent his last earthly penny to be there. Neither the president nor his brother was present at the ceremonies, but the influence of the administration had been powerfully evoked on the day before. John Lewis of SNCC had routinely distributed advance copies of his speech to the other speakers as well as to the press. When Cardinal Patrick O'Boyle, a close friend of the Kennedys, read it, he became apoplectic. He objected to such phrases as: "We are now involved in a serious revolution. This nation is still a place of cheap political leaders allying themselves with open forms of political, economic and social exploitation. . . ." Lewis was immediately smothered with pleas as well as demands from the black and the white leaders to tone down his language. Lewis stated:

> I think Rustin came to my defense and defended my position. On the other hand, some of the people were concerned about the use of the word "revolution"....Martin King, in effect, said, "John, I know who you are. I think I know you well. I don't think this sounds like you."[57]

Lewis did tone down his speech but not by much. Significantly he did not delete the word "revolution."

The high point of the March-on-Washington was the speech by Dr. King. "I Have a Dream" was not only the greatest oration ever delivered by a black American, but it was also one of the most moving experiences of modern times. Few who listened to it will ever forget King's ringing peroration:

> When we let freedom ring, when we let it ring from every village and every hamlet, from every state and every city, we will be able to speed up that day when all God's children, black men and white men, Jews and Gentiles, Protestants and Catholics, will be able to join hands and sing in the words of that old Negro spiritual, "Free at last! Free at last! Thank God almighty, we are free at last!"[58]

At the conclusion of the day's activities some of the black leaders were invited over to the White House for cocktails and a postmortem session on the march. The president was in a good mood. He had listened to most of the speeches, and he was especially enthusiastic over that by Dr. King. He had been fearful that the march would turn into a wild and violent attack on the city by angry and militant blacks. However, this had not happened and the black leaders and the black people were to be congratulated. But there were other views of the march. Malcolm X had not been one of the "black leaders" and he had not been invited to the White House, but he had been among the crowd at the Lincoln Memorial:

> Yes, I was there. I observed that circus. Who ever heard of angry revolutionists all harmonizing "We Shall Overcome . . . Suum Day . . ." while tripping and swaying along arm-in-arm with the very people they were supposed to be angrily revolting against? Who ever heard of angry revolutionists swinging their bare feet together with their oppressor in lilypad park pools, with gospels and guitars and "I Have A Dream" speeches?[59]

CHAPTER 4

The Mississippi Freedom Democrats

By the end of 1963 the black social revolution in the United States was about to enter the critical second stage of its metamorphosis. In the process it was to undergo substantive, not to say radical, alterations in its goals, strategies, and tactics. There were also to be wholesale changes in its bases of operation, in its leadership, indeed in its image itself. Needless to say, the changes were not to be popular with everyone. To some observers the movement would appear to have undergone a veritable Dr. Jekyl and Mr. Hyde transfiguration. What had once been dignified, nonviolent, and even exemplary would become militant, demagogic, and menacing. But there were reasons. In its second stage the black revolution would shift northward; that is to say, its new center of gravity would be the ghettos of non-Southern central cities. In this area the ills of the blacks were of a different genre—massive unemployment, shoddy housing, disease, and plain hopelessness—none of which could be successfully assaulted by sit-ins, kneel-ins, and boycotts. Instead, these conditions did invite attacks on the system, its symbols and its apparatus. In 1963, however, all of this was still a short distance in the future. The first phase of the black revolution still had one more milestone to reach.

The first phase of the black revolution, 1955 to 1965, was almost wholly Southern in scope. Beginning with the bus boycott in Montgomery and the desegregation battles of Little Rock and other Southern towns, it flowered into the sit-in crusade of 1960 and the freedom rides of 1961. The de facto desegregation of public accommodations and of interstate transportation in the South was the main goal. The victory at Birmingham and the celebration of the March-on-Washington marked the successful conclusion of the drive. Desegregation was ultimately to be legislated into public policy by the United States government. The final and what may yet be adjudged to be the most critical activity of the first phase of the black revolution was the black voter-registration operation conducted in the South between 1962 and 1964. In terms of its magnitude, its intensity, the turbulence it created, and finally its results, the registration drive was revolution in itself.

For more than seventy-five years Southern politics had been exclusively the white man's business. But in countless cities and towns and rural areas blacks for once found the courage to attempt to register. The result was that by 1964 the total black vote in a number of states had increased 40 to 50 and even 100 percent. In Texas, for instance, the black vote jumped from 111,014 in 1962, to 375,000 in 1964. In both Georgia and Florida, during the same period the net gains were about one hundred thousand. The one retrograde state was Mississippi. Here the increase was a mere 5,000 for a net increase of 5 percent. Mississippi was later to get special attention. In total figures the number of blacks registered to vote in eleven Southern states rose from 1,344,519 in 1962, to 2,074,461 in 1964. This was a gain of more than 700,000 or some 40 percent. But this represented merely the beginning.[1] In 1970 there would be better than 3,500,000 black voters in the South. They would elect some 700 black public officials.[2]

Interest in mounting a campaign to increase the political power of Southern blacks extended back into the early years of the black revolution. In the spring of 1957, a few months after the victory in Montgomery, Dr. King and the SCLC announced the launching of the Crusade for Citizenship, a drive to help millions of Southern blacks to qualify to vote. Addressing a mass rally in Washington, D.C., on May 17, 1957, Dr. King said:

> Give us the ballot. Give us the ballot and we will no longer have to worry the federal government about our basic rights. . . . Give us the ballot and we will quietly, lawfully, and nonviolently, without rancor or bitterness, implement the May 17, 1954, decision of the Supreme Court.[3]

However, the Crusade for Citizenship never got off the ground. The SCLC was still a fledgling organization, and at this early date its reach was clearly exceeding its grasp. Besides, Southern blacks were much too preoccupied with school desegregation to give their attention to any other cause.

By 1961 the situation had changed considerably. With the sit-ins and freedom rides in the background the Field Foundation made a grant of $100,000 for a black voter-education program to be operated jointly by the United Church of Christ and the SCLC. Andrew Young was named director. In September, 1961, Young and his assistant,

Wyatt Walker, set up a voter-education leadership training center in Dorchester, Georgia. With other SCLC staff members and volunteers courses were instituted in the teaching of reading, writing, civics, voter-registration techniques, and the political process in general. Many of the Dorchester graduates set up miniature institutes in their own communities. By the beginning of 1962, upwards of fifty "Dorchester Centers" had been established in Alabama, Mississippi, Georgia, South Carolina, and Virginia.[4] The Dorchester Centers were valuable as far as they went, but some critics felt that they placed greater emphasis on voter education than on voter registration. Under any circumstances they appeared not to have upset unduly the local white power structures. In the end a genuine grass-roots voter-education crusade had to await the coming of such SNCC stalwarts as Diane Nash, Marion Barry, Rev. James Bevel, Robert Moses, and others. These young people were capable of the kind of commitment, the sense of mission, and the raw courage needed to lead a file of blacks into a registrar's office in a Mississippi Delta town.

The most noteworthy of these young blacks was Robert Moses. He, more than any other single individual, was responsible for the success of the 1962–1964 registration drive in the hostile South. Indeed, he was so caught up in its day-to-day heartaches, its gains, its set-backs, and its survival that the story of the voter-registration crusade could well be captioned: "The Ordeal of Robert Moses." When the sit-in movement began to make headlines in early 1960, Moses was teaching in the school system in New York City. Hungry for involvement, Moses conferred with people in the New York office of the SCLC and worked out an agreement to come South and do volunteer work that summer.[5] In Atlanta, in June, Moses discovered that no plans had been made for him. However, his real interest was in the student movement anyway, and after a meeting with Jane Stembridge he wound up doing miscellaneous office chores in SNCC's Atlanta headquarters. Later during the summer Moses agreed to make a field trip in several Southern states to recruit black students for SNCC's October conference in Atlanta. In Cleveland, Mississippi, Moses struck up an acquaintance with Amzie Moore, the tough battle-scarred head of the local NAACP. Moses tells of their meeting: "He [Moore] wasn't very interested in the sit-ins and integration of lunch counters and so forth. So we mapped out the areas where a voter registration drive could take place and an idea for a program which I sent back to Atlanta."[6]

Moses returned South in July, 1961, but not to Atlanta. He had been invited by C. C. Bryant, head of the NAACP in McComb, Mississippi, to come to that city to start the voter-registration drive.[7] In McComb, Moses was joined by two other SNCC volunteers, John Hardy of the Nashville Movement and Reggie Robinson of Baltimore. There were more than a dozen other volunteers, mostly ex-freedom riders who had been released from the Parchman jail. Moses scurried about in the black section of town getting housing for his workers. Harry Belafonte and others were supplying the money. On August 7, the first voter-registration school went into operation. Instructions had to be given in the filling out of a twenty-one question registration form. Mississippi's law also required that a prospective voter interpret to the registrar's satisfaction one or more of the 285 sections of the state constitution. These were formidable if not discouraging requirements, but there were local blacks who considered voting important enough to take them on. Moses and his volunteers rolled up their sleeves and went to work.

On August 15, Moses accompanied three local blacks, two middle-aged women and an old farmer, to the nearby town of Liberty to register.

> We arrived at the courthouse about 10 o'clock. The registrar came out. . . . He asked them: What did they want? . . . They didn't say anything. They were literally paralyzed with fear. . . . I told him who I was and that we were conducting a school in McComb, and these people had attended the school, and they wanted an opportunity to register. Well, he said, they'll have to wait. . . . Our people started to register, one at a time. In the meantime a processing of people began moving in and out of the registration office: the sheriff, a couple of his deputies, people from the tax office, the people who do the drivers' licenses—looking in, staring, moving back out, muttering. Finally finished the whole process about 4:30; all three of the people had had a chance to register—at least to fill out the form. This was a victory.[8]

As the four were driving back to McComb, a highway patrolman who had seen them in the registrar's office flagged them down. He asked Moses if he was the one who had been "trying to register our niggers." All were taken back to Liberty. Moses was charged with interfering with an officer in the discharge of his duties, fined fifty dollars, and sentenced to two days in jail.[9]

Moses had been warned. When he first moved into McComb, the local whites did not know what he planned to do. After the brazen episode of August 15, however, the SNCC workers were to be treated as enemy infiltrators. They would be chased down, harassed, jailed, bloodied, and even murdered. Thus, on August 29, when Moses had the "affrontery" to show up in Liberty with three more blacks to register, he was given a savage beating. Eight stitches were required to close the wound in his head. On September 25, Herbert Lee, a black farmer who had worked with voter registration in Liberty, was shot and killed by E. H. Hurst, a white state representative. Hurst claimed self-defense. Less than a month later police in McComb shot and killed Eli Brumfield, a black whom they apparently thought to be a SNCC volunteer. Finally, in late October white officials in McComb took steps to rid themselves entirely of the local voter-registration movement. On October 4, nineteen students, including Robert Moses and ten SNCC workers, were arrested for leading a protest march of young blacks to the city hall. They were charged with breach of the peace and contributing to the delinquency of minors. At their trial on October 31, they were all found guilty and sentenced each to a $500 fine and six months in jail. In his remarks the judge said: "Some of you are local residents, some of you are outsiders. Those of you who are local residents are like sheep being led to the slaughter. If you continue to follow the advice of outside agitators, you will be like sheep and be slaughtered." [10]

In January, 1962, following his release from jail, Moses decided to move his entire operation north to Jackson, Mississippi. McComb and Liberty had served their purposes as proving grounds. Besides, intimidation and repression had been keeping the local blacks away from the voter-education schools. The time had come to depart. As Moses put it: "The movement from the rural to the urban is irresistible and the line from Amite to McComb to Jackson straight as the worm furrows. Accordingly, I have left the dusty roads to run the dusty streets." [11] Jackson quickly became a beehive of SNCC activity. Moses had not been able to get many blacks on the registration rolls in South Mississippi, but news of his valiant efforts had gone out to the country. Ex-freedom riders and sit-in people began to drift into Jackson to work with Moses in voter registration. With an enlarged staff Moses began to formulate plans for a summer campaign. Adequate funding was to come from unanticipated sources.

Since the summer of 1961, the Kennedy administration had been promoting its ideas for a well-financed and professionally directed voter-registration campaign throughout the entire South. The Field and Taconic Foundations and the Egar Stern Family Fund responded in early 1962 with grants of several hundred thousand dollars to the

Southern Regional Council (SRC) to set up and direct such a campaign.[12] In late March the SRC established the Voter Education Project (VEP) to run for two years, from the fall of 1962 to the fall of 1964. Wiley A. Branton, a black veteran civil rights lawyer from Pine Bluff, Arkansas, was named director. In addition to Mississippi, voter-registration activities were being carried on in other Southern states by the NAACP, CORE, SCLC, the National Urban League, and SNCC. The VEP critically reviewed and evaluated these programs and made initial grants to some of them. Branton was, however, to reserve his special attention for Mississippi.

Mississippi was the only state where four black organizations were attempting to carry on voter-registration work at the same time. Obviously the VEP would have to do something to coordinate the financing and avoid duplication of efforts with these groups. A meeting of the representatives of these groups was held in Clarksdale and the decision was made to adopt the Council of Federated Organizations (COFO) as an umbrella for all VEP activities. COFO had been a paper organization but it had had an interesting history. In February, 1960, Aaron Henry, state president of the NAACP, called a meeting in Clarksdale of the black Elks, Masons, teachers, and other groups. Adopting the name Council of Federated Organizations, they requested a meeting with Governor Ross Barnett. They wanted to discuss such black grievances as unemployment, welfare, education, and voter registration. Barnett received them at his office and listened to them. His reply was: "Nothing you ask, am I willing to do." [13] COFO did not meet again until the summer of 1961. At this meeting, Robert Moses of SNCC, Dave Dennis of CORE, and Medgar Evers of the NAACP decided to make COFO an umbrella organization for all civil rights groups in the state, but nothing was done to implement the decision. With the new COFO, Aaron Henry was named president and Robert Moses executive director. The group received a grant of $14,000 for the period August 1, 1962, to March 31, 1963.[14]

Greenwood was to be the focus of the new drive, but it was Mississippi itself that was being challenged. For more than a century that state had operated almost as a closed society. To outsiders its chief activities seemed to be the production of cotton and the suppression of blacks. To be sure, Mississippi's blacks had the highest illiteracy and poverty rates in the nation. They were a peasant class in every sense of the word. Since 1890, they had been almost totally disfranchised. They had been lynched by the hundreds, and they had been bloodied even for imaginary offenses against their white masters. The ancient dicta that a Negro has no rights that a white man was bound to respect was forever the rule in Mississippi. But Robert Moses and Aaron Henry knew Mississippi; they were under no illusions about the difficulties of their appointed tasks. During the summer of 1962, COFO proceeded to set up voter-registration centers in Greenwood and other towns in the Delta region of the state.

The white reaction to the COFO program was swift in coming. In Senator James O. Eastland's own bailiwick, Sunflower County, black tenant farmers who showed an interest in voting were driven off the land. Mrs. Fannie Lou Hamer, later to become legendary in the movement, reports:

> The thirty-first of August in '62, the day I went into the courthouse to register, well, after I'd gotten back home, this man that I had worked for as a timekeeper and sharecropper for eighteen years, he said that I would just have to leave. . . . So I told him I wasn't trying to register for him, I was trying to register for myself. . . . I didn't have no other choice because for one time I wanted things to be different.[15]

Violence was not being abandoned; the whites were merely supplementing it with other means. Banks and finance companies would not make loans; local credit for food, clothing, and gasoline was cut off and welfare checks were stopped. A black who had the courage to attempt to register to vote could be reduced to begging.

During the fall and winter of 1962, the whites in the Delta towns even further tightened the screws. The distribution of federal surplus food and other commodities was put under tight restrictions. In Senator Eastland's Sunflower County, blacks had to get "responsible persons" to countersign their applications. Those who couldn't were out of luck. LeFlore County took the ultimate step. Early in December free food distribution was cut off completely for thousands of people most of whom were black.[16] This of course meant starvation for people who were already in desperate straits. To meet the emergency, member organizations of COFO called upon their home offices to gather food and medicine for distribution in Greenwood and the surrounding area. The local whites tried to impede this effort. Two black students from Michigan were bringing a truckload of food, clothing, and medicine for distribution in the Delta. They were arrested in Clarksdale; and after their truck was searched, they were charged with the possession of narcotics and dangerous drugs. After spending almost two weeks in jail, they were released. The narcotics turned out to be a common medication. LeFlore County was finally given the choice of resuming the food program or having the federal government do it. It chose the former.[17]

During the early months of 1963 the Delta whites began to escalate their campaign of violence and harassment of voter-registration people. COFO offices were raided and ransacked, "stakeouts" were maintained, and telephones were "tapped." The police and highway patrol "tailed" COFO vehicles, making arrests for crossing the center line, weaving, or any seeming infraction of the traffic regulations. On February 20, in Greenwood four black business establishments located on the same street as the SNCC office were burned to the ground. The businesses were burned by mistake. A SNCC worker who witnessed the arson was jailed, beaten, and almost run down by a speeding truck. A little more than a week later an automobile carrying three COFO workers, Robert Moses, Jim Travis, and Randolph Blackwell, was fired upon by the occupants of a passing vehicle. Thirteen forty-five caliber bullets hit the car. One of the SNCC members, Jim Travis, was hit in the shoulder and neck. Angered and out of patience as a result of this and other incidents in LeFlore and Sunflower Counties, Wiley Branton, director of the VEP, sounded a new resolve:

> The state of Mississippi has repeatedly thrown down a gauntlet at the feet of would-be Negro voters, not only by the discriminatory practices of the registrar, but also by the economic pressures, threats, coercions, physical violence and death to Negroes seeking the right to vote. The time has come for us to pick up the gauntlet. LeFlore County has elected itself as the testing ground for democracy and we are accordingly meeting the challenge there.[18]

(Branton was, ironically, a mulatto descendant of the fabulous white Delta slave owner, Greenwood LeFlore, after whom both the city and county were named.)

Telegrams were dispatched to Governor Ross Barnett of Mississippi and Attorney General Robert Kennedy informing them that the registration drive would continue and that the VEP would expect full protection of the constitutional rights of the voter-registration workers as well as those they assisted in registering to vote. In its response to Branton, however, the Justice Department showed some anxiety about becoming involved in the Delta. Burke Marshall suggested, in effect, that the VEP officials await the outcome of a pending legal action that could force registrars to accept black registrants. But Branton was adamant—the drive would not be postponed. The SCLC, CORE, and the NAACP were directed to send additional detachments of workers to Greenwood. SNCC brought in staff from all over the state. The decision had been made to fight it out with the Delta whites. If federal protection were forthcoming, so much the better. If not, COFO and the VEP were preparing to go it alone. The right to vote, far more fundamental than the right to buy a hot dog in Woolworth's, was the issue.

The local whites lost no time in picking up the challenge. On March 24, the COFO office in Greenwood was completely gutted by fire with all equipment and records destroyed. Two days later a shotgun blast ripped into the home of one of the SNCC volunteers. And over in Clarksdale an attack was made on Aaron Henry's drugstore. Unintimidated by all of this, SNCC officials on March 27 led a small delegation of blacks up the main street of Greenwood to the courthouse to protest against the continued harassment of COFO volunteers. On the way they were joined by about a hundred blacks from the community. The police met them with riot guns and German shepherd dogs. Eight of the leaders were arrested and subsequently sentenced each to two hundred dollars fine and four months in jail.[19] No longer able to stand aside, the Justice Department now stepped into the picture. On March 31, United States attorneys went into federal court seeking a restraining order against local officials. Their petition not only sought protection for the right to register and vote, but also demanded in addition that the local officials release the eight registration workers, refrain from further interference with the registration campaign, and permit Negroes to assemble for peaceful protest demonstrations.[20]

These were strong and resolute words but unfortunately that was all they turned out to be—mere words. On April 4, the same day that Dr. King unleashed his Project C in Birmingham, the Justice Department announced its decision to drop its injunctive proceedings against Greenwood in return for a promise from local officials to permit the safe registration of blacks as long as they refrained from marching on the courthouse. Perhaps the Kennedy administration did not want to wage war on two fronts. It was deeply interested in the voter registration campaign, but King commanded national and world attention and where he pitched his tent was where the federal government would be, and in full force. The meaning of Greenwood and LeFlore was now to be lost in the explosion in Birmingham. It would ultimately mean the failure of the VEP campaign in all of Mississippi.

However, Robert Moses and his SNCC diehards were still in the Delta and they planned to stay there. They had never really counted on federal intervention and now they planned to go on as before. During the summer of 1963, a group of white law students working in the movement ran across a Mississippi election law which they thought could be useful to COFO. The regulation provided that a voter who had been omitted from the rolls by error could be permitted to vote upon the submission of an affidavit certifying that he was otherwise qualified to do so.[21] Robert Moses seized upon the idea and planned to "crash" the August 6 primary in the state. Affidavits were secured and local blacks were assisted in filling them out. Early in August, State Attorney General Joe T. Patterson warned that any blacks who attempted to vote would be promptly jailed and prosecuted. This warning frightened some but not all of the local blacks. On the day of the primary some 500 blacks "voted" in Greenwood, 430 in Jackson, 30 in Canton, and a lesser number in several other Delta towns. Stokely Carmichael, working in the field for SNCC, observed: "Two years ago we would have been shot for a stunt like this. . . ."[22] But there was no shooting—indeed, there was no violence. The white election officials simply threw out the black ballots.

During the fall of 1963, the COFO volunteers were to follow through on yet another idea. Since blacks could not participate in the regular state elections, a mock election would be held for blacks throughout the state. The idea had originally been tossed around by Al Lowenstein (later a congressman from New York), Robert Moses, Annelle Ponder of SCLC, and Dave Dennis of CORE. The groups got Aaron Henry to run for governor of Mississippi and Edward King, a twenty-seven-year-old white chaplain at the black Tougaloo College, to stand for lieutenant governor. Ballot boxes were placed in churches, meeting places, and wherever blacks could get to them. In a rather low-keyed campaign Henry and King hit at the subjection of both blacks and whites to the exploitive power structure in the state. Some 90,000 blacks participated in the election thus giving the lie to whites who insisted that blacks were not interested in voting.[23] But a mock election is not a regular election and in the case of the latter, Mississippi, in spite of the VEP and COFO, was still keeping black participation at the zero level.

It was for this reason that on November 13, 1963, Wiley Branton notified Aaron Henry and Robert Moses that the VEP was reluctantly cutting off all funds to the registration drive in Mississippi. He applauded the courage of the hundreds of people who had labored in the campaign, but he insisted that no registration drive could succeed in the state without vigorous and meaningful federal support. Branton noted also that more money had been spent with fewer results than in any other state and further spending in Mississippi would take money from areas where positive results were being obtained.[24] It was a hard choice for Branton but he was a realist. The VEP was backing voter-registration drives in ten other Southern states besides Mississippi. There was white opposition in all of them, but in no case did it reach the fanatical level of Mississippi. And in those ten other states some 700,000 new black voters were added to the rolls. The real meaning of all this of course was that Mississippi brutality and intransigence had prevailed yet again. It would take federal power and determination to register blacks in that state and this would not be forthcoming until August, 1965.

Shortly after the mock election in November, representatives of the member organizations of COFO held a six-day meeting in Greenville, Mississippi.[25] After the inevitable evaluations and postmortems on the mock election were made, the group got down to discussing COFO plans for 1964. Almost everyone at the sessions agreed that Mississippi blacks should have a political organization of their own for participation in the 1964 elections. Some of the members wanted the organization, later to be known as the Mississippi Freedom Democratic Party, to become a permanent political party. But Robert Moses, who dominated the sessions, wanted such an organization principally for the purpose of challenging the regular state delegation at the Democratic National Convention in August. Black voter registration was to be the objective during 1964, but it was agreed that this should be supplemented by a summer project to dramatize such things as illiteracy, poverty, poor health care, and social services to the black and the poor in Mississippi. This idea later blossomed into the program known as the "Mississippi Freedom Summer—1964."

During the spring of 1964 with planning already at an advanced stage, Robert Moses and his staff began sending out calls throughout the nation for volunteers for the Freedom Summer program.[26] Moses did not particularly want white volunteers for the program. He had said earlier that "very consciously staff people did not want whites to come to the Delta." In an undertaking of this kind, however, there was not much choice. White organizations and individuals responded as though they had been waiting for an invitation. The National Council of Churches virtually appointed itself as the Northern regional headquarters for the program. Early in May it initiated a widespread drive for young recruits. Because of the hazards to be faced in Mississippi, efforts were made to screen out the immature and emotionally unstable. Of three hundred applicants from Stanford University only forty-five eventually got to Mississippi, and at Wesleyan only half of those who applied were accepted.

In Mississippi they were to be housed with black families whenever possible. The recruits were principally idealistic and enthusiastic white middle-class students. They came from the Ivy League and eastern schools, as well as from midwestern liberal arts institutions. A training school was set up for them by the National Council of Churches at the Western College for Women in Oxford, Ohio. They were given two weeks' drilling in the techniques of nonviolence and were familiarized with the type of hardships to be encountered in Mississippi.

By Sunday, June 21, the first contingent, consisting of two hundred volunteers, was ready to depart for Mississippi. In the lobby of a hall at the Western College for Women where they were trained a red-lettered bulletin warned: "Before you leave Oxford, write your Congressmen asking them to act to insure your safety. Contact should be established with them before you reach Mississippi." [27] In Mississippi, on the other hand, a wholly different view was taken of the situation. Students or not, they were the enemy, and Mississippi officials prepared to treat them accordingly. "To meet the anticipated horde of barbaric invaders," writes an eminent observer, ". . . a furious Mississippi legislature enlarged local police powers to the point of legalizing home-grown vigilante committees, doubled the size of the state Highway Patrol and gave it police powers. . . ." [28] Running through the minds of white Mississippians was a fear reminiscent of the ancient terror of a slave rebellion. The *New York Times* reported: "The emergence of the Ku Klux Klan and the closely related Americans for the Preservation of the White Race has put thousands of white Mississippians into an armed camp." [29]

In Jackson with a new $2.2 million budget the police department bought two hundred new shotguns and supplied every man with a tear-gas mask. A new motorized corps was equipped with troop carriers, two half-ton searchlight trucks, and three trailer trucks to imprison demonstrators. To top it all off, the department added the so-called "Thompson Tank" (named after Jackson's Mayor Allen Thompson). The tank was an armored truck designed to hold twelve policemen.[30]

On the same day that the two hundred volunteers departed for Mississippi, three young COFO workers were shot and beaten to death in Neshoba County, Mississippi. Not missed immediately, their bodies were unearthed by FBI agents some six weeks later near Philadelphia, Mississippi.

With it all, however, the volunteers kept coming to Mississippi. By midsummer they numbered over one thousand. Seven hundred of these were students, about one hundred were clergymen, and 150 were lawyers. The lawyers were provided by the NAACP Legal Defense Fund, the Lawyers Constitutional Defense Fund, the Lawyers Committee for Civil Rights under Law, and the National Lawyers Guild. There were also more than a dozen other national organizations on the scene assisting the volunteers. There were about one hundred regular workers directing the program. Of these, about seventy-five came from SNCC and the remainder from CORE. The NAACP was apparently confining its participation to legal defense while the SCLC satisfied itself with a few representatives. All activities were directed from COFO headquarters in Jackson by Robert Moses and a SNCC staff. Indeed, the Mississippi Freedom Summer was essentially a SNCC enterprise.

In the field, work for the volunteers lay in three separate categories. The first of these was voter registration—the task of assisting blacks to qualify to vote. Secondly there were the community centers which conducted literacy classes and training in the various skills for adults, along with arts and crafts courses, and recreational programs for children. Thirdly, there were the freedom schools which offered remedial academic work and vocational training for black high school youth. The freedom schools were set up in church basements and other available spaces in the Negro communities.

The Mississippi Freedom Summer program came finally to a close at the end of August, and the hundreds of volunteers packed up their gear and prepared to leave the state. For the vast majority of white Mississippians it was none too soon. To them the summer volunteers were a bunch of "communist-inspired agitators, immoral, filthy, frustrated beatniks whose personal desires were limited to interracial fornication"[31] and whose avowed purpose was to see Mississippi occupied by the United States Army. The fact of the matter, however, was that these volunteers were highly disciplined, intelligent, courageous, and idealistic to a fault. More than one observer had described them as a super-Peace Corps. During the summer program they helped to add more than 1,200 blacks to the voter-registration rolls; in the freedom schools they accelerated the pace of 2,500 black high school students, and in the community centers they brought an appreciation of the arts and crafts to hundreds of youngsters and adults. In the final analysis, however, the worth of these volunteers would be judged not by the task they completed, but by the forces they released which fractured the status quo and set in motion a process leading to a freer society.

The departure of the volunteers from Mississippi marked only the conclusion of phase one of Freedom Summer. There was a second phase. It was to begin on August 21, with the arrival of the Mississippi Freedom Democratic Party at the Democratic National Convention in Atlantic City. Back in November, 1963, Robert Moses had been indeed earnest when he proposed that COFO take the initiative in building a grass-roots political movement in Mississippi. The objectives of such an organization would be to challenge and unseat the regular Democratic organization at the National Convention in August, 1964, and thereafter gain recognition as the legitimate Democratic party apparatus in Mississippi. Over the winter of 1963 the idea was thoroughly discussed, and by February, 1964, COFO had made the decision to establish the Mississippi Freedom Democratic Party. During the next few months the MFDP moved rapidly to get its house in order. In March, Robert Moses appointed Joseph L. Rauh as chief counsel for the party. Rauh, a nationally known labor lawyer, was a leader in the Americans for Democratic Action, counsel for the United Automobile Workers and a longtime friend of Walter Reuther. On April 24 Ella Baker along with Reggie Robinson, Frank Smith, and Walter Tillow, all students, were dispatched to Washington, D.C., to set up a MFDP office. They immediately got busy making arrangements for the MFDP delegation's stay in Atlantic City; they began to solicit support for the MFDP from the various state delegations throughout the country, and they sent letters as well as speakers out in a campaign to raise money. Back in Jackson on April 26, COFO officials called a press conference to launch officially the new political party.

To keep within the law, application was made to the state for a charter for the MFDP. And with the party's need for an official roster of members, a "freedom registration" drive was begun among the state's 400,000 unenfranchised blacks during the late spring. For all practical purposes the MFDP considered itself ready for business. In the June 2nd primary elections the party ran four black candidates for seats in the United States Congress. The best known of the four was Mrs. Fannie Lou Hamer, running for office from Senator Eastland's own district. No one was naive enough to believe that any of the black candidates could beat his entrenched white opponent, but their candidacies were expected to dramatize the basic issues, to point up the fact that blacks had been shut out of the political process and that these were the first black candidates to run for office since the Reconstruction period.

During mid-June the regular Democratic organization made ready to select delegates to its state convention. The law required that at 10 A.M. on June 16 precinct meetings were to be held in each of the state's 1,884 precincts. The MFDP planned to send delegates to these meetings who, among other things, would attempt to introduce resolutions calling for loyalty oaths to the national Democratic party. On the appointed day, however, the blacks found it impossible even to locate the meetings; indeed, in more than three-fourths of the precincts no meetings were held at all. In six counties blacks were simply refused entrance, and in ten others blacks were admitted but not allowed to participate in the proceedings. The white delegates selected at these meetings constituted the state Democratic convention which met in Jackson on July 28. They rejected an oath to support the national Democratic party and instead passed the following resolution:

We believe in separation of the races in all phases of our society. It is our belief that the separation of the races is necessary for the peace and tranquility of all the people of Mississippi and the continuing good relationship which has existed over the years. . . .[32]

In the meanwhile the MFDP was moving ahead with its own program. In July the Mississippi secretary of state had refused to grant the party a charter and ruled it illegal, but the party proceeded nevertheless with plans to hold a state convention. With upwards of 100,000 blacks registered on freedom ballots as members of the MFDP, a delegate-selection process was set in motion. Precinct meetings were held in twenty-six counties and county meetings were held in thirty-five. The three hundred delegates selected at these meetings made up the MFDP state convention held in Jackson on August 6.[33] It was a unique experience for most of those in attendance. The hall was decorated with bunting flags and posters; TV camera crews, lights, and bustling newsmen kept excitement high. The convention selected a delegation of sixty-eight people for Atlantic City, with Aaron Henry as chairman and Fannie Lou Hamer as vice-chairman. The platform they adopted pledged allegiance to the national Democratic party and called for support of the party platform during the national elections. It called also for firm and positive federal action to end segregation and brutality in Mississippi.

In all truthfulness the leaders of the MFDP did not expect to get favorable consideration from the Credentials Committee at the Democratic Convention. To get the party's case via a minority report on the convention floor and thereby before the nation at large, Joseph L. Rauh, the chief counsel, evolved what he called an "eleven and eight strategy." [34] Convention rules stipulated that a minority report of the Credentials Committee must have the backing of 10 percent or eleven of the committee's 110 members. The rules also required that eight delegations support a motion for a roll call. Beginning in early August, Rauh and MFDP leaders worked tirelessly at lining up the support of as many Credentials Committee delegates and full delegations as possible. By mid-August their efforts began to pay off. On August 15, the California State Democratic Convention adopted a resolution demanding the seating of the MFDP at Atlantic City. [35] Less than a week later twenty-five congressmen representing some seven states issued a statement calling for the seating of the MFDP. The statement declared that the regular Mississippi Democratic party "subscribed to 'repugnant principles' which distort the image of the party in the nation." [36] By convention time on August 22, Rauh had secured promises of support from eighteen Credentials Committee members and some ten state delegations. He was ready to put his "eleven and eight" strategy into operation if the occasion arose.

In the nation's capital President Lyndon Johnson was daily becoming more anxious over the developing battle between the rival Mississippi delegations. He was sympathetic with the claims of the MFDP, but he did not want to jeopardize the support of the white South. Most of all as the assured candidate of the party he wanted no squabble to mar or interrupt the proceedings leading to his nomination. At a meeting with party leaders on August 18, Johnson proposed a three-point solution to the Mississippi problem: (1) the regular Mississippi delegates would be seated provided they pledged to support the convention's nominees; (2) the MFDP delegates would be seated but would have no voting rights; and (3) a change would be made in the call of the convention in 1968 to make clear that the Democratic party in every state must be open to every registered voter without discrimination because of race and that any state party practicing discrimination would not have its delegation seated. The proposal got only a mixed reaction from the party leaders present. However, Johnson was the president and party leader, and his proposal became the guide for the Credentials Committee.

Led by Robert Moses, Aaron Henry, and Mrs. Hamer, the MFDP delegation arrived in Atlantic City on Friday, August 21. One of the delegates described its immediate activities:

> Every delegate from every likely state was provided with a copy of the [MFDP] brief to the credentials committee. . . . MFDP, with the help of SNCC, produced brochures, mimeographed biographies of the MFDP delegates, histories of the MFDP, legal arguments, historical arguments, moral arguments, and distributed them to the delegates.[37]

At an early caucus the delegation voted to reject President Johnson's proposal. Moses insisted that the MFDP had come to Atlantic City to unseat a regime of injustice, illegality, and immorality and that it would not allow itself to be limited to the token role of spectator. Besides, sentiment among delegates at the convention seemed to be moving in favor of the MFDP.

On Saturday, August 22, the MFDP began to present its case before the Credentials Committee. In his brief for the party, Chief Counsel Rauh concentrated on the disloyalty of the regular Mississippi Democrats and the brutal means they employed to stop the black voter-registration campaign. "Are you going to throw out of here the people who want to work for Lyndon Johnson, who are willing to be beaten and shot and thrown in jail to work for Lyndon Johnson? Are we for the oppressor or the oppressed?" he asked the committee.[38] Rauh then called up a stream of witnesses including Mrs. Fannie Lou Hamer, Dr. Martin Luther King, Aaron Henry, the Reverend Edwin King, and others. Mrs. Hamer gave a dramatic account of the brutality which she and other blacks had encountered in attempting to register and vote in the Mississippi Delta. Dr. King asserted that no state in the union had gone to "such extremes" as Mississippi to prevent black participation in political life.[39] Growing impatient with this type of recitation, the chairman of the Credentials Committee, David Lawrence, suggested that the witnesses of the MFDP confine themselves to the legal issue before the committee and not expatiate on the general subject of general life in Mississippi. Chief Counsel Rauh vigorously objected. He insisted that testimony dealing with conditions in Mississippi was pertinent to the point that blacks were deprived of participation in the Democratic party. The parade of witnesses was resumed.

On Sunday afternoon the Credentials Committee called a recess until Tuesday. A subcommittee was appointed to work out a compromise. Johnson and the party chiefs were resolved to bring the impasse to an end. They held no brief for the unreliable Mississippi white regulars, but they could not allow the MFDP to call the shots. No unofficial group, regardless of the merits of their case, could be allowed to pressure or panic a convention into a total capitulation to its demands. Hubert Humphrey, who was in hot pursuit of the vice-presidential nomination, was designated by Johnson to find a middle way. In the meanwhile Walter Reuther was called in from Detroit to use his influence with his longtime friend and colleague, Joseph L. Rauh.[40] Johnson moved also to decimate MFDP support on the Credentials Committee. Good jobs were offered to some members of the committee and dismissals from federal employment were held out to others. By Monday evening Johnson had smashed Rauh's "eleven and eight" strategy to bits. There would be no MFDP minority report and no roll call on the convention floor.[41]

By early Tuesday morning Humphrey and his subcommittee had produced a new proposal. In essence it provided for the seating of all regular Mississippi delegates who would accept the loyalty oath; it gave seats with full voting rights to the MFDP's Aaron Henry and Rev. Edwin King, and finally it stipulated that at all future conventions no delegations would be seated from states where citizens were denied the right to participate in party affairs by reason of race, creed, or color. During the two days in which he hammered out the provisions of the compromise, Humphrey was in constant consultation with black and white liberal leaders at the convention. The final product therefore had the prior approval of Walter Reuther, Bayard Rustin, Dr. Martin Luther King, Joseph L. Rauh, and several others.[42] Under any circumstances it represented the final position of the party leadership on the Mississippi question. The MFDP caucused at 10:30 A.M. Tuesday. The meeting was closed to all except members of the delegation. Robert Moses addressed the group pointing out that the MFDP had not been totally opposed to compromise and that in fact the delegation had earlier gone on record in favor of a proposal of Congresswoman Edith Green that any member of either Mississippi delegation willing to take the loyalty oath would be seated and given the vote.[43] The Humphrey proposal, however, was not a compromise; it was an abomination. It not only limited the MFDP to two token seats, but it had the affrontery even to name those two. The caucus voted to reject the Humphrey proposal.

For the better part of Tuesday afternoon MFDP delegates listened to people hoping to get them to reverse their earlier decision. Bayard Rustin spoke of the need to understand the art of compromise. Senator Wayne Morse of Oregon emphasized the critical need of all Democrats to unite against the threat of Barry Goldwater. And in a thinly veiled threat to the delegation the National Council of Churches averred that they might not be disposed to continue support of the programs of persons who did not "understand the national responsibility" of that organization.[44] When Dr. King appeared to address the delegation, the atmosphere became charged. To many of the delegates he was fast becoming a Judas. Advising acceptance of the compromise, King spoke of the efficacy, indeed the need, of pragmatism even in the most idealistic of situations. Robert Moses angrily disagreed. "This reasoning that you have been giving us here is inaccurate. We are not here to bring politics into our morality, but to bring morality into our politics."[45] The exchange continued with Moses becoming more bitter by the second. In the view of one observer he not only won the argument; "he tore King up."[46] In a final poll that Tuesday evening the delegation voted once again to reject the compromise. It was now up to the convention.

Temporary Chairman John O. Pastore banged his gavel several times and his voice sang out over the rising din, "The ayes have it." The time was approximately 9:30 P.M., and "the ayes have it" meant that the convention had just approved the report of the Credentials Committee, that is, the Humphrey compromise on the seating of the Mississippi delegations. MFDP delegates who had been in the gallery and on the outside of the convention hall now decided to voice their disapproval in the only way left to them. Linked arm-in-arm, solemn and determined, they moved upon the convention floor. They brushed aside protesting ushers and sergeant-at-arms and proceeded to occupy the vacant seats designated for the Mississippi delegation. Within seconds they were surrounded by reporters, radio and TV newsmen. Blacks from other state delegations began to arrive to cheer them.[47] In the meanwhile the regular business of the convention had come to a dead halt. It would be near midnight before the impromptu demonstration had run its course and Chairman Pastore could again bang his gavel. Sometime later Robert Moses explained his refusal to compromise:

> The FDP delegates were the only people at that whole convention who were free in any meaningful use of the term. The President told everyone else . . . what to do. All I cared about was the insides of those 68 delegates and the future of the FDP in Mississippi.[48]

Moses and the other leaders of the party had hoped to win at Atlantic City, but regardless of the outcome they planned to challenge the right of the regular Mississippi delegation to seats in the United States Congress. "This had been an integral part of the program from the beginning. Actually, planning had begun long before the convention."[49] From October 30 through November 2, the MFDP conducted its "Freedom Election" throughout the state. Ballot boxes were set up in barber shops, restaurants, churches, funeral homes, and even trucks to reach the outlying areas. When the returns had been counted, some 63,000 votes had been cast for Lyndon Johnson to 17 for Barry Goldwater. Three black women, including Fannie Lou Hamer, had been elected to the U.S. House of Representatives, and Aaron Henry was elected to the U.S. Senate. On January 4, 1965, the three black women appeared in the chamber of the U.S. House of Representatives demanding to be seated. Their counsel contended that since blacks had been "deliberately and systematically denied the right to register and vote" in the regular election in Mississippi, the seating of the five regular party congressmen would constitute a violation of the Constitution. Sentiment in the House of Representatives clearly favored the MFDP, but it was the vote that counted. The House voted 276 to 149 to seat the regular Mississippi delegation.[50]

In the aftermath of the Democratic National Convention the general consensus was that the MFDP had won an unprecedented victory at Atlantic City and should have accepted the compromise. Perhaps. But Robert Moses and his disciples had not come to the convention to win a political victory. They had come for *justice, for a denial to Mississippi of the fruits of barbarism and brutality.* This goal was not achieved. The issue was the crux of the matter. In the early sixties Moses and other SNCC volunteers had started coming into Mississippi. Fresh from the sit-ins and freedom rides, they had confidence in themselves and their mission; they gloried in nonviolence; and above all they still had faith in the "system." Democracy in America had ultimately to mean democracy in Mississippi and democracy for black people. It could not be selective, or so they thought. But frustration and disillusionment very early began to dim their hopes. The stark and ever-present terror, the visceral poverty, and destitution abounding in Mississippi were so new to the young radicals as to be unbelievable.

But others knew. They knew also that the cost of victory in Mississippi was almost prohibitive. This accounts for the reluctance of the federal government to back them, for Wiley Branton's decision to withdraw VEP funds from Mississippi, and for the less than enthusiastic support given them by the big four black civil rights groups. By the end of 1964 Moses and the young volunteers were giving up the struggle. Mississippi had given them a beating both physically and spiritually. In the process they had been shorn of their idealism and their optimism. They had become contemptuous of nonviolence, of love and Dr. King, and they had grown distrustful of the black middle-class and white liberal leadership alike. Most of all, they had lost faith in American democracy. The system, after all, *was* selective. It had refused to combat brutality and injustice in Mississippi, and moreover it had sustained that state at Atlantic City. To be sure, the Mississippi experience profoundly altered the thinking of all the young volunteers who shared it. Mississippi ultimately proved to have been one of the nation's greatest training grounds for revolutionary black nationalism.

In the rest of the South the story was much different. As a matter of fact, 1964 and 1965 proved to be banner years for the civil rights movement in Dixie. In the fall of 1964, Wiley Branton was able to report to the Southern Regional Council that the first Voter-Education Project had been a roaring success. During the period 1962 to 1964, more than 700,000 blacks had been added to the voter registration in the South. Black disfranchisement in the region was definitely being brought to an end. On July 2, President Johnson affixed his signature to the Public Accommodation Act of 1964. This law was to prove to be the most meaningful and effective piece of civil rights legislation ever enacted by Congress. Assistant Attorney General Burke Marshall was to state: "The thing that the Act reaches is the official caste system in this country."[51] Of the eleven sections or titles of the act, number VI was both the most crucial and controversial. It called for the elimination of discrimination in all federally assisted programs, authorizing termination of programs or withdrawal of federal funds for failure to comply. The provision applied immediately and directly to some two hundred programs receiving in excess of $18 billion of federal funds.

There was, perhaps, no man in the country who received greater satisfaction from the passage of the Public Accommodation law than Dr. Martin Luther King. Some nine years earlier he had initiated the movement that led ultimately to its enactment. To a very great degree the law was a monument to his leadership and the students and others whom he inspired. During the early fall Dr. King was to receive a more personal and more dramatic tribute to his greatness. On October 14, the Swedish government notified him that he was to be awarded the Nobel Prize for Peace. Members of the Swedish Parliament had selected him because he had succeeded in keeping his followers to the principle of nonviolence and because he was the "first person in the Western world to have shown us that a struggle can be waged without violence."[52] King was the youngest man, the third black, and the twelfth American to receive the honor.

Among the hundreds of congratulatory messages received by Dr. King those from the South were conspicuous by their absence. Down in Birmingham, Bull Connor remarked of the award: "They're scraping the bottom of the barrel when they pick him. He's caused more strife and trouble in this country than anyone I can think of."[53] On the other hand, it took the white establishment in King's own home city of Atlanta no little time to recover from the shock. Dr. King was anathema to many of them, and they stubbornly opposed any public honor by or in the city for him. Ultimately, however, more liberal counsels were to prevail. Mayor Ivan Allen was one of them: "It should be recognized that Dr. King has furnished the Negro people the leadership that a white leader would have given his race should it have been a minority seeking equal rights and full citizenship."[54] On January 27, 1965, some 1,500 Atlantans, mostly white, gathered at a banquet to pay tribute to King. He was presented with a Steuben glass bowl bearing the inscription: "To Dr. Martin Luther King, Jr., Citizen of Atlanta, Recipient of the 1964 Nobel Peace Prize, with respect and admiration, January 27, 1965." King's speech to the gathering was enthusiastically received. He said in part: "I must confess that I have enjoyed being on this mountain-top, and I am tempted to want to stay here and retreat to a more quiet and serene life. But something within reminds me that the valley calls. . . ."[55]

Some three weeks prior to the Atlanta testimonial Dr. King announced the kick-off of a voter-registration drive in Selma, Alabama. It was that campaign to which he was alluding when he said, "Something within reminds me that the valley calls." Dr. King and the SCLC went into the Selma campaign for several reasons. First, directly after Birmingham, the SCLC had decided on an "Alabama Freedom Summer" for 1964. It was to be essentially a voter-registration drive with Selma as its focus. However, the idea was dropped because of the big buildup of the COFO program in Mississippi. Second, the SCLC had earned something less than commendation for its token efforts in Mississippi. Besides, Dr. King had been severely criticized by SNCC delegates at Atlantic City. Third, it was common knowledge that Selma's sheriff, Jim Clark, was a potential Bull Connor. This meant that there was every likelihood that the city would commit the same blunders with the same national reactions as Birmingham. Indeed, the Selma White Citizens Council in 1964 had advertised itself as a group

> whose efforts are not thwarted by courts which give sit-in demonstrators legal immunity, prevent school boards from expelling students who participate in mob activities. . . . Law enforcement can be called only after these things occur, but your Citizens Council prevents them from happening.[56]

There were upwards of fifteen thousand blacks of voting age in Selma. A team of SNCC volunteers had been in the town since 1963 but had not been able to add more than two hundred of them to the registration lists. Prospective black voters could not come up with the required [white] reference. And those who could were unable to answer such voter-qualifying questions as: "If no national candidate for Vice-President receives a majority of the electoral vote, how is a Vice-President chosen? In such cases how many votes must a person receive to become Vice-President?"[57] Beyond this the local registration office was open only on the first and third Mondays of each month, thus greatly limiting the possibility of registration.

Dr. King had to be absent from Selma for most of January. During the interim his lieutenants, Hosea Williams and Andrew Young, held demonstrations and led mass marches to the courthouse. More than one thousand blacks were jailed. Sheriff Jim Clark was assisted in his tasks by a volunteer group of local whites who liked to call themselves squirrel shooters. Back in Selma at the end of the month Dr. King was prepared to begin the campaign in earnest. On February 1, he and Rev. Ralph Abernathy led one thousand blacks on a march to the courthouse. More than 750 of them, including King and Abernathy, were rounded up and jailed by Jim Clark and his "squirrel shooters." On the next day another five hundred marchers were intercepted and arrested. As Sheriff Clark was hauling King and his nonviolent followers off the streets, an acknowledged apostle of violence had flown into town. On February 3, Malcolm X walked into Brown's Chapel (Dr. King's campaign headquarters) and asked to be introduced. Giving his usual militant speech, he held the audience of local blacks spellbound, many of them breaking into applause. Informed of what was going on, Mrs. King went to Brown's Chapel to put in a defense for nonviolence. She was very effective. Later Malcolm X reassured her: "I want Dr. King to know that I didn't come to Selma to make his job difficult. I really did come thinking that I could make it easier. If the white people realize what the alternative is, perhaps they will be more willing to hear Dr. King." [58] Dr. King was released from jail on February 5.

As in the Birmingham campaign, the SCLC recruited young people for the mass demonstrations. On February 10, Sheriff Jim Clark compelled 165 of these children, some under twelve, to force march, mostly trot, more than three miles through the countryside on their way to jail for demonstrating. Riding along in automobiles and trucks, the sheriff's men beat at them with billy clubs and burned them with cattle prods to keep them on the run. Some of them collapsed by the roadside screaming. When a fifteen-year-old girl refused to march any farther, a member of the posse jabbed her with a prod shouting, "March, dammit!" Nearby a young boy chided him, "God sees you," and the white man turned around and hit him in the mouth with a billy club.[59] On February 18, in the nearby town of Marion, state troopers savagely beat up some four hundred demonstrators, fatally shooting one of them. The reaction to Dr. King's campaign was becoming bloodier by the day, but not all of the white citizens approved. Thus, on March 6, an organization calling itself the Concerned White Citizens of Alabama staged a march to the Selma courthouse. The group included some seventy businessmen, school teachers, professors, and housewives coming from Montgomery, Huntsville, Auburn, Tuscaloosa, and Birmingham. Demanding that brutality against blacks be halted and that a simplified registration be adopted for all, they declared: "We are sickened by the totalitarian atmosphere of intimidation and fear officials have purposefully created and maintained to discourage lawful assembly and peaceful expression of grievances against the existing conditions."[60]

An indispensable part of the SCLC's strategy for a successful campaign was coverage by the national and world press. To ensure this, the campaigns invariably featured a spectacular if not illegal demonstration or march. In keeping with this principle, Dr. King announced at Brown's Chapel on March 5 that on the following Sunday he would lead a grand march over the fifty-four mile route from Selma to Montgomery. The purpose was to lay before Governor George Wallace the many grievances of Alabama's long-suffering blacks. The governor's reaction to the idea was predictable. He immediately issued a directive to Colonel Al Lingo, head of the state troopers and to Sheriff Jim Clark to stop the blacks at any cost. Representatives of the national and international press began pouring into Selma. In the meanwhile Nicholas Katzenbach, newly appointed U.S. Attorney General, pleaded with Dr. King not to risk injury or possible death by leading the march. King's assistants in the SCLC voiced the same concern. They thought that it would be better for him to remain in Atlanta and work up national support. King eventually agreed to let his chief lieutenants lead the march.

Early Sunday afternoon with Hosea Williams and John Lewis in the lead, some 525 blacks headed up Sylvan Street and through town to the small concrete bridge that humped over the muddy Alabama river. The marchers included boys less than fifteen years old and women over sixty. Many of them carried satchels and overnight bags containing blankets, toothbrushes, and extra shoes. Moving close behind the marchers were four ambulances carrying three white doctors who had flown down from New York City the night before at their own expense. There were also several black nurses as well as white nurses whose fare had been paid by the Medical Committee for Human Rights. Walking two abreast, the blacks began to cross the bridge to get on U. S. Highway 80 leading east to Montgomery. When they reached the south side of the span, they were confronted by a battalion of state troopers in steel helmets plus a mounted company of the sheriff's posse armed with bullwhips.

When the marchers moved within fifty feet of the troopers, a voice barked out: "This is an unlawful assembly. Your march is not conducive to the public safety. You are ordered to disperse and go back to your church or to your homes." The voice was that of Major John Cloud of the state troopers. When Hosea Williams called out,

"May we have a word with the Major?" the answer was, "There is no word to be had. You have two minutes to turn around and go back to your church." In something less than sixty seconds the major gave the order: "Troopers, advance." [61] A man on the scene from the *New York Times* describes the charge: "The wedge moved with such force that it seemed almost to pass over the waiting column instead of through it." [62] The first ten or twenty marchers were bludgeoned to the ground screaming. Clark was preparing to chase the blacks all the way back to Brown's Chapel, but he was stopped by Police Chief Wilson Baker who reminded the sheriff that his jurisdiction ended at the city line.

By this time, the ambulances which had been stopped at the bridge were allowed to cross. The doctors found the highway littered with hats, handkerchiefs, overnight bags, umbrellas, and miscellaneous articles. They found several bleeding people still lying on the ground. All told, some sixty-six marchers were sent to the hospital, sixteen of these with serious injuries. John Lewis, who was one of those injured, declared: "I don't see how President Johnson can send troops to Vietnam . . . and can't send troops to Selma, Alabama. Next time we march, we may have to keep going when we get to Montgomery. We may have to go on to Washington." [63] Back in Atlanta, Dr. King was aghast at the news from Selma:

> When I made a last-minute agreement not to lead the march and appointed my able and courageous associate, Hosea Williams, for this responsibility, I must confess that I had no idea that the kind of brutality and tragic expression of man's inhumanity to man as existed today would take place. [64]

King immediately announced plans for a march on Tuesday from Selma to Montgomery and indicated that he would go into the federal court to obtain a writ to prevent Alabama authorities from interfering.

In the meanwhile, "Bloody Sunday" was producing a national reaction virtually unprecedented in the history of the civil rights movement. The *New York Times* in an editorial commented:

> If this is described as law enforcement, it is misnamed. It is nothing more or less than race-conscious officialdom run amuck. It disgraces not only the state of Alabama but every citizen of the country in which it can happen. [65]

In Harlem and other black communities across the nation blacks went into the streets to denounce the bloodletting at Selma. Local civil rights groups, hundreds of clergymen of all faiths, college deans and professors, cabinet wives, and just plain people made rush plans to come to Selma and walk with King to Montgomery. The Medical

Committee for Human Rights rented several ambulances and announced its intention to stay close to Dr. King. The SNCC organization also decided to join the march. With the exception of John Lewis, the hierarchy of the organization had been following a hands-off policy toward Dr. King's latest endeavor. Stokely Carmichael and James Forman were bitterly opposed to any further involvement with the SCLC.[66] However, when news was received of the beating of John Lewis (SNCC chairman) and other blacks at Pettus Bridge, SNCC headquarters in Atlanta chartered a plane for Selma.

Dr. King in the meanwhile was finding that it was much easier to schedule the second march than to carry it off. On Monday, March 7, SCLC lawyers went into federal court to ask that Governor Wallace's ban on the Selma to Montgomery march be lifted. Judge Frank Johnson, considered to be pro-segregationist, responded with his own restraining order against the march. From Washington, D.C., President Johnson was exerting influence on Dr. King to call off the march. Vice-President Humphrey was asked to do what he could, and Attorney General Katzenbach virtually kept an open line to Dr. King's suite at the Hotel Albert in Selma. Dr. King's initial reaction to this pressure was to call off the march. The SCLC staff joined in the pressure. They argued that the organization had never knowingly violated a federal court injunction and that to do so now would be to jeopardize the valuable if not indispensable support of the national administration for the movement. Dr. King was stuck squarely between "the Devil and the deep blue sea." Already suspicious and mistrustful the SNCC leaders were watching to see if Dr. King would "chicken out." Dr. King spent all of Monday night and early Tuesday morning agonizing over the alternatives. By 4 A. M. he had come to a decision. "I would rather die on the highways of Alabama than make a butchery of my conscience. I ask you to join me today as we move on."[67] When Katzenbach called at 5 A.M., King apprised him of the decision.

Convinced that King meant what he said, President Johnson now made inquiries to find out how far each set of leaders believed it had to go to meet its needs and to maintain the confidence of its supporters. The president also placed some seven hundred federal troops on the alert in Alabama. Finally, Leroy Collins, former governor of Florida and now head of the Community Relations Service, was dispatched to Selma under orders to get both sides to agree to a compromise. From

Colonel Lingo and Sheriff Clark, Collins got the agreement to allow King to cross the Pettus Bridge to a point one mile beyond. If King stopped here and turned back upon being ordered to do so, there would be no gas, no force, and no violence. Collins then hurried over to the Albert Hotel to confer with King. Dr. King accepted the compromise and Collins supplied him with a map of the designated route.

By noon on Tuesday Selma was jammed with people coming from more than thirty states in the Union. Newsmen and TV cameramen were quite busy. At 2:30 p.m. Dr. King showed up at Brown's Chapel ready to go. "We have gone too far to turn back now. We must let them know that nothing can stop us. Not even death itself." [68] Accompanied by Rev. Fred Lee Shuttlesworth, James Forman, and James Farmer, Dr. King moved out in front of 1,500 marchers. As they approached the bridge, a federal marshal stepped up to the leaders and read Judge Johnson's restraining order. Dr. King listened intently, then informed the marshal that the march would continue. The procession moved across the bridge and one mile up Highway 80 to the prearranged point. With troopers barring the road, Major Cloud barked out: "This march will not continue. It is not conducive to the safety of this group or the motoring public." Dr. King then requested permission for his group to kneel in prayer. When the prayer was finished, Dr. King noticed in surprise that the troopers had removed the barriers and the road to Montgomery was wide open. Refusing the obvious bait, King wheeled around and ordered his marchers: "Go back. Turn around and go back."

Back in Selma there was an immediate howl over the failure of the march to continue to Montgomery. The criticism of Dr. King and the SCLC leadership grew louder and angrier by the hour. Charges of duplicity, "Tomism," and rank cowardice were flung about. The young activists of SNCC felt confirmed in their suspicions. Eldridge Cleaver undoubtedly spoke for them when he wrote:

> Much of the anger which Negroes felt toward Martin Luther King during the Battle of Selma stemmed from the fact that he denied history a great moment, never to be recaptured, when he turned tail on the Edmund Pettus Bridge. . . . If the police had turned them back by force, all those nuns, priests, rabbis, preachers, and distinguished ladies and gentlemen . . . the violence and brutality of the system would have been ruthlessly exposed.[69]

On the day after the march, embittered SNCC activists brought off a demonstration of upwards of one thousand students in front of the state capitol in Montgomery. Several of them were jailed. Six hundred more of them were back the next day demanding that the governor accept a protest petition. When they refused to disperse, mounted posse men and troopers moved in on them with clubs and whips. James Forman now lashed out at President Johnson for the lack of protection in Selma. He called for a massive convergence of blacks upon Washington, D.C. Forman was trying to be as good as his word. During the next several days SNCC staged sit-ins in the corridors of the U. S. Justice Department building, around-the-clock picketing, a seven-hour sit-in in corridors of the White House, and a sit-in that temporarily blocked traffic on Pennsylvania Avenue. On Thursday, March 11, hearings were opened in the federal court to determine whether the SCLC had violated the court's order not to go ahead with Tuesday's march. Judge Frank Johnson asked Dr. King pointedly and directly: "Is it correct to say that when you started across the bridge, you knew at that time that you did not intend to march to Montgomery?" Dr. King answered: "Yes, it is. There was a tacit agreement at the bridge that we would go no further."[70] The SNCC activists in the courtroom listened in disgust.

Back in Alabama the way was being cleared finally for the twice-aborted march from Selma to Montgomery. On Saturday, March 13, Governor Wallace went to Washington for a three-hour conference with President Johnson. The president's approach to Wallace was in the spirit expressed in his 1964 campaign: "Let's move Alabama beyond 'nigra, nigra,' on to important things. "[71] When Wallace replied that he, too, wanted to stop violence in his state, Johnson suggested that the way to end demonstrations was to take action to remove Negro discontent that caused them. Wallace remained noncommittal on this point, but he was nevertheless impressed by the smooth-talking, resourceful chief executive. As he left the White House, Wallace told reporters: "I have much more respect for him than I thought I'd ever have. I can understand now why he gets legislation through Congress." After a short pause Wallace added: "If I hadn't left when I did, he'd have had me coming out for civil rights."[72] The president, however, had not simply been trying to seduce George Wallace; he had, as a matter of fact, become deeply committed to the cause of equal rights for black Americans. Addressing a joint session of Congress on March 15, Johnson made an impassioned and emotion-filled plea for his voting rights bill then up for consideration by that body. Interrupted by two standing ovations and more than thirty intervals of applause, the president said:

> What happened in Selma is part of a far larger movement which reaches into every section and state of America. It is the effort of American Negroes to secure for themselves the full blessings of American life.
>
> Their cause must be our cause too. Because it's not just Negroes, but really it's all of us who must overcome the crippling legacy of bigotry and injustice. And we shall overcome.[73]

On Wednesday, `March 17, Judge Johnson issued an order permitting the proposed march from Selma to Montgomery. He not only enjoined Governor Wallace, Colonel Lingo, and Sheriff Clark from interfering with it, but he pointedly ordered state officials to provide protection for the marchers against hostile whites. The number of marchers to be on the highway was limited to three hundred and the date was set for Sunday, March 21. Governor Wallace, who had by now recovered from his enchantment by the president, called a joint meeting of the Alabama legislature and declared to it that Alabama was too poor to pay the cost of mobilizing the National Guard to police the march. Wallace then dispatched a telegram to the president stating that since the proposed march had been approved by a federal court, the federal government should pay for the mobilization of the Guard.[74] President Johnson responded almost immediately by federalizing the Alabama National Guard and alerting nearby units of the United States Army. However, he observed: "It has been rare in our history for the governor and the legislature of a sovereign state to decline to exercise their responsibility."[75]

On Sunday, March 21, Selma took on the air of a festive city. Notables and celebrities, black and white and from every conceivable avocation and profession, were on the scene. Precisely at 12:50 P.M. the grand march moved forward from Brown's Chapel, out across Edmund Pettus Bridge and on to Highway 80. On the first day the marchers covered little more than seven miles. Chartered buses took the bulk of the people back to Selma while the three hundred designated marchers remained to pitch tents. By Wednesday night the marchers had come within three miles of the Montgomery city limits. Pausing here overnight, they were entertained and regaled by celebrities, such as Sammy Davis, Joan Baez, Leonard Bernstein, Harry Belafonte, James Baldwin, and others. On Thursday morning in a heavy downpour and with thousands from the city joining them, the marchers turned off Highway 80 and into Montgomery. Up Oak,

Jeff Davis, and Mobile streets the marchers reached Dexter Avenue, thence into the state capitol area. Some 25,000 people quieted down to hear Dr. King: "I stand before you this afternoon with the conviction that segregation is on its death bed in Alabama and the only thing uncertain about it is how costly the segregationists and Wallace will make the funeral."[76] Dr. King's speech was impressive as usual, but the remarks of James Bevel got closest to the whole point of the struggle. Waving up at the capitol, Bevel said: "Those police up there on the steps know we belong inside. Thirty-four per cent of the seats in there belong to us. We don't want these steps. We want the capitol."[77]

The grand march was now over, but it was to have a quick and tragic anticlimax. Mrs. Viola G. Liuzzo, a white woman and the wife of a labor union official, had been working with the movement in Selma since early March. On Thursday night she joined other volunteers in transporting demonstrators back from Montgomery to Selma. About twenty miles out of Selma a car drew alongside of hers, and a bullet crashed through the glass and into her temple. Her death brought the number of volunteers "killed in action" in Selma to three. On February 18, Jimmie Lee Jackson was fatally shot by state troopers in a town outside Selma, and on March 11 the Reverend James J. Reeb, a Unitarian minister from Boston, died from a blow on the head he received from local whites. When these three are added to the hundreds who were beaten and injured and the thousands who paid fines and served jail sentences, the cost of marching from Selma to Montgomery was not inconsiderable. But there was another side of the ledger, and on balance Selma proved, after all, to have been worthwhile.

On August 6, exactly five months after the bloody incident at the Edmund Pettus Bridge, President Johnson put his signature to the Voting Rights Act of 1965. For blacks, it was the most important political rights law since the enactment of the Fifteenth Amendment some ninety-five years before. The act: (1) suspended all tests and devices used as a prerequisite for voting in those states or political subdivisions which had made use of them and where *less* than 50 percent of the population voted or were registered to vote in 1964; (2) authorized the attorney general, under specified circumstances, to use federal examiners to register voters; (3) authorized the attorney general to send federal observers to watch polling places and the counting of ballots in affected states and political subdivisions; and

(4) prevented states and political subdivisions covered by the act from denying or abridging the right to vote by changing voting qualifications, standards, or procedures that were in force prior to 1964. The states and political subdivisions involved were Alabama, Alaska, Georgia, Louisiana, Mississippi, South Carolina, Virginia, twenty-six counties in North Carolina, and one county in Arizona. Less than a week after the law went into effect forty-five federal examiners had been dispatched to the affected areas. By the end of the year they had been instrumental in adding 250,000 blacks to the registration rolls in Dixie. The passage of the Voting Rights Act of 1965 marked the end of the first phase of the black revolution. It also marked the beginning of the eclipse of Martin Luther King and his brand of leadership. The mood of the nation's blacks was changing. From here on it would be black power, black nationalism, the black experience—just so it was *black*.

CHAPTER 5

Malcolm X

The time was approximately 3 P.M. and the date was February 22, 1965. The four hundred wooden chairs in the chilly auditorium were only partly filled but the program was running late; so Brother Benjamin concluded his introductory remarks and hurried off the stage. The main speaker, a big gaunt man in a rumpled suit and close-cropped reddish brown hair, stepped to the lectern. *"As-Alaikum,* brothers and sisters," he shouted. *"As-Alaikum-Salaam"* came back to him from the audience. At that moment a scuffle broke out in a row of seats down front. A male voice rang out, "Get your hands out of my pocket." On the stage the speaker counseled: "Cool it, brothers. Cool it." With the attention of the audience riveted on the melee, three armed black men in the front row stood up and began to blaze away at the speaker.[1] A shotgun charge plowed through the lectern hitting him full-on in the chest. One of his hands shot upward; the other clutched at his chest. With his eyes glazed and blood rushing from his mouth, the big man fell backward knocking two chairs about. His body hit the floor with a thud. A firing squad had been at work. This was an execution—the execution of Big Red, Detroit Red, El Hajj Malik El-Shabazz, best known as Malcolm X.

A considerable proportion of the American populace breathed a sigh of relief. They did not particularly relish the manner of Malcolm's demise, but they were glad that he was dead. They considered him evil, dangerous, and divisive. He had been contemptuous of the great gains made by the civil rights movement over the past ten years; he had equated nonviolence with cowardice and had called instead for race war and bloodshed. He considered most black leaders to be charlatans and "Toms," and he reserved a special place in his contempt for Dr. Martin Luther King. In the thinking of many of Dr. King's partisans the conflict between their hero and Malcolm X reached beyond the question of strategies and tactics and transcended even ideological difference—it was Manichaean in essence, involving the eternal struggle between good and evil, light and darkness. Dr. King was a man of God, an apostle of love, nonviolence, peace, and justice. As the antithesis to all of this, Malcolm X was viewed as representing conflict, hatred, vengeance, and evil. Robert Penn Warren was to sum him up: "Malcolm X is many things. He is the face not seen in the mirror. He is the threat not spoken. He is the nightmare self. He is the secret sharer." [2]

But there were those with a different view of Malcolm X. Indeed, at the time of his death he had a host of followers and supporters, all black, who looked upon him as the true "Deliverer" of the race. Malcolm X had a special appeal for the militants and student activists who had become disenchanted with the nonviolence philosophy of Dr. King. To these young blacks every word uttered by Malcolm was regarded as revealed truth. Tapes of his speeches were played and replayed; collections of his messages and addresses were passed from reader to reader; and after his death his *Autobiography* became hardly less important to the faithful than the *Spiritual Exercises* were to the Jesuits. Among blacks under thirty, Malcolm X by 1964 was easily the most venerated man in the country. Reputed to be "the only Negro in America who could either start a race riot—or stop one," [3] Malcolm was also the nation's number one demagogue, black or white.

Malcolm was born on May 19, 1925, in Omaha, Nebraska. His father, the Reverend Earl Little, was a native of Reynolds, Georgia, and had been among the million or so blacks who had fled the Deep South during the high tide of the Great Migration. Malcolm was the seventh of eight children. Three of them were the products of a previous marriage by his father and lived in Boston. Malcolm's mother, Louise, was a native of Grenada in the British West Indies. She was a mulatto with straight black hair and a white skin. Her mother had been raped by a local white man on the island. Malcolm attributed the reddish brown color of his hair and skin to him. Rev. Earl Little was a very big, very black man. When Malcolm was three years old, the family moved from Omaha to Milwaukee and finally to Lansing, Michigan. Mr. Little tried his hand at operating a grocery store and on Sundays he did some free-lance preaching. His main interest, however, lay in spreading the gospel of black nationalism in the black community.

Like thousands of other new black migrants in the "promised land" the Reverend Earl Little came ultimately to the conclusion that the Negro could never achieve independence and self-respect in America. Therefore, he should leave America and return to Africa. He became an organizer for the Garvey movement and took little Malcolm with him to the meetings.

I can remember hearing of "Adam driven out of the garden into the caves of Europe," "Africa for the Africans," "Ethiopians, Awake!" And my father would talk about how it would not be much longer before Africa would be completely run by Negroes—"by black men," was the phrase he always used. "No one knows when the hour of Africa's redemption cometh. It is in the wind. It is coming. One day, like a storm, it will be here."[4]

Thus, in what were his formative years Malcolm was given extensive exposure to the dogma, the catechism, and the mythology of the black nationalist creed. In his later years he would lapse, but he would never really lose the faith.

The first tragedy in young Malcolm's life occurred when he was six years of age. Rev. Earl Little had been warned repeatedly by local whites in Lansing about "disrupting" the blacks with his preachments of Garveyism and black redemption. When he persisted with his program, the whites responded by burning the family dwelling to the ground. The Little family escaped unhurt. Finally deciding to rid themselves once and for all of the black agitator and preacher, the local whites abducted Little, beat him brutally, then lay him, still alive, across the tracks of an oncoming trolley. His body was almost cut in half. Local whites, including the insurance company, insisted that the minister had committed suicide but every black in town knew that there had been a lynching.

After the death of the Reverend Earl Little the family's descent into poverty was precipitous. The federal and state welfare systems were not then in existence, and private charity for blacks was almost nonexistent. Malcolm recalls his mother being reduced to the point of boiling a pot of dandelion greens. The neighboring children accused the family of eating "fried grass." In 1934, like millions of other poor families, the Littles went on welfare. Ultimately the family was to come almost under the complete control of the welfare officials. It was at their insistence that in 1937 the family was broken up. Mrs. Little was suffering mental deterioration and was committed to the state mental hospital at Kalamazoo, Michigan. Malcolm and the other children were distributed to foster homes. Malcolm was to remain with foster parents until he was thirteen years old. At this time his deportment in school and his delinquency outside of it caused the juvenile authorities in Lansing to sentence him to spend his adolescence in a detention home.

At the age of fifteen, Malcolm was a tall, gangling, intelligent, and restless young man. He had been a source of much trouble for local authorities; thus when his sister Ella in Boston offered to take Malcolm to live with her, everyone readily agreed. For Malcolm this was to be the beginning of a new life. Boston was to prove to be everything that Lansing was not. It was a veritable wonderland and when Malcolm arrived, he was carrying the inevitable cardboard suitcase and was dressed in a pea-green suit with his wrists hanging out of his sleeves and his pants cuffs riding three inches above his ankles. Within one year, however, the situation would be entirely different. Malcolm did not resume his education in Boston. Instead he searched for employment. He quickly found work as a shoeshine boy, then as a soda jerk, and finally as a busboy in the restaurant of Boston's famous Parker House. In his spare time he became a habitué of the local dance halls. For friends, he picked up with the "slick cats" and "hipsters" in Boston's black ghetto. Within a few months he had become one of them. He had long ago discarded his pea-green suit for the latest in fashion, a zoot suit. To make his world complete, Malcolm managed to attract the attention of a pretty young white woman who became deeply infatuated with him. He became an object of envy in Boston's black ghetto, but he began to look beyond Boston to New York City and Harlem.

Malcolm took up residence in New York City in 1942 while working as a sandwich man on a New York, New Haven, and Hartford train running between New York and Boston. Just as he had once been a hick in Boston, he was now a hick in big-time New York. He became fascinated with the Harlem underworld and could not wait to get inducted into it. He listened raptly to every con man and hustler who would talk to him. Malcolm proved to be an apt pupil and by the age of eighteen he was becoming known in Harlem as "Detroit Red." He had also become a skilled, finished hoodlum. He hustled numbers and bootleg whiskey; he was a con man, stick-up artist, and burglar. He had no preferences. He worked for prostitutes and sex specialty houses, and at various times he employed as many as one-half dozen men peddling heroin, marijuana, and any other kind of narcotics he could get hold of. His earnings were fantastic, and he began to regard the law with contempt. "The only thing I considered wrong was what I got caught doing wrong."[5] By 1945, however, the police were making New York City a bit too hot for Malcolm. He moved back to Boston, and within months he was arrested and indicted as the mastermind of a burglary ring. In February, 1946, he was convicted and sentenced to serve ten years in prison. He was not quite twenty-one years of age.

In his cell in Charlestown Prison, Malcolm had ample time to review the closely packed years of his still youthful life. A murdered father, a broken home, a mother committed to a state mental institution, and finally a quick descent and entrapment in the vicious world of crime. There had not been much real happiness and pride and self-esteem in his life since those earlier days when his father had talked to him of Marcus Garvey and had fired his youthful imagination with visions of an Africa redeemed and of a world in which black men would be masters instead of slaves. A chance to reach back to those childhood sessions with his father, to resume a development long ago abandoned—this might be his salvation both in prison and after he got out. So when Malcolm's brother Reginald first visited him in the Norfolk Prison and discussed with him the teachings of Elijah Muhammad and the Nation of Islam, Malcolm responded like a sinner redeemed.

> When Reginald left, he left me rocking with some of the first serious thoughts I had ever had in my life: that the white man was fast losing his power to oppress and exploit the dark world; that the dark world was starting to rise to rule the world again, as it had before. . . .[6]

It was black nationalism once again, but in Malcolm's mind the old ideology would be fused with the malevolence that he had acquired while in the criminal world plus the hatred for whites that he had harbored since the killing of his father. Malcolm X would ultimately come forth with a brand of militant black nationalism new to black people altogether and frightening and unnerving to the whites. For young blacks it was to become the basis of revolutionary black nationalism.

The movement known as the Nation of Islam, or more commonly the Black Muslims, originated in Detroit, Michigan, during the summer of 1930. Its founder was an itinerant peddler by the name of Wallace Fard. As the prophet of a new creed Fard taught that the black man was introduced to Christianity while he was still a slave and that Christianity was a white man's religion. The white man was evil, the Devil incarnate. All black men were really members of Islam with Allah as their God. For the time being the white man's Devil ruled the world, but black men would return to power in the not-too-distant future. Within three short years the new religion had become firmly established in Detroit. In 1934, however, the Prophet Fard mysteriously disappeared from the scene, leaving the leadership of the movement to his chief disciple, Elijah Poole. Poole was subsequently to change his name to Elijah Muhammad. During the ensuing ten years Muhammad was to build the Nation of Islam into a movement of some three thousand members with more than a dozen temples scattered throughout the country. The Nation of Islam, however, was not just another run-of-the-mill black organization. It was a neo-Garvey movement—black nationalism operating under the aegis of a religion and tailored to meet the special needs of proselytes in the black ghetto.

Through a voluminous correspondence with Elijah Muhammad over a five-year period, Malcolm received a thorough indoctrination in the new creed. Thus, when he was released from prison in August, 1952, he headed straight for Detroit and his new master. He was ready to serve the faith; all he needed was to be anointed. During the late fall of 1952 he received his "X" to replace his white slave-master's name of "Little." He was assigned to recruit new members from the Detroit ghettos, bars, poolrooms, and street corners. He was indefatigable. He was made assistant minister of the Detroit Temple during the summer of 1953, and toward the end of the year he was called to Chicago to receive a course of special training from Elijah Muhammad himself. During the early months of 1954 Malcolm organized Temple Eleven in Boston and Temple Twelve in Philadelphia. However, his biggest challenge as well as his big chance for recognition came with the order in June to establish a temple in New York City's Harlem.

During the next five years Malcolm was to become the nation's best-known and most powerful Black Muslim after Elijah Muhammad. Louis Lomax was to describe Malcolm as the Saint Paul of the Black Muslim movement:

> Not only was he knocked to the ground by the bright light of truth while on an evil journey, but he also rose from the dust stunned, with a new name and a burning zeal to travel in the opposite direction and carry America's twenty million Negroes with him.[7]

Through diligent and resourceful "public relations" he managed to build the Harlem temple into the unofficial national headquarters of the movement. Used by Muhammad to set up new temples and to assist some already established, Malcolm was chiefly responsible for the growth of the movement's membership from a few thousand in 1954 to upwards of forty thousand in 1958. Early in 1959 Malcolm decided that a monthly newspaper would be useful to air the views of Elijah Muhammad as well as to bring news on the Nation of Islam to the public. Lacking the talents for such a venture, Malcolm called for assistance from such of his friends as the authors Louis Lomax and C. Eric Lincoln. For the first few issues, the newspaper was called the *Islamic News*. It was changed later to *Mr. Muhammad Speaks*. Within a few short years it was to become one of the most widely circulated black newspapers in the nation. Malcolm's services to the movement did not go unrewarded. During mid-1959 Elijah Muhammad sent him on a three weeks' trip to Africa as an emissary from America's Nation of Islam. Malcolm visited Ghana, Nigeria, Egypt, the Sudan, and Arabia. He had permission to visit Mecca also but decided to defer his pilgrimage until Elijah Muhammad had made one.

In spite of its expanding membership and the stepped-up activities of its ministers, the Nation of Islam remained a little-known movement nationally. It was still somewhat an exotic cult and its tight discipline and emphasis on secrecy kept it out of the public eye. Malcolm X was becoming widely known, but his reputation did not extend beyond the boundaries of Harlem. All this, however, was to change dramatically during the late summer of 1959. Malcolm was to become virtually an overnight phenomenon and the Nation of Islam the object of national curiosity, fear, and derision. In July, 1959, Mike Wallace presented a five-part television documentary entitled "The Hate That Hate Produced." Film clips for the program along with the vital interviews of Elijah Muhammad and Malcolm X were done by author Louis Lomax. Mike Wallace, however, did the editing of the documentary, and it was clearly his purpose to depict the Nation of Islam as a sinister, clandestine, and dangerous group of black racists. In the opening installment of the program he said:

> These home-grown Negro-American Muslims are the most powerful of the Black Supremacist groups. They now claim a membership of at least a quarter of a million Negroes. Their doctrine is being taught in 50 cities across the nation. Let no man underestimate the Muslims.[8]

Malcolm X accused the producers of the program of designing and editing it with the intent of shocking the public. Public reaction confirmed his estimate of the effect of the program.

The documentary had also the unintended effect of catapulting

Malcolm into the national spotlight. The news media descended upon him like a swarm of locusts. "The telephone in our then small Temple Seven restaurant nearly jumped off the wall. I had a receiver against my ear five hours a day." Calls came long distance "from San Francisco to Maine . . . from even London, Stockholm, Paris."[9] Articles featuring Malcolm X and the Nation of Islam appeared in *Time,* the *Reader's Digest, Cosmopolitan,* the *U. S. News and World Report,* and the *New York Times Magazine.* The Muslim organization also benefited tremendously. A month after the documentary was aired, membership in the Nation of Islam had jumped from thirty thousand to more than sixty thousand and by the end of the year it was moving past the one hundred thousand mark. During the following year Malcolm X and the Nation of Islam received additional attention as a result of the publication of C. Eric Lincoln's, *The Black Muslims in America* and E. U. Essien-Udom's, *Black Nationalism: The Search for an Identity.* Louis Lomax was to follow in 1963 with *When the Word is Given . . . A Report on Elijah Muhammad, Malcolm X, and the Black Muslim World.* As scholarly treatments of the Nation of Islam these books introduced the movement to social scientists, theologians, and other scholars on the nation's campuses. Dr. Lincoln first used the name "Black Muslim" and in effect renamed the Nation of Islam. Malcolm states: "From Mr. Muhammad on down, the name 'Black Muslims' distressed everyone in the Nation of Islam. I tried for at least two years to kill off that *'Black* Muslims.'"[10] But the name was to become permanent.

Beginning in 1961 the established black leadership in the country found it increasingly necessary to make room for Malcolm X. They did not welcome him. They did not like him, nor what he stood for, nor the people he represented. They considered him to be a voice from the gutter and an apostle of violence. In truth they were afraid of him. Thurgood Marshall spoke for a good many of them when he said: "The Muslims are run by a bunch of thugs organized from prisons and jails and financed, I am sure, by some Arab group."[11] Up until 1960 Malcolm had directed his fire principally at white devils and white racism and had spared traditional black leadership. He had been following the orders of Elijah Muhammad who felt that to "counterattack" the black leaders would be to play into the hands of the white devils who wanted to keep the race divided. After the attacks by Thurgood Marshall and others, however, Muhammad decided to "unleash" Malcolm X.

Malcolm rose to the occasion. He denounced the black bourgeoisie as a shabby miserable lot who had historically led the black masses down the path of servility, tokenism, and gradualism. Malcolm accused the United Nations Undersecretary, Dr. Ralph J. Bunche, of selling out the Arabs to the Jews; he labeled Roy Wilkins as a "Judas"; and he denounced the NAACP as a "freak" with "a black body with a white head." Malcolm's favorite nickname for Martin Luther King was the "Reverend Dr. Chickenwing." [12] During the summer of 1960 Malcolm challenged Dr. King to "come to Harlem and prove that 'peaceful suffering' is the solution to the atrocities suffered daily by Negroes throughout America." [13] Dr. King did not pick up the challenge. Malcolm later accused him of teaching a slave philosophy and of talking black people into giving up their God-given right of self-defense. "Martin Luther King is just a twentieth-century or modern Uncle Tom or religious Uncle Tom, who is doing the same thing today to keep Negroes defenseless . . . that Uncle Tom did on the plantation. . . ." [14]

By the beginning of 1963 Malcolm was being recognized and treated as a national celebrity. He was now being booked months in advance for speeches and appearances on the nation's campuses and at public and private meetings. The news media staked out his headquarters in Harlem when it was not dogging his footsteps in his travels about the country. Malcolm was developing a public image that was beginning to overshadow and diminish his role as a minister in the Nation of Islam. Detroit was taking notice and becoming increasingly apprehensive. Indeed, since 1961, there had begun to develop a serious divergence between the preachings of Malcolm X on the one hand and the canons of the Nation of Islam on the other. Malcolm had stretched the bounds of Muslim doctrine to their limits. He introduced new ideology and techniques, and he had *style*— something which the other Muslim ministers shunned like the plague. Henry X, assistant minister to James X, accused Malcolm of abandoning the religion of the Muslims and becoming a "political sociologist." [15] He insisted that it was Malcolm who injected the political concept of black nationalism into the Black Muslim movement, which when Malcolm first arrived was essentially a religious organization.

The truth of the matter was that in contrast to other black militant and protest groups in 1963, the Black Muslims were looking more and more like a reactionary organization. Before 1960, their emphasis on the need for black unity had been one of their main strengths and the basis of a good deal of their popularity. It had made them the number one black militant group in the relatively quiet ghettos of the North. Beginning in 1960, however, black students opened up with their sit-ins, freedom rides, and other protest activities. The black revolution picked up steam and began to roll throughout the country. Even the most hidebound and traditional "Negro" organizations felt impelled to pay at least lip service to the new crusade for freedom. All through 1963 and 1964, various black organizations approached the Black Muslim ministers appealing to them to participate in or to support blacks in various demonstrations. In a few instances the ministers, on their own responsibility, rejected the invitation, but on other occasions the statement was made that the matter would have to get the approval of Elijah Muhammad. In every such case, the answer was, "No, we cannot join you." The refusal was based upon the Muslim position that the objective of the demonstrations was integration with whites; and since the Muslims as separatists were unalterably opposed to integration, they could not support any group that worked for its attainment. Young black militants dismissed this explanation with contempt. With black people daily confronting the police, suffering injury, and going to jail, there was not time to discuss theoretical distinctions between objectives. The Muslims were called upon "to put up or shut up." Louis Lomax, who was then studying the movement, observed: "The Negro masses are beginning to indict the Black Muslims for impotence; they talk but cannot act; they criticize but cannot correct." [16] The view that the Black Muslims were paper tigers was becoming widespread.

Malcolm X, of course, took the brunt of the criticism. He began to sense that this accusation that the Muslim strength was only verbal could lead to a separation of the Muslims from the front line of the Negro struggle. A more immediate problem for Malcolm and for the movement as a whole, however, was the news of ugly revelations that were beginning to seep out about Elijah Muhammad's private life. Two former secretaries brought paternity suits against him. Malcolm states that as far back as 1955 he had heard "hints" of these indiscretions but that his mind simply could not accept anything "so grotesque." [17] Any Muslim guilty of adultery was "summarily ousted" in disgrace from the Muslims. Malcolm could not and would not believe that Muhammad would betray the mosques full of "poor, trusting Muslims nickeling and diming up to faithfully support the

Nation of Islam—when many of these faithful were scarcely able to pay their rents."[18]

Deciding to check out the story himself, Malcolm searched out the secretaries long since exiled from the movement. He talked to three of the young women. "From their own mouths I heard their stories of who had fathered their children." Malcolm also learned from these women that Muhammad considered him "dangerous" and expected him ultimately to turn against the movement. Malcolm, of course, was shocked. "I felt like a total fool, out there every day preaching, and . . . not knowing what was going on right under my nose, in my own organization, involving the very man I was praising so."[19] For all this, however, Malcolm still could not bring himself to accept the bitter truth. He searched for rationalizations. Was it not true that a man's accomplishments in his life outweighed his personal human weaknesses? Did not David's adultery with Bathsheba count for less with history than his killing of Goliath? And thinking of Lot, "we think not of incest, but of his saving the people from the destruction of Sodom and Gomorrah."[20] Rationalizations or not, the confrontation between the two could not be put off indefinitely. Malcolm finally visited with Elijah Muhammad in April, 1963, detailing the allegations and "pulling no punches." Muhammad denied nothing. Instead, he answered Malcolm:

> I'm David. When you read about how David took another man's wife, I'm that David. You read about Noah, who got drunk—that's me. You read about Lot, who went and laid up with his own daughters. I have to fulfill all of those things.[21]

For all practical purposes the twelve-year relationship between Malcolm and Elijah Muhammad was at an end. Malcolm continued to function as the national minister of the Muslims, but he knew that this would only be until Muhammad found a suitable and plausible cause to sack him. This came on December 1, 1963, nine days after the assassination of President John F. Kennedy. Malcolm addressed a rally at the Manhattan Center in New York City. During the question and answer period following his speech someone asked him what he thought about President Kennedy's assassination. Malcolm answered that President Kennedy had twiddled his thumbs at the killing of South Vietnamese President Ngo Dinh Diem and his brother Ngo Dinh Nhu and that he "never foresaw that the chickens would come home to roost so soon." Extending these remarks, a few moments later Malcolm cited the murder of Patrice Lumumba, Congolese leader; Medgar Evers, the civil rights leader; and the three black girls killed in the bombing of a Birmingham church in 1963. He pointed to these as other instances of "chickens coming home to roost." Within hours the news media was headlining the story that Malcolm X had dismissed President Kennedy's murder as "chickens coming home to roost."

Malcolm flew to Chicago the day after the speech to pay his monthly visit to Muhammad. After brief amenities Muhammad asked him: "Did you see the papers this morning?" It was then that Malcolm recalled that he and every other Muslim minister had been put under strict orders to make no remarks whatever concerning assassination. But it was too late. Muhammad continued: "That was a very bad statement. The country loved this man. The whole country is in mourning. That was very ill-timed. A statement like that can make it hard on Muslims in general." And before Malcolm could manage an excuse, Muhammad spoke: "I'll have to silence you for the next ninety days—so that the Muslims everywhere can be dis-associated from the blunder."[22] With the utmost contriteness Malcolm responded: "Sir, I agree with you, and I submit, one hundred percent." Flying back to New York, Malcolm gave thought to the problem of apprising his assistants and friends of his "silencing" and virtual suspension. Upon his arrival, however, he discovered that the news had preceded him—his assistants had already been informed. What was more, telegrams had been sent to New York newspapers and television stations. Calls had been coming to him to verify the story.

Weeks later when he had begun to recover from the shock, Malcolm insisted that his comments about the Kennedy assassination were not why he had been drummed out of the Muslims. "It wasn't the reason at all. Nobody said anything when I made stronger statements before." The real reason, he said was "jealousy in Chicago" and the fact that he had "objected to the immorality of the man who professed to be more moral than anybody."[23] Perhaps. But for those who knew something of Malcolm's career with the Muslims and of his relationship with Elijah Muhammad, this explanation was too pat and too self-serving. Elijah Muhammad had had too much ex-perience with younger men to allow the disenchantment of one of his protégés push him to rash action. What *would* disturb him or anybody in his position, however, would be a serious challenge by one of his lieutenants to his leadership and hegemony over his empire. By 1963 there could be no doubt that such a challenge did exist. Louis Lomax wrote: "Many of the strong men around Muhammad clearly understood that the organization would be "Malcolmized" if the fiery minister continued to dominate the headlines."[24] In short, the Black Muslims were in danger of becoming Malcolm's personal movement. Elijah Muhammad could stand by passively and see it happen, or he could follow Machiavelli's advice in such a situation and cut his rival down. He did not have much choice.

By March, 1964, Malcolm began to accept the idea that his suspension was permanent. Not only had the ninety-day period run out without any word from Elijah Muhammad, but he began to hear of threats against his life. Malcolm felt that any "death-talk" for him could have been initiated "by only one man." Malcolm now knew that he was out of the movement and on his own. For the first time since 1946, he was sole master of his destiny. But the task of restructuring his life would not be easy. One of his disciples, Eldridge Cleaver, writes:

> During the bitter time of his suspension and prior to his break with Elijah Muhammad, we had watched Malcolm X as he sought frantically to reorient himself and establish a new platform. It was like watching a master do a dance with death on a highstrung tightrope. He pirouetted, twirled, turned somersaults in the air—but he landed firmly on his feet and was off and running.[25]

The truth of the matter was that there was only one direction in which Malcolm could run. Since 1960 he had been building a reputation as the nation's most formidable black militant and there could be no turning back now. As he himself put it:

> I reasoned that the decision already had been made for me. . . . I felt a challenge to plan, and build, an organization that could help to cure the black man in North America of the sickness which has kept him under the white man's heel.[26]

At a press conference on March 12, Malcolm announced the formation of a new movement—the Muslim Mosque. It was to be *Muslim,* because while Malcolm had definitely put the Nation of Islam behind him, he could not bring himself to abandon the Muslim faith. Other than this, the nature of the new movement was to be crystal clear. Malcolm stated: "The political philosophy of the Muslim Mosque will be black nationalism, the economic philosophy will be black nationalism, and the social philosophy will be black nationalism."[27] His long-range program was to be the return of the Negroes to their African homeland. In the short range he called for complete political control of the Negro community by that community itself. The new movement was greeted enthusiastically by the disparate and unorganized elements of black nationalists throughout the country as well as by the growing number of black students and erstwhile members of SNCC who had given up on nonviolence as the road to freedom for America's blacks. Encouraged by these reactions, Malcolm decided to elaborate further on his movement. On April 3, in a speech in Cleveland, Ohio, Malcolm revealed plans for a black nationalist convention to be held in August, 1964. Delegates representative of all levels and divisions within the nation's black populace would be invited. Seminars, workshops, and discussions would be held. After this the basic decisions would be made.[28] Malcolm had not only joined the black revolution, but he was also clearly bidding for its leadership through the establishment of this new organization.

Before implementing any of his new plans, however, Malcolm decided to gratify a long-deferred desire, the undertaking of a pilgrimage or *hajj* to Mecca, which is the ambition, the dream, of all true Muslims. Thus, Malcolm left the United States on April 13 for Africa and the Middle East. He visited Saudi Arabia, Lebanon, Egypt, Nigeria, Ghana, Liberia, and Senegal. His reputation as a spokesman for America's black masses had gone before him. In the West African countries he was literally accorded a hero's welcome. In Ghana he was treated almost as royalty. Nothing made a greater impression on Malcolm, however, than the easy camaraderie, the brotherhood, and apparent absence of racism that he observed among Muslims of all races and colors.

> During the past eleven days here in the Muslim world, I have eaten from the same plate, drunk from the same glass, and slept in the same bed [or on the same rug] . . . with fellow Muslims, whose eyes were the bluest of blue, whose hair was the blondest of blond, and whose skin was the whitest of white. . . .
>
> We were *truly* all the same [brothers]—because their belief in one God had removed the "white" from their *minds,* the "white" from their *behavior,* and the "white" from their *attitude.*[29]

In a conversation with the Algerian ambassador while in Ghana, Malcolm enthusiastically discussed his philosophy of black nationalism. The ambassador, who was white, asked where that left him. Indeed, where did it leave revolutionaries in Morocco, Egypt, Iraq, Mauretania, and other countries? Would it not alienate people (white) who were true revolutionaries, dedicated to the overthrow of imperialism and exploitation the world over? "So," Malcolm stated, "I had to do a lot of thinking and reappraising of my definition of black nationalism." He added: "Can we sum up the solution to the problems confronting our people as black nationalism?"[30]

In a press conference in New York Malcolm revealed his new thinking. A reporter asked the question: "Do we correctly understand that you now do not think that all whites are evil?" Malcolm answered: *"True,* sir! My trip to Mecca has opened my eyes. I no longer subscribe to racism. I have adjusted my thinking to the point where I believe that whites are human beings, as long as this is borne out by their humane attitude toward Negroes."[31] In the past he had made sweeping indictments of *all* white people. He would not be guilty of this again. White and black reporters at the press conference were stunned. The news of Malcolm's adjusted views had a comparable impact on the public at large. Among blacks there was disbelief, confusion, and worse. In attempting to avoid alienating Moroccans, Egyptians, and others, he was doing a good job of alienating the young black militants and black nationalists who literally worshiped him. Eldridge Cleaver spoke for some of them:

> Many of us were shocked and outraged by these words from Malcolm X, who had been a major influence upon us all and the main factor in many of our conversions to the Black Muslims. But there were those of us who were glad to be liberated from a doctrine of hate and racial supremacy.[32]

As it was to turn out, Malcolm's trip to Africa was to do much more than alter his views and attitudes toward white people. Among other things it impelled him to reexamine critically his whole approach toward the solution of the Afro-American problem. The Afro-Asian leaders he met with and talked with were duly impressed with his dynamism and charisma and his leadership potential, but not many of them took seriously his so-called black nationalist ideology. They considered such ideas too provincial, too obscure, and above all too ethnocentric. Malcolm instead should work to link the Afro-American freedom struggle with those of the colonized and oppressed peoples of the Afro-Asian world, raise the struggle for civil rights to the level of human rights, and take it into the United Nations where the Afro-Asians could throw their weight on the side of the black Americans. Let the world know the hypocrisy and injustice that is practiced in the United States. Malcolm listened, he was humbled, he was convinced, and he was converted. Under any circumstances, when he returned from overseas in May, 1964, he was no longer a black nationalist.

Always a man to suit his actions to his beliefs, Malcolm lost little time in calling off the black nationalist convention he had scheduled for early August. He moved next to scuttle his vaunted Muslim Mosque. Neither of these ideas was feasible or useful for what he now had in mind. During the last week in June he released a letter which he had sent to the heads of civil and human rights organizations and the representatives of African nations who were present in the United States. In the letter he announced the formation of Organization of Afro-American Unity (OAAU) with the purpose of uniting Afro-Americans and their organizations around a constructive purpose for human rights. The letter went on to invite the recipients to a rally on Sunday, June 28, 1964, in New York City.[33]

In terms of attendance the rally was a disappointment. The "local and national heads" of black organizations were conspicuous by their absence. Perhaps Malcolm did not really expect them. At any rate, membership applications were taken from the faithful who did attend and the new organization got under way. Elected as its first president, Malcolm read and elaborated on the basic aims and objectives of the new OAAU. One of the things not mentioned by Malcolm, however, was his plan to use OAAU in his efforts to bring the United States before the United Nations for violating the basic rights of its black citizens. This of course would not be the first time American blacks had appealed to a world body for assistance in their struggle against domestic oppression. As early as 1919, Dr. W. E. B. Du Bois had written:

> A League of Nations is absolutely necessary to the salvation of the Negro race. Unless we have some supernatural power to curb the anti-Negro policy of the United States ... we are doomed eventually to *fight* for our rights. . . .[34]

On June 6, 1946, representatives of the National Negro Congress presented to the U.N. a document entitled: "A Petition to the United Nations on Behalf of Thirteen Million Oppressed Negro Citizens of America." It was addressed to Secretary-General Trygve Lie for submission to the General Assembly and to the Commission on Human Rights of the Economic and Social Council. No action was ever taken on the petition.[35] In October, 1947, the NAACP also submitted a petition. Prepared under the direction of Dr. Du Bois, this document consisted of six chapters totaling 155 pages. It was entitled: "An Appeal to the World, a Statement on the Denial of Human Rights to Minorities in the Case of Citizens of Negro Descent in the United States of America and an Appeal to the United Nations for Redress." On December 3, at the meetings of the U.N. Commission on

Human Rights the Soviet delegation moved for consideration of the petition. The motion was defeated by a vote of four to one.[36]

On July 9, Malcolm flew to Cairo, Egypt. The Organization of African Unity, founded in 1963, had scheduled an "African Summit" meeting for July 17–21. The heads of some thirty-four member states were in attendance. Employing all of the skills of a professional lobbyist, Malcolm managed to get himself admitted as an observer. In this capacity he was allowed to submit to the member states an eight-page memorandum appealing for their support in bringing the case of American blacks before the United Nations.[37]

For diplomatic and other reasons, not all of the delegates at the conference could be expected to favor Malcolm's plea. Nevertheless, there was sufficient accord to enable them to pass a resolution condemning racism in the United States. Indeed, some of the delegates assured Malcolm that they would assist the OAAU in its campaign and lend their support during the ensuing session of the United Nations. The language of the resolution was temperate. It observed "with satisfaction the recent enactment of the Civil Rights Act designed to secure for American Negroes their basic human rights," but it declared that the African states were "deeply disturbed . . . by continuing manifestations of racial bigotry and racial oppression against Negro citizens of the United States of America." The resolution restated the OAU's "belief that the existence of discriminatory practices is a matter of deep concern to member states of the Organization of African Unity," and it urged the U. S. government to intensify its effort to eliminate "all forms of discrimination based on race, color, or ethnic origin."[38]

Malcolm's activities in Cairo and his anti-American speeches in several African countries during the remainder of his trip on the continent were bound to arouse the interest of the United States government. A State Department spokesman expressed the concern that bringing the issue of the civil rights of American Negroes before the United Nations would only provide an opportunity for critics of the United States to undermine its position in that international body. Because of a heavy calendar of impending business, plus the deadlock over membership dues, there was no opportunity for OAU members to bring up Malcolm's proposal at the fall session of the U.N. However, during the acrimonious debate over the Congo question at the U.N. during December of 1964, the influence of Malcolm's memorandum could plainly be detected.

In the long run, however, the results of Malcolm's efforts in the international arena were bound to be marginal. For one thing, he absolutely did not have the support of domestic black leaders or of the masses in his United Nations venture. American blacks were never enthusiastic about identifying with Africans and Asians anyway; and in spite of their long and intense struggle against white racism, they were inclined to regard it as the internal affair of the United States and not the business of a "bunch of foreigners." Ultimately a recognition of this fact was to force itself upon Malcolm. "I must be honest. Negroes—Afro-Americans—showed no inclination to rush to the United Nations and demand justice for themselves here in America. I really had known in advance that they wouldn't." [39] Malcolm also began to become aware of a serious loss of supporters in the black community. Alex Haley writes that in the bars and restaurants and street corners of Harlem "there could be heard more blunt criticism of Malcolm X than ever before in his career." Blacks complained that Malcolm spent his time *talking* while other civil rights organizations were *doing*. "All he's *ever* done was talk, CORE and SNCC and some of them people of Dr. King's are out getting beat over the head." They complained also that Malcolm was too confused to be taken seriously any longer. "He doesn't know *what* he believes in. No sooner do you hear one thing than he's switched to something else." [40]

The truth of the matter was that while Malcolm had switched he was no longer confused. By the end of 1964 he had made the discovery, as would Huey P. Newton, Floyd McKissick, and others a few years later, that he had been running far too much ahead of the black masses. He had shifted from Black Muslimism to black nationalism and thence to Third-World revolutionary socialism, but he was still out of step. Malcolm reluctantly but realistically concluded that the Afro-American was a traditionalist and thus would accept no exotic solution to his problems. He asked:

> So how does anybody sound talking about the Negro in America waging some "revolution"? Yes, he is condemning a system—but he's not trying to overturn the system, or to destroy it. The Negro's so-called "revolt" is merely an asking to be *accepted* into the existing system! [41]

During the last couple of months of his life Malcolm sought not only to work with the established black leadership but also to promote cooperation between the races. As he now viewed it:

> . . . both races, as human beings, had the obligation, the responsibility, of helping to correct America's human problem. The well-meaning white people . . . had to

combat, actively and directly, the racism in other white people. And the black people had to build within themselves much greater awareness that along with equal rights there had to be the bearing of equal responsibilities.[42]

A number of black leaders welcomed the change and thought that had Malcolm lived he could have become extremely effective. John Lewis of SNCC, who had been close to both Malcolm and Dr. King, stated that "there could have been an alliance with a Malcolm and a Martin King pulling upon . . . the strength of the two. I think something like that was in the making."[43]

A few months after his expulsion from the Black Muslims Malcolm told his biographer Alex Haley:

> The first direct order for my death was issued through a Mosque Seven official who previously had been a close assistant. Another previously close assistant of mine was assigned to do the job. He was a brother with a knowledge of demolition; he was asked to wire my car to explode when I turned the ignition key.[44]

This particular "job" was, of course, not carried out, but Malcolm knew from this point on that he was a marked man. During the next fourteen months he was stalked and tracked like a hunted animal. One attempt after another was made upon his life until he was finally cornered and mercilessly cut down. It was at least the preliminary opinion of observers that he had been killed by Black Muslims. Indeed, on several occasions Malcolm had let it be known that his would-be killers were Muslims. However, shortly before his death his suspicions began to broaden. He told Alex Haley: ". . . the more I keep thinking about this thing, the things that have been happening lately, I'm not all that sure it's the Muslims. I know what they can do, and what they can't. . . . I think I'm going to quit saying it's the Muslims."[45]

The question "Who killed Malcolm X?" became almost a parlor game. If the Black Muslims did not kill Malcolm, who did? The Central Intelligence Agency, the FBI, the "white power structure," and the black bourgeoisie were all in turn accused of the assassination. Mrs. Ella Collins, Malcolm's half-sister, insisted that the murder of her brother was "much bigger" than the Black Muslims, that the "Black Muslims did the job, but with others." She felt that had Malcolm "lived through the summer of 1965," he would have influenced great changes in America. The power structure knew this. His death was planned by the power structure of the West.[46] James Farmer of CORE asserted that the "real story" of Malcolm's death would surprise those who considered it a case of Muslim revenge.

"Malcolm was warring on the international narcotics interests in Harlem and they were not pleased about it."[47] And so it went.

The New York City police, however, proved much less interested in those who plotted the assassination than in those who carried it out. Three men were arrested, brought to trial, and subsequently convicted. They were Talmadge Hayer and two avowed Muslims, Norman 3X Butler and Thomas 15X Johnson. Hayer confessed his part in the killing and a long line of eyewitnesses filled in the rest: A scuffle broke out in one section of the auditorium, causing much excitement and distracting the audience. Johnson, armed with a shotgun, and Butler and Hayer with pistols then moved forward and commenced firing. The time was approximately 3 P.M., and the date was February 22, 1965.

CHAPTER 6

Black Power

On May 17, 1966, a black Atlanta newspaper carried the headline: "Lewis, Forman Replaced in S.N.C.C.: West Indian Named Chairman."[1] The term "West Indian" was a reference to Stokely Carmichael, and its use was an indication of how little he was then known in black communities and in the nation as a whole. Extremely intelligent and a gifted rhetorician, Carmichael was also a superb manipulator of men. His leap from the ranks to the leadership of SNCC was a palace revolution, skillfully contrived and pitilessly executed. It caught the SNCC old regime almost totally unprepared. For several days during May, upwards of one hundred members of SNCC, staff, field, and undesignated, had been assembled at a vacation retreat outside of Nashville for the Sixth Annual Spring Conclave of the organization. On the night of May 14, the delegates finally got around to the business of electing its officers for the ensuing year. John Lewis was the incumbent chairman. He had held the post since 1963. His reelection seemed a foregone conclusion in spite of the fact that Carmichael had let it be known that he wanted the post.[2]

Lewis was quickly nominated. A militant minority, mostly Carmichael's supporters, then grabbed the floor, holding on to it for four hours in an attempt to discredit Lewis's leadership of the organization. SNCC's nonviolence stance was denounced as cowardly and outdated; Dr. King's influence with SNCC was deplored; and the MFDP's bitter experience in Atlantic City in 1964 was rehashed. The militants further insisted that black consciousness and black nationalism were the new moods among black people throughout the country and that SNCC must move with the tide. The discussion finally came to an end at 3 A.M. When the balloting had been completed, Lewis emerged the victor by a vote of 66 to 22. The delegates were proceeding with the election of lesser officials when a member, Worth Long by name, burst into the room and shouted: "I want to challenge this election. I think you're violating your own constitution, your own rules and regulations."[3] The fact was, however, that SNCC had no written body of laws and Mr. Long knew it. This was simply a ploy to set John Lewis's election aside and keep the way open for Carmichael. It worked. The debate was reopened and for five hot, humid, and sweaty hours the Carmichael and Lewis protagonists battled it out. Friends turned upon friends, promises were broken, and tears were freely shed. When the second vote was taken, Lewis went down to defeat. Carmichael was the new chairman of SNCC.

Mrs. Ruby Doris Robinson, a supporter of Carmichael, was elected to the post of executive secretary. James Forman, who formerly held the post and who was also a supporter of Carmichael, resigned to become a member of the executive committee, and Cleveland Sellers, also a Carmichael man, was continued in the position of program director. Finally, the membership of the organization's central committee was reduced from twenty-one to ten. In an obvious gesture of tokenism, one white member, Jack Minnis, was retained on the committee. Minnis incidentally had formerly been head of SNCC's research department. The Carmichael machine included several members with whom he had associated as a student at Howard University. Known within SNCC as the "Washington clique," they included Courtland Cox, Bill Mahoney, and Ivanhoe Donaldson. Cox, who reputedly invented the "Black Panther" label for Carmichael's political party in Lowndes County, Alabama,[4] was placed on the central committee; Mahoney was installed as SNCC press relations' officer; and Donaldson, who originally hailed from New York City, was appointed the new director of the SNCC office in that city. The Carmichael takeover represented no mere changing of the guard. SNCC was now to be rerouted from its nonviolence-civil rights course and sent hell-bent down the road of black nationalism. It was the end of an era.

As of May, 1966, SNCC had been in existence for upwards of six years. During this period it had achieved recognition as one of the nation's major civil rights organizations. Indeed, the term "Snick" had become a household word in black communities throughout the country. The organization's greatest period came between February, 1960, and July, 1961, when through the use of nonviolent tactics its members brought about the virtual end of segregation in public accommodations in the South. In a larger context SNCC activities precipitated a social revolution in the region, one which would see the Afro-American abandoning his age-old attitudes of docility and obsequiousness toward whites and moving forward to claim his rights as a man and a citizen. During the first year and a half SNCC was almost a totally Southern movement. The black students and the handful of white students who participated in the sit-ins were largely Southern born and for the most part Southern educated. Their philosophy and inspiration, coming as they did from Dr. Martin Luther King, were Southern based. But the movement quickly drew an interest beyond the region. Black students and white students and a miscellany of "liberals" saw it for the exciting, unprecedented, and dynamic cause that it was and hastened to "get involved."

The end of the age of innocence for the new movement came with its involvement in the Freedom Rides in the spring and summer of 1961. The Congress of Racial Equality which initiated this activity had long been wedded to the philosophy of nonviolence, but in mid-1961 it seemed, at least temporarily, to be more interested in ends than in means. In recruiting people for its program, CORE began to accept all those who volunteered regardless of their views on nonviolence.

Prior to the summer of 1961, the students had managed to achieve their goals without indulging in frontal assaults on the "system." Thus, while hundreds of them had been arrested and jailed, the bloodletting among them was kept at a minimum. The Freedom Rides, however, were to change all of this. Their involvement in the "kamikaze-like" activities at Birmingham and Montgomery brought the students into contact with the most brutal and savage aspects of Southern white racism. It was something they had been warned of but had never really experienced. To be accurate, however, CORE had not planned it this way; that is, they had expected to be roughed-up and jailed but not beaten, bombed, and even killed. So when the going really became dangerous, the CORE cut their involvement. If we may recall, the "first" Freedom Ride which was almost an all CORE venture ended really at Birmingham, Alabama. It had been scheduled to continue on to Montgomery and thence to Jackson, Mississippi, but confronted with the malevolence and brutality of Bull Connor and his men, CORE people forgot about the buses and instead flew on to Jackson, where they disbanded. (See chapter 3.)

At this point the students became involved. Determined not to allow violence to achieve an easy victory over nonviolence, SNCC activists resolved to complete the itinerary of the disrupted CORE effort exactly as it had been scheduled. Thus in what became known as the second Freedom Ride the students suffered through bloody beatings at Birmingham and Montgomery. When finally they arrived in Jackson, Mississippi, they were unceremoniously clapped into cells in the odious Parchman Prison. Even here, however, they were resolute enough to insist upon serving two-month sentences rather than paying the nominal fine.

But all men have their limits, and as excitement of the summer died down, many of the students began to reexamine their views on nonviolence. They were finding it difficult to follow Dr. King's dicta to the effect that they had to love the white racists regardless of the bestiality suffered at their hands. Besides, they were all troubled that Dr. King, for one reason or another, had avoided any direct involvement in the Freedom Rides. As John Lewis was to put it: "More and more people just could not . . . accept the non-violent philosophy."[5] With it all, however, nonviolence would for some time remain the dominant creed among them. It had been too deeply ingrained in the movement to be lightly or peremptorily discarded. As time passed, some of them would go in search of a larger frame of reference and more positive philosophical support for their belief in nonviolence. Among the intellectuals, Albert Camus' *The Rebel* became almost required reading. In an interview with Robert Penn Warren, Robert Moses mused:

> Camus talks a lot about the Russian terrorists—around 1905. What he finds in them—is that they accepted that if they took a life they offered their own in exchange. He moves from there into the whole question of violence and nonviolence and comes out with something which I think is relevant in this struggle. It's not a question that you just subjugate yourself to the conditions that are and don't try to change them. The problem is to go on from there, into something which is active, and yet the dichotomy is whether you can cease to be a victim any more and also not be what he calls an executioner. The ideal lies between these two extremes—victim and executioner.[6]

This "ideal" would remain the goal for Moses and many others until Malcolm X replaced both Dr. King and Camus as the philosopher-king of the movement. After that, young blacks sought to become "executioners" rather than "victims."

Aside from their problems with ideology the students in August, 1961, were confronted with the difficult task of restructuring the SNCC organization. At their meetings at the Highlander Folk School during that month the students argued for days as to whether the movement should involve itself in the voter-registration program urged upon them by the Kennedy Administration and by Dr. King. The question split the membership into two groups: the so-called "voter-registration faction" supporting the new program, and the "direct-action group" insisting instead that SNCC continue to devote all of its energy and resources to sit-ins, picketing, and local confrontations. The impasse was ultimately resolved by the "Ella Baker compromise" which in effect froze the two factions into two new divisions of SNCC. Diane Nash was given direction of direct action activities and Charles Jones was named to head up voter registration. While SNCC was to remain divided into two divisions, it was not to be along these lines. With students jumping back and forth between voter registration and so-called direct action, the distinction between the two quickly became blurred. With the emergence of a small but efficient bureaucracy after 1962, the more meaningful divisions became that of staff and field. Concentrated as it was in its Atlanta headquarters, the staff personnel came to be known as the "SNCC establishment." However, both staff and field produced young men and women whose names became legendary in the black revolution. Some of these were Ruby Doris Robinson, Julian Bond, James Forman, John Lewis, Robert Moses, Diane Nash Bevel, Charles Jones, and Stokely Carmichael.

When the first sit-in was staged in Greensboro, North Carolina, in February, 1960, Ruby Doris Smith was a seventeen-year-old sophomore at Spelman College in Atlanta. She could hardly control her excitement. "I began to think right away about it happening in Atlanta, but I wasn't ready to act on my own."[7] However, when the first student volunteers were selected for demonstrations in Atlanta, Miss Smith was in the vanguard. In mid-April of 1960 she attended the Raleigh Conference that brought SNCC into existence, and she was one of the ten students who initiated SNCC's jail-no-bail policy when they were arrested in Rock Hill, South Carolina. They each served thirty days in prison. She was one of the very few students willing to go on the second Freedom Ride. Indeed, when the Nashville students asked Atlanta for students for the ride, Miss Smith was the only one to volunteer. She even borrowed the money to travel from Atlanta to meet the group in Birmingham. At the end of the ride she, along with John Lewis and others, served out a two-month prison sentence in Parchman Prison. For a time in late 1961 she worked in McComb, Mississippi, with Bob Moses' voter-education program. After 1962, however, she settled down to become a mainstay in SNCC's Atlanta headquarters. She had long been a friend and supporter of John Lewis, but in 1966 she cast her lot with Stokely Carmichael, becoming executive secretary in his administration.

Aside from Miss Smith the most familiar figure in SNCC's Atlanta headquarters came to be Julian Bond. Like Miss Smith, Bond had been with the movement since its inception. When news of the Greensboro sit-ins reached Atlanta, he and a fellow student called a campus-wide meeting which led to the creation of the Atlanta Committee on Appeal for Human Rights. This group became an affiliate of SNCC and Bond was to work with it almost full time for the fifteen or sixteen months of its existence. When SNCC established its headquarters in Atlanta in August, 1961, James Forman, the new executive secretary, asked Bond to serve as public relations director. Bond enthusiastically accepted. In addition to his leaflets, topical pamphlets, and news releases Bond assumed editorship of SNCC's newsletter, the *Student Voice*. An English major at Morehouse College, he was soon to make good use of his talent and training. He was to convert the *Student Voice* from a carelessly mimeographed sheet into an imaginatively designed and beautifully printed publication.

Up until 1965, Bond, in contrast to Forman, Lewis, Moses, and others, operated in relative obscurity. He was totally unknown on the national scene, and in Atlanta he was dismissed as just another member of the local SNCC crowd. In June, 1965, however, Bond ran for election to the lower house of the Georgia state legislature. Waging an aggressive and intelligent campaign, he won by an impressive majority. This was the first step in his rise to prominence. On January 6, 1966, just four days before he was to take his seat in the House, SNCC's hierarchy, of which he was a member, issued a so-called "white paper" on the Vietnam war.[8] Along with a scathing denunciation of the United States for its conduct of the war, the paper called also for resistance to the draft. Sensing a story, the news media immediately descended upon Bond. On Monday, January 10, he was to be sworn into office and the newsmen asked: "You have an oath to take come Monday. Will you be able to take this oath with a clear conscience and endorse this statement?"[9] Bond's answer was simple and unevasive—yes, he endorsed the SNCC statement, and yes, he intended to take the oath to uphold the Constitutions of the state of Georgia and of the United States. In the Georgia House on Monday, however, the matter was not so simply to be disposed of. Opposition to Bond was bitter and intense, and he was roundly denounced as a traitor and a renegade. Many of his friends and supporters had urged him to withdraw his support of the SNCC statement, but Bond held to his convictions. By a vote of 184 to 12 the Georgia House refused to seat him.[10] Bond carried the case to the federal courts and a year later the United States Supreme Court ordered the Georgia House to seat him. He had, in the meanwhile, become a national figure.

At thirty-three years of age James Forman was in 1961 the oldest member of SNCC's Atlanta staff. He was SNCC's perennial executive secretary. Along with John Lewis, he constituted the organization's "top brass" until the Carmichael takeover in 1966. Unlike most of his younger colleagues Forman served a hitch in the Army, 1947–1950. He went from there to the University of California, Los Angeles, and then to Roosevelt University from which he received a B.A. degree. Forman also pursued graduate study at the Illinois Institute, Middlebury College, and Boston University.[11] He could not decide whether he wanted to teach or to write; so he tried his hand at both. In the summer of 1960, Forman was recruited by CORE to work with sharecroppers in Fayette County, Tennessee. He made frequent trips to Nashville where he made the acquaintance of Diane Nash. Forman greatly impressed her. A year later in helping to organize the staff for SNCC's headquarters in Atlanta, she prevailed upon him to accept the sixty-dollars-a-week post of executive secretary.

More than ten years older than most of his new colleagues Forman supplied an element of maturity to staff deliberations and decisions. Beyond this he was to display a level of courage and fortitude almost unmatched in the organization. Robert Penn Warren writes of him: "James Forman is a combat officer. His inner peace comes only, perhaps, in the immediate outer clash. He is bitter, or at least impatient, about those who do not have his special kind of total commitment.·. . ."[12] Forman was always to be found in the front line of a confrontation, whether it was Albany, Birmingham, Greenwood, Selma, or Washington, D.C. Those who knew him intimately questioned his commitment to nonviolence. Warren states: "He does not, in fact, first think in terms of the moral or psychological question or motivations but in terms of practical effect: 'It's what the social effect is of what a person is doing that's important.'"[13] By the beginning of 1966 Forman had had enough of nonviolence. He became a leader of the militant wing of the SNCC organization. And although he resigned his post of executive secretary during the May election, he stayed on to become one of Carmichael's top advisers. He was ultimately to wind up as an official in the Black Panthers.

When the decision was made at the Highlander Folk School meetings to split SNCC into two divisions, it was inevitable that Diane Nash would be placed in charge of direct-action activities. Bitterly opposed to changing the orientation and the directions of the organization, she had led the fight against adoption of the voter-education program. Diane Nash had been with the movement since its earliest days. As a student at Fisk University in 1959, she had participated in the nonviolence workshops conducted by the Nashville Christian Leadership Council. It was there that she met John Lewis, Marion Barry, James Lawson, and her future husband, James Bevel. In February, 1960, she took the lead in organizing the sit-in movement in Nashville. She was a founder and the first chairman of the central committee of the Nashville Student Movement. John Lewis, himself a product of Nashville movement, described her as "very courageous" and the "most beautiful" of the earlier leaders.[14] At the Raleigh Conference in April, 1960, the Atlanta delegation worked hard and long to secure the election of one of its members as the first national chairman of SNCC. The fact that Marion Barry of the Nashville Movement was named was due largely to the political skill of Miss Nash.

Her greatest work for SNCC, however, came with the Freedom Rides. Indeed, it is very probable that there would have been no continuation of the first ride had it not been for Diane. When the CORE riders got bogged down in Birmingham and decided to fly on to Jackson, Diane, up in Nashville, worked around the clock assembling students courageous enough to continue the ride. (See chapter 3.) In August, 1961, Diane, like a number of her colleagues, dropped out of school to devote full time to SNCC. During the early months of the next year she and her new husband, the Reverend James Bevel, moved to Jackson, Mississippi, to work with Robert Moses. In May, 1962, four months pregnant, she was jailed by the Jackson police for teaching the techniques of nonviolence to black children. The charge was contributing to the delinquency of minors. She insisted on sitting in jail rather than putting up bail. "I can no longer cooperate with the evil and corrupt court system of this state. Since my child will be a black child, born in Mississippi, whether I am in jail or not he will be born in prison." [15] Sentenced to two years in prison, she was released after a short stay. At the March-on-Washington rally during August, 1963, she was introduced by the chairman, A. Philip Randolph, as one of the outstanding women of the civil rights struggle. She had earned it.

At the Highlander Folk School meetings Diane's most skillful opponent was a fair-skinned black student from North Carolina by the name of Charles Jones. Jones had met frequently with Tim Jenkins and other advocates of voter registration, and he had become convinced that it was an area to which SNCC should devote some of its energy and dedication. In the divisional split of the organization, he was, of course, given charge of voter-registration projects. Jones was a product of Johnson C. Smith University in Charlotte, North Carolina, and he had been a leader in the student movement in that state. He served also for a time as youth secretary for the Fellowship of Reconciliation. During the first year and a half of the sit-in movement Jones was involved in almost all of its major actions. He was among the students who initiated the jail-no-bail policy at Rock Hill, South Carolina, and with the other male students involved he served his thirty days sentence on the road gang. Like Diane Nash and others Jones did not return to school in the fall of 1961, but *unlike* a good many of them he did not head for Jackson, Mississippi. Along with Cordell Reagan and Charles Sherrod he chose to work with the oppressed and voteless blacks of southwest Georgia. In spite of the great publicity given Dr. King, the Reverend Wyatt T. Walker, and the SCLC in general, Jones and his two colleagues were the motivating force behind the Albany Movement.[16] It was their work also which largely accounted for the great increase in black voter registration in southwest Georgia between 1962 and 1964. This achievement would have long-range consequences.

Of all of the young activists in the student movement perhaps none could boast of a longer or more intense commitment to nonviolent struggle than John Lewis. As a fifteen-year-old high school student in Troy, Alabama, Lewis kept abreast of the developments in the Montgomery bus boycott. He was captivated by Dr. King and his methods.

> What I saw in Montgomery during that . . . period, the whole idea of a people, in a sense, rising up and saying that they are not going to be adjusted to this system of segregation . . . and that they are going to take something from the heart of the Christian faith and make it real, and apply it, was very meaningful to me.[17]

In the years to come he was to remain unshakable in his devotion to the principles and practice of nonviolence. Like his friends Diane Nash, Marion Barry, James Bevel, and James Lawson he was a product of the Nashville Christian Leadership Council. And when the sit-ins came to Nashville, he took the lead with Diane Nash in organizing the Nashville Student Movement. For the next two years he shuttled back and forth between Nashville and Atlanta. He participated in the Raleigh Conference, and he was the only person to take part in both the first and second Freedom Rides. Lewis saw "service" at Birmingham, Montgomery, and Selma, Alabama; Albany, Georgia; and Jackson, Greenwood, and McComb, Mississippi. All told he was arrested twenty-two times, beaten more than twelve, and left for dead at least once.

In 1963, Lewis was elected third national chairman of SNCC. During his tenure, 1963–1966, the organization achieved its greatest power and influence in national affairs. Its budget, which stood at $250,000 in 1963, rose to nearly a million dollars in 1965.[18] The money was spent principally for staff operation and maintenance in Atlanta and field operations in southwest Georgia, Mississippi, and elsewhere in the country. SNCC was not a tax-exempt organization. After 1963, SNCC was accorded equal status with other national black groups, such as CORE, the NAACP, SCLC, and the National Urban League. Thus, the youthful and diminutive chairman of SNCC frequently trooped in and out of the White House in the company of such leaders as Dr. King, Whitney Young, James Farmer, and Roy Wilkins. Unlike the older and more stable black organizations, however, the youthful SNCC rank and file were restless and impatient for change. By 1965 it was abandoning nonviolence and civil rights for militant black nationalism. Lewis could not, and would not, go along. As he described it:

> It was the whole question of "who could be, in a sense, more militant than another, who can articulate the movement or make the most radical statement?" . . . I didn't want to be associated with it; I didn't want to be identified with it. I didn't want to be part of it; it was not me.[19]

A few weeks after Carmichael took over the organization, Lewis severed his connections. Julian Bond was soon to follow. The student movement that they knew and loved so much no longer existed.

Of the many regulars on the long roster of the SNCC organization, Stokely Carmichael was one of very few who had never subscribed to the nonviolence philosophy. When he did observe it in practice, it was because the starkness of white Southern terror left him little choice. Unlike his Southern-bred colleagues in the movement Carmichael was crass, cynical, "hard-nosed," and opportunistic. He was also an extremely courageous man. Like most other Freedom Riders, Carmichael was locked up when he got to Jackson, Mississippi. Here was where the Carmichael story began. Howard Zinn writes:

> In Parchman jail ... Stokely almost drove his captors crazy: when they decided to take away his mattress because he had been singing, he held tightly to it while they dragged it—and him—out of the cell, and they had to put wristbreakers on him to try to make him relinquish his grip; after six fellow Riders had been put in solitary confinement, he demanded the same treatment, and kept banging loudly on his cell door until his wish was granted. When, after 49 days, Stokely and the others left Parchman, the sheriff and his guards were somewhat relieved.[20]

Stokely was eleven years old when his family moved from Trinidad, B.W.I., to New York City. He was a bright young lad, and in 1956 he was accepted as a student in the elite Bronx High School of Science. He was a senior in high school when Ezell Blair and the others began the sit-ins at Greensboro. Unimpressed he looked upon it as a prank or a stunt. As the black student movement grew, however, Carmichael become more interested. While a student at Howard University, he helped to organize the Non-Violent Action Group (NAG). Quickly affiliating with SNCC, the NAG took on the task of desegregating public accommodations in the nation's capital. In the summer of 1961, a number of the NAG members, Carmichael, Bill Mahoney, John Moody, and Dion Diamond, joined the Freedom Rides. They all served time in the Parchman State Penitentiary.

Unlike a number of students who dropped out of school, some permanently after joining the movement, Carmichael continued his education. However, during his four years at Howard University he spent his vacations and whatever other time he could spare doing fieldwork for SNCC in the Deep South. He worked hard in Greenwood and Jackson and other Mississippi towns in the voter-registration program, and like others in the MFDP he entertained an outside hope that the group would be seated at the 1964 Democratic National Convention. However, when this did not happen, Carmichael was not as shattered as were many of the other young people. Summing it up later, he stated:

> The lesson ... was clear at Atlantic City. The major moral of that experience was not merely that the national conscience was generally unreliable but that, very specifically, black people in Mississippi and throughout this country could not rely on their so-called allies.[21]

Along with a considerable number of SNCC personnel, Carmichael abandoned Mississippi at the end of 1964. During the spring of 1965, he and a few of his close friends proceeded to set up shop in Lowndes County, Alabama.

Located in south central Alabama, Lowndes County was traditional "black-belt" country. Blacks constituted 81 percent of the population, but, typical of this region, political and economic control of the county rested firmly in the grip of the white minority. Beyond this, Lowndes County had a reputation for brutality and repression that made it unique even in Alabama. Mrs. Viola Liuzzo had been killed in this county while returning from the Selma rally. In moving into this county, Carmichael and his fellow activists were motivated by a desire to avenge the death of Mrs. Liuzzo. They wanted also to break or at least to fracture the tight, almost totalitarian control that whites maintained over the region. As Carmichael put it: "The history of the county shows that black people could come together to do only three things: sing, pray, dance. Any time they came together to do anything else, they were threatened or intimidated."[22] Thus, early in March of 1965, the Carmichael group along with a few local blacks set up the Lowndes County Christian Movement for Human Rights. John Hulett, a well-known local black, was named chairman.

The SNCC activists went to work in the county with the same courage and energy that they had displayed in Mississippi for almost four years. They visited homes, shops, and farms and called local meetings. They broadcast such slogans as "Political power is the first step to independence and freedom" and "You can control this county politically."[23] As in Mississippi also, the students found that the local blacks were apathetic and fearful. Taught that politics was the "white man's business," most of them did not want even to be seen publicly talking to a student activist. Thus, during the first six months of the drive, as Carmichael himself admits, not more than fifty or sixty local blacks could be induced to go to the polls and attempt to qualify to vote.[24] As in other sections of the South the big change in Lowndes County was to come after the passage of the Voting Rights Act. In August, 1965, federal examiners and registrars, as provided by the act, moved into the county and began to add blacks to the registration rolls. By the spring of 1965, some 2,700 had been qualified to vote. The white vote stood at 2,800. Heartened by the new situation, the students began to step up their political activity. They discovered an unusual Alabama statute which permitted any group of voters to establish a county-wide political party. To be so recognized, the group had to receive 20 percent of the votes cast in elections for county offices.[25] It was with this law in mind that the students in March, 1966, organized the Lowndes County Freedom Organization (LCFO). The emblem of the new group, *not* its name, was the Black Panther.[26]

The county had seven positions to be filled in a regular election. These were: sheriff, coroner, tax assessor, tax collector, and three members of the Board of Education. Carmichael's party planned first to qualify black candidates in the county's primary on May 3, then to conduct an all-out campaign to elect them in the November regular election. In the weeks before the primary, however, the local whites employed every stratagem including, of course, violence to keep local blacks from signing up as members of the LCFO. After an appeal to the United States Department of Justice, local whites reluctantly permitted the LCFO to hold its nominating convention. During the summer of 1966, both the LCFO and the local white Democrats competed for the black vote. Carmichael's workers moved around the county holding rallies, workshops, and mass meetings while the local whites warned the blacks of possible economic and physical reprisals. As was generally expected, the black candidates did not win in the November elections. However, because of Carmichael and his LCFO, blacks participated in the local political process for the first time since Reconstruction. "November 8, 1966, made one thing clear: Some day black people will control the government of Lowndes County. For Lowndes is not merely a section of land and a group of people, but an idea whose time has come."[27]

Months earlier Carmichael had decided also that the time had come to unseat John Lewis as chairman of SNCC. He knew that the mood of the organization had changed, and he was convinced that Lewis would no longer be able to lead it. The truth of the matter was that by mid-1965, the SNCC values, discipline, high dedication, and selflessness had all but disappeared. In the aftermath of the MFDP's defeat at the Democratic National Convention, the erosion had begun to set in. In Mississippi many of the young radicals had put their lives on the line and had given their all in the belief that the "system" could be made to look, listen, and respond. Now there was alienation, despair, frustration, and rage. There was the growing disposition to give up the useless struggle and to "chuck it all." John Lewis, who was still the chairman, was deeply disturbed: "The staff was just disintegrating altogether. People had just come out of the Mississippi

Summer Project; people were bitter, frustrated, torn apart, battle fatigued and everything else."[28] Indeed, the stalwarts of SNCC had reached the point that they no longer wanted to participate in marches, demonstrations, or any kind of direct action. When Lewis went before the group in March, 1965, to ask for volunteers for Selma, he was met by bitter opposition. The complaint was that there had been too many beatings already. In the end, of course, the membership relented and SNCC went on to play a leading role at Selma.

The collapse of discipline in the organization led ultimately to the interlude known as "freedom high." And once again the intellectuals in the movement turned to Camus' *The Rebel* for philosophical support. They had their favorite passages in the work, thus:

> No man considers that his condition is free if it is not at the same time just, nor just unless it is free. Freedom, precisely, cannot even be imagined without the power of saying clearly what is just and what is unjust, of claiming all existence in the name of a small part of existence which refuses to die.[29]

In its literal application, however, the new meaning of freedom in SNCC was an approach to nihilism. Robert Moses, the leading disciple of Camus and a main advocate of "freedom high," wanted no national office, no hierarchy, and no structure. All should be able to "go where the spirit say go, and do what the spirit say do."[30] The results for the organization were almost disastrous. John Lewis was aghast:

> People were so high with freedom that they didn't do anything. They were no longer functional. . . . So, during that whole period while a few of the SNCC staff were working very hard in Selma . . . other people were on this "Freedom High" kick. They were drunk, in a sense, with freedom.[31]

The attention of the young radicals was being drawn at this time also to the newly translated works of Frantz Fanon, the young psychiatrist from Martinique. In his *The Wretched of the Earth*, Fanon clinically examined the oppressive, brutal, and dehumanizing treatment accorded "colonized peoples" the world over at the hands of the Western imperialist nations. Especially important to the young radicals was Fanon's identification of America as one of the Western imperialist oppressors and American blacks as one of the colonized peoples.[32] In the matter of freedom or liberation the students were interested in Fanon's warnings against the compromising weakness of nonviolence. Fanon characterized this tactic as "an attempt to settle the colonial problem around a green baize table, before any regrettable act" had been committed.[33] Most interesting were Fanon's views on the therapeutic value of violence: "At the level of individuals, violence is a cleansing force. It frees the native from his inferiority complex and from his despair and inaction; it makes him fearless and restores his self-respect."[34] By the beginning of 1966 there was hardly a black student radical anywhere who could not quote literally from *The Wretched of the Earth*. (See chapter 12.)

Malcolm X had, of course, been gaining in popularity among the student radicals since 1963. Even the comparatively conservative John Lewis could state that "Malcolm, perhaps more than any other person, was able to articulate the feelings of the Negro sharecropper in Mississippi, and at the same time . . . express the bitterness and frustrations of the Negro in . . . Chicago and Philadelphia."[35] More important to the militants in SNCC was the fact that Malcolm before his death seemed to be marching in lockstep with Fanon on the questions of colonialism and Third-World liberation. They applauded Malcolm's attempt to have the United States brought before the United Nations and condemned for its oppression of American blacks. By the time of its elections in May, 1966, therefore, SNCC had moved a long way from the philosophy of love and nonviolence. It was adopting new creeds and new heroes. Dr. King, they reasoned, was a sincere and dedicated man, but he was no longer relevant. No doubt he was going to hold on to his doctrine of love until the day he died, but "that day . . . would not be long in coming because some redneck was almost certain to love him back with a shotgun full of 'double-ought' buckshot and that would be the end of Dr. King and nonviolence."[36]

Carmichael's ascendancy to the chairmanship of SNCC was only part of the larger program that he had visualized for himself in the immediate future. True, he now held a relatively important position of leadership among blacks, but he was a man in a hurry. He needed a means by which he could leapfrog and propel himself upon the national stage and thereby command national attention. It was soon to be forthcoming. On May 29, 1966, Congressman Adam Clayton Powell delivered the baccalaureate address at Howard University. He said in part:

> Human rights are God-given. Civil rights are man-made. . . . Our life must be purposed to implement human rights. . . . To demand these God-given rights is to seek *black power*— the power to build black institutions of splendid achievement.[37]

There were a number of SNCC activists in the audience who heard this address. That evening in Washington, D.C., some of these SNCC members attended a dinner dance given by local residents to raise funds for the organization. John Lewis and Carmichael were among those present.[38] A main topic of conversation was Powell's use of the term "black power." The term had not before been used publicly, and Carmichael was quick to seize upon its possibilities. For his purposes, he now had his gimmick. What he needed now was a suitable occasion on which to use it. This was to be provided by the "Meridith Mississippi Freedom March."

Paul Good, covering the march for the *New South,* stated:

> The march gave the new SNCC chairman a great opportunity to get his philosophy across to America because everything he said was delivered within earshot of Dr. King and Dr. King's presence insured fullest press coverage. Not necessarily enlightened but full.[39]

Meridith began his "Memphis to Jackson March" on Sunday, June 5, 1966. His avowed purpose was to dramatize the fear that dominated the day-to-day life of blacks in the Deep South. He hoped by his action to encourage timid Mississippi blacks especially to overcome their docility and go on to exercise the right to vote. Something like a dozen of his cronies accompanied him as he set out on U.S. Highway 51. On Monday, June 6, about ten miles inside Mississippi a white man stepped from the underbrush on the side of the highway and blasted Meridith with three rounds from a shotgun. It appeared to some of those at the scene, including one or two newsmen, that Meridith had been killed; but upon his arrival at a hospital in Memphis, it developed that he had been only superficially wounded. Even this news, however, was enough to shock the nation.[40]

Early the next morning Dr. King and Floyd McKissick of CORE visited Meridith at the hospital in Memphis offering sympathy and vowing to continue the march for him. As they were about to leave, in walked Carmichael and his militant associate, Cleveland Sellers. Carmichael came ostensibly to bring the well wishes of SNCC, but he had guessed that King intended to continue the march and he did not intend to be left out. In a brief conference between Dr. King, McKissick, and Carmichael it was agreed that CORE, SNCC, and the SCLC would jointly sponsor the march and that other civil rights organizations would be invited to join. They agreed also to send out a national call for support and participation. Later that morning, "march" headquarters were set up in the Reverend James Lawson's church in Memphis. Staff assignments were made and the news media were alerted. Dr. King, Carmichael, and McKissick with four automobiles of volunteers then set out for the spot on Highway 51 where Meridith had been shot the day before. "So began the second stage of the Meridith Mississippi Freedom March."[41]

As Dr. King trudged along in the broiling sun that afternoon, he was to discover that he was traveling with ideological strangers—even enemies. Nonviolence was not on this march. Instead the youngsters about him were militant, black conscious, and violence oriented. "If one of these damn white Mississippi crackers touches me, I'm gonna knock the hell out of him," shouted one.[42] And when someone suggested singing "We Shall Overcome," some refused, saying: "This is a new day, we don't sing those words any more. In fact, the whole song should be discarded. Not 'We Shall Overcome,' but 'We Shall Overrun.'"[43] At a meeting in a Negro motel that evening, Dr. King worked hard to get the march back on a nonviolent track. He said: "I tried to make it clear that besides opposing violence on principle, I could imagine nothing more impractical and disastrous than for any of us, through misguided judgment, to precipitate a violent confrontation in Mississippi."[44] Carmichael took the floor. Enjoying his new role, he shouted: "I'm not going to beg the white man for anything I deserve, I'm going to take it." He insisted also that the march was a black affair and that whites should be completely excluded.[45] After a lengthy and bitter discussion Roy Wilkins, Whitney Young, and Floyd McKissick joined in support of Dr. King's contention that the march must be nonviolent as well as interracial. Charles Evers had his own doubts about the march: "I don't want this to turn into another Selma where everyone goes home with the cameramen and leaves us holding the bag."[46] The meeting also evolved a manifesto which stated: "This march will be a massive public indictment and protest of the failure of American society, the Government of the United States, and the state of Mississippi to 'fulfill these rights.'"[47] Roy Wilkins and Whitney Young did not sign the manifesto.

Jackson was two hundred miles from Memphis, and it was estimated that the march would be in progress for some two or three weeks. As the group, some 350 of them, moved down the highway, it was spearheaded by a couple of automobiles and a truck rented by the wire services and TV networks. State patrol cars moving up and down the highway kept them under surveillance. During the night the marchers slept in sleeping bags or under tents carried on the truck.

With the national and international news media closely observing the progress of the march, Mississippi officialdom was anxious to avoid trouble. Thus, when the marchers reached the outskirts of Grenada, word was quickly spread by the city fathers to avoid incidents wherever possible. While the marchers were in the city, local officials allowed more than 1,300 blacks to become registered to vote, with the county even adding temporary black registrars. The march had hardly moved out of town, however, before blacks were jailed for attempting to integrate a local theater.

Thus far on the journey Carmichael had kept his plans under wraps; but as the procession neared Greenwood, he prepared to go into action. Paul Good reported: "Stokely spread the word to his many followers on the march that Black Power would be the slogan from there on in."[48] In Greenwood on the night of June 16, the police warned the marchers against erecting tents in a school yard without the permission of the school board. Carmichael abruptly countermanded the order saying, "That ain't no problem. We'll put them up anyway."[49] He was immediately arrested. Out on bail a short time later Carmichael addressed a rally of marchers and local blacks: "This is the 27th time I have been arrested—I ain't going to jail no more."[50] As to what followed, a *New York Times'* man on the scene reports:

> Five times Mr. Carmichael shouted, "We want black power! And each time the younger members of the audience shouted back, "Black power!" Almost before Carmichael had finished, Willie Ricks, who was one of his close associates, leaped to the platform shouting, "What do you want?" The crowd roared back "Black Power." Again and again Ricks cried, "What do you want?" and the response grew louder and louder until it had reached fever pitch.[51]

The rest was the work of the mass media. Carmichael had given it a slogan, simple, terse, and unencumbered with explanations and qualifications. Black power was sent screeching across the land, frightening some, intriguing others, but enlightening none at all. To Dr. King the term "Black Power" had a menacing, ominous ring, threatening to nonviolence as the dominant technique of the black protest in America. In a kind of quiet but controlled desperation Dr. King requested a conference with Carmichael and McKissick, who himself was now a Black Power advocate. Dr. King stated:

> For five long hours I pleaded with the group to abandon the Black Power slogan. It was my contention that a leader has to be concerned about the problem of semantics. Each word, I said, has a denotative meaning—its explicit and recognized sense—and a connotative meaning—its suggestive sense.[52]

King insisted that the group must "work to build racial pride and refute the notion that black is evil and ugly. But this must come through a program, not merely through a slogan."[53] Carmichael was ready with a rejoinder: "How can you arouse people to unite around a program without a slogan as a rallying cry? Didn't the labor movement have slogans? Haven't we had slogans all along in the freedom movement? What we need is a new slogan with 'black' in it."[54] But not really interested in debating with Dr. King, Carmichael decided to let him in on something: "Martin," he said, "I deliberately decided to raise this issue on the march in order to give it a national forum, and force you to take a stand for Black Power."[55]

Out of this meeting Carmichael emerged as clearly the dominant figure. On the remainder of the march his voice would attract the greater attention and speak with the greater authority. In Canton, Mississippi, he ordered the marchers to pitch their tents on a school grounds in defiance of a police order not to do so. As the marchers prepared to obey Carmichael, the police went into action. They were not arresting anyone—they were out to punish disobedience to their orders. Tear gas was hurled into ranks of the marchers after which the police moved in with flailing clubs, black jacks, and whips. It was Selma all over again but with fewer casualties. There was, however, no panic, and in spite of all the talk about violence and defiance no marchers fought back. Indeed, even Carmichael seemed to have temporarily lost his belligerency. In fact, Carmichael was ultimately led from the scene by Dr. King, himself red-eyed from tear gas but steady as usual under attack.

On the day before the Canton confrontation Dr. King had wired Washington for federal protection against the threat of violence in the Mississippi Delta, but the administration pointedly ignored him. President Johnson was not only exasperated by the seemingly endless petitions for federal protection from Dr. King, but he was miffed also by the latter's denunciation of America's involvement in the Vietnam war. Thus in Washington on the day following the Canton troubles, Attorney General Katzenbach dismissed a group of protesting clergymen with the observation that the marchers had brought the trouble on themselves by refusing to move from the school grounds where they had no right to be. Important to Dr. King's mystique among blacks and whites was his apparent ability to deliver federal assistance virtually upon demand. This time, however, he seemed to have gone to the well once too often. Worse yet, in ignoring Dr. King now, the Johnson administration was in effect helping to promote the burgeoning image of Stokely Carmichael.

On Sunday, June 28, in Jackson, the termination of the march was marked by what was billed as the greatest turnout of blacks in Mississippi's history. To many of the weary marchers and newsmen who had accompanied them, however, it was but a tiresome anticlimax. Aside from a handful of nationally known celebrities there was a list of speakers that included Whitney Young, Stokely Carmichael, and Dr. King. Carmichael was running the show. He was supreme commander with Dr. King serving in the role of a mere adviser. Hot and tired the marchers remained unmoved by the speeches, and many of them drifted away before the conclusion of the program. But the young SNCC activists remained. They sang songs, they danced, and they chanted: "Black power, black power."[56] Things were never again to be the same in the civil rights struggle.

By August, 1966, Carmichael had become the most talked about black man in the United States. Black Power had become almost a household term. Unlike Dr. King, James Lewis, Whitney Young, and Roy Wilkins, Carmichael was a successful and skillful demagogue rather than a proven leader. As a recent student activist himself, he was alert to the subtle but swift changes taking place in the nature and direction of the black revolution. Rather than follow sheep-like in the new path, he was determined to lead. His blueprint for success called for the cooperation of the news media and especially of television. He was aware that the price for any such cooperation would be demagoguery and sensationalism. He paid the price, and in the end he may have gotten the better of the deal.

Once on top, one of Carmichael's basic objectives was to break up the three-year-old coalition of black civil rights organizations and to force each of them to take a stand, one side or the other, on the question of militant black nationalism. Endorsement of the Black Power concept was to be the test. Those organizations that refused to do so were to be labeled white oriented, bootlicking, and "Tomist." The strategy was successful. Floyd McKissick was the first to unfurl the Black Power banner over his organization. In January, 1966, he had become the national director of CORE, replacing James Farmer who had resigned in December, 1965. McKissick had been a virtual confidant of Carmichael on the Meridith March, and he had eagerly assisted in the projection of the Black Power slogan in Greenwood, Mississippi. At the opening of its Twenty-third Annual Conference at

Baltimore on July 4, 1966, it was clear that black nationalism had replaced CORE's old image of nonviolence, love, and Christian humanity. The list of convention speakers not only included James Farmer and Mrs. Fannie Lou Hamer but also Stokely Carmichael, Lonnie Shabazz of the Black Muslims, and James Gray, a New York militant. Whites were conspicuous by their absence. In a series of resolutions adopted at a working session, the new CORE leaders declared themselves in opposition to the Vietnam war and to nonviolence as a protest technique. They declared Black Power rather than integration to be the new goal of the organization.[57]

In the aftermath of the convention a number of longtime white members resigned—some in exasperation, some in disgust, and some in sorrow. Among the latter was the noted author Lillian Smith. Miss Smith, whose book *Killers of the Dream* dealt with Southern white racism, accused McKissick and other CORE leaders of being new killers of the dream. She charged that the organization had been infiltrated by "adventurers and by nihilists, black nationalists and plain old-fashioned haters, who have finally taken over."[58] Stung by the backlash and alarmed at the prospect of diminishing financial contributions due to the flight of white members, McKissick later clarified his position on Black Power. At a press conference on July 7, he stated: "Black power is not black supremacy, does not mean the exclusion of white Americans from the Negro revolution, does not advocate violence and will not start riots."[59] Whatever else it did or did not mean, with McKissick's "clarifications" it was no longer the Black Power the militants had in mind. Under the shrewd and masterful leadership of Whitney Young, there was no chance at all that the National Urban League would look favorably on the Black Power concept. As the nation's largest and most powerful black social service organization, the League has always been system oriented. It has focused its efforts on making the system work for blacks. At its annual convention in August, 1966, the League reemphasized its dedication to programs which "bring jobs to the unemployed, housing to the dispossessed, education to the deprived, and necessary voter education to the disfranchised."[60] The League was not oblivious to the controversy over Black Power, but as executive director of the organization Young saw no point in becoming involved in "the fruitless dispute over the value of a slogan which has not even yet been clearly defined by its originators."[61]

Like the League in the field of social service, the NAACP was the oldest and most powerful black organization in the area of civil rights. Very definitely system oriented, the organization long held reservations about accepting the young SNCC activists as civil rights bedfellows. Thus, while the NAACP willingly provided financial and legal aid to student activists during critical situations, it freely and openly criticized them when it thought that their activities were too radical or extremist. Little knowledge of the NAACP was necessary, therefore, to predict what its reaction to Black Power would be. At the organization's annual convention in July, Executive Director Roy Wilkins spoke for the record:

> Though it be clarified and clarified again," black power" in the quick, uncritical and highly emotional adoption it has received from some segments of a beleaguered people can mean in the end only black death. Even if, through some miracle, it should be enthroned briefly, the human spirit, which knows no color or geography or time, would die a little, leaving for wiser and stronger and more compassionate men the painful beating back to the upper trail.[62]

Wilkins insisted further that the abandonment of nonviolence by CORE and SNCC could lead ultimately and directly to white counterforce, lynchings, and repression. Wilkins and other officials at the convention did not call for the NAACP's withdrawal from the coalition. They concluded that for all practical purposes Carmichael had already killed it.

As if waiting the word from Roy Wilkins, a host of traditional black groups and organizations built up in opposition to Black Power. The redoubtable Bayard Rustin spoke for most of these groups when he said:

> "black power" not only lacks any real value for the civil rights movement, but . . . its propagation is positively harmful. It diverts the movement from a meaningful debate over strategy and tactics, it isolates the Negro community, and it encourages the growth of anti-Negro forces.[63]

At a meeting in Chicago one hundred black clergymen representing the five-million-member National Baptist Convention issued a manifesto denouncing Black Power.[64] In what was almost a full-page advertisement in the *New York Times,* a committee of forty-eight nationally prominent black churchmen insisted that black power or any other kind of power was "not a thing lying about in the streets to be fought over." They held that if blacks were seriously concerned about power, they must build upon that which they already had. "'Black power' is already present to some extent in the Negro church, in Negro fraternities and sororities, in our professional associations, and in the opportunities afforded to Negroes who make decisions in some of the integrated organizations of our society." [65]

During and after his debate with Carmichael in Greenwood, Mississippi, Dr. King continued to tell himself and others that Black Power posed only a problem in semantics. He could not bring himself to believe that the student activists were really abandoning non-violence or that Black Power was anything but a new bottle for old wine. However, as the slogan gained in notoriety, and as it became the rallying cry of militant black nationalists and would-be ghetto revolutionists, Dr. King began to have second thoughts. In his book, *Where Do We Go from Here: Chaos or Community?* published early in 1967, Dr. King devoted almost fifty pages to a discussion of Black Power.[66] His views had changed considerably. He now insisted that while the slogan was an understandable response to a racist white power structure, it did not have the substance and program to become the basic strategy for the civil rights movement. He concluded that at bottom Black Power was a "nihilist philosophy" and that it carried the "seeds of its own doom."

Back in Atlanta, the SNCC office was taking on more and more the appearance of a black nationalist headquarters. The organization was using its field secretaries less in the field and more in the propagation of its new black militant ideas. Its presses worked full time in turning out Black Panther bumper stickers depicting a lunging black panther. The scholarly *Student Voice* was replaced by the angry and militant *Nitty Gritty,* and Malcolm X's philosophy was available in an abundance of pamphlets. But along with its new image SNCC had new problems. In letter after letter coming into the organization's headquarters, former contributors, disturbed by the exclusion of whites or by the Black Power slogan, cut off their financial support. Following are excerpts from some of the letters:[67]

When you talk about "white America," you are talking about me too. . . . And I have a strong prejudice against being bad-mouthed with my own money.[68]

I am a white liberal. . . . My purpose in writing you is to tell you bluntly to take my name off your mailing list. I want no part of S.N.C.C.[69]

Until you orient your organization more towards humanity, and less toward a select and unfortunate segment of an ethnic minority, you will not get any more money from me than the 5¢ stamp on this envelope.[70]

When the name and type of person like Stokely Carmichael are no longer associated with your cause, I will be happy again to contribute. As a Jew, I could hardly feel myself divorced from civil rights.[71]

Amid the whole raging controversy over Black Power there was one central, vital question which almost everybody asked: What did it *really* mean? What everyone wanted, ghetto-dweller and university professor alike, was a terse, concise, working, official or party-line definition of Black Power. But this was never forthcoming. What little that Carmichael did offer was invariably shrouded in bombast or lost in ambiguity. Because of this situation there were literally dozens of differing, even competing, definitions of Black Power current during the latter part of 1966. Most of them spoke vaguely of some indeterminate thrust that black people could or should make in one direction or another. All of this is understandable, however, in view of the calculating and cynical stratagem employed to promote the slogan on the Meridith March. The point to be made is that Black Power was, at the time, nothing more than naked rhetoric. Its authors had not yet had time to work out a supporting thesis.[72] It was, in short, a slogan in search of a meaning.

With pressure for some definition continuing to mount, SNCC in early August "leaked" a so-called position paper to the *New York Times*. While the document did not do much to clarify Black Power per se, it provided considerable insight into the thinking of the new leaders of the movement. For one thing, black "liberation" had become solidly entrenched as the new goal of the organization. Integration had become reactionary. "We had fallen into a trap whereby we thought that our problems revolved around the right to eat at certain lunch counters or the right to vote, or to organize our communities." This, SNCC believed, was a result of the influence and power of the "myth of 'Negro citizenship.'" The fact of the matter was that the broad masses of black people react to American society in the same manner as colonial peoples in Africa and Asia react to the West. In order to bring about the liberation or decolonization of American blacks, SNCC would work to promote black consciousness and glorify the black experience. "We allowed them [white people] to tell us what was good about our Afro-American music, art and literature." Whites would "no longer designate roles that black people play" but rather blacks would define the roles that whites would play. Under any circumstance: "The reality of the colonial people taking over their own lives and controlling their own destiny must be faced."[73] The authors of this document conceded that they were moving in the direction of black nationalism. The nonviolent, naive, and integrationist student movement had ceased to exist.

CHAPTER 7

The Long Hot Summers

In a little less than a month after the Black Power slogan made its debut at Greenwood, the long hot summer of 1966 broke loose upon the nation. Beginning on July 13, the blacks in Chicago went on a week-long rampage. Three blacks were killed; scores were injured; and property damage ran into the millions of dollars. During the next ten weeks the story was repeated in more than forty cities and towns throughout the country. With leaders such as Roy Wilkins denouncing Black Power as the "father of hatred and the mother of violence" and with the news media highlighting stories of sniper fire and guerrilla warfare, the conclusion would be obvious—Black Power was leading directly to violent black revolution. Stokely Carmichael was almost daily being depicted as a black Robespierre or Lenin, and black nationalists everywhere were being regarded with deep fear and suspicion. What was being overlooked in this semi-hysteria, of course, was the fact that the long hot summers did not begin in 1966. They had been recurring annually since 1963, long before the advent of Carmichael and Black Power. To blame the riots on a slogan was the easy and popular thing to do, but it was overlooking the deep racial causes and as such was both naive and dangerous.

Oddly enough, there were those, on the other hand, who were insisting that not only was the Black Power slogan not the cause of the riots, but also that race itself was only an incidental factor. Edward C. Banfield in his *The Unheavenly City*, published in 1970, states: "Almost everything said about the problems of the Negro tends to exaggerate the purely racial aspects of the situation." On this basis Mr. Banfield rejects the thesis that the riots were essentially a rebellion against the evils of white racism. In his thinking the problems of the blacks "are seldom purely racial and very often have little or nothing to do with race."[1] A ghetto is a ghetto, and given the same socioeconomic conditions comparable disorders will occur anywhere at any time. "It would appear, then , that what requires explanation is not so much rebellion by Negroes . . . as it is outbreaks of animal spirits and of stealing of slum dwellers, mostly boys and young men and mostly Negro."[2] Against this analysis is to be pitted the weight of evidence accumulated from the study of riots occurring over a fifty-year period, that is from East St. Louis in 1917 to Newark in 1967. What is clearly indicated is that a black ghetto is something more than an accumulation of statistics or a geographical location. It is a unique type of community—a concentration of socioeconomic maladies compounded by the factor of race. It is, in the words of Dr. Kenneth B. Clark, nothing short of "institutionalized pathology."[3]

Racial disorders in the Northern black ghettos began to occur during and immediately following World War I. They were to erupt spasmodically during the next four decades until 1963 when for five consecutive years they exploded into "long hot summers." While all of the disorders have had the same root causes, they have not all displayed the same profile. Sociologist Morris Janowitz divides the riots into two basic categories: (1) communal riots and (2) commodity-type riots.[4] The communal or "contested area" riots are "ecologically based" struggles involving direct confrontation between residents of black and white neighborhoods. Because of the bloody clashes such confrontations invariably incur, they have historically been referred to as race riots. The first important communal riot of this century occurred in East St. Louis during the summer of 1917. As is invariably the case, the disorders had been preceded by a protracted period of interracial tension. On July 2, mobs of whites roamed the black neighborhood assaulting and killing blacks without regard to age or sex. The blacks retaliated as best they could. When it ended, eight whites had been killed and over one hundred Negroes had been shot or beaten up.[5]

The racial disorders of the "Long Bloody Summer" of 1919 belong in the communal category. Because of the classical study made by Charles S. Johnson, the Chicago riot of that summer is most widely discussed.[6] Johnson's report revealed that while there had been enough jobs to go around for both races, the burgeoning black population had created a housing shortage. Thus, the bloody clash that broke out in the city on July 27 was essentially "ecological warfare." For almost two entire weeks Chicago was a city without law and order. When the final count came in, fifteen whites and twenty-three blacks had been killed; some 537 of both races had been injured and more than one thousand families, mostly blacks, had been rendered homeless. The last of the so-called communal riots was that which occurred in Detroit during the summer of 1943. In the background of these disorders were the fifty thousand black migrants who had recently come into the city from the Deep South and who had been pressing for jobs and housing—neither of which were available. The eruption which began on June 20 resulted in the killing of twenty-five blacks and nine whites and a very large property loss.[7]

The commodity-type riot is essentially an attack on property. It is almost never a conflict between black and white civilians. Such deaths and injuries as do occur are usually the result of confrontations between the rioters and the police. This type of riot is, in the first place, set off by a real or rumored incident of police brutality some place in the ghetto. Crowds collect, tension mounts, and the police are insulted or attacked. Local control begins to break down in the second stage. Plate-glass windows are smashed, and ghetto residents recognize that food, liquor, and merchandise are there for the taking. If order is not restored at this point, a third stage is reached where arson, molotov cocktails, and sniper fire become the order of the day. The Harlem riots of 1935 and 1943[8] were the first important commodity-type riots of record in black communities. In the first of these there was a property loss of some two million dollars, and in the second the loss was a quarter of a million dollars. With the white flight to the suburbs accelerating after World War II, the causes of "ecological warfare" or communal riots were diminished. Thus, all of the disorders of the long hot summers fall in the category of commodity-type riots.

When viewed as a whole, however, the long hot summers cannot be classified as simply a series or collection of riots. These disorders persisted over a period of six successive years; they extended over a wide area of the nation; and they were conflagratory in nature. In short, they verged on open rebellion. From the longer view they were an extension of the black revolution that had begun in the Deep South some eight years earlier. Widespread discontent and frustration among Southern blacks had been brought on by the failure of the great promises of the *Brown* decision. But segregation was not an issue in the Northern states; and while Northern blacks were duly sympathetic with their Southern brethren, they did not feel impelled to become otherwise involved. Toward the end of the decade of the

1950s, however, Northern blacks were beginning to experience reversals of their own. The unemployment rate among blacks had begun to climb rapidly until by the early 1960s it was at 9.3 percent as compared with 3.3 percent for whites throughout the country. Along with mounting poverty there was an acceleration in the deterioration of ghetto housing plus a rise in crime and in narcotic addiction. The optimism of the early 1950s was turning into hopelessness and despair. And as the gap between expectations and actuality widened, there was an increased alienation and hostility toward the white power structure and the institutions of law and government which it controlled. Among young blacks especially there was a growing conviction that there was no effective alternative to violence as a means of obtaining redress and moving the system.

Along with everything else Northern blacks were becoming increasingly sensitized by the growing violence committed against black activists in the South. The cry for retaliatory violence against "whitey" began to be sounded in black ghettos throughout the nation. Contrary to what is generally assumed, however, the first of the long hot summers, that of 1963, was largely Southern based. Dr. Martin Luther King was fond of saying that "as Birmingham goes, so goes the nation." Ironically, the blacks of Birmingham made the first decisive break with the nonviolence tradition and thereby inaugurated the first of the long hot summers. On the night of May 12, in retaliation for the bombing of Rev. A. D. King's home, blacks set out to sack and burn the city. That they did not succeed was due largely to the tact and forbearance of the police along with the diligence of firemen and civilian defense workers. The main casualty of the eruption was nonviolence. When the Reverend Wyatt T. Walker attempted to calm the enraged blacks, he was shouted down: "Tell it to Bull Connor. This is what nonviolence gets you!"[9] In Savannah, Georgia, a few weeks later more than one thousand blacks impatient with the slow pace of desegregation went on a destructive rampage through the city. In Jackson, Mississippi, blacks armed with weapons for a riot were barely dissuaded from retaliating for the killing of Medgar Evers. All told, there were more than thirty demonstrations in the South in 1963.[10] Some were *not* nonviolent.

In the North, in the meanwhile, blacks were asserting themselves in what someone called "aggressive nonviolence." In New York City, members of CORE dumped truckloads of debris at City Hall Plaza in protest against filthy conditions in Harlem. A few days later other demonstrators had to be forcibly removed from the mayor's office. In Detroit, demonstrators who had "occupied" a bank in protest for its failure to hire black tellers had to be removed on stretchers. And in Chicago black demonstrators relaxed in thick mud, blocking the construction of mobile schools for black children as a means of keeping them out of the white ones. If violent disorders did not break out in the North in 1963, it was due in large measure to the tireless efforts of the major civil rights groups. Malcolm X was doing his level best to discredit them, but at this point they still retained some prestige among the black rank and file. Moreover, as the summer passed the midpoint, blacks everywhere became preoccupied with preparations for the upcoming March on Washington. The Kennedy administration promoted this venture as an alternative to violence by blacks. Thus, when September arrived without there having been a major ghetto upheaval, the nation breathed a collective sigh of relief.

By the sheer violence of the disorders of 1964, Northern blacks seemed to be making up for what they failed to do in the previous year. This was in reality the first long hot summer for the North, and it brought dismay to the nation at large. Theodore White, the historian, has commented: "The riots of the summer of 1964 were not race riots. They were worse: they were anarchy, a revolt led by wild youth against authority, against discipline, against the orderly government of a society that had taken too long to pay them heed." [11] The first, as well as the worst, of these disorders was to take place in Harlem. This community had been a veritable tinderbox for more than a decade. Since 1953 it had been the headquarters for Malcolm X. In addition it was the home of more than a score of black nationalist organizations, some serious and dedicated, and others hustling and pandering black nationalism for a living. Beyond this Harlem had long prided itself in being a militant community. It would not long remain quiescent in the midst of a national black upheaval. In 1959, Malcolm X almost precipitated a riot himself when he marched some fifty Muslims to a police station and compelled the police to agree to hospitalize an injured brother Muslim. During the spring of 1964, New York blacks were still limiting their activities to "aggressive non-violent demonstrations." The Brooklyn chapter of CORE announced a "stall-in" to block traffic approaches to the New York World's Fair scheduled to open on April 22. [12] The national headquarters of CORE disapproved, and other major black organizations turned thumbs down on the idea. With far more rhetoric than planning, the

Brooklyn CORE chapter persisted in what was bound to end in a fiasco. The police had little trouble in keeping the accesses to the fair wide open.

The city's black militants finally got their chance for action on July 16 when a white off-duty policeman shot and killed fifteen-year-old James Powell. Neither the Harlem nor the Brooklyn disorder which followed this incident was spontaneous. On the day after the shooting, the Progressive Labor Movement, a Marxist-Leninist group, circulated inflammatory leaflets denouncing police brutality.[13] Local black militant groups worked overtime to keep the incident alive in the community. On Saturday, July 18, a crowd gathered as usual at Harlem's "Hyde Park" on 125th–126th streets and Seventh Avenue. Speakers took turns addressing the listeners, all of them demanding some form of retaliation for the "murder" of James Powell. In a short while, the crowd, numbering some 250 people, with several black nationalists in the vanguard converged on a police precinct about two blocks away. Forewarned, a handful of policemen moved out in the street to confront them. The spark was set to the tinder. In a little more than one hour, what had been merely a noisy demonstration had grown into a mob of more than a thousand howling, excited, and angry human beings. From the police station the mob moved up to the business district of the community and began to sack and loot the shops. As news of the rioting spread, people hastened to "get a piece of the action." During early Sunday morning there were three or four independent mobs roaming Harlem.[14]

By Tuesday, July 21, the rioting had leaped the East River to flare anew in the Bedford-Stuyvesant section of Brooklyn. And in this blighted community incitation of the riot clearly appeared to be the work of CORE militants.[15] The chapter in Brooklyn had been suspended for its failure to call off the abortive stall-in of April. Once the riot had gotten started in Harlem, its members waited in the wings. On Monday, July 20, CORE staged a rally at the popular northeast corner of Fulton and Nostrand avenues to protest the killing of Powell. One after another, the speakers pilloried the New York police for their continued brutality against blacks. Aroused and excited, people in the audience began to shake their fists and chant: "Killer cops must go." When the police began to beef up their forces around the rally, tension began to mount. CORE leaders now asked the police to withdraw "so the people would not have anything to be infuriated by."[16] When the police refused to do so, CORE leaders urged the mob to disperse but it refused. A few minutes later the mob was racing up and down Fulton and Nostrand avenues smashing windows and looting on the run. The rioting in Brooklyn was to continue sporadically until late Wednesday night when a heavy downpour drove everyone off the streets.

By Thursday, July 23, both Harlem and Bedford-Stuyvesant had quieted down. City officials began the task of assessing the damage and laying the blame. The latter was to prove a difficult task. Once the riot had gotten started, CORE withdrew from the scene. The Black Muslims had not been visible at any point in either disorder, and Malcolm X was out of the country. During most of the rioting Mayor Robert Wagner had also been out of the country. When he returned on Tuesday, July 21, his first action was to call on Dr. Martin Luther King for help. Harlem, however, was in no mood to listen to the apostle of nonviolence.[17] Both King's visit and his suggestions to the mayor were ignored by the black community. With the exception of Bayard Rustin, all of the other black leaders in the city stayed out of circulation until the riots had run their courses. They probably would have been ineffective anyway.

In the meanwhile the scene shifted to a city several hundred miles to the north of New York. During the evening of July 24, a young black who had been drinking very heavily proceeded to disrupt a street dance in the black community of Rochester, New York.[18] When the police attempted to arrest him, they met violent interference from an assembled crowd. The usual cry of police brutality was raised, and the crowd quickly grew into an angry mob. When the local chief of police arrived, he was promptly attacked and his car overturned. Rumors spread like wildfire among the city's thirty-five thousand blacks, and as is usual in such cases the young blacks took to the streets. Within a few minutes Rochester began to experience the worst ordeal in its history. During three days of rioting, pillaging, and arson some 350 persons were injured, with one killed. More than one thousand people were arrested, with property loss totaling in the millions of dollars. Order was restored finally with the assistance of the New York State National Guard. During the next few days racial disorders were to erupt in rapid succession in three New Jersey cities: Paterson, Jersey City, and Elizabeth. In each of the cities there was a repeat of the usual pattern of the police brutality incident followed by rumors, rioting, looting, and arson. Order was restored in all of these cities by mid-August.

The last of the season's major disorders was to occur in Philadelphia in late August. In this city the black community was commonly referred to as "The Jungle." Blacks from the Deep South had squeezed into this area, giving it a density of some 2,000 residents to the city block. Along with this density came unemployment, poverty, disease, and crime. On the afternoon of August 28, a black woman sat in a stalled automobile at an intersection, refusing to move or to allow the vehicle to be towed. When the police placed her under arrest and began physically to remove her, she began screaming and shouting obscenities. Onlookers immediately became involved.[19] A black militant leaped upon the porch of a nearby house and began to harangue a crowd, urging them to attack the police. After this the pattern of New York and Rochester was repeated with two exceptions: (1) employing minimal force in restoring order, the police used no firearms or tear gas, and (2) the city's black leaders moved upon the scene almost immediately to assist in controlling and stopping the disorder. The result was that no one was killed and injuries were kept to a minimum.

As the autumn months approached and the disorders began to recede from the front page, the question on everybody's mind was what could have been the cause of such an unprecedented eruption of violence and disorder among the nation's blacks. For many the answer was simple: Since blacks had lived with unemployment, poverty, and squalor up to the present without rebelling, the riots had to be inspired by outside forces, such as Communists, black nationalists, or even parties unknown. Under any circumstances, it was reasoned, conspiratorial forces were at work since the riots showed every indication of having been planned, scheduled, and executed with precision. Early in September, however, the Federal Bureau of Investigation disappointed a good many pundits when it announced that it had not been able to discover any evidences of conspiracy behind the riots. Like almost all other agencies studying the riots, the FBI found the dehumanizing conditions of life in the black ghetto to be the root cause.

Aside from the law enforcement agencies, no group in the nation agonized more over the disorders than the leaders of the Democratic party. With national elections impending, party strategists were fearful of the impact that the riots might have on the "ethnic" and lower white middle-class vote in the Northern states. Moreover, the blacks were proving difficult in yet another area. The intransigence of

MFDP could well lead to an alienation of much of the Southern white vote. Summed up, it all spelled "backlash." Its possibilities produced prodigious countermeasures on the part of the Democratic leaders. Theodore White states:

> Every form of pressure—political, financial, investigative . . . was quietly applied to the problem. . . . White liberals who normally finance Negro movements in the North were brought to heel and persuaded to threaten to cut-off all moneys. The large sums of money appropriated for registration of Negro voters by the Democratic National Committee were held up long enough to make sure that every penny so directed would go to registration and not into hell-raising.[20]

As a result of considerable White House persuasion, leaders of the major black civil rights groups, including A. Philip Randolph, conferred in New York City on July 29 and agreed to issue a call to the nation's blacks "to observe a broad curtailment, if not total moratorium, of all mass marches, mass picketing and mass demonstrations until after Election Day."[21] Dr. King, Wilkins, Young, and Randolph signed the statement. James Farmer and John Lewis demurred. But the "call" notwithstanding, there were no disorders after September 1. Rioting was a summertime activity among blacks, and furthermore, most blacks, including those in the ghetto, considered the election of Lyndon Johnson vital to the welfare of the race.

While none of the black militant groups was in 1964 organized sufficiently to operate on a national level or to engage in effective conspiratorial work, the racial disorders were of considerable benefit to many individual members of these groups. For one thing, a good many of them received what they considered to be "battle training," and for another it enabled them to begin to formulate what could be called a riot ideology. The typical militant was a young black male, very probably born in the ghetto, who had achieved a high school education. He was alert, politically sophisticated, and in possession of a strong self-image. As a group, the militants were thoroughly imbued with the teachings of Malcolm X. They made extensive use of revolutionary terminology. Under any circumstances, they despised the traditional black organizations, such as the NAACP and the National Urban League. And they insisted that though nonviolence had produced limited results in the South, it would be totally ineffective against institutional racism in the North. The riot ideology dictated that the only thing the white man understands is force and that violence, pillage, and arson in the ghetto brought a quick and ultimately a positive response. In the wake of the 1964 riots, young militants began to project this view in a growing number of black communities across the nation.

One such community was the area known as Watts, located in Los Angeles County, California. *Ebony* magazine in March, 1965, listed Watts as being one of the ten top cities in the nation for the percentage of blacks who were gainfully employed. One-fourth of Los Angeles municipal employees were black: one third of the City Council's members were black, and Los Angeles had elected one black man to the United States House of Representatives. Better than 10 percent of Los Angeles black families earned more than $10,000 a year. And along with its clusters of dilapidated and overcrowded houses and dingy business places, Watts boasted of a representative number of modern homes, attractive gardens, and well-dressed black citizens. Thus Watts was a ghetto but not a teeming, sleazy, deteriorating "jungle." And yet for seven terrible days this community was wracked by one of the most savage and destructive racial disorders ever to occur in the United States.[22] Between August 11 and 17, 1965, the riot accounted for some thirty-five million dollars in property loss, 997 buildings damaged or destroyed, 1,032 persons injured, and thirty-four persons killed.

The incident that sparked the disorder involved the usual charge of police brutality. Far more important than the incident, however, was the ideological content in the thinking of the black community at the time of the riot. A study of the riot by a team of social scientists from the University of California at Los Angeles suggested that not a tiny fraction but better than 15 percent of the people in the community participated in the riot; that 34 to 50 percent supported the rioters; that 62 percent approved of it as a Negro protest; and that 64 percent thought that the victims of the riot deserved what they got. Finally, some 38 percent of those interviewed described the riot in "revolutionary rhetoric" using such terms as "revolt," "insurrection," and "revolution." To a considerable proportion of the people in the community the riot was viewed as a legitimate protest against white racism, and it was expected to result in improvements in the condition of blacks generally. They were not at all concerned over the possibility of white retaliation.[23] To a large number of blacks the name Watts became symbolic of the black protest but to the nation as a whole it became synonymous with ghetto anarchy.

Even as late as 1965, not all of the nation's black leaders knew or understood the true dimensions of the mood among the black rank and file. When Dr. Martin Luther King first learned of the outbreak in Watts, his initial reaction was one of shock. He termed the riot "a blind and misguided revolt against authority and society" and insisted that the authorities were justified in using whatever force necessary to restore order. However, this did not mean that he was washing his hands of the matter. Leaving San Juan, Puerto Rico, where he had been attending a conference, Dr. King arrived in Los Angeles on August 18. He planned to set up a "'constant dialogue' between friendly whites and the Negro community; and to help Negro leaders formulate remedial programs." [24] Touring the side streets and avenues of Watts in the company of Bayard Rustin and Andrew Young, Dr. King was in for another shock. When he discussed the riot with a group of youngsters, they shouted gleefully: "We won." King then asked them: "How can you say you won when thirty-four Negroes are dead, your community is destroyed, and whites are using the riot as an excuse for inaction?" Their reply was: "We won because we made them pay attention to us." [25] A little later in attempting to address a group in the Westminster Community Center, Dr. King was shouted down: "Get out of here, Dr. King!" [26]

Disillusioned and obviously frustrated, Dr. King left Los Angeles much before he had intended. But he now resolved to accept the challenge of the black ghetto. As he put it: "A riot is at bottom the language of the unheard. It is the desperate, suicidal cry of one who is so fed up with the powerlessness of his cave existence that he asserts that he would rather be dead than ignored." [27] But violence has its limitations—it can be put down with superior force. Nonviolence, on the other hand, can mobilize "numbers so huge" that there is no counterforce. Dr. King reasoned that the critical task would be to convince blacks that "nonviolence can win." Resolved to profit from his experiences in Watts, Dr. King proceeded to blueprint a nonviolent program for Chicago's black community. Along with other observers he was convinced that this metropolis was next in line for a racial explosion. In October, 1965, he dispatched a team of fourteen SCLC staff people, headed by the Reverend James Bevel, to do a detailed study of the social and economic conditions of that city's black community. They set up the West Side Christian Parish as an organizational base for their operation.

On Sunday, January 23, 1966, Dr. King and his family took up residence in a slum tenement on Hamlin Avenue in Chicago. As soon as the landlord discovered that King was a tenant, he rushed a crew to clean up the building and remove long-standing violations of the building code. The word was passed along and other slum lords did likewise. A local newspaper observed that if King would simply move from block to block, he might "stimulate the same sort of healthful and helpful shock wave" in each case that could result in cleaning up the city's slums.[28] Dr. King's own plans, while being less dramatic, were more comprehensive. He had three objectives in view: (1) to educate blacks in the city about slum conditions, (2) to organize blacks into a tenants' union to compel landlords to obey the law and meet their obligations, and (3) to mobilize black slum dwellers into a huge force of nonviolent crusaders. King changed the name of his West Side Christian Parish to the more secular Union to End Slums. It became a member organization of the local Coordinating Council of Community Organizations which included such other groups as the NAACP, SNCC, CORE, and the National Urban League. King became the accepted spokesman for the CCCO.[29]

On February 23, Dr. King visited Elijah Muhammad with a view toward bringing the Black Muslims into the group, but the Muslims preferred to continue going it alone. In the meanwhile Mayor Richard E. Daley and his lieutenants were keeping close watch on the new developments in the black community. On February 10, the city officials had announced the hiring of fifty additional housing inspectors. Landlords guilty of violating or ignoring the housing code would be prosecuted to the fullest extent of the law. Indeed, some twenty-five of the worst offenders had already been marked for prosecution. A little more than a month later Daley summoned a group of black ministers (King was out of town) to City Hall to fill them in on what the city had been doing about poor housing, segregation, and discrimination in employment. The ministers drew up a list of recommendations for the city's immediate consideration. During most of the spring months Dr. King had to be away from Chicago, and the activities of the CCCO were limited to skirmishing with the slum lords and City Hall.

During the last week of May, however, Dr. King announced plans for a massive march on City Hall to take place on June 26. He said: "We've been studying to see exactly what's needed and now we've emerged with concrete demands. Chicago will have a long hot summer, but not a summer of racial violence."[30] During the ensuing weeks King was out of town again and the march on City Hall was postponed. He was involved with the Meridith March where he became the unwitting midwife to the birth of the Black Power slogan. In the interim the city of Chicago had been granted a huge federal loan for the purpose of renovating five hundred substandard apartment units. Daley proudly announced that slums would be cleared from Chicago by the end of the decade. For Dr. King, however, this was too little, too late. Addressing a kick-off rally at Soldier Field on July 10, King proclaimed: "We will be sadly mistaken if we think freedom is some lavish dish that the federal government and the white man will pass out on a silver platter while the Negro merely furnishes the appetite." [31] At the conclusion of the rally, King led a procession of five thousand marchers through the streets to City Hall where, in emulation of his sixteenth-century namesake, he posted a list of demands on the door of a main city building. It did not escape the attention of the militants that Dr. King decided to lead the procession in a sleek air-conditioned limousine. In their thinking this was "nonviolent riding" in style.[32]

Two days later the militants decided to call an end to Dr. King's experiment in peaceful nonviolence and give the city a taste of a genuine long hot summer. Beginning on July 12 and continuing for the next three days, this was precisely what the blacks on the city's West Side attempted to do. Armed with molotov cocktails, knives, bricks, and even ash cans, the blacks stood off the police and looted stores and shops at will. Before some 4,200 National Guardsmen could restore order, scores of civilians and police had been injured; three blacks had been killed; and an uncalculated amount of property had been damaged or destroyed.[33] At the conclusion of the disorders Dr. King continued to press his program on the city, but the riot should have indicated to him that he was out of step with the times and certainly with the mood of the nation's blacks.

If any additional evidence was needed, it was provided in mid-July when blacks in the relatively affluent Hough community in Cleveland, Ohio, went on a four-day rampage.[34] When asked why they were rioting in this type of black community, one man answered that it was "a question of dignity." Blacks felt that they had been shabbily treated by the city administration and by the police in particular. Before the summer of 1966 bowed out, a total of forty-three riots and assorted disorders had occurred throughout the country. Although there had been substantial variations in setting, duration, and intensity, they were invariably ignited by a minor incident or a rumor of one and aggravated by antagonism between the police and the black community. Beyond this there was the new and rising hostility against whites in general. Blacks everywhere were angry. It was a time of militancy rather than of marching, of the clenched fist rather than the bended knee. As the year drew to a close, the image of Stokely Carmichael had almost completely blocked out that of Martin Luther King. The Black Power cry became the *"Sieg Heil"* of young black militants all over the country. Portents for the immediate future in the black ghettos were truly ominous.

For one surveying the national scene in the late summer of 1967, it would have been difficult not to conclude that blacks in America were in open rebellion. For the first nine months of the year there had been a total of 164 riots and racial disorders.[35] Upwards of two thousand people had been injured, with more than eighty killed. Property damage reached the astounding figure of $664 million. The worst of the rioting occurred during a two-week period in July when Newark and then Detroit became veritable battlegrounds. The intensity of the rioting and the stark anarchy made these two weeks unique in American history. Black militants and members of the new and old Left were quick to proclaim the existence of insurrection, revolt, and revolution. *Ramparts* called it: "wild and suicidal and romantic and very irrational. It is the spirit of revolution. . . ."[36] H. Rap Brown, newly elected chairman of SNCC, boasted that "as counterrevolutionary violence escalates against black people, revolutionary violence will rise to meet it."[37] And from the frightened leaders of the Republican party came the cry:

> Leaders of violence are publicly proclaiming and advocating future riots and the total defiance of all government. Hate mongers are traveling from community to community inciting insurrection. . . . We are rapidly approaching a state of anarchy. . . .[38]

1967's insurrectionary two weeks began in Newark, New Jersey, sometime during the late evening of July 12. Newark was one of the black communities described by Dr. King as having a "short fuse and a long train of abuses." At the time of the riot 52 percent of the city's 400,000 was black with a high percentage of these recently removed from the South. Over half of the adult blacks had less than an eighth grade education. The typical ghetto syndrome of unemployment, family breakup, and crime was present in all of its elements. More than 40 percent of all black children lived in broken homes. Newark had the highest incidence of substandard housing and the lowest per capita income for cities of comparable size. Its crime rate was high and a majority of its criminals along with the preponderance of their victims was black. A native of Newark himself, LeRoi Jones wrote of the city in 1967:

> Get to the tone of this place, this Black colony. Where liquor stores close at 10, and they cant even sell beer on Sunday.
> You can pay off anything in Newark, so completely rotten and graft-ridden is the place.[39]

Given these conditions, Newark constituted a fertile area for black militancy. Indeed, for almost a decade, several black nationalist groups operating out of New York City had been working to sensitize, politicize, and organize the seemingly apathetic blacks of Newark. A main center of these activities in Newark was the "Spirit House" established by LeRoi Jones in 1965 as a center for black art and community activities.

By the spring of 1967 local black activists had two hot issues going for them. One of these was the refusal of Mayor Hugh Addonizio to appoint a black man to the post of secretary of the Board of Education despite the fact that 70 percent of Newark's school children were black. The second of these was the announced intention of the authorities to move blacks out of 150 acres in the city to make room for a medical school. Militants regarded this as an attempt to dilute black political power in the city. All through the spring and early summer, tension in the black ghetto continued to mount. The incident that precipitated the riot involved the perennial charge of police brutality. The forcible arrest of a black cab driver led quickly to rumors that the man had been beaten to death by the police. In short order, militants had put together a crowd of blacks with which to confront the police. The time was approximately 10:30 P.M. From the precinct house the crowd proceeded on a mass march to the city hall. On the way, someone threw a rock; someone else set an automobile on fire. The riot had begun.

On the first evening, however, the looting and pillage was limited to a few stores and shops. During the next twenty-four hours the busiest place in town, aside from the police department's Fourth Precinct Station, was Spirit House. Local black militants were working feverishly to keep tension in the black community as high as possible. On the next day, Thursday, July 13, the community was inundated with inflammatory literature. Militants passed the word that a "Police Brutality" protest rally would be held during the early evening in front of the Fourth Precinct Station. Newsmen and TV cameramen were alerted. The crowd began to assemble early. By 7:30 P.M. it had become a milling, nervous mass of blacks; and when the police attempted to disperse them, it quickly became a mob. With teenagers in the vanguard, sacking, pillaging, and arson began. In less than three hours a large section of the city had been reduced to ashes. Between 2:00 and 2:30 A.M. Friday, Governor Richard B. Hughes, declaring the city to be in "open rebellion," called out the National Guard.

For the next two days a situation of near anarchy prevailed in the city.[40] Contributory causes were the lack of effective liaison between the local police and the National Guard plus the Guardsmen's lack of riot training. A third and new factor for ghetto riots was the reported appearance of organized sniper activity. While neither the police nor the guardsmen were ever able to round up the alleged snipers, a team of reporters from *Life* magazine was able to hold a clandestine meeting with a group of young activists who admitted to sniper activity during the riot. From the interview it was revealed that these young snipers had been organized by several activists who had served as civil rights workers in Mississippi in 1965. Becoming disenchanted, they had all decided to give up nonviolence. There were approximately fifty members of this sniper team active in and around the city, with more than half of them from Newark. "Others had been moved in for the action from California, Ohio, Pennsylvania."[41] Presumably they would move to other cities as the occasion and/or need arose. In a statement made to the press on July 26, Stokely Carmichael was apparently referring to these activists when he said:

> In Newark we applied war tactics of the guerrillas. We are preparing groups of urban guerrillas for our defense in the cities. The price of these rebellions is a high price that one must pay. This fight is not going to be a simple street meeting. It is going to be a fight to the death.[42]

On Monday afternoon, July 17, the state police and the National Guard forces were withdrawn from the city. During the four days' disorder there had been more than 250 fire alarms, many of which had been false. Of the ten million dollars in property loss, two million dollars was in damage to buildings; the rest was due to looting and pillage. The twenty-three persons killed included twenty-one blacks, one white fireman, and one white detective. More than two thousand people suffered injuries. Newark had truly gone through an ordeal. In appearance the sprawling black ghetto with its gutted buildings and its rubble was reminiscent of eastern European towns that had been hit by the Nazi blitz. For a few days it would replace Watts as the symbol of ghetto anarchy; then it would have to share that dubious honor with Detroit.

In the matter of living conditions for blacks, Detroit in the mid-1960s was considered to be a model city. Enjoying high employment in the automotive industry, Detroit blacks were considered to be among the most affluent in the nation. More than half of them owned automobiles and almost half of them owned their own homes. But there were also lesser blacks in the city—those who because of urban renewal had been moved out of the city's "Black Bottom" and into the Twelfth Street neighborhood. Here, rather than affluence, the blacks evidenced the common disabilities of all ghetto dwellers. The population density in this area was 21,000 to the square mile. Unemployment was estimated to be between 12 and 15 percent for adult black men and 30 percent for those under twenty-five years of age. Crime and narcotic addiction were rampant. Indeed, the conditions seemed to be ripe for a riot.

At approximately 3:45 A.M. on July 23, the Detroit police raided a black-owned after-hours drinking establishment known in that city as a "Blind Pig."[43] The police proceeded to lock up all eighty-two persons found on the premises. As early as it was on Sunday morning, the activity drew a crowd of some two hundred onlookers, and when the police had pushed the last arrestee into the waiting van, someone smashed a rear window. Within minutes rumors began to race up and down Twelfth Street. A young militant known about as "Mr. Greensleeves" shouted, "We're going to have a riot," and he urged the swelling crowd to vandalism. Within a couple of hours, more than three thousand blacks were out on Twelfth Street smashing store windows and looting at will. Obviously under orders, the 540 policemen detailed to the area refrained from interfering with the pillaging. Indeed, a good deal of bantering took place between the police and the looters, some of whom were still in their pajamas. Shortly before noon Congressman John Conyers, Jr., climbed atop an automobile in the middle of Twelfth Street to address the people. As he began to speak, he was challenged by an angry middle-aged black who shouted, "Why are you defending the cops and the establishment? You're just as bad as they are!"[44] Conyers made no further attempt to stem the tide. By his own admission it was a futile task.

As in Watts and Newark, a spirit of nihilism seemed to be taking hold. Middle-class blacks were jostling with the "slum folks" in the pillaging of the shops. Late Sunday afternoon it appeared to some observers that the young people "were dancing amidst the flames." With conditions becoming worse by the hour, Mayor Jerome Cavanaugh issued a proclamation instituting a 9 P.M. to 5 A.M. curfew. Following an aerial survey of the city, Governor George Romney shortly before midnight proclaimed that a state of public emergency existed in the cities of Detroit, Highland Park, and Hamtramck. Around 9 P.M. the first sniper fire was reported by the police. Quite possibly the "brothers" whom *Life* magazine had interviewed during the Newark disorders had arrived on the scene. At any rate, during the next forty-eight hours there were to be several hundred reports of sniping. One such report led to the police action that is so dramatically recounted in John Hershey's *The Algiers Motel Incident.*[45]

By 2 A.M. Monday some twelve hundred National Guardsmen and eight hundred state troopers were assisting the Detroit police. An additional eight thousand guardsmen were on the way. Still apprehensive, Governor Romney and Mayor Cavanaugh decided to call Washington for federal assistance. The United States Attorney General's office advised the governor that the law required that before federal troops could be dispatched, he would have to state that the situation had deteriorated to the point that local and state forces could no longer maintain law and order. Romney interpreted this to mean that he would have to declare that the city was in a state of insurrection. He was unwilling to make such a declaration, insisting that the insurance companies would not pay losses due to insurrection. However, contact with Washington was maintained and by twelve noon on Monday, President Johnson had authorized the sending of a task force of paratroopers to Selfridge Air Force Base near the city. By Thursday, July 27, the disorders had been brought to an end. During the four days of rioting forty-three persons, thirty-three of them black, were killed; 2,000 persons suffered injury and some 7,200 were arrested. Estimates of property damage originally set at better than $500 million was quickly scaled down. The final figure was put at $85 million. On Tuesday, August 1, the curfew was lifted and the National Guard moved out.

Like all racial disorders since those of 1963, the Detroit riot raised the specter of conspiracy. To a great many Americans it was absolutely incredible that such massive eruptions could be spontaneous. The National Advisory Commission on Civil Disorders was particularly interested in conspiracies as a possible cause of the riots. It obtained "documents, numbering in the thousands," from the Federal Bureau of Investigation, the Central Intelligence Agency, the Departments of State, Treasury, and Defense, the Internal Revenue Service, and the Post Office Department. In addition, the commission established a special examination staff that made on-the-spot examinations of riots in twenty-three cities. Beyond this, the commission "studied the role of foreign and domestic organizations, and individuals dedicated to the incitement or encouragement of violence." And finally, it looked into the organizational affiliations of those who preached violence, "their contacts, sources of financial support, travel schedules and so far as possible, their effect on audiences." In its 250,000 word report issued on March 2, 1968, the commission stipulated that "militant organizations, local and national, and individual agitators, who repeatedly forecast and called for violence were active in the spring and summer of 1967," and that "they deliberately sought to encourage violence, and that they did have an effect in creating an atmosphere that contributed to the outbreak of disorder." [46]

However, on the basis of all available data, the Commission concluded that "the urban disorders of the summer of 1967 were not caused by, nor were they the consequence of, any organized plan or 'conspiracy.'" More specifically, it "found no evidence that all or any of the disorders or the incidents that led to them were planned or directed by any organization or group—international, national, or local." [47] So much for the conspiracy theory, and if there were those who were disappointed by these findings, they were to be even less enchanted by the commission's finding that a fundamental cause of ghetto unrest was the "racial attitude and behavior of white Americans toward black Americans. . . . White racism is essentially responsible for the explosive mixture which has been accumulating in our cities since the end of World War II." [48] It is to be noted that nowhere in its report did the commission use the terms "insurrection," "rebellion," or "revolution" in referring to any of the disorders it discussed. By definition all of these terms involved organized activity, planning, and conspiring. The commission found none of this in its investigations.

Other groups and individuals, however, were less discriminate in their characterization of the disorders. Among these were the sensationally minded TV commentators, newspaper reporters, and columnists. Police officers and public officials with a "law and order" orientation demanded rigorous suppression of "ghetto insurrection" and "black revolt." On the other hand, both Governors George Romney and Richard Hughes used the terms "insurrection" and "open rebellion" until each was advised that insurance companies would balk at paying off damages caused by disorders of these descriptions. Perhaps no group of whites was more avid in its adoption and use of the terms "black revolt," "insurrection," and "rebellion" than the so-called "New Left." Members of this group had long identified with the programs and even the rhetoric of the black militants.

To black militants and black nationalists everywhere there was no doubt about what happened in Newark and Detroit. The terms "riot" and "disorder" were rejected out of hand.

> They are, in fact, revolts. By this we mean that they are acts which deny the very legitimacy of the system itself. . . . They are revolts because the black people are saying that they no longer intend to abide by an oppressive notion of "law and order."[49]

To the extremists and the millennium-minded young blacks, the hour had struck. H. Rap Brown exultantly declared black Americans to be in a state of open rebellion. "If America don't come around, we're going to burn America down, brother."[50] And LeRoi Jones, the bard of the black revolution, mused:

> The war on the devil has begun throughout this land! We begin to feel ourselves again, and know the passion of righteous action.
> We are not murderers. We have oppressed no man. We seek only to rule ourselves. . . .[51]

Obviously desiring to celebrate and to mark the outbreak of the "black rebellion," leading black militants decided to hold the first National Conference on Black Power in Newark, New Jersey, July 20 to 23. As it turned out, this was during the interim between the Newark and the Detroit riots. Pressured by anxious city and state officials to select another date or place or both, the directors of the conference refused. They reasoned that such a conference "held amidst yesterday's ashes of Newark's scorched black community would represent a phoenix of tomorrow's black power for all black communities."[52] The idea for such a conference originated with

Congressman Adam Clayton Powell during the summer of 1966, and under his directions plans were finalized early that fall. The objectives of the conference were not clearly spelled out, but given its "Black Power" title it was fairly predictable that certain black organizations would not be represented, as indeed they were not. One of the conference participants put it this way: "Whitney Young, Roy Wilkins, Rev. Martin Luther King, Jr., and Bayard Rustin were not there and nobody missed them. Floyd McKissick's presence more than equaled their collective absence." [53]

The one thousand delegates attending the sessions represented upwards of two hundred organizations and groups. While several of the delegations included whites, the most obvious thing about the conference was its dominance by militant black nationalists. After four days of fiery speeches and revolutionary rhetoric—what one observer described as "ideological eclecticism"—the delegates got down to the business of adopting resolutions. Chief among these were calls for:

> Establishment of "black universities" to make "professional black revolutionaries" of "revolutionary black professionals."
> "Black national holidays" to honor such "national heroes" as Malcolm X. . . .
> Refusal to accept birth-control programs, on the basis that they seek to exterminate Negroes.
> Paramilitary training for Negro youths. . . .
> There was enthusiastic support for a resolution for "starting a national dialogue on the desirability of partitioning the United States into two separate nations, one white and one black." [54]

Writing about the conference some months later, Chuck Stone suggested that while the country was not yet aware of it, it was going "to feel for a long, long time the effects of what those 1,000 independently minded black folks did in Newark, New Jersey, for four fateful days." [55] Time was to prove Mr. Stone's forecast as something less than accurate. Five years later what the country remembered about Newark was the riot of 1967 rather than the conference which followed it. Newark was still a gutted, burned-out black ghetto; the percentage of black residents was still rising; and the whites were still fleeing to the suburbs. The city was still financially bankrupt, and all of this was presided over by a sincere but impotent black administrator. The impact of July, 1967, was still felt, but it was the impact of the riot rather than the "ideological eclecticism" of the first National Conference on Black Power.

CHAPTER 8

Revolutionary
Black Nationalism

In January, 1967, the results of a Gallup poll indicated that Dr. Martin Luther King was no longer included among the ten men most admired by Americans. He had begun to slip rather badly. A chief reason for this development had been his stand against the war in Vietnam. Since 1965, his support for the peace forces had progressively become more vocal. In late March, 1967, he delivered an anti-war speech to a massive crowd at the Chicago Coliseum, and a little more than a week later he addressed an audience of three thousand in New York's Riverside Church. On Sunday, April 16, Dr. King in the company of Dr. Benjamin Spock headed a march of 125,000 demonstrators through New York's Central Park and across town to the United Nations Plaza. A few days later Dr. King was asked to run for president of the United States on a "peace ticket" with Dr. Spock. As a direct result of these activities Dr. King managed to alienate an important element of his white support. The White House warned him more than once to stay away from the war and stick to civil rights. And as was to be expected, he became *persona non grata* to Lyndon Johnson.[1]

To a few of the recognized black leaders, Dr. King's alliance with peace activists was political expediency pure and simple. For others, King was becoming a "patsy" for the skilled and cynical operators of the New Left. Under any circumstances black leaders were appalled by this new commitment. Whitney Young was quite pointed about it. During a fund-raising dinner at which they both had been speakers, Young loudly berated King for his anti-war activities. King angrily retorted: "Whitney, what you're saying may get you a foundation grant, but it won't get you into the kingdom of truth." Young replied that he had maintained a hard commitment in the ghetto while King's program was a humbug. "You're eating well," he told Dr. King.[2] The argument between the two became so heated that bystanders had to break it up. At a board meeting in mid-April, Roy Wilkins castigated King for his anti-war stand. Jackie Robinson joined the chorus of critics, and the polite and discreet Dr. Ralph Bunche suggested that King should "'positively and publicly give up one role or the other,' that of civil rights leader or that of international conciliator."[3] As always, however, Dr. King had the courage of his convictions. He was to continue to hold on to his new alliances in spite of the campaign against him.

In the matter of the civil rights movement, however, Dr. King's approach began to undergo some fundamental alterations. He was in fact beginning to move toward an accommodation with the black militant position. He had come to accept the view that the white power structure was evil and corrupt and incapable of reform; that the system needed substantial restructuring; and that the ghetto represented "domestic colonialism" for its black inhabitants. The idea of "love" was to be discarded but nonviolence was to be retained. King would embrace neither black insurrection nor black separatism, but his views had changed sufficiently for one observer to suggest that he had become a nonviolent Malcolm X. By the beginning of 1968, King and his staff had evolved a new program—a new synthesis:

> I think we have come to the point where there is no longer a choice now between non-violence and riots. It must be militant, massive non-violence, or riots. The discontent is so deep, the anger so ingrained, the despair, the restlessness so wide, that something has to be brought into being to serve as a channel through which these . . . deep angry feelings . . . can be funneled.[4]

The new program was to be known as the "Poor People's Campaign." The plan called for three thousand poor people, blacks, Indians, Mexican Americans, and whites, to converge on Washington, D.C., from ten cities and five rural areas. Some of them would make the journey on foot and others would use conventional means of transportation. They would all assemble in a shantytown in the nation's capital, and during a three-month period squads of demonstrators were to make daily sorties to the U. S. Senate and House of Representatives and the offices of selected federal agencies and bureaus. Dr. King's objective was the enactment of an "Economic Bill of Rights for the Disadvantaged" budgeted at ten to twelve billion dollars. Dr. King's invitation to the other black civil rights organizations to join or to support the new campaign was either rejected or ignored altogether. To several of them King was becoming simply a nuisance. Nevertheless, the SCLC during the months of

February and March proceeded with its scheduled workshops to train people who were to serve as marshals and team leaders in the campaign. The kickoff date was set for April 22.

In the meanwhile, Dr. King's attention was drawn to Memphis, Tennessee. Back in January the SCLC's Memphis affiliate, headed by the Reverend James Lawson, had become involved in a strike of black public works and sanitation employees. Dr. King was, in due course, called upon to lend his prestige and assistance to the cause. On March 28, he answered the call to lead a massive demonstration on behalf of the black sanitation workers. However, the demonstration was quickly to turn into a riot. With Dr. King and Rev. James Lawson in the lead the procession had barely traveled three blocks before young militants shouting "black power" began smashing store windows, looting, and pillaging. National Guardsmen brought the riot under control. Dr. King was becoming visibly weary, tired, and frustrated. Beyond this the number of threats to his life were increasing. To close friends it appeared that King was beginning to have premonitions of an impending tragedy.[5]

In Memphis again on April 3, King addressed an audience at the Mason Street Temple. He said:

Like anybody, I would like to live a long life. Longevity has its place. But I'm not concerned about that now. I just want to do God's will. And He's allowed me to go up to the mountain. And I've looked over, and I've seen the promised land.[6]

One listener at the Temple remarked that King "sounded as though he were giving his own eulogy." On the next day Thursday, April 4, Dr. King spent most of his time in his room at the Lorraine Motel in Memphis. Toward 6 p.m. he readied himself to go to dinner at the home of a local black mortician. Earlier that evening a man calling himself John Willard checked into a nearby motel. He rented a room which gave him an unobstructed view of Dr. King's balcony. The distance was little more than two hundred feet. Willard later brought to his room a pair of Bushnell binoculars, a Remington 30.06 telescopic rifle and a box of soft-point bullets. Shortly after 6 p.m., all dressed and ready to go to dinner, Dr. King moved out to the balcony of his room. Across the way Willard took careful aim and squeezed the trigger. A bullet was sent crashing into the right side of Dr. King's face shattering his jaw. The time was 6:04 p.m. The Reverends Jesse Jackson, Ralph Abernathy, Billy Kyles, and Andrew Young rushed to King's assistance. At 6:15 he was rushed to a local hospital. He died some forty-five minutes later.[7]

In its almost two hundred years of existence as a nation, anarchy never strode so boldly in the United States as it did in the wake of Dr. King's assassination. Grief-stricken, bitter, and vengeful millions of blacks took to the streets to even up the score any way they could. In Washington, D.C., a wall of fire raced up a ghetto block; in Chicago whites were indiscriminately beaten and pummeled; and in New York's Harlem Mayor Lindsay was driven to cover. For seventy-two long hours arson, pillage, violence, and wild disorder prevailed in upwards of 125 American cities and towns. In the nation's capital reporters spoke jokingly of the "second sacking of Washington, D.C." On the minds of many were the questions: "Is this the real revolution?" "Is nonviolence at an end?" When finally the disorders had subsided and the trauma had passed, the nation turned its attention to the worldwide manhunt for James Earl Ray, the man who had registered in the sleazy motel as John Willard.

In spite of his fading aurora, Martin Luther King to the very moment of his death had remained a giant among men. As a black leader he had absolutely no peers. By his unceasing devotion to nonviolence, he inhibited the growth of militancy and nihilism among the nation's frustrated blacks. With his death the door was flung open to the apostles of violence. From an eminent sociologist came the warning: "I think that one of the next big steps among black nationalists will be the development of more systematic, controlled disruption of the operation of our white society. There will be terrorism, and there will be sabotage. . . ."[8] Stokely Carmichael seemed to be confirming these predictions with his statement: "We have to retaliate for the deaths of our leaders. The execution for those deaths will not be in the courtrooms. They're going to be in the streets of the United States of America."[9] Following the funeral of Dr. King, however, the great majority of the nation's blacks eschewed further violence and returned to their daily pursuits. There was not to be any mass black rebellion nor any predatory killing of whites. Nevertheless, beginning with April, 1968, and continuing for some two years thereafter, the black nationalists were to dominate black America with their incendiary rhetoric, their unorthodox styles, and their militant, menacing posturing.

During the decade of the 1950s there were upwards of twenty-five black nationalist organizations in the United States, almost all of them located in New York's Harlem. They boasted a combined membership of not more than five thousand, and with the exception of the Black Muslims none of them was known outside that community. In the main these organizations were storefront movements or "hustles" operated by and for a leader and a handful of lieutenants. About a half dozen of the groups originated during the late 1920s as offshoots of Marcus Garvey's movement. Some of the leaders definitely qualified as crackpots; all of them fantasized about the glories of Black Africa; and they all paid lip service to a common objective: Afro-American liberation. Following is a brief description of six of these groups:[10]

The Universal African Nationalist Movement. Founded in 1930, this was one of the numerous splinters that survived the breakup of Garvey's Universal Negro Improvement Association. During the early 1950s, the group pressed a bill introduced by Senator William Langer, Republican of North Dakota, providing for a congressional appropriation to promote voluntary emigration to Liberia. The organization propagated Garvey's old cry: "Africa for the Africans—those at home and those abroad."

The Garvey Club. Built also out of the remnants of the Garvey movement, this group taught pride in African ancestry, African history, and African culture. The group encouraged those who could migrate to Africa to do so. Not essentially anti-white in orientation the Garvey Club advocated "friendly and business-like" relations between the races.

The United African Nationalist Movement. This movement was founded by James Rupert Lawson, a native of Georgia and a former official in the Harlem Labor Union. The group maintained a liaison with African missions to the United Nations for the purpose of exchanging information and promotion of the common cause. In 1954, Lawson was decorated by Emperor Haile Selassie. The movement was interested generally in promoting independent black nationhood along with economic self-determination in all black communities.

United Sons and Daughters of Africa. While "Buy Black" was the main cry as well as the main objective of this group, it was particularly interested in providing aid for the emerging black African nations. Locally it advocated equality of the races through separatism, the establishment of Afro-American business enterprises, Afro-American schools, and the promotion of Afro-American unity.

The Cultural Association for Women of Afro-American Heritage. Headed by the well-known singer Abby Lincoln, this was one of the newer groups that surfaced right after the first African states were admitted to the U.N. The group led the highly publicized demonstrations at the U.N. in February, 1961.

The National Memorial Book Store. Also known as the "Home of Common Sense and Proper Propaganda," this was a main gathering place for New York black nationalists and the Black Liberation movement. The store contained books and other materials dealing with every aspect of African and Afro-American history and culture.

During the late 1950s and the early 1960s black nationalist doctrines and especially their pan-African element began to attract increasing interest in black communities throughout the country. There were several important reasons for this new development. Beginning in 1957, successive black African states were admitted to the United Nations. The appearance of stately and colorfully garbed black delegates in New York City greatly impressed the local blacks. The result was a heightened sense of kinship and a newfound pride in "our brothers" and "our homeland" in Africa. The Africans were wined and dined by local black dignitaries, and they were featured as VIP's in black communities everywhere in the nation.

The new identification with Africa on the part of local blacks led to an unprecedented disruption of a United Nations Security Council meeting early in 1961.[11] During the afternoon of February 15, some sixty black men and women burst into the Security Council chamber interrupting the meeting and tussling with the guards in a protest against U.N. policies in the Congo. They accused the U.N. of complicity in the death of Patrice Lumumba, former premier of that country. Late the same evening more than two hundred activists took over East 42nd Street in a noisy demonstration chanting, "Congo, yes! Yankee, no!" Several local black nationalist groups were found to have "sponsored" the demonstration. Several days later these same groups held a three-hour funeral service for Lumumba at a black nationalist meeting place in Harlem. Speakers at the funeral denounced the United States, white people, Jews, and black leaders such as Dr. Ralph Bunche and Roy Wilkins.[12] One of the important aspects of the new development was the interest and involvement of young educated blacks. Though he could not make it, James Baldwin had planned to take part in the disruption of the U.N. Security Council's meeting. James Reston summed up the new mood:

We are beginning to see a confluence of the world struggle for freedom in Black

Africa and the struggle for equal rights in the Negro communities in America. No longer is the American Negro asking as Countee Cullen did thirty-five years ago, "Copper sun, scarlet sea, what is Africa to me?"[13]

Perhaps the greatest factor for the resurgence of black nationalism during this period was Malcolm X. Indeed, he was to become the symbol and the voice of that ideology for a new generation of blacks in America. During the years that he preached black nationalism, he was almost the equal of the legendary Marcus Garvey. Up until 1963, virtually all black nationalist leaders in the United States, including Malcolm X, subscribed to the classical Garvey thesis that the integration of blacks into American society was neither possible nor desirable and that blacks should, therefore, emigrate to Africa and build a powerful nation of their own. In his version of this doctrine Malcolm X stated that the government should provide everything that would be needed for blacks to establish themselves as an independent people in Africa.[14] This was what was known as *emigrationist* black nationalism, and it had been around a long time.

The young black militants coming along after 1960 gave the doctrine a thorough and critical examination. They approved its emphasis on black pride, black self-esteem, and veneration for Africa both past and present. As a whole, however, they could not and would not accept the notion of mass black emigration to Africa. If American blacks wanted to reject integration, to protect their own subculture, indeed to be masters of their own destiny, the answer was to demand a separate state within the continental United States. The race deserved no less for the four hundred years of oppression and slavery it had suffered at the hands of a racist white power structure. "Back-to-Africa" was adjudged therefore to be unnecessary, impracticable, and obsolete. In other words, separatism was "in," emigrationism was "out." The new trend took hold quickly. In January, 1963, a New York black nationalist group known as the Alajo party issued a "Declaration of Self-Determination" in which it demanded that all land south of the Mason-Dixon line be set aside for an African nation in the United States.[15]

Early in 1964, Malcolm X began to back away from emigrationism. In a speech on March 12, he stated: "Emigration back to Africa is a long range program, and while it is yet to materialize, 22 millions of our people who are still here in America need better food, clothing, housing, education and jobs, right now. . . ."[16] On December 12, several months after he had split from the Black Muslims and created his own movement, Malcolm moved even further away from emigrationism. Malcolm X was ultimately to espouse a doctrine of black nationalism freed of emigrationism and calling for the cultural, spiritual, and physical liberation of the black "colonial peoples" *within* the continental United States. Malcolm's disciples, the new, young black nationalists, were separatists. They insisted that Garvey wanted "to go back to Jordan" and that was never really possible. "We do not want a Nation, we are a Nation," said LeRoi Jones.[17] "Look down! Pick up the earth, or jab your fingernails into the concrete. It is real and it is yours, if you want it."[18]

By the beginning of 1966, it became apparent that the black nationalist movement in the United States was being taken over by young educated black militants. The new crowd had no interest whatever in the already existing black nationalist organizations. They either established new organizations, such as the Revolutionary Action Movement, the Black Panthers, and the New Republic of Africa, or they proceeded to convert their own membership organizations to the ideology. Among the first of these to do so was SNCC. James Forman identified several factors which brought about a change of thinking among SNCC members. These included: (1) "a growing awareness of the importance of Africa" to the cause of black liberation in America, (2) "the influence of the ideas of Malcolm X," and (3) the "increased study of the works of Frantz Fanon."[19] More directly, however, a serious campaign was begun in early 1966 to convert the organization to black nationalism. The so-called "position paper" leaked to the *New York Times* in August, 1966, was essentially an argument for black nationalism and had been in circulation among SNCC members since January, 1966. The chief advocate of black nationalism in the organization was of course Carmichael, and his election as chairman in May, 1966, marked the triumph of the ideology. Carmichael resigned the office in 1967 after having served only one term. The switch by CORE to the black nationalist ideology was clearly indicated at its 1966 annual convention. The new chairman, Floyd McKissick, later claimed: "Black People in the United States live in a state of *de facto* nationhood."[20] He felt that black control of a few states would bring about better treatment of blacks in American urban centers as well as influence "the exercise of American foreign policy."[21]

As of the summer of 1966, black nationalism was not only becoming more youthful in appearance, it was developing a distinct style and a new image—an African image. The guidelines for the new image could well have been set by a New York black nationalist leader:

> We must Africanize everything! Our names . . . our manners and customs. . . .
>   Begin with yourself today. You have nothing to lose or fear. It is as natural for persons of African descent to take and maintain the customs, dress and traditions of their motherland, as it is natural for people of European descent to continue European customs and traditions in America. It is distinctly unnatural and degrading, even ridiculous, for persons of African descent to have and keep European customs and habits forced upon them during their enslavement. Our liberation must be complete. Every technique of slavery must be wiped out. . . . Support Africanization! Note to men: adopt the African look. . . .[22]

Young black militants all over the country began to be caught up in the idealization of almost everything African. African tribal dress—dashikis, bubas, jewelry, and accessories were worn by young blacks everywhere and on almost all occasions. Not the least of the new styles was the new natural or "Afro" hair style for both sexes.

All of this was viewed as part of a mounting psychological and ideological revolt against Western white imperialist and racist culture. Rounding out the new trend, there was a new emphasis on the term "black," a demand that it be substituted for "Negro" or "colored" as a general designation for the race. "Black is beautiful" became the cry. Beyond this there was a new glorification of black female beauty and an idealization of black skin. Indeed, a veritable cult of blackness arose. While the "Back-to-Africa" doctrine was abandoned as anachronistic, Marcus Garvey himself was included in a new black nationalist hagiology alongside W. E. B. Du Bois, Malcolm X, and Frantz Fanon. Literature on Marcus Garvey went into reprinting. Garvey paraphernalia, such as red, black, and green flags and buttons, reappeared, and black nationalist scholars began beating a path to the door of his still living widow. It was inevitable perhaps that the preoccupation with blackness would lead to what one observer described as "black skin chauvinism." As Harold Cruse put it, the new cult led "to the reasoning that 'I'm blacker than you, and so is my mama, so I'm purer than you and your mama. Therefore, I am also more nationalistic than you, and more politically trustworthy than you and your mama, in the interests of Black Power.'"[23] The game of comparative and competitive blackness led to the introduction of such dubious and odious distinctions as "black-on-black" and "black-on-brown."

But there were additional problems for the new cult. Black people in the United States have been historically conditioned to accept white standards and white values. Against this rather formidable entrenchment the caveat "celebrate your blackness" was bound to encounter rough sailing. For young black men, especially the militants, it posed some difficult choices. It was one thing, for instance, to sing the praises of female black beauty, but it was quite another to date or to marry the very dark ones. Long after the cult took hold there was every indication that young black males, militants. included, continued to prefer the "tans" and "yellows" in preference to the black-on-blacks, as beautiful as any of them might have been. As one black girl put it:

> There's that whole business of if you're yellow you're mellow. Any black who says it's dead is lying. You hear it in very subtle ways: "Oh man, you know I saw a chick I could really dig. She was black, but man she was pretty." It is there.[24]

Nor was there any diminution of the black male's preference for white girls when they were available. On almost any college or university campus in the North or East one could hear the remark: "A dashiki, an Afro, the clenched fist, but look what's on his arm." Black girls became increasingly embittered. What was true on the college campuses was true, if to a lesser degree, elsewhere among blacks in the United States. Despite the sincerity of some of its advocates, to a majority of black Americans "black is beautiful" was no more than a catchy slogan.

   The one thing in which the young black nationalists of the 1960s were more or less original was their espousal of the use of violence as a means of achieving freedom or, as they termed it, black liberation. At no time in the past had any major black protest group advocated an armed onslaught against the established order. Some observers viewed this new trend as the work of the Marxists or other professional revolutionists among the young blacks. The consensus among social scientists, however, was that the new development was due to "desperation born of the apparent failure of both conventional politics and non-violent direct action to secure significant changes in the condition of the American Negro."[25] Now of course there were many young militants in the movement who subscribed to Marxist beliefs, some even to nihilism. There could also be found among them a good deal of desperation and disenchantment if not disillusionment, but the advocacy of violence by the movement had more specific causes. As it arose in the South, the movement was nonviolent both in theory and practice. When it moved North, nonviolence encountered not so much the desperation as the contempt of the ghetto blacks. To the young blacks in these areas violence was attractive, spectacular, and virile; nonviolence was equated with cowardice, "Tomism," and traditionalism. New leaders of the movement, such as Huey P. Newton, Eldridge Cleaver, LeRoi Jones, and H. Rap Brown, all recognized the value of an appeal to violence among the black ghetto militants.

Of major importance in the movement's switch to violence, guerrilla warfare, etc., were the speeches and writings of Malcolm X and the works of Frantz Fanon, especially his *The Wretched of the Earth*. Everyone of the young militant leaders could be counted a disciple of both Malcolm X and Fanon. Both of these men denounced nonviolence as emasculating, cowardly, and nonproductive. True liberation, they insisted, could be achieved only through the spilling of blood. From Malcolm X for instance, the militants learned that:

> Revolution is never based on begging somebody for an integrated cup of coffee. Revolutions are never fought by turning the other cheek. . . . And revolutions are never waged singing "We Shall Overcome." Revolutions are based upon bloodshed. . . . Revolutions overturn systems.[26]

And from Fanon they learned that violence is a "cleansing force" freeing the oppressed individual from "his inferiority complex and from his despair," making him "fearless," and restoring "his self-respect."[27] The writings of Malcolm X and Fanon provided the theoretical foundations of revolutionary black nationalism, which was what the movement was ultimately to be called.

Beginning in 1966, the leading exponent of revolutionary black nationalism in the country was to be the Black Panther Party. A program for black guerrilla warfare and other insurrectionary activity, however, had been drawn up by another militant group some three years earlier. This was the Revolutionary Action Committee (Movement). The RAM first surfaced during the winter of 1963. From its earliest inception the organization had maintained a close liaison with Robert F. Williams, a black expatriate residing in Cuba until 1966 and thereafter in Tanzania and the Peoples Republic of China. During the late 1950s Williams had been director of the NAACP branch in Monroe, North Carolina. In a reaction to the activities of the local Ku Klux Klan, Williams had organized the blacks into a rifle club, later converting it into an armed defense force.[28] During a racial clash in Monroe in April, 1961, Williams and his wife gave shelter to a white couple who were fleeing a local mob.

The local police promptly filed charges of kidnapping against Williams, and when the FBI entered the case on the side of the local police, Williams fled to Cuba.[29] He subsequently became an out-and-out revolutionist.

From Cuba Williams schooled the RAM in the new techniques of revolution. In 1964, he wrote:

> The new concept of revolution defies military science and tactics. The new concept is lightning campaigns conducted in highly sensitive urban communities with the paralysis reaching the small communities and spreading to the farm areas. The old method of guerrilla warfare, as carried out from the hills and countryside would be ineffective in a powerful country like the U.S.A. Any such force would be wiped out in an hour.[30]

Under Williams' sponsorship, the RAM took on a Marxist-Leninist orientation. During the next couple of years the organization kept out of the public eye. Its small number of hard-core members, about fifty, maintained a liaison with other black militant groups. In the meanwhile, members of the group worked as advisers to ghetto youths, attempting at the same time to recruit them into underground guerrilla bands. Overall the RAM's intention was to build a black liberation army consisting of local and regional groups held together under a tight chain of command.[31]

Terror was to be a major weapon. There was also to be selective assassination of national leaders, both black and white. On June 21, 1967, police in New York City and Philadelphia rounded up sixteen members of the RAM. Seized along with them were a number of rifles, shotguns, carbines, a machine gun, radio receivers, and transmitters, walkie-talkie sets, 275 packets of heroin, and 1,000 rounds of ammunition. Two of the arrestees were charged with plotting to assassinate Roy Wilkins, of the NAACP, and Whitney Young, head of the National Urban League. All sixteen were charged with advocating criminal anarchy and other offenses.[32] Early in September, 1967, four more members of RAM were arrested in Philadelphia and charged with conspiring to foment a riot during which time they would poison the city's water supply. The arrest yielded some 300 grams of potassium cyanide. In 1968, with its top leadership under indictment and its ranks thoroughly infiltrated by informers, the RAM quietly passed from the scene.[33]

A new group known as the Republic of New Africa was to take up where the defunct RAM left off. Indeed, a few former members of the RAM were among the founders of the latter group. The RNA was set up at the National Black Government Conference held in Detroit in April, 1968. The conference proposed the taking over of all of the territory comprising the states of South Carolina, Georgia, Alabama, Louisiana, and Mississippi for a new black separate nation. Robert F. Williams, the expatriate, then residing in Tanzania, was designated as president of the new "nation." Williams took his new office seriously.

In May, 1969, an official of the RNA made a "formal" visit to the United States Department of State in Washington, D.C., to present a note demanding $200 billion in indemnity or "damages" for Afro-Americans and the ceding of the five southern states of South Carolina, Georgia, Alabama, Mississippi, and Louisiana.[34] The RNA held a four-day legislative conference in Washington, D.C., in late August, 1969. It was well attended. A *New York Times'* reporter observed "hundreds of delegates, many in African garb and head-dresses and almost all of them wearing the black, green and red buttons favored by many black militants."[35] The conference set up an official governmental structure including a council of ministers. Its military arm was known as the Black Legion. Members of this force scrutinized delegates and visitors attending the session. They wore black uniforms with leopard-skin epaulets, black combat boots with white laces, and white pistol belts.

In the absence of Robert F. Williams, Milton R. Henry was the guiding spirit of the RNA. In the event that the United States government ignored the demands of the RNA, Henry and his followers were prepared to put a liberation program into operation. As detailed by Henry, the campaign would be begun in Mississippi. In the initial stages at least, it would make use of the political process. Through the use of the ballot, blacks would take control of county after county in Mississippi, installing black sheriffs in the process. The black sheriffs would then proceed to deputize the RNA's Black Legion thus giving the RNA both political and police control of the county. Ultimately, the entire state would come under black control. This process would be repeated in the other four Southern states. Vice-President Henry did not anticipate intervention on the part of the U.S. government. He anticipated that the U.S. government would be ready to negotiate with the RNA.[36]

In the event that the U.S. government proved hostile the RNA had an alternative plan: If the United States government started to interfere with RNA activity in the South, their guerrilla groups in urban areas all over the country would act.[37] In the meanwhile the

RNA considered itself an independent sovereign state, the government for blacks in the United States who had no control over their lives. The new "government" had even set up "consulates" in such cities as New York, Chicago, Philadelphia, Baltimore, Pittsburgh, Washington, D.C., and Cleveland. The issuance of passports was postponed until relationships with the U.S. government were normalized.[38]

While it all appears to be a bit bizarre in perspective, there is little question about the seriousness with which the young black men and women of the RNA took themselves and their so-called nation. Yet the vast majority of blacks in the country were almost totally oblivious of their existence, and the United States government never considered their claim of "sovereignty" as anything but a bad joke. Indeed, the "special assistants" to the secretary of state who received their demands in August, 1969, were nothing more than security men sent to head off the RNA emissary. A final ignominy came to them in December, 1969, when Robert F. Williams resigned as president.

Williams had just returned to the United States from exile abroad and was fighting North Carolina's effort to extradite him back to the state to face eight-year-old kidnapping charges. Williams explained, "I want a broader base, a coalition of organizations, to fight extradition."[39] Following Williams' resignation, Richard Henry, the brother of Milton R. Henry, became president of the RNA. Richard subsequently changed his name to Imari Obadele. During the fall of 1970, Obadele moved the group's headquarters from Detroit to New Orleans and thence to Jackson, Mississippi. Determined to get its program going, the RNA in the spring of 1971 took an option on twenty acres of land near Jackson and consecrated it as El Malik, the capital of the Republic of New Africa. Weeks later, however, Lofton Mason, the black farmer who owned the land, refused to go through with the sale. Mason in fact obtained a court injunction forbidding the RNA to set foot upon his land. The RNA then held a "people's court" and found Mason guilty of fraud. In the continuing battle Mason filed a one-million-dollar damage suit against some RNA leaders alleging he was slandered and harassed.[40]

The last battle for the RNA, probably its "Götterdämmerung," occurred on August 18, 1971, in Jackson, Mississippi. Seeking to serve fugitive warrants on three members of the group, a party of fifteen local police and fourteen FBI agents, using the city's armored vehicle, raided RNA headquarters. A twenty-minute gun fight erupted which resulted in the wounding of one of the FBI agents and two of the policemen, one of them fatally. None of the RNA members were injured. The police reported that the front door of the headquarters had been boobytrapped to explode when the door was opened. All in all, eleven members of the RNA, including President Obadele, were taken into custody. Denouncing the eleven blacks as "armed insurrectionists," the local district attorney filed charges of treason, in addition to murder, against them. They were accused of violating a Mississippi statute making it a capital offense to participate in armed rebellion against the state.[41] Still playing the game of sovereignty, an official of the RNA announced the initiation of a "prisoner-of-war fund" to finance the legal defense of the "insurrectionists."

If the Republic of New Africa represented the most extreme expression of revolutionary black nationalism, the Black Manifesto movement was its most brazen and most calculating. The prime mover in the Black Manifesto movement was James Forman. During the shake-up in SNCC in May, 1966, Forman resigned his post of executive director but retained his membership. In 1967 he became the organization's director for international affairs. During the next year Forman joined the Black Panther Party where he was quickly appointed minister of foreign affairs. Still restless, Forman quit the Panthers in 1969 to travel and write. In the early spring of 1969, Forman, along with several hundred other black leaders and activists, was invited by the predominantly white Interreligious Foundation for Community Organization (IFCO) to participate in a proposed National Black Economic Development Conference to be held in Detroit from April 25 to 27. IFCO was a cooperative group engaged in funding projects in poor communities. In 1969, the twenty-five participating denominations included the American Baptist Home Mission Societies, the Executive Council of the Episcopal Church, the American Jewish Committee, and the National Catholic Conference for Interracial Justice.[42]

In Detroit a few days before the opening of the conference, Forman held discussions with a number of blacks including leaders of the League of Revolutionary Black Workers. With the black revolution running at high tide in the country, Forman and these black activists began planning for a black-dominated conference, with minimum white input and participation. Even the white press was to be excluded. The group also discussed the old idea of reparations for black people; and since this was a church-sponsored conference, they decided that a demand should be made upon American churches for reparations. Under Forman's direction this demand was incorporated in a lengthy document that was to be known as the Black Manifesto. The group decided also that following the takeover, the NBEDC should be made a permanent organization, presumably for the purpose of handling the expected reparations. Everything was ready. Forman stated: "On April 26, 1969, at 7:00 P.M., the hour arrived for me to address the conference with the Manifesto. We had completed all the arrangements for taking it over."[43]

Forman's speech to the conference was entitled "Total Control as the Only Solution to the Economic Problems of Black People." The Black Manifesto, which was the main body of the speech, was couched in typical black revolutionary rhetoric.[44] It denounced the United States as a racist, capitalistic nation which had "systematically tried to kill all people and organizations opposed to its imperialism." Under such circumstances the ideal thing for Afro-Americans to do would be to migrate back to Africa, but since this was not feasible, the manifesto was advising blacks to begin preparations to "bring this government down."[45] In this connection, the blacks must, in fact, take the initiative. "We say that there must be a revolutionary black vanguard, and that white people in this country must be willing to accept black leadership. . . ."[46] The manifesto insisted further that the new order that was to be established must be a black one because only an "armed, well-disciplined, black-controlled government can insure the stamping out of racism in this country."[47] Blacks, therefore, must prepare to seize the state power. "We work the chief industries in this country, and we could cripple the economy while the brothers fought guerrilla warfare in the streets."[48] This, of course, would involve some long-range planning "but," said the manifesto, "whether it happens in a thousand years is of no consequence."

During the meanwhile, the revolution would need financing, at least in its preparatory stages. To meet this problem, the authors of the manifesto felt morally justified, even duty bound, to call upon the nation's white churches and synagogues:

> We are therefore demanding of the white Christian churches and Jewish synagogues, which are part and parcel of the system of capitalism, that they begin to pay reparations to black people in this country. We are demanding $500,000,000 from the Christian white churches and the Jewish synagogues. This total comes to fifteen dollars per nigger. This is a low estimate, for we maintain there are probably more than 30,000,000 black people in this country. . . . We are . . . not unaware that the

exploitation of colored peoples around the world is aided and abetted by the white Christian churches and synagogues.[49]

The manifesto specified nine projects to which the reparation funds would be allocated. These included $200,000,000 for the establishment of a Southern land bank to help poor blacks organize cooperative farms; the creation of a black university to be located in the South, $130,000,000; and the creation of an International Black Appeal chiefly to promote the establishment of cooperative business enterprises among blacks in the United States as well as in Africa, $20,000,000. Finally, the manifesto called for the recognition of the NBEDC as the permanent agency for the implementation of its program. All black people were urged to become members. Blacks were further urged to stage sit-in demonstrations at selected churches, to seize the offices and other properties of church-sponsored agencies, and to hold them in trusteeship until the demands of the manifesto were met. Sunday, May 4, 1969, was the date set for the beginning of hostilities.

James Forman and the NBEDC were not, of course, the first to demand that reparations be paid to black people for their 250 years in chattel slavery and for the century of exploitation thereafter. During the latter part of the nineteenth century Bishop Henry McNeal Turner had demanded forty billion dollars in reparations for blacks from the federal government. By the mid-twentieth century the payment of reparations had become a rather common demand by black nationalist organizations. And from its very inception the RNA had demanded $200 million from the United States government. What was new about the Black Manifesto's demands was that they were not made upon the federal government as had heretofore been the case but upon a nongovernmental institution—the church. Forman talked about the church's role as an agent of the capitalistic system, but there were those who wanted to know why his demands were not made more directly upon the system itself, for instance, the banks and the great corporations. Perhaps susceptibility rather than culpability was the more important consideration in determining who should pay the piper. At any rate, the threat against the churches began on schedule.

On Sunday morning, May 4, Forman paid a call on New York's wealthy and prestigious Riverside Church. As the worship service began. he strode down the aisle brushing two ushers aside. Ascending the half dozen chancel steps, he turned around to face the congregation. Leaning on a cane with his legs wide apart, Forman waited until the organ quieted down. As he began to read his demands, Riverside's senior minister, Dr. Ernest Campbell, with his sixty-member choir at his heels, left the church. Some fifteen hundred of those in attendance followed quickly. Forman continued to read his demands. He said that Riverside Church would have to pay extra reparations to black people because of its heavy endowment by the Rockefellers who were still exploiting people of color all over the world. He then made five specific demands upon the church:

1. Sixty percent of the yearly income from all church security and real-estate investment payable to the N.B.E.D.C. on or before January 3rd of each year.
2. A list of all church assets. The proportion of these funds to be donated to the Negro group to be negotiated.
3. Rent-free office space for the group, with unrestricted right to use the telephone for local and long-distance calls.
4. Classrooms for the use of Harlem residents.
5. Unrestricted use of the church's FM radio station, WRVR, for twelve hours a day and weekends. The director of programming and staff to be selected by the Negro group.[50]

The public reaction to Forman's audacity was one of shock and disbelief. Mail and telephone calls poured into Dr. Campbell's office at Riverside Church for the next several days. As Dr. Campbell described it: "Some of the letters were so hot they should have been sealed in asbestos. The predominant reaction to what happened to Riverside on the 4th of May can be summed up in five words: 'The Shame Of It All.' 'The Shame Of It All.' "[51] The *New York Times* in an editorial stated:

The unreasonableness of the demands was exceeded only by the outrageousness of the episode. . . . The spirit of worship, even more than the spirit of scholarship, forbids violence. Protection must be given when needed, but the much greater need is for reasonable men to begin to set some acceptable limits for social action.[52]

In New York's City Hall, Mayor John Lindsay offered the protection of his police department against any future disruption and intimidation of the churches. "I am inviting a cross-section of New York religious leaders to City Hall this week to advise them on the procedures they should follow when faced with the threat of intimidation."[53]

Come what may, however, Forman was determined to follow through with his campaign. On Tuesday, May 6, he posted a demand for $50 million on the door of the New York headquarters of the Lutheran Church in America. On May 9, when he received an injunction against further interruption of Riverside Church, he publicly burned it. During the next three weeks Forman and his associates in the NBEDC made demands on religious organizations totaling more than one billion dollars. Some of the denominations upon whom demands were made were the Episcopal Church, the Lutheran Church in America, the United Presbyterian General Assembly, the United Church of Christ, the United Methodist Board of Missions, the American Baptist Convention, the Christian Science Church, the Roman Catholic Archdiocese of New York, the Reformed Church in America, and the Unitarian Universalist Association. No direct demands were made upon Jewish synagogues, but, when it was rumored on May 9 that Forman would appear at New York's Temple Emanu-El during worship, thirty-nine members of the militant Jewish Defense League surrounded the area.[54] In the meanwhile members of affiliates of the NBEDC were busy disrupting services and demanding reparation from churches all across the nation.

As the drive continued, however, not all of the reactions were negative. The United Methodist publication, *World Outlook*, suggested:

> If we cut through the revolutionary rhetoric of the Black Manifesto (which isn't easy to do), it is clear that the churches have not begun to repent of their complicity in slavery, in the enslavement of the black man.... The only thing surprising about the call for reparations is that no one thought of it sooner.[55]

In a lead editorial, *The Christian Century* said:

> We do not believe that the idea of reparations is ridiculous. This generation of blacks continues to pay the price of earlier generations' slavery and subjugation; this generation of whites continues to enjoy the profits of racial exploitation. The real problem is not in the *idea* of reparations: it is in effective implementation of the idea.[56]

And from the *Commonweal,*

> The church has been an all too willing accomplice in the subtle and unsubtle shapes of racism. From segregated communion rails to shady business associations, a goodly number of God's people have come on like a brood of light-skinned vipers. As the keys to the kingdom are inserted deeper into corporate America, the harder it is to avoid laying up those earthly moth-eaten treasures.[57]

Sympathizing with the plight of the black people was one thing. However, the handing over of a billion dollars to one who, to the white churchmen, was an obscure black militant was quite another. The white church was bound to seek less expensive and more conventional means of assuaging their collective guilt. The Jewish and Roman Catholic officials were the first to turn thumbs down on the demands of the Black Manifesto. While no direct demands were ever made upon the Jews, on May 12 national Jewish leaders issued a policy statement which included the following: "Two separate issues have been raised by the 'Black Manifesto': one by the substance of the demands, the other by the tactics employed to advance them. We find the demands and the tactics objectionable on both moral and practical grounds."[58] About a week later, the Roman Catholic Archdiocese of New York issued a similar statement. It found the political concepts of the Black Manifesto contrary to "our American way of life." For this and other reasons it rejected the demands.

While the Protestant denominations were generally not as peremptory in their responses, few of them could stomach the inflammatory rhetoric of the manifesto, and in all but a few cases they refused to recognize or to do business with the NBEDC. Instead, most of the Protestant churches and agencies either increased their aid to their own existing programs for blacks, or they set up and funded new ones entirely. Typical of this approach was the decision of the trustees of Union Theological Seminary to invest $500,000 in black business in neighboring Harlem, and further to raise one million dollars to support Union's involvement in community programs.[59] In writing the Black Manifesto several years later, Forman stated that the BEDC "actually received less than $300,000 in reparations" by mid-1970. "Most of the money voted," he said, "was carefully turned over to organizations *other than* BEDC." Forman stated further that "of the funds received by the BEDC, the great part was invested in a revolutionary publishing house called the Black Star Publications. . . ."[60]

Reaction to the manifesto in the black community was divided. Traditionalist leaders, such as Roy Wilkins of the NAACP and the Reverend J. H. Jackson of the black National Baptist Convention, were opposed to the demands. Speaking from the other side of the ideological spectrum, Milton R. Henry of the RNA denounced the manifesto as counter-"revolutionary idiocy." Not only had the RNA anticipated the manifesto with its own reparations demand but also it considered Forman's group to be system-oriented rather than truly revolutionary. Other black organizations were more cautious and circumspect in their approaches to the manifesto. Without taking a positive stand one way or the other the Reverends Ralph Abernathy and Andrew Young of the SCLC thus went on record: "There can be but one question to debate in regard to the so-called Black Manifesto: Is our lord speaking to us through it?"[61] Among the black churchmen, generally there was positive support for the manifesto. However, Forman was severely critical of the so-called "black caucuses" within the white denominations:

> At first they did help us . . . but most of them later began to pimp off our efforts and to take money for their own programs in very opportunistic ways. Some of them rewrote parts of the programs in the Manifesto and presented them for funding from their own denominations.[62]

The RAM, the RNA, and the Black Manifesto movement collectively presented the nation with a brand new type of black radical. Thinking of themselves as "black revolutionists," they called for a new concept of black liberation plus new tactics and strategies to bring it about. The older militant groups were contemptuously dismissed as "cultural nationalists" capable only of indulging in endless rhetoric. The new breed was affected with a paranoic hatred of the white power structure, white people, and white racism. And whether it be the aberrational activities of the RAM or the well-planned and efficiently executed assault of the Black Manifesto movement, the idea was to deal a blow at the system, at its personnel, and at its symbols. There was to be no compromise, no negotiations, and no backing off. After 1967 the standard-bearers of the new breed were to become the members of the Black Panther Party.

CHAPTER 9

The Black Panther Party

In its report on the Black Panther Party published in August, 1971, the House Committee on Internal Security stated:

It is hard to believe that only a little over a year ago the Panthers, despite their small number, ranked as the most celebrated ghetto militants. They fascinated the left, inflamed the police, terrified much of America, and had an extraordinary effect on the black community.[1]

The committee felt, however, that the "Panthers . . . through their own excesses" did much to destroy their image. "Most of those liberals and idealists who once sympathized with the Panthers have realized that the Panthers are not so much Robin Hoods as they are hoods. . . ."[2] The committee concluded that never at any time had the Panthers "constituted a clear and present danger to the continued functioning of the U.S. Government or any other institutions of our democratic society."[3] Based upon the data it undoubtedly had at its disposal, the committee could also have concluded that a substantial percentage of the criminal indictments and prosecutions of the Panthers throughout the nation had been malevolent in nature and inspired by a vigilante sense of justice. Victims of a veritable inquisition, the Panthers had been prosecuted, persecuted, and proscribed as had been no other group in the history of the United States.

Two youthful black ghetto militants, Huey P. Newton and Bobby Seale, were the co-founders of the Black Panther Party. Newton, the younger of the two, was born in Oak Grove, Louisiana, on February 17, 1942. He was one of seven children. Two years later Huey's father went to California in search of wartime employment and wound up working for the Naval Supply Depot. During the following year he moved his family from Louisiana and settled them in Oakland. Young Huey was to become a product of Oakland's tough black ghetto. After graduating from high school in nearby Berkeley,

California, Huey registered in Oakland's two-year Merritt Junior College. Attending only as a part-time student, Newton took five years to earn the Associate of Arts degree. He also took some courses at a law school in San Francisco, but after a year he dropped out.[4]

Bobby Seale was born in Dallas, Texas, on October 22, 1936. His father was a master carpenter, but jobs for black craftsmen were few and far between and the family lived constantly on the edge of poverty. After World War II the family moved to California, and young Bobby Seale was enrolled in Oakland High School. During the mid-1950s Bobby was inducted into the United States Air Force. In 1958, with more than three years of service behind him, Seale apparently became fed up with routine, discipline, and military life in general. To his superior officers he became almost unmanageable. At Ellsworth Air Force Base in South Dakota he was court-martialed and dismissed with a bad conduct discharge. During the next three years Seale found work as a comedian, a musician (he played the drums), a carpenter, a mechanic, and a mechanical draftsman. He worked also in a couple of aircraft and electronics plants until the personnel managers discovered that he had lied about his discharge from the service.

In September, 1961, Seale enrolled in Merritt College, but not until a year later did he meet the fellow student who was to become his ideal and his leader. Newton was speaking at a campus rally of the Afro-American Association when Seale first came upon him. Seale was immediately and completely captivated. "I think that when I met Huey P. Newton, the experience of things I'd seen in the black community . . . and my own experience, just living, trying to make it, trying to do things, came to the surface."[5] Largely because of Newton, Seale joined the Afro-American Association. The association was in reality an Oakland community organization with a chapter or branch on the Merritt College campus. Its founder was a young black attorney named Donald Warden. The association was not black nationalist in orientation though Warden preached black dignity and black self-esteem. He insisted that young blacks should strive for a growing role in the political activities of the community and that black people should spend their money with black businessmen. Warden soon began to attract support for his program from local whites who approved of his ideas of black self-help.

Although neither or them approved of Warden's philosophy, both Seale and Newton continued as members of the association. Early in

1963, Newton led the black students at Merritt in a demand for the establishment of a black history course. Surprisingly enough the college administration readily agreed to the demand. When the course was set up, however, it did not meet with Seale's specifications. Newton did not enroll. The course bore the title "Negro History," and it was taught by a white instructor. Seale almost immediately cried "Foul." "The cat that was teaching it didn't know what he was doing. He really wasn't teaching Black History; he was teaching American history and reiterating slavery...." [6] By 1964 both Seale and Newton had become sufficiently disenchanted with the Afro-American Association to leave it. Shopping around for something with a more radical orientation, Seale took up with the local chapter of the RAM. He was soon to discover, however, that the local branch of that organization was far more proficient with rhetoric than with revolution. Newton, in the meanwhile, was having difficulties with the law. Invited to a so-called "mixed" party, Newton became involved in a heated argument with a tough ghetto black. In the altercation that ensued, Newton inflicted a knife wound on his opponent. He was subsequently convicted of assault and sentenced to serve eight months in prison with three years on probation. In the years which followed, prison was to become a very familiar place to young Huey.

Like hundreds of other young black activists in 1965, Seale became a disciple of Frantz Fanon. He was so enthralled, that he read *The Wretched of the Earth* six times and encouraged Huey P. Newton to read the book. In the days that followed, Fanon became the chief topic of conversation between them. (See chapter 12 for extended discussion of Fanon's influence.) With new ideas and a broadened vision of the black struggle, Seale and Newton decided to establish a new black organization on the Merritt College campus. It would be called the Soul Students' Advisory Council. Its demands would include a comprehensive black curriculum instead of a "Negro History" course, recognition of the rights of black students, and provisions for their special needs and social programs. The SSAC was to become the prototype for the black student unions that were to usher in "Black Studies" a few years later.

Once the SSAC became established, Seale and Newton became more ambitious in their plans for the black struggle. They insisted upon a close reading of Frantz Fanon, and they assigned especial importance to Malcolm X's catechisms on violence and self-defense. But they intended to move beyond mere rhetoric to follow the teaching of Malcolm X, but not his personal example. Newton wanted to convert the SSAC into a black militant group that would look and act as though it meant business, even to the point of displaying loaded weapons. He had carefully researched California law and knew it was entirely legal for any citizen to have in his possession, unconcealed, a fully loaded weapon.

At a meeting during the spring of 1966, Seale and Newton proposed to the SSAC's central committee that for the commemoration of Malcolm X's birthday a squad of disciplined armed young blacks from the ghetto be brought upon the campus.

> We could reach the community (because the press would be hungry for it) and show them, on Malcolm X's birthday, May 19, that Malcolm X had advocated armed self-defense against the racist power structure and show the racist white power structure that we intend to use the guns to defend our people.[7]

The members of the central committee were stunned. They considered the SSAC to be an organization of black militants, not black insurrectionists. What they had in mind was an educational program that would stress black self-esteem, black pride, and the black experience. If the black masses ultimately called for armed revolt, that was one thing; but to parade in public like black storm troopers was to court disaster. The central committee backed away from the idea. In a fit of temper Seale jumped up and yelled: "We resign. . . . We don't have time for you. You're jiving in these colleges."[8] Seale and Newton quit the SSAC and the college community for good. "We just went to the streets, where we should have been in the first place—those four or five years that preceded this showed us that—and Huey, the brother off the block, had never really left the streets at all."[9]

Up until 1966 the black ghetto or so-called "brothers off the block" had not been generally represented in the leadership of the black revolution. The movement had originated among and had been dominated by young middle-class blacks turned black militant. There was no end of talk about the ghetto and the "jungle" but never any real effort to recruit its members. The truth of the matter was that there was a hard and fast bias against the "block boys." They were considered to be too vulgar, too gross, and too prone to violence. Whenever they made their appearance, the atmosphere became charged with a sense of foreboding, fear, and general discomfort. They were never really welcome. A realization of this fact finally forced itself upon Seale and Newton and impelled them to return to their roots in the ghetto.

During the late summer of 1966, Seale and Newton decided to put together their own movement. From here on in they would rely upon brothers from the block, not college students. Between October 1 and October 15, they hammered out a program for the new organization. As Seale recalls it: "Huey himself articulated it word for word. All I made were suggestions." [10] The program read as follows:

1. We want freedom. We want power to determine the destiny of our Black Community.
2. We want full employment for our people.
3. We want an end to the robbery by the capitalists of our Black Community.
4. We want decent housing, fit for shelter of human beings.
5. We want education for our people that exposes the true nature of this decadent American society. We want education that teaches us our true history and our role in the present-day society.
6. We want all black men to be exempt from military service.
7. We want an immediate end to POLICE BRUTALITY and MURDER of black people.
8. We want freedom for all black men held in federal, state, county and city prisons and jails.
9. We want all black people when brought to trial to be tried in court by a jury of their peer group or people from their black communities, as defined by the Constitution of the United States.
10. We want land, bread, housing, education, clothing, justice, and peace. And as our major political objective, a United Nations-supervised plebiscite to be held throughout the black colony in which only black colonial subjects will be allowed to participate, for the purpose of determining the will of black people as to their national destiny.[11]

Seale was satisfied that he and Newton now had a program which spoke to the needs of the black ghetto. As he described it: This is "what the people want and not what some intellectual personality wants or some cultural nationalists, like LeRoi Jones," or anybody else remote from the ghetto who tried to prescribe a program.[12] The name of the new organization was to be the Black Panther Party for Self-Defense.

Seale and Newton, however, were not the first ones nor the only ones to use "Black Panther" as the name of a black militant group. The Black Panther party of San Francisco headed by Ken Freeman came into existence in and around the same time as Seale and Newton's organization.[13] The Black Panther party of New York City, however, was older than both the California groups. Organized during the summer of 1966 the New York Panthers were heavily engaged in community action by the early fall. The group was, for instance, pushing a boycott of a Harlem school in demand of the establishment of community control of schools and the teaching of

African and Afro-American history. It had a roster of more than one hundred members and an executive commitee of fifteen. Eddie Ellis was temporary chairman of the Party.[14]

Seale and Newton's Black Panther party was launched on October 15 in a Poverty Program office in Oakland, California. Seale was acting as chairman of the Party, and Newton was its minister of defense. Seale's wife and Newton's girl friend typed and ran off one thousand copies of the program for distribution among the brothers on the block. From mid-October until the end of the year the Black Panther party was essentially a two-member organization—Seale and Newton, with a member-to-be, Bobby Hutton, tagging along. The first order of business was to get the organization known in the local community. Street-corner meetings and rallies were held. The brothers on the block wanted discussion about the executing of racist cops and the dropping of molotov cocktails into strategic industrial installations, but Seale and Newton did not oblige. Instead, they talked about the community-level functions of the organization, the protection of black people against police brutality and harassment, arbitrary arrest and imprisonment, and social injustices generally. Finally, they stressed the fact that the Party was organized for self-defense rather than for offensive activities. As Seale put it: "The nature of a panther is that he never attacks. But if anyone attacks him or backs him into a corner, the panther comes up to wipe that aggressor or that attacker out, absolutely, resolutely, wholly, thoroughly, and completely."[15]

Toward the end of November, Seale and Newton decided that the time had come for them to implement article seven of the Party program. This called for the establishing of armed patrols "or policing the police" in the black community. Thus from an extremist acquaintance of theirs, they obtained two weapons, an M-1 rifle and a 9mm pistol. They then proceeded to do further research on California gun laws as well as on federal court decisions on the Second Amendment to the United States Constitution. Newton was still on probation, and his probation officer warned him that while he could carry a rifle or a shotgun, he could not be in possession of a handgun. As a result Seale displayed the 9mm pistol and Newton the loaded M-1 rifle. They were now ready to institute their armed patrol. They trailed the police cars through streets, avenues, and back alleys of the Oakland black ghetto. Whenever they saw the police apprehend a black person, they would stand a legal fifteen feet away from the officers to avoid being charged with interfering and read aloud relevant passages of the laws assuring the arrested persons of their rights.

Inevitably, of course, a confrontation with the police was bound to occur. Thus, while Seale and Newton were attending a party one night in the community, the local police were waiting for them on the stairway and vestibule of the building and out in front on the street. When the two young militants emerged, loaded weapons in hand, the police pressed in on them demanding to know where they got the weapons and what they planned to do with them. Newton gave a recitation of the California gun law and relevant sections of the Bill of Rights. He and Seale then walked between the lines of the frustrated police to their Volkswagen and drove off into the night.[16] Word of the incident quickly spread throughout the black communities in the Bay area. The reputation of the Oakland Black Panthers had been made.

On January 1, 1967, Seale and Newton set up the first official headquarters of the Black Panther Party for Self-Defense. Regular meetings were immediately scheduled for the new headquarters. Beyond this, plans were made for an expansion and intensification of the armed patrols along with a stepped-up recruitment of new members. Bobby Hutton, the fifteen-year-old youngster who had been tagging along with Seale and Newton, was inducted as the first regular member of the Party. The recruitment of new members was to be confined exclusively to the ghetto. Seale states:

> Huey wanted brothers off the block—brothers who had been out there robbing banks, brothers who had been pimping, brothers who had been peddling dope, brothers who ain't gonna take no shit, brothers who had been fighting pigs—because he knew that . . . once you organize those brothers, you get niggers, you get black men, you get revolutionaries who are too much.[17]

During the first three weeks of January, upwards of twenty-five "brothers off the block" were induced to join the organization.

The problem now became that of finding the money to provide the new members with weapons. A solution soon suggested itself. Newspapers, television, and periodicals were then featuring a new and unique literary work: "the little Red Book," *Quotations from Chairman Mao Tse-tung*. English translations were available but still scarce. Seale and Newton recalled that they had seen a supply of the books on the counters of a Chinese bookstore in San Francisco, selling at thirty cents a copy. It was Newton's idea that they could sell the books at a profit on the Berkeley campus of the University of

California. The pair went to the bookstore and bought two packages of the books. "We sold the Red Books inside of an hour, at a dollar apiece and that shocked us. So we took all that money and we went back to the bookstore and bought all the Red Books the man had left in the store."[18] In a few days the pair had amassed enough money to provide almost every new member of the Party with a weapon.

Before receiving the weapons, however, all new members had to go through a period of indoctrination and training. Each man was taught the use and safety features of weapons and how to fieldstrip rifles and shotguns. They were taught never to point, much less fire, a weapon at anyone "other than the enemy, and never accidentally or unnecessarily." No member of the Party could be under the influence of alcohol or narcotics while doing Party work or in possession of a weapon; indeed any member caught "shooting narcotics" would be expelled. And lastly, party members were prohibited from committing any crimes against black people.[19] The Party at this time also adopted an official Black Panther uniform. This consisted of black trousers, powder-blue shirt, black leather jacket, black beret, and black leather shoes. Many of the members wore dark eyeglasses or "shades" to "roundout" the Panther image.

The Party now decided to beef up its armed patrol in the Oakland black ghetto. As many as five cars were out on the streets on a given evening each carrying armed Panthers with a camera, a law book, and sometimes even a tape recorder. Every Panther also carried on his person a copy of "Legal First Aid," a printed list of thirteen basic legal and constitutional rights. The police were in the meanwhile increasing their surveillance of the Party. Lists of Black Panther automobiles and photographs of Panther leaders were posted in police stations. Party members were picked up as suspects in robberies, assaults, and other offenses and invariably detained for the maximum period allowed by the law.

One afternoon as Seale and Newton and other Party members were seated in a car in front of their headquarters, several police cars pulled up alongside. Bent upon harassment the police began asking the now familiar questions about the weapons the Panthers had with them. Exasperated and angry Newton got out of the automobile loading his M-1 rifle as he did so. When a policeman asked him, "What are you going to do with that gun?" Newton shot back: "What are you going to do with *your* gun? Because if you try to shoot at me, or if you try to take this gun, I'm going to shoot back at you, swine." The other

Panthers sat quietly in the car but with firm grips on their weapons. Watching Newton closely, Seale said to himself: "This is the baddest motherfucker in the world! This nigger is telling pigs, 'If you draw your gun, I'll shoot you.' Telling this to the pigs standing there." Hampered by the law and unable to frighten or face down the Panthers, the sullen police backed off and drove away.[20] After this incident the Oakland police stepped up their campaign for a change or a repeal of the California law on unconcealed weapons.

In the meanwhile, word of this latest confrontation had spread throughout the Bay area. The Black Panthers were becoming lords of the black ghetto. Applications for membership in the Party began to pour in. One of the new applicants was Eldridge Cleaver, a parolee from Soledad Prison, then working for *Ramparts* magazine as senior editor. By background Cleaver was eminently qualified for membership. Born in a small town in Kansas, Cleaver moved with his family to Los Angeles when he was ten years old. At the age of thirteen, he was sent to reform school for breaking into a store. This was merely the beginning. As one of his biographers put it: "There was never again a day in his life that he was not either a fugitive, incarcerated, on probation, or on parole."[21] While in Folsom Prison during the early 1960s, Cleaver became a Black Muslim minister. However, when Malcolm X broke with the Muslims and later denounced black racism, Cleaver followed suit. Among other things Cleaver possessed considerable natural ability as a writer. While in Folsom and Soledad prisons, he wrote a number of articles, some of which were later published in *Esquire* and *Ramparts* magazines. Some of the articles were to become part of his best-selling book, *Soul on Ice*. Prison officials became impressed with Cleaver's budding career. In December, 1966, he was paroled to become a senior editor and contributing writer of *Ramparts*.

While in prison Cleaver had closely followed the development of the black liberation movement. Once out, he could not wait to become involved. Thus in January, 1967, he and three other young blacks, Marvin Johnson, Ed Bullins, and Willie Dale, teamed up to establish Black House in San Francisco. Black House quickly became the center of so-called "non-establishment" black culture throughout the Bay area. Cleaver also had other ideas. One of these was the revival of the Organization of Afro-American Unity which had folded so quickly after the demise of Malcolm X. Cleaver stated: "I was amazed that no one else had moved to continue Malcolm's work in the name of the organization he had chosen, which seemed perfect to me and also logically necessary in terms of historical continuity."[22] Cleaver conceived of a three-day program for February, 1967, that would memorialize Malcolm's assassination and serve also as a forum for the resurrection of the OAAU. Malcolm's widow, Betty Shabazz, would give her blessing to the idea in a keynote speech on the final day of the program. Thus late in January, Cleaver sent out a call to black organizations in the Bay area asking them to assist in setting up a steering committee to plan for the memorial.

Responding to Cleaver's invitation, several organizations came together to form a temporary coalition known as the Bay Area Grassroots Organizations Planning Committee. It was at the initial meeting of the group that Cleaver got his first look at the Black Panthers. "I spun round in my seat and saw the most beautiful sight I had ever seen: four black men wearing black berets, powder blue shirts, black leather jackets, black trousers, shiny black shoes—and each with a gun! . . . Where was my mind at? Blown!"[23] For some time to come Cleaver could think of little else than the Black Panthers. The planning committee drastically modified Cleaver's proposal for the memorial. The program was extended from three days to a week, and Mrs. Shabazz's keynote address was scheduled for the opening session. Finally, the Panthers were asked to provide an honor guard for Mrs. Shabazz during her stay in San Francisco.

On February 21, twenty impeccably uniformed Black Panthers with pistols strapped to their sides marched in formation into the San Francisco airport. Completely ignoring the startled security guards and the crowds of shocked and frightened onlookers, the Panthers greeted Betty Shabazz and escorted her out to the waiting automobiles. She was scheduled for an interview at the offices of *Ramparts*, and when the Panthers arrived there with her, they were greeted by some thirty members of the San Francisco police. Another confrontation was in the making. As the Panthers were leaving the *Ramparts'* office, one particularly beefy policeman blocked Newton's path and stood there facing him. Newton stopped in his tracks and returned the stare. From the sidelines Seale yelled: "Let's split, Huey! Let's split!" Ignoring him, Newton stepped up closer to the policeman and said: "What's the matter, you got an itchy finger?" When the policeman did not answer, Newton challenged him, "You want to draw your gun?" The policeman's colleagues called out to him to call it off, but he apparently did not hear them. "O.K.,"

Newton said. "You big fat racist pig, draw your gun!" When still there was no move, Newton jacked a round of ammunition into the shotgun and sneered: "Draw it, you cowardly dog! I'm waiting." Finally, the policeman let out an audible sigh and left the scene. Watching the entire incident from outside the *Ramparts'* office, Cleaver was overwhelmed. "I went back into *Ramparts* and we all stood around chattering excitedly, discussing what we had witnessed with disbelief."[24] Within a few weeks Cleaver himself would be wearing the Panther uniform.

As the Panther versus police confrontations continued to occur in the Bay area, a public clamor began to arise for a change in the gun laws of the state. Don Mulford, who represented the Oakland district in the state legislature, responded by introducing a bill "prohibiting the carrying of loaded firearms on one's person or in a vehicle in any public place or on any public street."[25] Floor discussion of this legislation was scheduled for Monday, May 2, and a notice to this effect was carried in the local newspapers. Newton read the notice and decided upon immediate action. The Panthers would go en masse to the state capitol in Sacramento to bear witness against a law which was obviously directed against them.[26] On May 2, therefore, he dispatched some five automobiles carrying some thirty Panthers to Sacramento. Twenty of them were armed with assorted weapons. Still on parole, Cleaver tagged along as a representative of *Ramparts*. Newton did not go.

With Seale in the lead the armed Panthers marched into the capitol building, past gaping tourists and frightened clerks and up a flight of stairs. On the second floor, with TV crews, photographers, and newsmen scrambling and twisting for vantage points, Seale asked directions to the Assembly Chamber. Actually he wanted the spectators' gallery. But newsmen and TV crews were either oblivious to his queries or they had their own ideas. Thus, facing Seale and moving backward down the corridor, the newsmen led the gun-toting uniformed Panthers directly upon the Assembly floor. This, of course, was a violation of the basic rules, customs, and traditions of the state legislature. After considerable shouting and confusion, the Panthers and the newsmen were herded off the floor and into a room off the corridor. Guards seized some of the Panther weapons but later returned them. In the meanwhile Seale managed to read to the reporters a statement protesting the Mulford bill. He had carried out at least part of his mission.[27]

The group was able to leave the capitol grounds unmolested, but as they were preparing to drive off in their automobiles, they were halted by the police. Twenty-six of them, including Seale and Cleaver, were arrested on charges ranging from disturbing the peace to violation of the fish and game laws. Seale and five other Panthers ultimately received jail sentences, Seale for violation of section 9051 of the Code of California which prohibits "the willful disruption of a State of California legislative body assembly." He was to serve five months in prison. Charges against Cleaver were dropped when it was ascertained that he had been representing *Ramparts* magazine.

The Sacramento invasion resulted in tremendous national publicity for the Party. Representatives of large metropolitan dailies and major TV networks descended upon Black Panther headquarters in Oakland for interviews, stories, and photographs. Almost overnight the news media transformed the Panthers from a local black militant organization into "America's Black Guerrillas." Legends about Black Panther exploits began to circulate in black communities throughout the nation. On May 25, in San Francisco Stokely Carmichael loudly proclaimed SNCC's support of the Black Panthers. He praised the Party for scaring the wits out of an "anti-black" American society. The Sacramento affair, however, marked the end of the first period or phase of Panther development. It would become known as the "era of the gun." As one ex-Panther was to put it, "The gun had overnight capitulated the Party into the vanguard of the black liberation movement, thereby shoving the black liberation movement into a new era."[28]

But if the gun had been the key to the rise of the Party, it was also becoming its Achilles' heel. If the public display and brandishing of loaded weapons was not a violation of the letter of the law, it certainly was a violation of its spirit. The Panthers had every appearance of a paramilitary force, and the police were using their appearance and posturing to brand them as outlaws. Beyond this there appeared to be increasing evidence that the police were looking for a pretext to shoot them down publicly. The Panther leadership was not oblivious to the situation. It regarded Sacramento as a dramatic achievement, but it began to feel that continued armed confrontations would prove counterproductive. During mid-May, therefore, the Party banned the public display of all weapons, and it called a halt to the armed patrol of the police. As one Party member put it: "Suicide was not what the Party was about."[29]

By the summer of 1967, the Black Panther Party had reached an impasse in its development. Newton and Seale had been worshipers of Malcolm X. Together they had built an organization of young ghetto blacks whose individual life-styles had been similar and in some cases almost identical to that of young Malcolm. They had devoutly followed his precepts as to the assertion of black manhood, courage in the face of physical danger and armed self-defense. They had unconsciously made their Black Panthers into a reflection of the character and personality of Malcolm X. When they were moved to put down the gun in the spring of 1967, they as an organization had approximated that stage in Malcolm's career where he at least figuratively put down the gun—his break with the Black Muslims. Malcolm thereafter struck out on a path which led to a rejection of black racism and black revolutionary nationalism in favor of a Third-World socialist revolution. The Panthers were ultimately to travel this same road, but they needed new leadership for the new direction. Seale and Newton were men who tended to value action over ideas.

The breach was filled by Eldridge Cleaver. If anything, Cleaver had been a far greater disciple of Malcolm X than either Seale or Newton. In the Soledad and Folsom prisons Cleaver had been a Muslim minister, but when Malcolm left the movement, Cleaver followed suit. Out of jail he was to continue his devotion. "I had come out of prison with plans to revive the Organization of Afro-American Unity, the vehicle finally settled upon by Malcolm X to spearhead the black revolution."[30] In San Francisco in early 1967, he looked over several groups of so-called black liberationists and concluded that none of them would do for his purposes. In February when he got his first view of the Panthers, he knew that he had found what he wanted. "The only hangup I had was with its name." He wished that the Panthers had named themselves after Malcolm's organization. With the rest, however, Cleaver was more than satisfied. He discovered that to a very large extent the Panthers had adhered to the teachings of Malcolm X. Taking it from there, he could work to fashion the Panthers into the type of organization he believed that Malcolm would have built had he lived. For their part the Panthers were equally satisfied with Cleaver. In recommending him for membership, Seale described him: "This nigger from prison, this nigger is tired of shit. This nigger is like a Malcolm X to us, and voom! This nigger can write."[31] Cleaver was immediately installed as a sort of resident theoretician and ideologist for the Party.

Even before the advent of Cleaver, however, Black Panther thinking and beliefs were to be distinguished from that of other black liberationist groups. From their very beginning, they had rejected the shopworn clichés, the bombast, the bubas, and the dashikis of the so-called cultural nationalists. They were critical of what they considered to be an overemphasis on African culture, and they flatly rejected black mass emigration to the mother country. In his shaping of Panther ideology, Cleaver was also to downgrade the importance of the African homeland idea. He felt that the emigration idea was obsolete. To Cleaver, America and not Africa was the mother country, the white mother country of American blacks.[32]

In Cleaver's view blacks in America were a captive colonial people who stood in the same relationship to America as Algerians to France and as some former African colonial peoples to Great Britain. The land the Afro-Americans must look to, the land to which they were entitled, therefore, was the land beneath their feet. To get it, however, Cleaver insisted that the Afro-American must be prepared to fight; he cannot wait for the "pigs" to give him "five or six states." After the blacks had put themselves by means of revolutionary struggle into a position from which they were able to inflict a political consequence upon America, then the land question could be brought out. To Cleaver the forcible overthrow of the American state became priority number one. Since blacks could not do the job alone, the assistance of sympathetic white revolutionists was to be welcomed, even cultivated. The revolution would have to be interracial. "It makes no sense to holler for freedom for the black community and have no interconnection with white groups who also recognize the need for fundamental change."[33] In Cleaver's scheme of things there could be no place for the crippling black racism of the cultural nationalists. Finally, since capitalism was the root cause of both imperialism and white racism, the basic goal of black liberation had to be the ultimate establishment of a socialist society.

In the pragmatic readjustment of the Party's program induced by Cleaver, there was a new and greater emphasis on propaganda and political work. In this connection, the Party devoted more time and energy to developing its newsletter, the *Black Panther Community News Service,* into a full-blown newspaper. Without any funds at their disposal and with ample time on their hands, the Party members produced the paper themselves. Bobby Seale did the layouts and Cleaver functioned as editor.[34] The first printed issue of the paper appeared on May 15, 1967. It was issued once or twice a month thereafter. It was also in the issue on May 15 that the *Black Panther* carried the first cartoon in which police officers were referred to as "pigs." The first cartoon bore the caption: "Support your local police." Emory Dawson, the Panther minister of culture, was the cartoonist. His drawings regularly depicted pigs in policemen's uniforms committing various types of physical violence against black individuals. In its earlier issues the paper also featured a "bootlickers gallery" in which were posted pictures of Roy Wilkins, Martin Luther King, Whitney Young, Senator Edward Brooke, Floyd McKissick, Bayard Rustin, and James Baldwin.

The police, in the meanwhile, were stepping up their surveillance of the Party. Individual Panthers were arrested on weapons charges, for minor traffic violations, and even for spitting on the sidewalks. One Party member writes: "After Sacramento, the Establishment in California had succeeded in dissipating the strength of the Party by arrests, bail, and constant pressure. That is how they work—not to destroy you overnight, but by the process of attrition."[35] On October 28, the "process of attrition" caught up with Huey P. Newton. Early that morning, the Oakland police stopped an automobile known to them to be a Panther vehicle. Newton, who had been driving the car, was ordered out as an officer named John Frey began to write out a citation. As Newton began to walk to the waiting police car, shooting erupted. A few moments later Frey lay dead with a second policeman wounded. Newton wound up with four slugs in his abdomen. He was subsequently charged with murder, assault with a deadly weapon, and kidnapping and was held in the Oakland County jail without bail.[36]

The incident of October 28 had a most profound impact upon the fortunes of the Black Panther party. With both Newton and Seale in jail (Seale was serving his six months' sentence for the Sacramento incident) the leadership of the Party fell squarely upon the shoulders of Eldridge Cleaver. Since joining in the early spring, he had remained in the background working on the development of Party ideology. Now with almost total control he skillfully piloted the Party on a course of his own choosing. In so doing, he achieved a notoriety even above Huey Newton and one that he retained even while in exile.

In the immediate aftermath of Newton's imprisonment, Cleaver moved to organize a "Free Huey" campaign. More than one hundred black liberation leaders were called to a meeting to establish a Huey Newton Defense Fund. An elaborate organization was set up with key personalities serving as chairmen of the numerous committees. Commitments and pledges were made to work until Huey was set free. However, the old rancor against the Panthers could not be erased. After all, these leaders were the "jiveass cultural nationalists" whom Newton had so savagely and scornfully attacked in the past. Thus, in less than a month the "Free Huey" movement had collapsed. The publicity committee composed of six active black writers had not composed even a solitary sentence. However, almost all of the chairmen managed to show up at press conferences when the TV cameras began to grind. Observed one Party member: "TV nationalism is a form of entertainment that is very popular."[37]

The Party did not have much better luck with a group of black lawyers whom they considered retaining to defend Newton. Earl Anthony, who was among the Party members to interview the lawyers, concluded that they were nothing more than a group of incompetents and opportunists who saw a chance to gain some publicity. "Entrusting Huey's defense to a few of these men would have been tantamount to putting his life in the hands of fools."[38] From here on in and largely through Cleaver's influence the Party relied increasingly upon services and cooperation of white individuals and organizations. Through Cleaver's influence Charles R. Garry, a white lawyer, was hired to defend Newton. A well-known leftist, Garry had a background of successfully representing trade unionists and assorted radicals. In place of the committee of black liberationists, the Party accepted the assistance of a group of young whites who adopted the name "Honkies for Huey." The group immediately took on the task of writing and printing leaflets publicizing the Newton defense campaign.

Of great importance to the Party was the alliance it consummated with the largely white Peace and Freedom Party. The first meeting of the two groups, however, could have been abortive. Cleaver and Anthony had been driving in San Francisco one day when their attention was attracted to a P.F.P. sound truck announcing an impending voters' registration rally in the city. It occurred to them that the truck would be an invaluable asset in their "Free Huey" campaign. The two discussed the possibility of coercing the P.F.P. into turning it over to them, but they discarded the notion as being politically unsophisticated. Instead the decision was made to rely upon Cleaver's acquaintance with some of the members of the organization. "Eldridge," says Anthony, "definitely had the knack of handling white radicals." It was Anthony's view also that Cleaver's "ascendancy as a key figure in the black liberation movement was due" in large part "to the support for him on the white Establishment Left."[39]

Cleaver went to work through his New Left contacts to arrange a meeting with the P.F.P. Actually, the P.F.P. had already planned to contact the Panthers. The group was trying to get on the California ballot as a third party for the 1968 elections, and it needed assistance to obtain the necessary signatures. These were available in the black community. At the meeting with the Panthers the P.F.P. expressed the desire to hold rallies in the Bay Area black communities with the Panthers assisting as registrars and making brief talks. Cleaver countered with the suggestion that the Panthers take over the whole task of registration in these communities. Whites were not needed or wanted. In return the P.F.P. would assist in all ways possible in the campaign to free Newton. After considerable haggling, the P.F.P. agreed.

When the Black Panther-P.F.P. coalition was announced on December 22, the black liberation community was aghast. Distrustful of the Panthers, many of the black leaders cried betrayal. Others denounced Cleaver and the Panthers as a simple-minded bunch of ghetto hoodlums who had been taken in by slick, conniving New Left radicals. But the Panthers remained unruffled. They insisted that their basic objective was to free Newton and that they would do whatever it took to bring this about. To prevent further isolation and ostracism, however, the Party decided to mend its fences in the black community. An uneasy peace was established with Ron Karenga's organization in San Francisco, and the Party began to think in terms of a national alliance with SNCC. During the summer of 1967, the Party had drafted Carmichael to serve as Panther field marshal for the eastern half of the United States. Early in January, 1968, Cleaver and Seale, who was now out of prison, flew to Washington, D.C., to talk with Carmichael and to invite him to speak at an upcoming rally for Newton in Oakland. The talks with Carmichael were expanded to include other members in the SNCC hierarchy. The upshot was the establishment of an alliance with SNCC. Carmichael was made Honorary Prime Minister of the Panthers; James Forman, Minister of Foreign Affairs; and H. Rap Brown, Minister of Justice.

Word of the Panther-SNCC alliance caused almost as much shock among black militants as had the Panther-P.F.P. coalition. SNCC was certainly the leading "jiveass cultural nationalist" group in the country, and who was Carmichael if he was not the nation's leading practitioner of black racism? It seemed as though the Panthers were running from one extreme to the other. Not all in the SNCC hierarchy were happy about the "alliance," but the top leadership was enthusiastic. James Forman states: "I was probably the one who wanted most to see this alliance develop. I saw working with the Black Panthers as . . . a way of fighting our mutual repression and a way of implementing decisions SNCC had reached but could not carry out. . . ."[40] As it developed, however, the Panthers were looking beyond mere friendship and cooperation with SNCC. What they had in mind was not an alliance but a merger—a merger by which the Party would absorb the SNCC membership and inherit its national contacts and a national apparatus which it now so badly needed. The Panthers let the cat out of the bag during a briefing session with SNCC leaders. Shock and disbelief prevailed. James Forman, who was in attendance at the meeting, states: "I was stunned to hear Eldridge [Cleaver] insist that our relationship was that of a merger."[41]

After this meeting relationships between the two organizations rapidly deteriorated. Cleaver did not help matters much in a speech he made on the merger:

> It is very important to realize that SNCC is composed virtually of black hippies, you might say, of black college students who have dropped out of the black middle class. And because that is their origin and that is where they came from, they cannot relate to the black brother on the block in a political fashion. . . .
>
> Most people don't know this, but a lot of the rhetoric you hear from Stokely Carmichael and Rap Brown these days . . . was adopted precisely because they had come to the West Coast and spent a little time with the Black Panthers out here.[42]

SNCC had no intention of allowing itself to be merged out of existence by the Panthers or anybody else, but it especially resented the methods adopted by Cleaver and others to bring this about. Beyond this the SNCC members, like a lot of other people, found themselves intimidated by the tough-looking ghetto-hardened Panthers. As one member put it, "I can't work with anybody I don't feel right turning my back on."[43] By mid-July, H. Rap Brown and Forman had come to the conclusion that they had best resign their posts in the Party. Resenting the authoritarian nature of Panther leadership, Forman insisted that his "political integrity" had been challenged. "Within the Black Panther Party I was not about to become the patsy of anyone. . . ." Finally Forman, like many others, felt ill at ease in working with the Panthers. He states: "I had never worked in an organization where I felt my personal security and safety were threatened by internal elements and I did not intend to start doing so then."[44]

The Panthers for their part were equally distrustful of Forman. Seale considered him to be a crafty manipulator whose basic strategy was an attempt to keep the Panthers weak. Thus in late July when the Party high command got word that Forman was "bad-mouthing them" up and down the country, it decided to do something about it. Led by Cleaver and Seale a squad of eighteen Panthers burst into the SNCC office at 100 Fifth Avenue in New York City and ordered the panic-stricken staff "up against the wall." Cleaver, Seale, and Hilliard then herded James Forman into a side room. One of the members of the Panther squad reports: "I could hear someone telling Forman they would end his actions right there. The muffled sound of what appeared to be pleading was followed by the crashing of furniture."[45]

A few weeks after this incident the SNCC central committee voted to terminate its so-called alliance with the Panthers on the grounds that it had been consummated by individuals acting on their own rather than by the organization as a whole, and that the exact nature and mechanics of the alliance had never been thoroughly discussed. For his own reasons Carmichael alone, among other SNCC leaders, maintained an amicable relationship with the Panthers. By the summer of 1969, however, he had become convinced, as had all other black liberationists, that there could be no association with the Panthers except on *their* terms. After a lengthy and fruitless discussion with Cleaver, who was then in Algiers, Carmichael resigned.

Along with their problems with SNCC, the Panthers were continuing to have their difficulties with the law. During the early months of 1968 the Oakland and the San Francisco police combined and intensified their efforts to drive the Panthers out of the Bay Area or out of business. Thus, on January 16, at 3:30 A.M., the Tactical Squad of the San Francisco police decided to surprise Eldridge Cleaver. Without a warrant and offering no explanation, they kicked in the door of his apartment and proceeded to dump and scatter the furnishings and papers about. When nothing incriminating was found and no resistance was offered, they withdrew. On February 25,

David Hilliard and three other Panthers were picked up in Berkeley and charged with carrying concealed weapons and conspiring to commit murder. The same police officers later called upon Bobby Seale in his apartment in Berkeley. They kicked the door down and proceeded to manhandle both Seale and his wife. Two guns were found and Seale and his wife were booked on gun charges.

When Martin Luther King was killed on April 4, the haggard Panther leadership came to a quick and critical decision. They knew that if the blacks in the Bay Area erupted into violence as had others throughout the country, the Panthers would inherit the blame and thereby become legitimate targets for an overeager police. To prevent this development, Party members were sent out to patrol the streets and to tell people to "hang loose" and "cool it." As Anthony states it: "Our people kept stressing the fact that we were not against burning the 'motherfucker' to the ground. But it was not a correct revolutionary tactic at that time."[46] Nevertheless, on April 6, the police cornered Bobby Hutton and Cleaver in the basement of a house on 28th Street in Oakland. In the battle that ensued, Cleaver and Hutton found themselves becoming overcome by tear gas. With the police obviously bent upon killing them, Cleaver decided that the only way for them to survive even a surrender would be to take off their clothes and present themselves buck naked and defenseless on the open street. Young and somewhat shy, Hutton rejected the idea. When the two reached the street, the nude Cleaver was taken into custody. Hutton, fully clothed, turned and ran. He was promptly cut down by a hail of gunfire.[47] Cleaver was charged with assault and attempted murder. His parole was revoked, and he remained in jail from April until June 12 when he was released upon $63,000 bail.

As brutal as it was, however, the harassment and persecution of the Panthers were not without benefits to them. Hardly a day passed that some Panther exploit was not dramatized on the TV evening news or splashed across the front pages of local newspapers. Cleaver, Newton, and Seale were lionized by fawning, impressionable, and news-hungry reporters. Waiting for an interview with Cleaver at the offices of *Ramparts,* Don Schanche reports the following: "Most of the white press in the room seemed so awed by C. that they over-acted a great show of loud camaraderie, like Southern deputies kissing the ass of a particularly mean sheriff."[48] In the black community the Panthers became folk heroes and their exploits were made into legends. No black organization of any stripe could compete with them in terms of prestige and glamour. The black leather jacket and the black beret and shades became status apparel in the black community. Between January and June of 1968 a dozen new Panther chapters were established throughout the nation. During a single month, June, 1968, upwards of a thousand new members flocked into these new chapters.

From July 15 to September 8, the trial of Huey Newton served to keep the Panthers before the public eye. In addition to the work of the Party, prodigious efforts were expended in Newton's behalf by the P.F.P. and other New Left organizations. Testimony in the trial amounted to more than four hundred pages. Newton's attorney, Charles Garry, followed the line that Newton was a political prisoner and that the trial was a political trial. In his own defense Newton insisted that he had been "framed." He denied having fired any shot or having a gun in his possession at the time of the incident. After deliberating for some twenty-four hours, the jury found Newton guilty of voluntary manslaughter in the death of one policeman and innocent of shooting the second. On September 27, Newton was sentenced to serve two to fifteen years in the state penitentiary. On the same day the court revoked Cleaver's parole, giving him sixty days to wind up his affairs and return to prison.

For Cleaver these were sixty busy and hectic days. Among other things he was running for president of the United States. Back in January, 1968, the Panthers had assisted the P.F.P. in obtaining the signatures (105,000) necessary to get on the California ballot for the November, 1968, elections. As time passed, the Panthers began acting as though this assistance gave them a proprietary interest in the new party. This, at any rate, was the manner in which the Panther delegation conducted itself at the P.F.P. founding convention held in mid-March at Richmond, California. Cleaver literally intimidated the convention into accepting as candidates of the P.F.P., Huey P. Newton for Congress and Bobby Seale and Cleaver's wife, Kathleen, for the California State Assembly. The convention also adopted a whole slate of Panther resolutions. At the P.F.P. national convention in August, Cleaver received the party's nomination for president. There were those in the party, however, who were dismayed at the easy capitulation to Cleaver and his Panthers. Late in October this group pulled out and established the Freedom and Peace Party with the comedian Dick Gregory as their candidate for president.[49]

Beginning on June 12, when he was released on bail from prison,

Cleaver began to campaign in earnest. As the author of the best-selling *Soul on Ice*, Cleaver was already fairly well known in the country. In early October, however, he received further national publicity when Governor Ronald Reagan attempted to block his appointment to teach a course at the University of California at Berkeley. On the local level in California, Newton, Seale, and Kathleen Cleaver were all running against black opponents. With black extremists thus pitted against black moderates the campaign became exceptionally vicious. Party member Anthony comments:

> The spectacle of black leaders feuding at a petty level created bad vibrations in the black community. When I think back, I believe the Party lost more than it gained, for they sacrificed their image in the community for token white radical support.[50]

As the final returns came in on election night, November 5, Cleaver received something less than 200,000 votes nationally. Newton, Seale, and Kathleen Cleaver running locally, all did poorly. Three weeks later, on the day he was to return to prison Cleaver dropped out of sight. Months later he surfaced in Havana, Cuba. From there he fled to Algiers. A second phase in the history of the Party had come to an end.

With the coming of the new year the Party moved to make a wholesale change in its image. With the rest of the top leadership in jail or in exile, Seale was now at the helm. Early in January he announced a new four-point program for the Party with emphasis upon "serving the people."[51] The four activities listed were: (1) free breakfasts for children of welfare recipients, (2) free health clinics in black communities, (3) black liberation schools, and (4) a campaign to bring about the decentralization of urban-area police forces. As time passed, the free breakfast programs turned out to be the most successful and praiseworthy. By the end of the year free "breakfasts were being served in 19 cities under the sponsorship of the national headquarters . . . and 23 local affiliates." As a consequence, "more than 20,000 youngsters received 'full, free breakfasts' before going to their grade school or junior high school classes. . . ." The program was not rigidly confined to black neighborhoods. One of the Seattle programs, in fact, operated in a predominantly white middle-class community. After its initial introduction in some communities by the local Panthers, the program was taken over or subsidized by other individuals or community groups.[52]

The liberation schools were designed to replace the free breakfast programs when schools closed for the summer recess. The first such schools were opened in Berkeley, Oakland, and San Francisco in late June, 1969. Black Panther ideology was taught to the youth through songs, talks, films, field trips, and miscellaneous activities. In two or three of the Panther affiliates elsewhere in the country, the school was held for teenagers during the afternoon, after a hot lunch, or during the evening after a free supper. Describing the activity of the schools, Seale states: "The youth have to understand that the revolutionary struggle in this country that's now being waged is not a race struggle but a class struggle. This is what the Liberation Schools are all about."[53]

The free health program of the Party was inaugurated on August 20, 1969, when the Kansas City, Missouri, affiliate announced the opening of the "Bobby Hutton Community Clinic." A "People's Free Health Clinic" was opened in Brooklyn, New York, in November, to be followed by the "Sidney Miller Medical Clinic" in Seattle, Washington, on December 1, 1969. Ultimately, however, the free health clinic proved to be one activity in which the Panthers overreached themselves. Opening the centers was one thing, but providing them with medical services proved to be impossible. By mid-1970 the activity was largely abandoned.[54]

During 1969 and 1970 the Black Panther party affiliates in about a dozen cities circulated petitions seeking referenda on the decentralization of the local police. These efforts met with failure in all but one city. In 1971, after two years of campaigning, the Panthers and their white supporters obtained sufficient signatures to force the issue to a vote in Berkeley, California. The referendum actually called for the establishment of three separate police departments, one each for the black community, the white community, and a "hippie" and student community near the university campus. When the vote was counted on election day, April 6, 1971, the proposition was defeated by a vote of almost two to one.[55] Viewed as a whole, the conclusion must be that to "serve the people" was a good, positive thrust in a new direction. It helped to change the Party's old image, and it won them some new friends and new support. The gains for the Party would have been even greater had not the new program been so obviously and so crudely used to propagate Black Panther ideology.

Aside from its "serve the people" program, the Party in 1969 made a fundamental alteration in its political ideology. In the process it discarded its black nationalist orientation and moved squarely into the camp of revolutionary socialism. David Hilliard, Chief of Staff of the Party, put it succinctly: "The ideology of the Black Panther Party is the historical experience of the Black people in America translated through Marxism-Leninism." The class struggle was thus given preeminence over black liberation. The legitimate aspirations of the "black colony" were not to be disregarded; indeed, they were to be achieved through the overthrow of capitalism in the white mother country. There was, in fact, no other way, for even if blacks achieved a separatist independence in the United States, they would in Newton's view "be unable to function side by side with a capitalistic imperialistic country."[56] Thus, all logic now dictated that the black liberation movement abandon its racist parochialism and combine with the white Left in pursuit of a common goal.

To be sure, the leaders of the black liberation movement, the so-called "cultural nationalists," remained unconvinced. Their thoughts on the matter were perhaps best spoken by Stokely Carmichael:

> The ideologies of communism and socialism speak to class structure, to people who oppress people from the top down to the bottom. . . . We are facing something much more important, because we are the victims of racism. In their present form neither communism nor socialism speak to the problem of racism. And to black people in this country, racism comes first, far more important than exploitation.[57]

There were even members in the Panther high command who could not accept the new dogmas. Deputy Minister of Education Earl Anthony was expelled from the Party in March, 1969, principally because of his refusal to toe the new ideological line. He said: "I had *never* been committed to the political concept embraced by the Party that blacks and whites *should* and *could* integrate their efforts to work toward revolution in America."[58]

During the spring of 1969, the Panthers expanded and intensified their involvement with the Left. The Party severed its remaining ties with the black liberationists, and it denounced as counterrevolutionary all those who criticized its new departure. On March 30, at Austin, Texas, the Party entered into an alliance with the forty thousand-member Students for a Democratic Society. Jubilant SDS spokesmen declared: "We must keep in mind that the Black Panther party is not fighting black people's struggles only, but is in fact the vanguard in our common struggles against capitalism and imperialism."[59] The national office of the SDS agreed to print and distribute information about the history, development, and programs of the Black Panther party. Local chapters were directed to develop and strengthen formal and informal relationships with the Panthers.

During the midsummer the Party ambitiously convened a National Conference for a United Front Against Fascism in America. The three-day conference held in Oakland, California, was attended by some three thousand delegates, 75 percent of whom were white. The Panthers displayed their new mood by consenting to participation by members of the American Communist party. They had previously held this group at arm's length. Perhaps the chief result of the conference was the decision to establish "National Committees to Combat Fascism." The young white delegates enthusiastically embraced the idea. The Panthers, however, had other purposes in mind for these committees. As Seale put it: "We see the National Committees as the political organizing bureau of the Black Panther Party." [60] Within the year fifteen of these committees were set up in about a dozen cities across the nation. They functioned as satellites of the Panthers, and they were kept under tight reins.

While the making of alliances with Marxist groups was one thing, a genuine understanding of and commitment to Marxist doctrine was another. On the evidence it would appear that the Panthers achieved neither of the latter. Basically the Party was not noted for its respect for orthodoxy. Panther ideologists thus interpreted, deleted, and rearranged Marxist-Leninist tenets at will. This do-it-yourself approach to the ideology was best expressed by Eldridge Cleaver: "I think we are developing now, in the United States, a new and uniquely American Marxism, an indigenous Marxism. It's not Chinese Marxism or Russian Marxism. It's American Marxism. Yankee Doodle Dandy Socialism." [61]

In the fall of 1970, Panther ideology underwent yet another alteration and Yankee Doodle Dandy socialism, whatever it was, was scrapped. The change was dictated by Huey Newton, now back at the helm of the Party after having been released from prison on August 5. Under the new ideology which was known as "Intercommunalism," [62] the Party would no longer regard black Americans as a colony or an oppressed nation. Indeed, the concept of nationhood was abandoned altogether. With North American imperialism running across national boundaries, the nation/state idea had become meaningless. The Black Panther Party would therefore advocate the disappearance of all national boundaries and national sentiments. The world, in Newton's view, would be a collection of free communities, an intercommunal framework, based upon proportional representation and providing for equal distribution of the world's wealth. Newton felt that a revolution would be necessary to destroy American imperialism and put the means of production under the control of the people. Then war would cease, the state would no longer exist, and there would be communism. Newton concluded that this new objective would correspond with Marx's "withering away of the state."[63]

The Party hierarchy appeared unconcerned, almost uninterested in the new ideology. Among other things it was terribly preoccupied with the internal affairs of the organization. During the several years of Newton's imprisonment the Black Panther party had become a truly national organization. By the fall of 1970, the Party was operational in some thirty-five cities in nineteen states and the District of Columbia. This activity was controlled by thirteen Party chapters and five branches, twenty National Committees to Combat Fascism, and two information centers.[64] In January, 1969, Party headquarters in Oakland, California, promulgated a code of twenty-six rules for the expanded organization. Actually, the code was a combination of new rules with the original ten-point program. Among the new provisions was the requirement that Party leaders devote at least two hours per day to reading in order to keep abreast of social and political developments. All chapters, branches, and affiliates were required to submit a monthly financial report to the Party's Central Committee and the Ministry of Finance. Party leaders were required also to adhere to policy and ideology promulgated by the Central Committee. Violations of Party rules and regulations led to suspension, expulsion, or other disciplinary actions. The Party initiated its first purge in January, 1969, under the direction of Seale and Hilliard. Admission of new members was halted for three months in order to facilitate the weeding out of undesirables.[65]

By the spring of 1969 the Party's tabloid newspaper, *The Black Panther*, was offering competition to the Black Muslim *Muhammad Speaks*. From a sleazy newssheet in 1967, it had grown into a well-turned-out weekly with a circulation of upwards of 100,000. The paper sold for 25 cents per copy with 12.5 cents going to the national office. After production and shipping costs were deducted, the national office realized a profit of five cents per copy. Sales of the newspaper became perhaps the most reliable and lucrative source of income for the Party. The House Committee on Internal Affairs estimated that during the eleven months preceding October, 1970, the

Panthers' national office banked close to one-half million dollars, presumably from the sales of the newspaper.[66] Each chapter of the Party had its quota of the newspaper to sell, and the national office insured remittances by requiring payment for a previous week's papers before new deliveries were made. This arrangement assured some income to the Party chapters, but most of them had to rely upon other sources for their general maintenance.

As the Party chapters mushroomed throughout the nation, police activity against them assumed national proportions. By 1969, there seemed good reason to believe that this activity was coordinated if not inspired and directed by one or more federal police agencies. For instance, on February 7, 1970, Mayor Wes Uhlman of Seattle, Washington, disclosed that he had refused a proposal from the United States Treasury Department officials to conduct a raid on Black Panther party headquarters in his city.[67] During 1968 and 1969, some thirty raids, most of them without warrants, were carried out against Panther chapters in cities across the nation. Perhaps the most spectacular of these was the predawn assault carried out against the Party's Chicago chapter on December 4, 1969.[68] When some of the facts concerning this incident were ferreted out by a grand jury, the *New York Times* was moved to comment: "The story unfolded by the Chicago grand jury makes it appear that the law-enforcement agencies, more than the Panthers, were acting out a conspiracy."[69] By summer of 1970, the number of Black Panthers netted in raids began to make it appear that an "inquisition" was in progress. The FBI reported that 348 Panthers were jailed in 1969 alone.[70] To many observers it appeared that the "establishment" was attempting to transfer the black revolution from the ghetto streets to the penitentiaries. At any rate, the American prison system for the first time in history had to deal with a new kind of inmate—the black political prisoner. The Black Panther party incidentally established its first prison chapter in San Quentin State Penitentiary in February, 1971.[71]

In article 9 of their original platform and program the Panthers state: "We believe that the courts should follow the United States Constitution so that black people will receive fair trials."[72] In their determination to implement this belief Panther defendants and their legal counsel helped to bring about some of the most bizarre and spectacular court trials in the history of the American judicial system. The most noteworthy of these was the trial of Bobby Seale in the Federal District Court in Chicago in 1969. Seale, along with seven other non-Panthers, was charged with conspiring to cross state lines with intent to riot at the 1968 Democratic National Convention. In the absence of his lawyer, who was ill, Seale attempted to act as his own counsel. His request was not only denied, but when he persisted, Judge Julius Hoffman angrily ordered him chained and gagged in open court.[73] Hoffman finally severed Seale's case from that of the others and sentenced him to four years in jail for contempt of court. None of the subsequent Panther trials was as uproarious as that of Bobby Seale's. As time passed, Party members became more interested in staying out of prison than in baiting and frightening trial court judges.

On February 9, 1971, several Panthers from the national office distributed mimeographed handbills in front of a courthouse in downtown New York announcing the expulsion of nine members of the Party's New York chapter. The nine were members of a group of twenty-one New York Panthers who in April, 1969, had been charged with conspiracy to blow up several buildings in the city. Specifically, nine were being expelled because they had signed an "Open Letter" criticizing the national leadership for being soft and insufficiently militant.[74] The letter contended that chances for a genuine revolution with armed struggle were reduced when so-called revolutionaries spent their time publishing newspapers and holding conventions and rallies. "We desperately need more revolutionaries who are completely willing and ready at all times to KILL to change conditions."[75] The national office subsequently expelled three others of the twenty-one for bail jumping, and when the New York chapter leaders attempted to intervene, the entire chapter was cashiered.

In truth, the New York chapter had long been something of a maverick group. They were convinced that theirs was the premier chapter in the Party and should therefore house the national headquarters. Beyond this the New Yorkers felt that Oakland had been paying far more attention to the legal defense of national officers than to the twenty-one local members who had been in jail since April, 1969. On March 1, the New York chapter took it upon itself to "expel" Huey Newton and David Hilliard. To further complicate and intensify things, Eldridge Cleaver from Algeria thrust himself into the matter. In an intercontinental telephone conversation, Cleaver, taking the side of the New Yorkers, called for the expulsion of Hilliard and the reinstatement of the New York chapter along with all expelled members. The national office was quick to react to

Cleaver; on March 6, the *Black Panther* carried a lengthy story entitled "Free Kathleen Cleaver." Eldridge, in the article, was accused of keeping his wife a virtual prisoner and of beating and abusing her on several occasions. Eldridge was further accused of having killed a black escaped convict, Clinton (Rahim) Smith, for showing a romantic interest in Kathleen. To wind the matter up, the national office on March 20 decreed that the entire "Intercommunal Section" in Algeria had defected from the Party. Thus Cleaver and his group were no longer members of the Black Panther organization.[76]

Weeks later in a lengthy review of the Party's history Newton held Cleaver responsible for many serious mistakes and misjudgments in Party policies. He suggested that Cleaver had joined the Party in the first place because of his fascination for armed confrontation with the police. He defected from the Party, said Newton, because "we would not order everyone into the streets tomorrow to make a revolution." The Party made a basic error in accepting Cleaver's suggestion to ally with elements of the New Left. "Our hook up with white radicals did not give us access to the white community because they do not guide the white community." The result was the placing of the Party in a "twilight zone" in which it was unable to mobilize whites yet incapable of influencing blacks. The use of profanity in speech and publications resulting in the alienation of the black community was also blamed on Cleaver. Newton conceded that the Black Panther Party had defected from the black community long before Cleaver had defected from the Party, but the departure of Cleaver would permit the Party to end its isolation from the black community.[77]

By the end of the year 1971 the general public had all but lost interest in the Panthers. These were no longer the armed tough-looking ghetto blacks of a few years earlier. Besides, they were no longer preaching revolution or threatening guerrilla warfare, and they were attempting to avoid all confrontations and other involvements with the law. As Newton put it: "The Party was very wrong to think that it could change the police forces in the way we tried to do it. All we got was a war and a lot of bloodshed." The Party had considered itself to be the vanguard of a people who wanted change. "However, when we looked around," said Newton, "we found we weren't the vanguard for anything."[78] There had to be a return to the people to hear from them their needs and their desires and to regain their favor. This is what the Party set about doing at the beginning of 1971.

CHAPTER 10

Black Studies

Along with the spectacular activities of the Black Panther party, a major focus of the black revolution after 1968 was the Black Studies movement. The movement began as a demand for the inclusion of courses in Afro-American history in the curricula of predominantly white colleges and universities. While many of the young blacks in the movement considered the field to be a wholly new one, the fact is that the study of Afro-American (Negro) history and culture dated back a half century. Over these years a dogged, determined interest in the field was kept up by two distinct and dissimilar groups of blacks. The first and by far the most competent and learned was the group of black scholars and teachers who labored in the tradition established by Dr. Carter G. Woodson and the Association for the Study of Negro Life and History. Beginning in the post-World War I period and for better than two generations thereafter, courses in black history and culture were taught on the campuses of predominantly black schools throughout the South. While the vast majority of black historians could not find publishers, the discipline still managed to produce such brilliant scholars as Dr. Woodson himself, William E. B. Du Bois, John Hope Franklin, Benjamin Quarles, and Lorenzo Greene.

The second group with an interest in black history was composed of black nationalists. Unlike Woodson, Du Bois, and the others, the nationalists concentrated on African history and culture and the African origins of American blacks. As separatists rather than integrationists they were not particularly interested in the participation by blacks in the building of American civilization. The propagation of African history and culture was an important facet of the Garvey movement. As the chief heirs of Garvey tradition the Black Muslims continued and expanded this activity. To the thousands of converts they made and the other thousands who read their literature, the Muslims proclaimed that the black man was the primogenitor of all civilization and that the Caucasian had developed out of the weak and cast-off of the black race. They taught also that black men ruled Spain and Southern Europe, reigned as popes in the Vatican, and built great civilizations on the west coast of Africa. Essentially, however, Black Muslim and other black nationalist teaching was largely confined to the ghetto. The black middle class knew and heard little of it.

Malcolm X was the first to generate real interest among black students in black history and culture. He linked his demands for black liberation to the claim that black people possessed a dazzling and glamorous heritage and that they had been tricked into slavery three centuries ago by the "white devil." Malcolm taught his history not only to the ghetto youth but also he was self-confident enough to carry his message directly to black college students.

Largely as a result of the influence of Malcolm X militant black students and intellectuals began to conclude that the propagation of black history and culture was necessary to the success of the black liberation movement. Their interest, however, was in a *new* or *revised* treatment of the black man's past. The traditional "Negro History" of the Carter G. Woodson school was rejected as system-oriented, integrationist, and servile—the product of those whom Malcolm X called "brainwashed black Ph.D's." Specifically what was wanted was *militant* history—history that depicted the black man's 350 years in America as a valiant struggle against enslavement, white racism, repression, and even genocide.

Picking up this theme in the early 1960s were a number of bright young black writers, a few with a background in journalism, but none with training as a professional historian. Their articles appeared in such black periodicals as the *Negro Digest, Ebony,* and *Freedomways.* Most notable among these was a series of articles on Afro-American history written for *Ebony* by its young and brilliant senior editor, Lerone Bennett. Bennett wrote glowingly of the African heritage of black Americans; he emphasized the indomitable resistance of blacks to the institution of slavery; and he paid high tribute to such nineteenth-century black militants as David Walker and Henry Highland Garnett. Bennett's articles sang of the militancy and courage of black Americans. It was popular rather than scholarly history, but it was reflective of the mood of the black Revolution. The articles were subsequently published in book form under the title

Before the Mayflower: A History of the Negro in America. Quickly becoming a best seller among blacks, the new book soon replaced John Hope Franklin's *From Slavery to Freedom* as the standard text in black history.

The demand for courses in black history and culture, or Black Studies as it was soon to become known, was first to be heard on the predominantly white campuses. As we have noted, Merritt Junior College as early as 1960 boasted an Afro-American society. The black history course which Huey Newton, Bobby Seale, and other members of AAS forced Merritt College to adopt in 1963 proved unsatisfactory, but it was a pioneer effort in the Black Studies movement. Of greater importance was the Soul Students' Advisory Committee organized on the Merritt College campus, again by Newton and Seale. The SSAC demanded not only a full black curriculum, but it designated itself as the representative and sole bargaining agent for all of the needs of all of the black students enrolled at the institution. The organization became the model for the black student unions that proliferated on white campuses between 1966 and 1970.

Across the Bay at San Francisco State College the black students were thoroughly familiar with the activities of the black militants at Merritt Junior College. And while they rejected Seale and Newton's blandishments to join in forming a liaison with the ghetto "block boys," they looked favorably upon the idea of a black student organization as represented by the SSAC. During the spring of 1966 the black students at San Francisco State persuaded the college to offer a course in black nationalism. By midsummer they had organized themselves into the Black Student Union and began campaigning for a full black curriculum. To them, the issue was clear. As black students, they were made to survey *white* civilizations, read and write *white* prose and poetry, study *white* families, analyze *white* music, examine *white* cultures, and think in *white* psychological terms. This was no longer acceptable. What the students wanted was the *black* perspective whenever and wherever possible.

The academic year 1965–1966 was known as "the year of student revolutions" at San Francisco State. The college was besieged by the multiple and often nonnegotiable demands of several radical student organizations. In an effort to accommodate the more reasonable of these demands and to involve students and faculty in joint efforts, the college set up three new areas of activity. These were: (1) the Experimental College which broke new ground in the type of courses offered; (2) the Community Involvement Program which put students to work with residents of the ghettos and slums; and (3) the Tutorial Program which concentrated in helping children to learn to read and write and in motivating them to remain in school. The curriculum demanded by the Black Student Union was carried through in the Experimental College during the fall semester of 1966. A Black Arts and Culture Series was introduced for the purpose of giving due weight and recognition to the "black experience." Courses dealt with the areas of history, law, psychology, dance, social science, and the humanities.[1]

During the following year, 1967–1968, a comprehensive Black Studies program was adopted which included a total of eleven courses each carrying three-hours credit. Among the courses listed were the following:[2]

ANTHROPOLOGY: Historical Development of Afro-American Studies
DRAMATIC ARTS: Improvisation of Blackness
EDUCATION: Miseducation of the Negro
ENGLISH: Modern African Thought and Literature
HISTORY: Ancient African History
PSYCHOLOGY: Workshop in the Psychology of, by, and for Black People
SOCIOLOGY: Sociology of Black Oppression.

This was the first such curriculum ever adopted by any institution, black or white, in the United States. It was an achievement in which any group of students could have taken deep pride and satisfaction. But not so the B.S.U. of San Francisco State. To the militants who dominated the organization this was only a down payment. What they really wanted was an autonomous department of Black Studies coupled with B.S.U. control of black student life on the campus. During the fall of 1967, the organization, then directed by Black Panther leader George S. Murray, began to make things difficult for the college's new president, John H. Summerskill. In November they invaded the office of the campus newspaper, the *Golden Gate*, and physically assaulted the editor for his alleged insulting remarks about blacks. Resulting suspensions led to a B.S.U. demonstration followed by an attempt to burn the bookstore down.[3]

Summerskill was San Francisco State's sixth president in eight years. He appeared to be genuinely committed to Black Studies, but he was also badly frightened by the guerrilla-type activities of the militant black students. Thus, on February 9, 1968, without the knowledge of the other administration officers or the faculty he appointed a Coordinator of Black Studies, Dr. Nathan Hare, whose task was to structure an autonomous Black Studies department. Dr. Hare, a sociologist, had recently been fired from Howard University for excessive black militant activity. He enthusiastically accepted the new appointment and by April 16, he was ready with a proposal for a department of Black Studies.[4]

His program called for twenty-two black-oriented courses falling under three basic areas:[5] Black Arts Concentration, Behavioral and Social Sciences, and Core Courses. Each course carried four units of regular college credit. The program envisioned also full autonomy for the department, a full professorship for the director, who presumably would be Dr. Hare, and the right to hire a faculty of some twenty instructors. Basic to Hare's whole proposal was a component called "community development." Students and "other interested parties" were to be organized into Black Cultural Councils which would sponsor cultural affairs in the black community in addition to establishing black holidays, festivities, and celebrations. His other suggestions included Black Information Centers, a Black Community Press, and a Bureau of Black Education.[6]

Summerskill accepted Hare's program almost in its entirety and worked hard for its implementation. As the months passed, however, he became tired, exhausted, and a bit frustrated. One day during the early summer he simply walked off the job. He had not lasted a full year as president. The San Francisco State Board of Trustees lost no time in naming his successor. The new president was Robert R. Smith, formerly Dean of the School of Education of San Francisco State. Smith immediately plunged into work on the Black Studies problem. By September he was ready to move with decisiveness. He created a Department of Black Studies with Dr. Hare as chairman; he provided for the admission of special students for the program; and he proposed to the board of trustees that the college award the Bachelor of Arts degree in Black Studies. This program included, in fact, all of the demands of the militant wing of the Black Student Union.[7]

The board of trustees, however, was not disposed to move with such dispatch. During the late months of the fall, the board found one reason after another to delay implementation of the program. On November 6, the Black Student Union called a strike which resulted in the closing down of the school. Two weeks later, with the school still closed, Smith resigned. He had had as much as he could take. The board now faced the task of recruiting a third president in little more than a year. Out of it all, however, San Francisco State emerged at the end of the year as the first institution of higher learning in the nation to establish a Black Studies program under the direction of a Black Studies Department. The department was given full faculty power commensurate with that accorded other departments at the college.[8]

No group in the nation paid more attention to the drama unfolding at San Francisco State than the black students on the predominantly white campuses. They were fascinated by what appeared to be the easy capitulation of a college administration to the demands of a radical student group. Thus, by the fall of 1968, the experiences of San Francisco State were being duplicated on dozens of campuses throughout the country. Indeed, since 1967 black students had been organizing under such names as the Onyx Society, United Black Students, the Association of African and Afro-American Students, and Black Students Union.[9] In almost every instance confirmed militants, including an occasional Black Panther, constituted the core of these organizations. While Black Studies was the professed objective of almost all of these groups, they perceived Black Studies as an aspect of black liberation. The overriding desire was to achieve a victory against the white power structure as represented by the big predominantly white college or university.

In truth, a large percentage of the nation's black students after 1967 was caught up in the genuine anticipation of an apocalypse—the impending black revolution that would topple the racist imperialist white establishment and thrust black people into positions of power. One young black student thus remembers his feelings and experiences:

> We learned the handshake and we learned the terminology: rap, relevant, culture, ad hoc, unity, bourgeoisie, revolution, black and beautiful, genocide, Malcolm X, black community, neo-colonialism, pan-Africanism, this monster called America, right on, etc. We went to rallies, we listened to Stokely, and we quoted Garvey, Du Bois, Frantz Fanon, and of course Malcolm X (by the book, chapter, page, and paragraph). And as to Black Studies? This would provide the vehicle for our preparation for the revolution.[10]

In general, Black Studies achieved a rapid if unenthusiastic acceptance on the major white campuses of the nation. Administrators and faculty everywhere had been softened up by four years of assault and abuse by the Students for Democratic Society

(SDS) and other white radical student groups. They were plagued also by a gnawing sense of guilt brought on by charges of racism, and many of them were willing to accommodate Black Studies as a means of expiation. To be fair, however, there were a significant number of white academicians who viewed the "Black Experience" as a legitimate corrective and needed addition to the teaching and study of American civilization.

On the other hand, most of these professors were aware of the other purpose for which Black Studies could be employed. Some realized that under the guidance of the militants the so-called Black Experience could become black racism and could be made to serve an explicit ideological end—namely the promotion and propagation of revolutionary black nationalism. Thus, Professor David B. Davis of Cornell warned:

> We must insist on maintaining the distinction between political ideology and education. There is a serious danger of allowing our educational machinery to become an instrument for propaganda. On this issue we must hold firm and not retreat. . . . It will be all too easy for whites who are burdened by fear and guilt to shrink from defending their essential beliefs and values. . . . One must be absolutely clear about distinguishing free intellectual inquiry from a party line, no matter how justified the party line may be.[11]

Yale University was the first prestigious institution in the land to establish a Black Studies curriculum. The program did not result from a confrontation between black students and the university officials and faculty. Rather, it was peacefully negotiated over a period of several months. As early as 1966 the handful of black students at Yale had been holding issue-oriented conferences during which the teaching of the Black Experience was a chief topic. During the fall of 1967 the black students had firmly committed themselves to the adoption of a Black Studies program by the university. However, faculty and administrative inertia was considerable. As one of the black student leaders put it: "After several months of determined effort, we discovered that little progress was being made in the struggle to convince the faculty at large of the validity and importance of our concerns."[12] Unlike the black students on many other campuses during this period the blacks at Yale did not "revolt." Instead, they took the initiative in calling for a symposium on Black Studies which was held on the Yale campus in early 1968. Papers and discussions by black and white academicians and administrators attending the symposium were impressive and convincing and built up considerable faculty support for a Black Studies program there.

The upshot was the creation by the university of an African-American studies committee consisting of four black students and four faculty members. This committee worked throughout the summer and fall of 1968 and by early December, it had evolved a Black Studies program that was markedly different from that of San Francisco State College. For one thing, the admonitions of Professor Davis had been adhered to. The committee had evolved a genuine Afro-American studies program rather than a platform for Black Liberation. Nor was there to be a separate or autonomous department for the new discipline. Administration of the program was to be entrusted to a faculty committee, representing several departments and special studies programs. Beyond this the program was inter-disciplinary and was to be based upon the forty-five existing courses in the university curriculum which could be related to the Afro-American experience.[13] Teaching personnel were required to hold appointment in one of the formal disciplines participating in the program. The committee had the responsibility to see that the program at all times conformed to the academic standards of Yale University. On December 12, the faculty unanimously approved Afro-American Studies as a degree-granting program. It was put into operation in September, 1969. During the next three years the Yale program served as a model for a large number of institutions throughout the country.

In the earlier stages of its development the movement for Black Studies at Harvard University paralleled that at Yale. During the fall of 1967 a handful of black students in the "Yard" began to take a serious interest in instituting the program at the college. An informal faculty group headed by Economics Professor Dr. Henry Rosovsky was also interested in promoting the idea. The first direct action to initiate the program, however, came on April 4, 1968, the day of Dr. Martin Luther King's assassination. That evening a group of black students marched to the dean's office with a list of demands calling for the end of the quota limitation on black students and the establish-ment of Afro-American Studies Department. One of the students in the group reports:

> A striking indication of the administration's disrespect for the black students was the fact that the Dean told the students that things were not done like that at Harvard; that you did not make demands but polite requests and that they should come back when they had reworded the petition.[14]

This was done and the administration responded by appointing a faculty committee on Afro-American Studies with Professor Rosovsky as chairman.

Taking his mandate seriously, Rosovsky pushed his committee hard throughout the summer and fall of 1968. Black students were part of all planning and deliberations, and two of them, though they declined, were offered voting membership on the committee. In January, 1969, about a month after Yale had adopted its Black Studies program, Rosovsky's committee reported to the Harvard faculty. Some of its recommendations[15] were:

1. The establishment of a research center in Afro-American Studies
2. A social center for black students
3. Fifteen to twenty fellowships worth $5,000 each to be granted annually to black students
4. The creation of a combined major in Afro-American Studies leading to a Bachelor of Arts degree in the field
5. The establishment of a faculty committee on Afro-American Studies.

February 11, the Harvard faculty approved the report without amendment. The administration followed by creating a standing committee on Afro-American Studies with instructions to get the program operational by September, 1969. Rosovsky was appointed to the standing committee, but Franklin L. Ford, Dean of the Faculty of Arts and Science, was named chairman. Black students at both Harvard and Radcliffe studied and debated both the Rosovsky report and the administration's decisions. They withheld any reaction until April 9 when the standing committee issued a directive to prospective students outlining requirements for the major in Afro-American Studies. The Association of African and Afro-American Students, as the blacks called themselves, now bitterly denounced the program for its recommendation of a combined major rather than a department of Black Studies, for its failure to include black students in the administration of the program, and for its omission of any programmatic tie-in with the black community of Greater Boston. They refused to accept the program.

April 9 also happened to be the day the SDS and members of other white radical groups seized Harvard's University Hall and kicked off a student revolt on the campus.[16] Preferring, however, to keep its grievances separate from those of the whites, the AAAS did not join the general revolt. It had prepared its own Afro-American Studies

program, and it now called upon black students at Harvard and
Radcliffe to boycott classes in support of it. As a result of the black
boycott and the radical student strike, Harvard was in a turmoil.
Rumors flew widely about the campus. With fear of a black student
"putsch" spreading, faculty members mounted an all-night guard to
protect the holdings of Widener Library.[17]

On April 22, the faculty held a meeting at Loeb Hall to hear and
consider the demands of the black students. An AAAS spokesman
called for the following:

1. The establishment of a Black Studies "department" in place of the combined
   major
2. The development of an Afro-American research institute and a greater Boston
   consortium of university Afro-American resources
3. Expansion of the standing committee to include six students—three from black
   student organizations and three from potential candidates in the field. Full voting
   rights for all of these students.
4. The committee to have the right to nominate the first four to six appointments in
   the department, two of which must be tenured
5. Responsibility for the new field to be vested ultimately in an executive committee
   consisting of four faculty members and four students, two of whom are to be
   elected by black student organizations and two by potential candidates in the
   field.[18]

The AAAS spokesman warned the assembled faculty: "Not to make
a decision in favor of the proposal that we have put here before you is
to commit a serious mistake, to perhaps play a part in creating a tragic
situation which this university may never be able to recover from."[19]
After some discussion and debate the faculty voted 251 to 158 to adopt
the AAAS demands. The entire proceedings of the meeting were
broadcast over WHRB, the university student radio.

Reaction to the "capitulation" of April 22 was swift and mostly
angry. Harvard alumni were astounded by the fact that black
undergraduates had been given powers hitherto held only by Harvard
senior faculty and denied to junior faculty, graduate students, and
non-black undergraduates. Professor Rosovsky resigned from the
standing committee. In the New York Times James Reston suggested
that the Harvard faculty had supinely submitted to the "use and
threat of force." He warned that "some authority must oppose
anarchy" and that if university teachers and administrators couldn't,
the police and the politicians would have to do it for them.[20]

On the other hand, the Loeb Hall decision had its defenders. Thus,
one of the professors stated:

This program is really a different matter, in the sense that the country has to make the utmost effort to find constructive solutions to the race problem, which is the great tragedy of American history. One has to be prepared to do things which one would not do in other circumstances.[21]

In the final analysis, however, there was no way to diminish the fact that the Harvard faculty in one of the most unique meetings in its history had made a substantive alteration in its educational program on the basis of political expediency rather than on academic merit. It had been moved to share its precious sovereignty with exponents of the Black Liberation.

Black Liberation advocates achieved their most spectacular on-campus victory at Cornell University, however. The specter of black students wearing bandoliers and waving twenty-gauge shotguns on a university campus demonstrated as never before the political nature of the Black Studies movement. During the last ten days of April, 1969, Cornell became a university where violent confrontation replaced rational dialogue and where fear, panic, and terror gripped almost everyone except a handful of militant black students. Historically, Cornell had never enrolled more than a handful of black students, but like most of the other "Ivy League" schools, Cornell moved to correct this situation during the early 1960s. In 1963, the university established a scholarship fund for culturally disadvantaged students with marginal credentials, "but who otherwise give evidence of being able to compete at Cornell."[22] As a result of this program the black student enrollment at the university increased from twenty in 1964 to 250 in 1968. As many as 180 new black students were enrolled in 1968 alone. A considerable proportion of these were "block boys" from the urban black ghettos.

During the spring of 1968 the Cornell Afro-American Society began pressing the administration for a Black Studies program. In response, the university's president, James Perkins, appointed an advisory committee composed of students, faculty, and administrative officials. Laboring throughout the summer, the committee put together a black curriculum similar to that of Yale University. The program was to have a governing board of eight black students plus nine members from the faculty and the administration. It was funded by a one-million-dollar gift from the chairman of Cornell's board of trustees and was scheduled to go into effect in September, 1969. The response of the black students to the new program was enthusiastic.

During the fall of 1968, however, hard-core militants took over the leadership of the AAS. They did not want to wait a year for the inauguration of a Black Studies program. Thus on December 6, about fifty black militants invaded the meeting of the Black Studies Advisory Committee and announced the body's dismissal. The militants declared that from here on the AAS alone would issue directives. On December 9, they presented the university with a nine-point nonnegotiable ultimatum which called for the establishing of a *separate* and *autonomous* degree-granting black college within the Cornell complex. All student fees received from black students were to be paid to this new black college by Cornell University on or before March 1, 1969. Finally, black students designated by the AAS were to operate within the offices of admission and financial aid, with full control over the allocation of financial aid for their assistance.[23] One of the militants thus rationalized the demands: "The validity of a program is determined by those who have the power to define and set up its limits and goals. If blacks do not define the type of program set up within an institution that will be relevant to them it will be worthless."[24] Not yet intimidated, President Perkins responded to the AAS with a statement stressing the unfeasibility of a totally independent black college and the fact that its establishment far exceeded his limited authority. Such an act, he said, would require the consent of the trustees, the regents, and the legislature of the state of New York. Perkins then moved to appoint a high administrative official to work out a new compromise Black Studies program with the AAS.

Rejecting Perkins' response as totally unacceptable, the militants now mounted a stepped-up campaign of harassment, threats, and insults of university officials and faculty. During mid-December, about fifty black students staged a sit-in at Perkins' office; they staged a "run" through the clinic; they danced on the tables in the student cafeteria; they disrupted the library stacks; and they overturned furniture in two administration buildings. On February 28, a black student physically removed Perkins from a microphone where he was explaining university policy toward investments in South Africa. At the other end of the stage during the same meeting a black nonstudent was threatening another university official with a 2" x 4" plank of wood. Six members of the AAS were subsequently cited for their conduct on this occasion.[25]

In the meanwhile, President Perkins was rapidly losing his will to stand up to the AAS. On April 10, without any prior consultation whatever with the faculty, Perkins decided to capitulate to the militants. He announced plans for the establishment of an inter-college Center for Afro-American Studies. The AAS would select the director of the Center who in turn would recommend faculty appointments and administer the program generally. The sum of $215,000 was allocated to the Center for the academic year 1969–1970.[26] For the AAS this should have been regarded as total victory, but unbelievably it was not. The militants sensed that they had the university in full retreat before them and that they could probably bring it to its knees. They, therefore, kept up the pressure.

At 6 A.M. on Saturday, April 19, about eighty unarmed members of the AAS moved into Willard Straight Hall on the campus and ordered everyone out. This included about forty employees and thirty parents staying in guest rooms over the weekend. Later during the day, an AAS spokesman announced over the campus radio that the action had been taken because of the university's racist attitude and because the faculty had refused to drop proceedings against the six black students who had been charged in December. In the meanwhile, a considerable number of rifles and shotguns had been brought into Willard Straight Hall.[27] After a good deal of pleading, university officials finally got the militants to agree to negotiate the matter. A settlement was reached at 3:30 P.M. the next day. At 4:10 P.M. 120 members of AAS with guns raised high marched in military fashion out of Willard Straight Hall.[28]

In essence the administration had agreed to recommend to an April 21 faculty meeting that all charges against the six students be dropped and that no action, civil or criminal, be taken against the AAS for occupying Willard Straight Hall. The faculty incidentally had stood by helplessly while the administration had capitulated to the black militants with regard to the Center for Afro-American Studies. Many of them now found this latest surrender utterly impossible to countenance. Thus, the faculty meeting of April 21 was marked by what one professor termed an "incredible hostility" to the administration. "After four hours of bitter debate . . . open jeering and catcalls," the faculty rejected the administration's peace offer to the AAS by a vote of 726 to 281. Frightened and anticipating the worst from the black militants, the administration now called in the police.[29]

On April 22, one hundred well-armed sheriffs and deputy sheriffs from eleven upstate New York counties reported for duty in Ithaca.

The AAS watched these events with rising contempt and anger. At 6 P.M. that evening a militant leader went on the campus radio with the announcement: "Cornell has three hours to live!"[30] He named three professors who had voted against the resolution suggesting that they would be dealt with later. At 8 P.M. the AAS again went on the radio, this time with the statement: "We are moving tonight. Cornell has until 9 to live."[31] For all practical purposes this warning marked the high point of the crisis. During the evening the faculty council met and decided to recommend to a faculty meeting on Wednesday that its action of Monday be reversed. When word of this decision reached the militants, they decided to hold up any action until after the scheduled meeting. On Wednesday, by a voice vote the faculty dropped the charges against the AAS. There was nothing more to concede. The university was now prostrate at the feet of the black militants. It was a situation from which Cornell would ultimately recover, but it was not one that it would soon forget.[32]

By the fall of 1969 the black student organization operating from a headquarters known as the Black, Afro, or Soul House had become a standard feature on predominantly white campuses throughout the country. These were new centers of power, a power that frequently rivaled that of university or college administrative officials. In essence the typical black student union was not a democratically oriented organization. Decision making invariably rested in the hands of a militant clique that evolved policy, programs, strategy, and tactics. The group was politically rather than academically motivated, and it never accepted compromise when it sensed that it could compel capitulation. In a few notable cases black student organizations were beset by power struggles between rival factions. The issue could be ideological with so-called cultural nationalists on one side with the more violence-prone militants on the other. Another possible issue was the control of patronage. Patronage in this case was no mere metaphor. It consisted of Black Studies budgets often running into thousands of dollars, directorships, and administrative and faculty appointments for these programs.

That the fight for control could be deadly was amply demonstrated on the UCLA campus in January, 1969. Beginning in the fall semester of 1968, control of the BSU at UCLA was split between two factions, Ron Karenga's US and the Black Panthers. Karenga's people included Donald Hawkins, Claude Hubert, Harold Jones, and the brothers George and Larry Stiner. Panther members were Captain

John Huggins and Deputy Minister of Defense Alprentice "Bunchy" Carter. Trouble began when the university established an Afro-American Studies Center and asked the BSU for its advice in naming a director. The position paid $20,000 a year. The Karenga group nominated Charles Thomas, then Education Director of the Watts Health Center. The Panthers did not have a candidate of their own, but they, nevertheless, opposed the appointment of Thomas. The impasse continued until January 17 when the BSU convened a meeting to settle the matter once and for all. After lengthy and acrimonious debates the meeting ended with the question still unresolved, but during the postmortem discussions outside of the meeting hall, Huggins and Carter were shot to death. The assassins lost themselves in the crowd. The shooting so outraged the Panthers that, for the first time ever, they became willing assistants to the "pigs." They provided the police with photographs and names of suspected assailants, all members of Karenga's US.[33] Three of Karenga's men were ultimately convicted and sentenced to life imprisonment for the murders.

Viewed as a whole, however, black students showed considerable restraint in their campaigns to establish Black Studies programs on the predominantly white campuses of the nation. In all but a few cases they did not engage in wanton destruction of school property or prolonged disruption of academic routines. And while it might not be entirely accurate to say that black students wanted to reform the universities while the white students were bent upon destruction, the blacks were single-minded enough to resist the embrace of the anarchist faction of the radical white Left. The blacks refused to be used or manipulated—they were determined to "do their own thing." To the militant minority among the black students, the achievement of a Black Studies program represented symbolically the liberation of the black captive nation from its white oppressors.

The Black Studies program on the black campuses was a different kettle of fish. If the white campus was a hostile environment, indeed, enemy territory, the black campus was not; it was a black world. On the other hand, it was not an ideal black world, and it most certainly did not meet the specifications of the Black Liberation movement. For one thing, the academic programs of the black institutions were not much more than replicas of their white counterparts. A few of them claimed a long tradition in teaching the Black Experience, but what they actually taught was "Negro History," and this was both quantitatively and qualitatively different from the broad-based Black Studies programs of the late 1960s. The African Studies programs offered by two or three of these black institutions were not only not part of any program of the Black Experience, but they also were dwarfed by the larger and better-financed African programs of the white institutions.

Militants on the black campuses demanded changes and reforms far more fundamental than Black Studies. What they wanted was a basic restructuring of the *entire* curriculum to make it more relevant to the Black Experience. They wanted innovative instructional and operational techniques in place of moth-eaten methodologies and procedures. If the instructional staff was too hidebound to change its ways, then they should be replaced with paraprofessionals. Indeed, it was the view of some militants that a few years of experience as an SNCC field worker should be considered more important than a Ph.D. for the teaching of the Black Experience. Beyond all this, the militants demanded a positive commitment from the black college to the ideology and objective of Black Liberation.

However, even if they were so inclined (and they were not), the nation's black institutions would have found it difficult if not impossible to respond positively to the militant demands. For one thing, the black institutions could not have afforded it. Professor Tobe Johnson of Morehouse College stated:

> Negro colleges, like the Negro middle class, are for the most part, marginal institutions. . . . Only two Negro colleges—Hampton and Tuskegee—have substantial endowments. Hence the penury of the Negro college is one of the central facts of the black experience in the United States as it relates to higher education. White philanthropy has supported the Negro colleges at the poverty level. Thus the Negro college, in the main, has lived a from hand-to-mouth existence. One unfortunate result is that innovation and experimentation have tended to be seen by many Negro administrators as a risky business.[34]

Secondly, black college administrators recognized, as others did not, that the militant faction on any black campus seldom constituted as much as 10 percent and quite often less than 5 percent of the student body.

In the matter of campus revolutions, most of the students in the black colleges were little more than "summer-time soldiers." Afros and dashikis notwithstanding, the students were middle class in orientation, with a basic objective of finishing school and getting on with the business of getting their share of the gross national product.

Ultimately they, rather than the administrative officials, constituted the chief frustration for the militant faction. A third barrier to Black Liberation on the black campus was the instructional staff, particularly that portion of it that qualified as senior faculty. These academicians were noted for their bourgeois mentality. Beyond this, most of them had been reared in the paternalistic, genteel, missionary tradition of Southern education. They could not abide the "four-letter words," the disrespect for authority, indeed, the "utter barbarism" of the militant students. Committed to working within the system, most of them completely rejected the notion of Black Liberation.

Black Studies did not fare much better with these professors. They regarded the program as the bastard offspring of a liaison between Negro History and the Black Liberation. Nevertheless, after Harvard, Yale, and Columbia universities provided "legitimacy" by their adoption of such programs, black opposition diminished considerably. By the fall of 1969, Black Studies programs had been adopted by such leading black institutions as Howard, Morgan, Tuskegee, Atlanta, Fisk, and Lincoln (Pennsylvania). The programs were not markedly different from those in operation on the white campuses. They consisted principally of the regular curriculum plus a few additional courses in black history, politics, art, religion, and the like. None of them appeared to reflect a genuine, long-term commitment to the teaching of the Black Experience. To be candid, however, this was true also of the majority of the predominantly white institutions. Thus, in its early stages there seemed to be substantial truth in the remark that Black Studies was the first academic field "for which burial was in order before the labor pangs subsided." [35]

While the Yale and San Francisco State programs served as national models for the Black Studies curriculum, there were a few innovative approaches. Most notable among these were Dr. Vincent Harding's ideas for the Black University. For a number of years Dr. Harding served as chairman of the Department of History at Spelman College in Atlanta, Georgia. During this time he was faculty adviser and confidant of a large number of students including many who were involved in the "movement." By the late 1960s Harding, himself, had become prominent as a Black Liberationist. As was true of a handful of other young black intellectuals, Harding rejected the prevailing models and concepts of Black Studies as being totally inadequate to treat the Black Experience. Calling for a different approach, Harding said that in the arts, the humanities, and the study of social organization, research and teaching and writing focused on the peoples of African descent could actually substitute for the total curriculum that exists in most colleges today.

This, in essence, was the Black University. In Harding's view it would be an institution in which the concept of a "Universal Black Man" would replace the traditional one of "Western Man." The institution would be devoted to the task of developing a black humanities and comparative studies of black expression in music, dance, drama, and literature. There would be a reordering of the values, goals, and perspectives of black students so that they could come to understand and celebrate their blackness. In 1969, Harding received an opportunity to move concretely toward his goal. He was appointed Director of the Institute of the Black World, which was then a division of the new Martin Luther King Memorial Center in Atlanta. Under Harding's able guidance, the institute quickly gained prominence as a center for research and the study of Afro-American history and culture. It acquired a staff of instructors and scholars in residence which enabled it to offer lectures and seminars in a variety of black subjects; it developed educational materials on Afro-American history and culture for use in black ghetto schools; and it accepted cooperative arrangements with a half dozen white and black colleges and universities for research in the Black Experience.[36]

In the whole history of higher education in the United States there is nothing to equal the dramatic emergence of Afro-American Studies. Most of the institutions that adopted the program did so out of political expediency rather than the conviction that it was a worthwhile cultural investment. It was everywhere rushed into operation before its ideological and administrative complexities could be resolved. One of the major problems was whether the program should be administered by an autonomous department or by an interdisciplinary, coordinating committee. This question went right to the ideological heart of the matter and brought on some of the ugliest confrontations. The militants insisted that no Black Studies program could have integrity unless it had full autonomy which meant control of admissions, faculty, curriculum, research, and budget. Autonomy further meant that the program would be administered by people who were committed to its success and who would have the mandate to give it first priority over other matters.

The vast majority of the universities and colleges successfully resisted the demand for an autonomous department and gave the program over to multidisciplinary coordinating committees. This was the soundest and most practicable procedure. Black Studies are by nature interdisciplinary and would present hard problems under ordinary circumstances. Under the so-called autonomous department arrangement, the difficulties were bound to be compounded. There was the possibility, even the probability, that the program would be isolated from the more traditional programs and labeled the "black department" and treated with derision and contempt.

The second most important problem for the Black Studies programs was the shortage of competent personnel. The militants demanded that the racial yardstick be applied to the hiring of faculty for these programs. They reasoned that because all blacks, teachers included, had suffered racial oppression and had lived the Black Experience, they would be ready and willing to teach Black Studies from the proper perspective. This proved to be both a superficial and fallacious assumption. As Professor Johnson observed: "The overwhelming proportion of Afro-American teaching at colleges and universities in the United States fit the bourgeois model described by [E. Franklin] Frazier rather than the activist model of revisionist black intellectuals." Johnson concluded that these bourgeois blacks would find it "as difficult to analyze and explain social phenomena from a black perspective" as would white professors.[37]

But there was even more to this problem. Black professors could not be persuaded to take employment in Black Studies programs even when offered salaries and fringe benefits much beyond that which they had been accustomed to receive. There were several reasons. On. many of the predominantly white campuses the Black Studies director amounted to little more than the administration's "head nigger." His major tasks were often that of running interference for frightened white officials or keeping the peace among unruly and potentially dangerous campus black militants. The role could be dangerous and demeaning, and most of the black academicians refused it. On the other hand, there was the black institution's demand upon the "loyalty" of the black professor. Traditionally the black college was perceived by black people to be more than a mere educational institution. It was viewed, and rightly so, as the main mechanism for racial uplift and advancement, and the black faculty was vital to its continued existence. To switch to a white institution, no matter how attractive the inducement, smacked of desertion. The white institutions were able to recruit a number of unattached black scholars in addition to a number of marginal black instructors, but the much discussed "brain drain" from the black institutions never materialized.

Another serious problem raised in the Black Studies programs was the demand on the part of black student groups that white students be excluded from the programs. At Antioch College during the summer of 1968, the black student union induced the administration to establish an autonomous Afro-American Studies Institute. This included a black student center called Unity House plus the right on the part of the blacks to exclude white students from the total program. A black student offered the rationalization: "For a white student to be in any of these sessions would only blunt the knife, and inhibit fundamental emotions from being expressed."[38] However, the "blacks only" regulation was quickly to bring the federal government into the picture. Title VI of the Civil Rights Act of 1964 prohibits discrimination in schools receiving federal funds, and these funds constituted about 20 percent of Antioch's operating budget. When investigators from the Department of Health, Education and Welfare visited the campus, Antioch officials insisted that a white student could not be excluded because of his race, but he could be excluded because his background was not relevant to special courses which in this case were Afro-American Studies. To the surprise of many observers, including some black Antioch students, HEW accepted this explanation and subsequently gave its approval to the exclusion. One HEW official explained it as "The black students . . . doing their thing under an open policy."[39]

The public reaction to the HEW ruling was swift and angry. In an editorial, the *New York Times* stated: ". . . the decision places the Federal Government in the dangerous role of aiding and abetting a new chapter in academic Jim Crow policies."[40] The eminent black psychologist Dr. Kenneth B. Clark, a member of the Antioch board of trustees, drew national attention with his letter of resignation from that body. Stung by this criticism, the Antioch board of trustees reconsidered its policies. In January, 1970, the president of the college announced that Unity House had been closed down "by mutual agreement of the college community, Negro students and the Antioch's board of trustees."[41] The Antioch action brought an end to the movement to exclude white students from Black Studies programs. If nothing else, it was impracticable. If white students generally had no desire to live in campus "Soul Houses," many of them did have a genuine interest in Afro-American history and culture. Indeed, by the end of 1970, on a growing number of campuses throughout the country the number of white students in these courses was equal to if not greater than that of blacks.

Beyond the ideological and administrative problems posed by Black Studies, colleges and universities had to contend with the formidable task of funding these programs. It was a standing joke that black student organizations had worked out every detail of the Black Studies programs except that of paying for them. The cost of these programs varied from a few thousand to as much as one-half million dollars. Some of the small, private liberal arts colleges had no clearer idea of how to raise the money than did the black student organizations. During the earlier years of the movement the foundations provided assistance to a selected number of institutions. The Ford Foundation, for instance, provided "seed money" for Black Studies to upwards of fifteen colleges and universities. After 1970, the foundation apparently decided to confine its support to graduate level activities in Afro-American Studies. The Danforth Foundation also took a serious interest in Black Studies. In 1969 the foundation established a program of postgraduate Black Studies fellowships designed to provide a year of study at a major university for instructors who were key personnel in Black Studies programs at their own institutions.[42] Both the Ford and Danforth foundations foresaw that for a long period of time the most critical need of the Afro-American Studies programs would be that of competent and trained instructors. In concentrating their assistance on study at the graduate level, they were addressing themselves to this problem.

By the fall of 1971 Black Studies departments and programs were no longer becoming political bases and cadre training grounds for the Black Liberation. The militants were no longer in the ascendancy. Their efforts at intimidating and politicizing black students were meeting with increased resistance, with the result that they were losing their control of black student organizations. On the other hand, Afro-American Studies on the high school, college, and university levels were steadily coming under the control of instructors and administrators both black and white who were genuinely committed and who were determined to establish the discipline as a standard facet of American education. There still remained a good deal to be done, but McGeorge Bundy spoke to this point when he said of Afro-American Studies: "It seems to me dead right to have come this far—and dead wrong to suppose that there is no rough country ahead." [43]

CHAPTER 11

Black Politics and the Black Center City

When Stokely Carmichael set up shop in Lowndes County, Alabama, in March, 1965, not a single local black was registered to vote. Though they constituted 81 percent of the population, blacks had been crippled by fear and apathy extending back to the post-Reconstruction period. Most of them would not even discuss voting. The SNCC activists mounted an intensive voter-education drive in March, but by August, Carmichael was complaining that not more than "fifty to sixty black citizens made their way to the courthouse to register and successfully passed the registration 'test'." [1] Lowndes County was of course typical of a large number of areas in the Deep South, but the whole picture was to change abruptly and dramatically during the first week of August, 1965.

On Friday, August 6, President Lyndon Johnson signed the Federal Voting Rights Act and by Monday morning, August 9, federal examiners had been dispatched to nine hard-core segregationist counties in Alabama, Louisiana, and Mississippi. By the end of the week these examiners were registering as many as eighty-two blacks a day in Lowndes County itself. Carmichael stated: "No longer did a black man face literacy tests or absurdly difficult questions about the Constitution or such tactics as rejection because a 't' was not properly crossed or an 'i' inadequately dotted. The voting rolls swelled by the hundreds." [2] Carmichael moved quickly to organize the new black registrants. In truth, therefore, it was "federal power" (federal examiners) rather than black power which enabled Carmichael in 1966 to build his Lowndes County Freedom Organization with the Black Panther symbol.

The Federal Voting Rights Act of 1965 was a revolutionary piece of legislation. Unlike the Civil Rights Acts of 1957, 1960, and 1964, this law provided for *direct* federal intervention to enable blacks to register and vote. There was no longer any need to resort to the courts and to engage in protracted litigation. The act also suspended literacy tests and other discriminatory requirements in the six Southern states of Alabama, Georgia, Louisiana, South Carolina, Mississippi, and Virginia. During the first year of the operation of the law no federal examiners were sent into Georgia and Virginia. Georgia's exemption was attributed in part to the immense power and influence of her senior United States Senator Richard B. Russell. By the beginning of 1967, however, federal examiners were working in all six of the designated states. Almost everywhere the examiners encountered devices and practices, some dating from Reconstruction, designed to prevent blacks from participating in the political process. These included the omission of the names of registered blacks from the voter lists, the refusal to render any assistance to illiterate black voters, the failure to provide blacks with the opportunity to cast absentee ballots, and the tendency to disqualify black ballots on flimsy and technical grounds. Blacks were almost universally excluded from precinct meetings and county and state conventions.

With their number steadily increasing after August, 1965, it was inevitable that the newly enfranchised blacks would begin to think of electing blacks to local public offices. Local white politicians anticipated this and moved quickly to head it off. Thus in July, 1965, a month before enactment of the Voting Rights Act of 1965, whites in Bullock County, Alabama, introduced local legislation to increase the term of office of county commissioners by two years. The law was passed by the Alabama legislature and signed by the governor just two weeks after the Voting Rights Act went into effect.[3] In other localities the stratagems included changing the law to make formerly elective office appointive, increasing filing fees, stiffening requirements for getting on the ballot, and even abolishing the office itself. And if after all of these difficulties a black was successful in getting himself elected, the state might, as in the case of Mississippi, make it virtually impossible for him to obtain the bonding required of all officials before they are sworn into office.[4]

With all their stratagems, however, the whites proved unable to prevent the mass enfranchisement of blacks. In order to keep themselves from being overwhelmed at the polls in black belt areas, the whites finally turned to measures designed to dilute or reduce the effectiveness of this vote. One of these involved the switching of an election from a ward to an at-large basis in counties with heavy black registrations. Early in 1966, Mississippi thus changed six such counties without giving them the benefit of referenda. Alabama did likewise in at least two of its counties. Main reliance, however, was placed upon the ancient device of the gerrymander. During the earlier part of the century it proved to be an effective means of fracturing the new black vote in the Northern urban areas. In the fall of 1965, Alabama employed the gerrymander against blacks when it combined black Macon County with white Elmore and Tallapoosa counties into a single legislative election district with the stipulation that representatives thereof be elected by a majority vote on a district-wide basis. In 1966, Mississippi cut up a solid block of nine black Delta counties and distributed them among three congressional districts where they would become mere appendages to white majorities.[5]

Under Section 5 of the Voting Rights Act, the six states or their political subdivisions are required to submit all new or revised election codes to the United States Attorney General or to the United States District Court for the District of Columbia for a determination that such codes or plans do not have the purpose or effect of denying or abridging the right to vote on account of race or color. However, during the early years of the Voting Rights Act the six states quite generally ignored the requirements of Section 5. A 1968 Civil Rights Commission report stated that "there have been many laws affecting voting procedures which have not been submitted."[6] The office of the Attorney General could have availed itself of Section 12D of the Act and brought suit to prevent the implementation of these procedures, but it generally neglected to do so. It was apparently willing to rely upon private civil rights organizations to act in these cases. The fact is that the fierce hostility of Southern whites had made the Voting Rights Act a difficult law to enforce, and the federal government was welcoming all the help it could get.

In the matter of voter registration, for instance, Attorney General Nicholas Katzenbach made the point that while federal examiners were necessary, they were not the crucial factor:

> Counties which have seen extensive Negro registration, whether by local officials or by federal examiners, are counties in which registration campaigns have been conducted. In counties without such campaigns, even the presence of examiners has been of limited gain.[7]

The registration campaigns Katzenbach alludes to were conducted principally by the Voter Education Project. As we have noted, the VEP was inaugurated by the Southern Regional Council in 1962. (See chapter 4.) Initially its purpose was to inquire and conduct research into the causes and remedies of the abnormally low black registration in the South; however, its main focus was soon switched to the actual task of registering the region's voteless black population. Under its first director, Wiley Branton, the VEP persuaded the five major black "rights" groups to abandon their independent efforts and to work jointly as the Council of Federated Organizations (COFO). Funded and directed by the VEP, COFO was directly responsible for the registration of nearly 700,000 new black voters between 1962 and 1964.

The first VEP came to an end in 1964 with no plans for the immediate future. However, with the passage of the Voting Rights Act a second effort was launched in 1966 under a new director, Vernon E. Jordan. The new VEP evolved a brand new set of techniques and approaches. Instead of relying upon a few black organizations to do the main job, the organization searched out and encouraged local black leaders to conduct the drives. It funded registration campaigns in dozens of black communities, and it sent along paid field workers to provide the necessary guidance and assistance. Most important, the new VEP became something of a pilot and/or sustaining agency for the Civil Rights Commission in its efforts to enforce the Voting Rights Act. Between 1965 and 1970, these two organizations working in tandem put almost a million blacks on the registration rolls in the Deep South. The number of blacks holding elective office rose from fewer than one hundred in 1965 to well over six hundred in 1970. These included mayors, state senators and representatives, city councilmen, county officials, law enforcement officers, and school-board members. However, these gains were not uniform throughout the region. In deep black belt areas the legacy of the past still tended to inhibit the growth of political activity among blacks. After the poor showing of black candidates in the 1971 local and state elections in Mississippi, a local newspaper commented:

> The election, in our view, proves that an historic relationship of paternalism of the whites for blacks still exists in Mississippi; that the blacks still look upon the whites for leadership, for guidance, for favors, for loans, for friendship.[8]

The new black political power reached its greatest potential in the urban areas of the South. People in the cities and towns were, of course, easier to register and to mobilize into political action. In Atlanta, which had become the bellwether of the urban South, less than 30 percent of the eligible blacks were registered to vote in 1960. By 1969, however, this figure had shot up to 65 percent. Paralleling this, the proportion of blacks in the city's *total* registration increased from 29 percent in 1960 to almost 41 percent in 1969. From the mid-1950s through 1968, the black vote functioned as part of a city-wide coalition, which included middle-class whites, the Jewish population, and the intellectual community. Opposing this group were most of the city's lower income and predominantly "redneck" whites. The dominant influence in the coalition was wielded by the middle-class whites. They provided the money and they selected the main or city-wide candidates. The blacks invariably followed their leadership. For more than twenty years this coalition provided the city of Atlanta with its governing officials and political leadership.

In 1969, however, this arrangement was abruptly terminated. A new generation of young and highly sophisticated black leaders arrived on the scene with new ideas. They insisted that with blacks constituting 50 percent of the city's population and over 40 percent of its registered voters existing political arrangements had become inequitable and obsolete. They called upon blacks to abandon their junior-partner role in the coalition, indeed, to abandon the coalition altogether. Self-determination was to become the new political path for the city's black population. The influence of the new leadership was clearly demonstrated in the municipal elections of 1969. The black community politely but firmly rejected the "establishment" choice for mayor; it cast the decisive vote for a black vice-mayor, two black members of the Board of Education, and four black members of the City Council.[9]

Unlike some Northern cities the breakup of the coalition in Atlanta did not result in the freezing of the city along hard racial lines. For one thing the whites did not react to black self-determination by forming an anti-black alignment. Black candidates received considerable and even decisive white support during the 1969 elections. On the other hand, blacks passed up the possibility of electing a black mayor during the same election. Black unity and black independence were desirable goals, but the blacks considered "black control" of the city to be of questionable value. Dr. Vivian Henderson, a leading member of the community, insisted that blacks must have control of their own culture, educational, and business institutions, but he warned that "blacks simply don't have economic muscle to keep Atlanta viable if the city becomes all black."[10] (In 1973 a black man, Maynard Jackson, was elected mayor of Atlanta.)

At a meeting of the Institute for Black Elected Officials held in Washington, D.C., in September, 1969, Mayor Richard G. Hatcher of

Gary, Indiana, recalled his first few days in that office:

> By attitude, temperament, experience and age, I assumed the office of Mayor as a kind of black militant, whatever meaning can be accorded that amorphous term. Previously as a councilman I had been an irritant to the Establishment, earning its enmity, but along with it enough confidence of black people to win the Mayor's seat. I see now that I did so with a few illusions. . . . Black political power is essential but in and of itself it is not enough.[11]

It is very probable that these same disillusionments were experienced by Carl Stokes in Cleveland, Kenneth Gibson in Newark, and a score of other blacks across the nation. These men were not only black mayors, but they were mayors of so-called "black cities." As such they were caught up in situations for which there were few guidelines and no models. They were in fact operating upon a new sociopolitical frontier.

The black city was the end product of some fifty years of demographic shifting and change within urban America. From 1910 through the mid-1920s upwards of a million marginal blacks came up out of the Deep South to settle in the Northern metropolises. These first migrants established the black ghettos in New York City, Newark, Philadelphia, Washington, D.C., Chicago, Cleveland, and other cities. The in-migration continued through the next two decades albeit on a much reduced scale. However, during and immediately following World War II, events were conspiring in the Deep South to precipitate a second and even greater migration. These included the wholesale displacement of sharecroppers and tenant farmers brought on by the rapid mechanization of cotton, the almost total exclusion of blacks from employment in new Southern industrial plants, low welfare payments as compared with the North, and the availability of employment opportunities for unskilled labor in the North. The result was fairly predictable.

During the ten-year period between 1950 and 1960 nearly two million Southern blacks moved into the nation's twelve largest non-Southern cities. The already overcrowded black ghettos began an almost irreversible expansion in all directions within the city. During the same ten-year period almost two million middle-class whites fled these cities to the suburbs. As long as they had held their ground in the cities, they constituted a middle ground between the blacks and the lower-class whites.[12] As they left, however, a situation of polarized confrontation developed. Long-existing and patiently developed interracial contacts were broken off. Scores of cities around the country became armed camps of nervous black and white citizens. White communities were particularly edgy. In Cleveland, Ohio, for instance, an Italian-American neighborhood set up an "ingenious" alarm system that alerted every house that "the colored are coming" as soon as a black crossed the neighborhood bridge. The local "minute man" organization vowed that "Not one of them will get out of here alive." [13]

In the area of politics the emergence of the so-called black central city signaled the end of the old Democratic coalition in urban America. Put together during the Great Depression by Franklin D. Roosevelt, the coalition was a political amalgam of middle-class whites, blacks, and working class, ethnic whites. For more than thirty years the coalition constituted the backbone of the Democratic party. In the big cities it made the Party almost invincible. During the early 1950s, however, the coalition began to suffer from the defection of middle-class whites. Between 1952 and 1968, the vote in the suburbs rose 37 percent while that in the center cities dropped by 21 percent. Indeed by 1968, the suburbs had surpassed the cities in voting power. During the national elections of that year the total vote cast in the suburbs of the nation's twelve largest non-Southern cities was 8,591,000 as compared to 8,112,000 for the cities themselves. Moreover, reapportionment had given the suburbs electoral power commensurate with the size of their vote.[14] They sent twenty additional representatives to the House in the Ninetieth Congress. And compounding the damage to the Democratic party, eighteen of these new congressmen were Republicans.

The working class or "ethnic" whites who remained in the center cities continued to vote Democratic in national elections but in decreased proportions. In 1968, the Democratic party received 28 percent, or 12,000,000, fewer votes than it did in 1964. The urban ethnics constituted a considerable proportion of this bloc. In local and state elections the ethnic defection from the coalition frequently became wholesale. So-called liberal white candidates had little or no chance of attracting the support of this group. After 1967 this vote invariably went to the "law-and-order" candidates. If there was no such candidate in the running, the ethnics voted Republican as the next best thing. In the final analysis the blacks were the only group to stick with the old coalition throughout its more than thirty years of existence. Psychologically some of the older ones were still voting for Franklin D. Roosevelt. Even so there were occasional and temporary defections. In New York, for instance, the blacks unfailingly supported the Republican John Lindsay in his successful campaigns for mayor. And while they might prefer not to be reminded of it, blacks in Baltimore in 1966 went all out for Spiro Agnew as governor of Maryland in order to defeat a law-and-order Democrat, George Mahoney.[15]

As the black population of the center cities continued to grow, urban blacks began to look toward the election of black candidates, with less attention going to party labels or the coalition. Indeed, the coalition was increasingly coming under the attack of black dissidents and militants. Stokely Carmichael, while acknowledging the necessity of coalitions in a pluralistic society, questioned their value for blacks. He felt that too often such coalitions followed objectives set by others. Rather, Carmichael argued:

> Let black people organize themselves *first*, define their interests and goals, and then see what kinds of allies are available. Let any ghetto group contemplating coalition be so tightly organized, so strong that—in the words of Saul Alinsky— it is an "indigestible body" which cannot be absorbed or swallowed up.[16]

In truth, however, Carmichael, as most black revolutionists, was opposed to any black participation in any coalition with whites for any purpose whatever. Instead, blacks were to use their political power to rout the whites and seize control of the city. The "liberated city" became the militant cry.

As loud and persistent as it was, however, militant rhetoric had but a secondary influence upon black political behavior during the 1960s. The results would very probably have been the same without it. Since emancipation, blacks have seldom passed up the opportunity of electing members of their own race when there was a reasonable chance to do so. Not only does the Reconstruction period provide testimony to this, but also in the first half of this century black electorates in Illinois, New York, and Michigan have sent numerous members of the race to city councils and state legislatures. The black bloc vote antedates the black revolution by more than a half century. The elections of Carl Stokes, Richard Hatcher, and Kenneth Gibson, therefore, owed far less to militant rhetoric than to the ancient pride in race achievement. Besides, the militants as a whole seldom bothered to register and vote.

Up until the mid-1960s the blacks in Cleveland, Ohio, remained an integral part of the local Democratic coalition. Since Frank Lausche's days they had not been very enthusiastic about the local Democratic machine, but they could still count upon it for needed small favors plus some local and state employment. Anyway, the blacks who in 1955 constituted less than 17 percent of the total population considered the city a fairly good place in which to live. Like the whites they subscribed to the slogan that Cleveland was the "best location in the nation." By 1965, however, the local situation had changed drastically—Cleveland was well on its way toward becoming a black city. The black population had shot up to 279,000 or 40 percent of the total. The white flight, on the other hand, was accelerating—more than 100,000 of them leaving during the five-year period 1960–1965. The city's credit rating in the meanwhile was slipping; its crime rate was spiraling; and its ghetto was bursting at the seams.[17]

During the local elections of 1965 black leaders decided that the time had come to buck the local coalition. The immediate objective was the defeat of a racist, Mayor Ralph S. Locher, who was running for reelection on the Democratic ticket. Blacks were preparing to support one of Locher's opponents, Mark Elroy, who also was white. The picture changed completely, however, when the attractive, young, and black Carl B. Stokes made his decision to enter the mayoralty race. Then serving in the state's House of Representatives, Stokes decided to avail himself of a city-charter provision which allowed for a candidate to file as an independent and bypass the partisan primaries. With a black candidate now in the race, black leaders moved to organize a black bloc vote. The strategy was to eliminate Locher in the primaries and then to defeat Elroy and the Republican candidate in the general election. For this election, however, the city's ethnic bloc plus the remnants of the white middle class stayed with the local Democrats.[18] Locher took the Democratic primary election and went on to beat the field in the general election. His margin over Stokes, the runner-up, was 2,110 votes.

Two years later, in 1967, Stokes decided to try again. This time, however, he had to enter the Democratic primaries. Seth Taft, the young and attractive Republican nominee, warned Stokes that he would withdraw from the race entirely if Stokes skipped the primaries for the general election. Taft saw no chance in winning a three-man race which included Stokes with his black bloc vote and Locher with his ethnics. The Democratic primary would eliminate one of these. Stokes, for his part, concluded that it would be best to eliminate Locher in the primaries and go on to face Taft alone in the general elections. With the matter thus settled, the Stokes organization with the help of Martin Luther King and his SCLC mounted a massive registration campaign in the black community. Stokes then carried his campaign into the city's white wards where he had received only 3 percent of the vote in 1965. His reception was not overly enthusiastic, but neither was he run out of the community. Not a militant, Stokes discussed the race issue on its merits. His campaign received a shot in the arm when the city's largest newspaper, the *Plain Dealer*, endorsed him. The *Cleveland Press* gave him limited support when it called for a change in the City Hall. In the Democratic primary election, Stokes received some 52 percent of the vote for a plurality of 18,000 over Locher. The third man, Frank P. Celeste, received a mere 4 percent of the vote, a low point in the city's election history. Stokes received approximately 16,000 votes in the white community. Blacks constituted only 40 percent of the registered vote, but 73 percent turned out in the election as compared with only 58 percent for the whites.[19]

Seth Taft, the Republican candidate for mayor in the general election, was neither a bigot nor a racist. He was the nephew of a distinguished United States Senator, Robert A. Taft, and a grandson of the even more distinguished President William Howard Taft. To win against Stokes, the young Taft would have to garner the bulk of the city's ethnic backlash vote. Of the 326,000 registered voters in the city only 10 percent, or 34,000, were Republicans. Stokes, on the other hand, went into the election with 90,000 black votes virtually in his pocket. As the campaign moved into high gear, he picked up the support of the AFL–CIO in addition to the unqualified endorsement of both the *Plain Dealer* and the *Cleveland Press*. Stokes was an attractive, exciting candidate. He was relatively uninhibited, self-confident, and indefatigable in his campaigning.

This campaign was Seth Taft's maiden effort, but what he lacked in experience he more than made up for in hard work. To offset his image of Ivy League aloofness, he undertook a rigorous campaign of handshaking and personal appearances in every corner of the city. His campaign staff made upwards of 200,000 personal telephone calls to voters in an attempt to close the gap. On the day of the election some 257,000 voters went to the polls. Returns indicated that the vote was almost split down the middle. Stokes emerged with a plurality of a little better than 2,500. As expected, he carried close to 100 percent of the black vote. The surprise was, however, that he received some 30,000 white votes, twice the number he had gotten in the primary.[20] The old coalition was on its last legs, but a good deal of its spirit was still around. In the meanwhile Cleveland had become the first major city in the nation to elect a black mayor.

While blacks were toasting Carl Stokes in Cleveland, an almost identical celebration was being staged in a city some three hundred miles to the west. Gary, Indiana, on November 7, had also elected the first black mayor in its history. Less than one-third the size of Cleveland, Gary's recent racial and political history had closely paralleled that of the larger city. For more than thirty years the local Democratic coalition had functioned like the well-oiled machine that it was. Race relations in the city were good. Blacks and ethnics worked side by side in the plants of the United States Steel Corporation and on election day went out to vote the straight Democratic ticket. Like most other Northern cities, conditions in Gary remained fairly stable until the mid-1950s, that is, until the black in-migration began to accelerate. Between 1950 and 1965 the city's black population increased from 38,000 to 85,000. And with the white middle class fleeing helter-skelter to the suburbs, Gary quickly joined the ranks of American cities whose population was split down the middle with ethnics on one side and blacks on the other.

In 1967, there were 45,000 blacks and almost an identical number of white registered voters in Gary. Studying these figures very carefully a bright young black lawyer, Richard G. Hatcher, decided to run for mayor of the town. Like Stokes over in Cleveland, he was counting on a modicum of support in the white wards. The first hurdle was the city's Democratic primary which was held on May 2, 1967. In that contest Hatcher took on A. Martin Katz, the incumbent mayor of Gary, and a second candidate, Bernard Konrady. Out of the 50,595 votes cast in the election, Hatcher received 20,272 as against 17,190 for Katz and 13,133 for Konrady. Hatcher and his supporters now hoped that the local and county Democratic organizations would rally behind him if only to defeat the Republican candidate in the general election. But this was not to be.

In an attempt to win the war though having lost the battle, the white Democratic leaders made their support of Hatcher conditional upon his agreement to allow the machine to appoint his police chief, fire chief, comptroller, and other key officials. When Hatcher refused, the white Democratic leaders virtually read him out of the Party. John G. Krupa, chairman of the Party's county committee, explained that Hatcher "was not the 'right kind' of Negro." He promised to "groom" one for mayor after Hatcher was defeated.[21] For the next several months Hatcher was denounced as a stooge for black militant and left-wing revolutionary groups. Krupa and others called upon Hatcher to repudiate publicly H. Rap Brown and Stokely Carmichael. Hatcher answered simply that he opposed the advocacy of violence by anyone.

As the election approached, evidence mounted that the Democratic election officials were planning to resort to fraud in their determination to defeat Hatcher. On the basis of suits brought by Hatcher as well as by the U. S. Department of Justice, a special three-judge court ordered the election officials to strike from the election rolls some 1,039 names found to be fictitious. It also ordered the restoration to the rolls of 5,000 black ghetto residents whom election officials had declared ineligible. On the eve of the election, tension in the city became so great that Governor Roger B. Branigan called out the National Guard to "drill" in locations near the city. With it all, however, Hatcher emerged victorious. He received a total of 39,330 votes to 37,941 for his Republican opponent, Joseph B. Radigan. The margin of victory was small, but the black bloc vote was the all important factor.[22]

On May 9, 1966, election returns in Newark, New Jersey, indicated that Hugh D. Addonizio in his bid for reelection as mayor had failed to get the required majority of the total vote and would, therefore, have to go into a runoff contest. Running against Addonizio were Leo P. Carlin, a former mayor of the city, and Kenneth A. Gibson, a relatively obscure black civil engineer. Addonizio went on to win the runoff election, but there were numerous indications that the next contest would find him in even more serious trouble. For one thing, Gibson, in the runoff, had taken almost half the black vote, and there was every reason to believe that on the next go-around he would receive all or almost all of it.

In 1960, Newark's nonwhite population stood at 34 percent of the total. During the ensuing decade the in-migration of blacks and Puerto Ricans helped drive it up to 70 percent. The white flight, which moved at a steady pace until 1967, became a mad rush during the months following the "July rebellion." Entire blocks in the white neighborhoods became depopulated almost overnight. The "old Newark" was fast disappearing. LeRoi Jones thus describes the changes:

> Downtown is a ghost town after 5 because the Crackers live off somewhere WestOrange-SouthOrange-Teaneck-Montclair-Bloomfield-Maplewood, &c.&c.&c.,

a hundred suburbs dripping with money taken out of Newark. And the downtown's for white people in daylight, long gone by fingerpoppin night.[23]

The old coalition which had bound the Italians, the blacks, and the Irish to the local Democratic machine had begun to crack during the election of 1966. It collapsed completely by 1968 at which time the black city was to include more than half of Newark's precincts. Black leaders in the meanwhile began to prepare to come into political control of the city. On November 14, 1969, a Black and Puerto Rican Convention, attended by more than a thousand delegates, "nominated" Gibson to run for mayor in the 1970 primary elections. The delegates made it clear that they wanted a candidate who could unify the nonwhite community. Money for Gibson's campaign was to be raised by the Newark Fund, a group organized by LeRoi Jones. Addonizio and the Italian-American leadership were extremely concerned over the breakup of the Democratic coalition. They had hoped to hold at least half of the black vote for the 1970 election and thus stave off disaster until 1974. What worried them even more, however, was the trouble that Addonizio and others of their group were getting into with the United States government. In December, 1969, federal indictments were handed up charging Addonizio and fourteen others with extorting a total of $253,000 from a construction firm that did business with the city.[24] Addonizio feared that this action might cost him some support among the non-Italian whites.

Aside from Gibson and Addonizio there were five other candidates running for mayor of Newark in the May 12, 1970, city primary elections. They were John P. Canfield who had previously been fired from his post as fire chief by Addonizio; Anthony Imperiale, a leading militant Italian-American for law and order; state Senator Alexander Matturi, a nonmilitant Italian; George C. Richardson, a black state assemblyman; and Harry L. Wheeler, a black former schoolteacher. Out of the 88,000 votes cast in the primary Gibson received 37,666 as against 17,925 for the incumbent Addonizio. The three other white candidates shared some 30,000 votes, with the two black candidates totaling 2,000. Gibson did not pull the majority vote needed to win the office, but his 43 percent of the total made him an odds-on favorite to win the runoff. The end was now in sight for Addonizio and his regime. Not only did the black vote appear irretrievably lost, but the non-Italian white populace of Newark was becoming increasingly hostile.

Addonizio's trial on the extortion charges began in the federal courts at the beginning of June. During the month between elections he would have to face criminal charges during the day and devote a good part of each night denying them. In desperation, Addonizio, like Krupa in Gary, turned to the politics of polarization. The strategy was to whip up anti-black sentiment among the already frightened and panicky whites. LeRoi Jones was portrayed as the sinister mastermind behind a black plot to take over Newark, after which there would be looting, raping of white women, pillaging, and murder.[25] Gibson, like Hatcher and Stokes in their campaigns, attempted to soft-pedal the race issue. He was aware that seven out of every nine voters, black or white, had voted against Addonizio. There was also the fact that John P. Canfield, the dismissed fire chief, was campaigning vigorously among the Irish in his behalf. Logic therefore dictated that, with the black bloc vote secured, he work to attract sufficient white votes to give him his needed majority.

As the returns came in from the runoff election, Gibson's strategy was proved to be the correct one. He received 54,892 votes as against 43,339 for Addonizio. Gibson's jubilation was matched by Addonizio's despair. This had been his "last hurrah." After having served fourteen years as a congressman and two terms as mayor, he had now not only been repudiated at the polls but was facing the possibility of being sentenced to a term in a federal penitentiary. Gibson's 11,000 vote margin was provided by the middle-class Irish who were turned off by Addonizio's black "bogeyman" rhetoric and who were also bent upon settling a political grudge that dated from 1962 when Addonizio and his fellow Italians knocked the ruling Irish out of City Hall. At any rate, Newark had now become a black city complete with a black political administration. Addressing the victory crowd, the Reverend Jesse Jackson declared: "What you saw here three years ago [referring to the Newark riot] were people running from genocide to suicide. What you see now is people talking about a tomorrow which we are going to control."[26]

As of February, 1970, black mayors presided over forty-seven municipalities in the United States. Even before 1970, however, there was every indication that the black mayors and the black center cities over which they presided were in deep trouble. Aside from their fiscal problems resulting principally from rapidly diminishing tax revenue, there appeared to be definite moves afoot to dilute and/or to restrict the autonomy of these municipalities. The business interests and white residents remaining in these cities invariably have proposed the annexation of adjacent territory ostensibly as a means of broadening the tax base but also with an eye on diluting the power of the black electorate. With few exceptions these proposals have been scuttled either by referenda which vote them down, or by the combined pressure of the white suburbanites and black political leaders who want no diminution of their power base.

It seems, however, that what cannot be accomplished by local authorities will be brought about by federal intervention. As some observers perceive it, federal agencies are beginning to compel municipalities to subordinate themselves to new regional-planning bureaucracies. Those that hesitate to establish "cross-jurisdictional agencies" will find it increasingly difficult to obtain federal grants-in-aid. What is emerging here is a new power—metropolitan or regional government. Francis F. Piven and Richard A. Cloward have pointed out that if such federally· sponsored attempts to establish metropolitan government succeed, blacks will suffer because the use of urban redevelopment to suit the commercial needs and professional interests in the center city will continue.

Another objective appears to be the imposition of a social quarantine around the black center city. The black blight is not to be allowed to spill over into the surrounding white suburban areas. Metropolitan government will, of course, maintain programs within the black center city. There will be minimal building of low-cost housing, housing rehabilitation, expanded educational programs, and beefed-up social services. In short, the emphasis will be placed on "human renewal" rather than dispersal. The question that suggests itself here is: "What is the attitude, the plans of the black community, toward this encroachment by metropolitan government?" The answer, up to now, seems to be that the black leadership has been concentrating on other things and is dimly if at all aware of the new challenge. There are pitifully few blacks seated with metropolitan or regional councils, and metropolitan government is almost never included on the agenda of local meetings in the black community.

To be utterly candid, much of the new black political leadership appears to be cripplingly myopic. In its frantic desire to maintain itself in power, it often mistakes form for substance. The net result is that the long-range interests of the black community are invariably neglected.[27]

By the beginning of 1969 there were upwards of 1,200 black elected officials in the nation ranging from justice of the peace to United

States senator. In more than a dozen states these officials were numerous enough to organize themselves into so-called "black caucuses" and leadership conferences. With so many state and local groups springing up, it was inevitable that they would come together in a national organization. The idea for such an amalgam originated with Dr. Kenneth B. Clark. In September, 1969, Clark got his agency, the Metropolitan Applied Research Center, to join with several other organizations in sponsoring a conference of black elected officials in Washington, D.C. In Dr. Clark's view the chief objectives of such a conclave would be "to make the black officeholder more effective in dealing with the complex and diverse problems facing him in his job."[28] During its four-day conference the group adopted the name "The Institute for Black Elected Officials." Four cochairmen were elected. They were Woodrow Wilson, a Nevada state assemblyman; Louise Reynolds, a Louisville, Kentucky, alderman; Percy Sutton, borough president of Manhattan; and state Senator Mervyn Dymally of Los Angeles.[29]

During the fall of 1970, with its membership reaching almost 2,000 the Institute decided to establish itself on a more permanent basis. It created a formal administrative structure including a new seven-member steering committee, and it changed its name to the National Black Caucus of Local Elected Officials. While a significant percentage of the new organization was comprised of state officials, its basic orientation was municipal. Indeed, the first two annual meetings of the N.B.C.L.E.O., 1970 and 1971, were held in conjunction with those of the National League of Cities. As "black cities" in the nation continued to proliferate, there was the distinct possibility that both organizations would be dominated by black officials.[30]

During the decade of the 1960s black membership in the United States Congress slowly but steadily increased. In 1962 Edward W. Brooke was elected to the Senate from the state of Massachusetts. Of the black delegation in the House, newer members included Augustus Hawkins of California, Robert Nix of Pennsylvania, and John Conyers of Michigan. The black veterans in the House were William L. Dawson of Illinois, Charles Diggs of Michigan, and Adam Clayton Powell of New York. Powell was far and away the best-known black member of Congress.

Powell first came to public attention in New York City during the mid-1930s. As a young black militant he led demonstrations and boycotts against department stores, public utilities, hotels, and the public transportation system, forcing all of them to hire their first black employees. In 1941, Powell was elected to New York's City Council, receiving the third highest vote ever cast for a candidate in city elections. During the next few years, Powell busied himself as a city councilman, as pastor of the big Abyssinia Baptist Church, and as a leader of Harlem's young black militants. In 1945 he was elected to Congress from Central Harlem, a district of some 300,000 people 90 percent of whom were black. He was the first black congressman from the East.

Carrying his militancy into the United States House of Representatives, Powell engaged in heated debates with Southern segregationists. In what was to become known as the "Powell Amendment," he sought consistently to deny federal funds to any project which allowed segregation and discrimination. As he grew in seniority, Powell fought to get black newsmen admitted to the House and Senate press galleries, and he introduced legislation outlawing segregation in interstate commerce. In 1956, Powell supported the Republican presidential candidate, Dwight D. Eisenhower. He insisted that he was protesting control of the Democratic party by Southern racists and demagogues. Post-election attempts to punish him for his defection failed, and Powell retained his seniority. By 1960, Powell had moved up to become chairman of the House Committee on Education and Labor. During his seven-year tenure in that post, Powell's committee helped enact forty-eight major pieces of social legislation. These included the National Defense Educational Act, the Anti-Poverty Act, the Manpower Development and Training Act, the Juvenile Delinquency Act, the Vocational Educational Act, and the Minimum Wage Act of 1961.

During the late 1960s Powell's career began to run into rough sledding. He was adjudged in contempt by a New York court for refusing to satisfy a $55,787 judgment against him;[31] he was criticized for excessive absenteeism from Congress; and he was accused of flagrantly misusing congressional funds. Early in 1967, a Select Committee of the House of Representatives recommended public censure and loss of seniority for Powell. On March 1, 1967, however, the House went beyond the Select Committee's recommendation and expelled Powell from the House by a vote of 307–116.[32] During a special election to fill his seat two months later, Powell beat out his opponent 27,900 votes to 4,091. However, the expulsion still stood.

Reelected to the House again in 1968, Powell this time was seated by a vote of 254 to 160. He was, however, fined $25,000 and stripped of all seniority.[33] Several months later the United States Supreme Court ruled that the House of Representatives had violated the Constitution in excluding him two years before. In the meanwhile, however, black Harlem had become bored and impatient with "Adam." There was a rising demand among the younger blacks that one of their generation be sent to Congress. The result was that in congressional elections of 1970, Powell lost out to the popular, forty-year-old Charles B. Rangel. An era had come to an end. Looking back, however, Powell was easily the most illustrious and most effective black ever to serve in the Congress of the United States.

In February, 1970, the nine black members of the U.S. House of Representatives, then organized loosely as the Democratic Select Committee, formally requested a meeting with President Richard Nixon to discuss his administration's policies vis-à-vis blacks in the nation as a whole. The request was almost peremptorily rejected. The president was reported to be much too busy for a chitchat and his assistant, John D. Erlichman, characterized the request as simply a bid for publicity. During the ensuing twelve months, more black members were elected to the House making for a grand total of thirteen—all Democrats.[34] There was one black member in the U.S. Senate, Edward W. Brooke, a Republican. In January, 1971, the black House members again sought a meeting with Nixon and were again turned down. This time, however, they decided to do something besides sulk and criticize the president.

With their more militant colleagues taking the lead, they organized themselves into a tight group known as the Congressional Black Caucus. Under the aegis of the new caucus, Nixon was notified that all black House members would boycott his January 22 State of the Union Message to be delivered to Congress. In a letter initiated by Congressman William L. Clay of Missouri the president was charged with "pitting the rural areas against the cities, the rich against the poor, black against white, and young against old."[35]

When the black caucus continued to publicize its disenchantment with Nixon by refusing, for instance, to attend the traditional White House breakfast for congressmen on February 10, the president began seriously to reappraise the situation. Word was sent to the black congressmen through Senator Brooke that the president might meet with them sometime in March. On February 15, at a press conference Nixon himself expressed hope that a meeting could be held.[36] Nixon's reluctance to meet with the black congressmen was not difficult to understand. As a public figure he had never been esteemed by blacks. They had voted against him overwhelmingly in the national elections of 1960 and 1968. The hostility that the black congressmen had held for him since the beginning of his administration had been ill disguised and could not be accounted for entirely on partisan grounds. What Nixon had been avoiding for almost a year, therefore, was not so much a conference as a confrontation. Nevertheless, the White House finally set the meeting for March 25.

In preparation for the occasion the Black Caucus compiled and printed a thirty-two page booklet which listed some sixty demands upon the Nixon administration. The actual meeting itself, however, was cordial enough. Nixon listened politely to the demands of the caucus and then announced the appointment of a five-man White House panel to study the recommendations and seek ways to implement them. But if for the Nixon administration this was to be the end of the matter, the black congressmen had other ideas. At a press conference called on the day after the meeting Congressman Charles C. Diggs of Michigan, Chairman of the Black Caucus, announced that if Nixon had not begun to act upon the demands by May 17, the caucus would take the matter to the people. May 17 was the anniversary of the historic *Brown* v. *Board of Education* decision. Congressman Clay perhaps best summed up the reaction of the caucus to the meeting with the president: "He listened, but we don't know if he heard. If he did not hear, he and the country will suffer."[37]

In spite of their publicly expressed misgivings and skepticism, however, the black congressmen were really pleased with themselves. None of them was so politically naive as to expect any positive, concrete results from one formal session with Nixon. What they had been really aiming for was an event that would dramatize the emergence of the Black Caucus on the national scene, and this was what the meeting achieved. After this, they began to work to establish themselves among blacks as a new kind of leadership by committee. Less than a week after the meeting with Nixon, Congressman Clay made the projection: "We want to set up a national system of communications with the black community to allow us to touch base with black businesses, the black press and all other black organizations."[38] By the summer of 1971, the Black Caucus felt sufficiently well established to venture a $100-a-plate fund-raising dinner. The affair was attended by more than 2,800 persons and netted upwards of $250,000 for the caucus.[39] With this working capital the group now hired a permanent staff with Howard T. Robinson, a former foreign service officer, in charge.

The question quickly arose as to whether the caucus would become just another clique of prestigious but self-serving blacks or whether it would fulfill the leadership role so critically needed by the nation's blacks. Representative Charles B. Rangel of New York spoke to the point: "The challenge has been thrown to us and we must deliver. Whether we can or cannot deliver, black people think we can and they expect us to."[40] Ultimately, however, there was the strong probability that the caucus would prove disappointing to the politically naive black electorate. The caucus, after all, consisted of only 13 delegates in an assembly of 437. And while all of them were black, none of them represented an all-black constituency. Thus, even if a man's rhetoric in Congress was black oriented, his voting record would have to reflect the interests of the white votes without which he would not be in Congress. Beyond this, there was the important consideration of election campaign funds. With blacks the notoriously poor givers which they have been known to be, there had to be a widespread dependence upon willing white financial sources.

Indeed, one of the most significant things about the caucus's fund-raising dinner was the purchase of $2,400 tables by corporations, such as General Motors, Gulf Oil, R. J. Reynolds Tobacco, Phillip Morris, Inc., Stax Records, and the Great Atlantic and Pacific Tea Company.[41] Black congressmen, like most politicians, are system-oriented individuals whose first obligation understandably is to get themselves reelected. As such, most of them can be counted upon to make deals and politically expedient compromises. They will, for instance, make concessions to black militancy while avoiding its embrace; some of them will join the separatist call for a black third party, but none looking to a future in Congress will work for its actual establishment. For all this, however, the black congressmen as well as the black caucuses on the state and local level can perform a vital function for black citizens. They can break the grip of the white power brokers both North and South and for the first time in the history of this country give the black electorate direct representation on the decision-making councils of American politics. Happily, there appears to be some development in this direction.

Along with their stepped-up activities in the field of politics, blacks in the center cities began to take an increasing interest in the economic development of the black community. This, of course, was not a wholly new departure. As early as 1900, Booker T. Washington sought to promote black economic self-sufficiency through the organization of the National Negro Business League. A generation later, Marcus Garvey not only called for the establishment of a separate black economy, but also his organization, the UNIA, established numerous black business enterprises in several eastern cities. The Black Muslims, an offshoot of the Garvey movement, moved furthest on the economic front. By the mid-1960s, the Muslims were the owners and operators of supermarkets, farms, restaurants, airplanes, and a newspaper.

During the black revolution, black economic development came generally to be known as "black capitalism." Floyd McKissick, one of its leading advocates, stated:

> Black Capitalism is so long overdue and of such importance that it takes precedence over job training programs and general education. Until now, Black People have been relegated to the bottom of the economic ladder. The only way to reverse this trend is to firmly establish Black People on every level of the capitalist structure— thereby guaranteeing organizations receptive to the Black Community and willing to aid in the training and education of the masses of Black People.[42]

The idea of black capitalism was supported by President Lyndon Johnson. Richard Nixon not only endorsed the concept during his 1968 campaign, but also during his first administration the Small Business Administration and other branches of the federal government were directed to aid in the establishment of black businesses through advice and the investment of government funds. Some private institutions, notably the Ford Foundation, also got behind the idea.

However, in spite of all of the initial enthusiasm behind the movement, black capitalism was bound to run afoul the hard realities of the black economic potential. Almost every black community in the nation was a poverty area, beset by low incomes, heavy debts, high unemployment, negligible savings, and financial assets. Blacks in 1970 constituted 11.3 percent of the total population, but their share of the national income was a scant 6.5 percent.[43] Beyond this, black-owned restaurants, motels, and other enterprises have been forced to compete with white establishments for the available black patronage. One observer made the wry comment:

> These mom-and-pop style Black firms cannot compete successfully due to their size,

inefficiency and inability to expand sufficiently to realize the economies of the scale that prevail in the larger more affluent operations of their white competitors.[44]

Andrew Brimmer, the first black member of the board of governors of the Federal Reserve System, felt that black capitalism did not promise a big enough "payoff" to do blacks much good. Even worse, he argued, it "may retard the Negro's economic advancement by discouraging many from full participation in the national economy with its much broader range of challenges and opportunities."[45]

In some other areas of black economic self-help the results were far more encouraging. The most notable of these were perhaps the ventures of the Reverend Leon Sullivan, pastor of the Zion Baptist Church in Philadelphia. Inspired by the activities of Dr. Martin Luther King and his SCLC, Sullivan and some four hundred black preachers in 1960 organized the Selective Patronage Program. Consisting essentially of a succession of black boycotts of major businesses in Philadelphia, the program met with great success. By 1963 it had opened up some two thousand skilled jobs to black workmen in that city. In 1962 the Reverend Leon Sullivan was invited by Dr. King to come to Atlanta to talk about his program to a group of local ministers. Sometime later King's own group, the SCLC, launched a similar program known as "Operation Breadbasket." Under the Reverend Jesse Jackson's leadership, the Chicago Operation Breadbasket was to receive national attention.[46]

In 1963 Sullivan went on to establish the Opportunities Industrialization Center, a job-training program for blacks and other minorities. The idea quickly earned the support of Philadelphia's white business leaders as well as that of the black community. Black leaders in other urban areas became interested in Sullivan's job-training ideas, and in a short time the OIC had become a national movement. By 1969 there were upwards of one hundred OIC programs in the country with twenty thousand trainees, some three thousand instructors and employees, and some forty thousand volunteers assisting the programs in various ways. The programs were collectively receiving some $18 million from such federal government sources as the Departments of Labor; Commerce; Health, Education and Welfare; and the Office of Equal Opportunity.[47]

In June, 1967, President Lyndon Johnson visited Sullivan's OIC in Philadelphia. Visibly impressed, Johnson remarked; "I have heard about this center for many months. Friends and associates of mine came here to see it and returned to tell me the good news—of how a movement born of protest has taken the next logical step—to preparation. . . ."[48] A few months later, the Johnson administration launched the "Philadelphia Plan" whereby all low bidders on federally financed hospitals, highways, colleges, and other projects were required to submit tables indicating the number of minority workers they would hire from a half dozen skilled trades. The plan was adopted and continued by the Nixon administration.

Sullivan's endeavors were not confined to job-training activities. In mid-1962 he persuaded fifty members of his congregation to put ten dollars a month each for thirty-six months in an investment cooperative program to be called the "10–36–50 Plan."[49] By 1965 the Plan had grown to six hundred members with investments for individual members worth as much as six thousand dollars. The 10–36 Plan paved the way to the more business-oriented Zion Investment Associates. Growing rapidly, the Zion Investment Associates between 1965 and 1970 was to acquire a seventy-five-thousand dollar apartment building, a million-dollar apartment complex, a shopping center with sixteen stores, an aerospace manufacturing center with $2,600,000 in subcontracts for the General Electric Corporation , and a garment manufacturing center supported by the Singer Corporation and the International Ladies' Garment Workers Union.[50]

The Reverend Leon Sullivan had been nurtured in the time-honored tradition of black Baptist preachers, but he managed nevertheless to move out and to exemplify a new and unique type of leadership in the black community. His OIC provided new hope and opportunities for thousands of unskilled blacks across the nation. His Zion Investment Associates represented the most successful black economic development enterprise in the nation's history. It was perhaps the only viable alternative to the abortive attempts to establish black capitalism.

CHAPTER 12

Black Literature and the Black Revolution

Although it was written some twenty years earlier, no book had a more profound influence on the literature of the black revolution than did Richard Wright's *Native Son*. In fact, the claims for the book are even greater than this. Thus, Irving S. Howe writes:

> The day *Native Son* appeared, American culture was changed forever. No matter how much qualifying the book might later need, it made impossible a repetition of the old lies. In all its crudeness, melodrama and claustrophobia of vision, Richard Wright's novel brought out into the open, as no one ever had before, the hatred, fear and violence that have crippled and may yet destroy our culture.[1]

In the sullen, seething, hate-filled Bigger Thomas, *Native Son's* main character, Wright created a prototype of the black militants, the "block boys," and the insurrectionists who were to frighten so badly white America during the late 1960s. But more than this, *Native Son* anticipated some of the major themes of the Black Liberation movement. The hypothesis that American blacks are a colonized nation within a white mother country is reflected in a statement made by Bigger Thomas's lawyer: "Taken collectively they [black people] are not simply twelve million people, in reality they constitute a separate nation, stunted, stripped and held captive *within* this nation, devoid of political, social, economic and property rights."[2] Frantz Fanon's "therapeutic value of violence" is suggested in Bigger Thomas's colloquy: "What I killed for must have been good. . . . I didn't know I was really alive in this world until I felt things hard enough to kill for 'em. . . ."[3]

Finally, the hatred, indeed the black rage, that became a hallmark of the Black Liberation movement is allegorically depicted by Wright in the following:

> It has made itself a home in the wild forest of our great cities amid the rank and choking vegetation of the slums. It has forgotten our language! In order to live, it has sharpened its claws. It has grown hard and calloused. It has developed a capacity for

269

hate and fury which we cannot understand. Its movements are unpredictable. By night it creeps from its lair and steals toward the settlements of civilization. And at the sight of a kind face it does not lie down on its back and kick up its heels playfully to be tickled and stroked. No, it leaps to kill.[4]

Native Son was an accurate and genuine reflection of conditions in the black community of 1940. But these conditions underwent a swift but temporary change for the better. Hence the impact of the book was delayed. World War II brought an end to much of the unemployment and poverty not to say the despondency in the black community. The decade which followed was one of optimism and hope for black people everywhere. The ancient walls of segregation seemed to be developing cracks, and the economic level of the race was perceptibly on the upgrade. Toward the middle of the 1950s, however, this period of rising expectations began to taper off. The future was arriving empty-handed, its promises unfulfilled. By the end of the decade the old conditions for black Americans were creeping back and the bitter reactions to these conditions were beginning to be heard.

The new generation of young black writers who were now to portray life in black America could turn only to Richard Wright as their guide. The author of *Native Son* and *Black Boy* had singlehandedly closed out an era. He had wrung down the curtain on the plaintive themes and moods of the Harlem Renaissance. During the 1940s and early 1950s no major black writers appeared on the scene save Ralph Ellison, and though his prize winning novel, *Invisible Man*, barely reveals it, he himself had been a protégé of Richard Wright. It was no mere coincidence, therefore, that Bigger Thomas, though much more urbane and sophisticated, should appear in some of the works of James Baldwin, LeRoi Jones, and other black writers.

A central fact of life for all black writers—novelists, poets, and playwrights—during the decade of the 1960s was the black revolution. Willingness to pay obeisance to the black experience was in fact a test of loyalty, and those who demurred were dismissed as irrelevant. The result was a veritable torrent of black revolutionary rhetoric, doggerel, or just plain trivia making claims on the black reading public. On the other hand, the period did witness the emergence of a handful of black writers whose works almost immediately marked them out as creative artists of the first rank. Chief among these was James Baldwin.

Like Ralph Ellison, Baldwin had been a protégé of Richard Wright. As a matter of fact, Wright did more than any other individual to launch Baldwin on his career. He read the preliminary draft of Baldwin's *Go Tell It on the Mountain* and subsequently used his influence in helping Baldwin win the Eugene F. Sarton Memorial Award for the completion of this novel.[5] Like many other budding young black artists, Baldwin desperately wanted to transcend the limitations imposed because of his race. He was determined to become something more than "merely a Negro or even merely a Negro writer." Finding it difficult or even impossible to achieve this aim while living in black Harlem or even in Greenwich Village, Baldwin took himself to Paris where he remained from 1948 to 1958. During this expatriation he polished up and published *Go Tell It on the Mountain.* This first work is essentially autobiographical. It reproduces Baldwin's early religious experiences in Harlem and tells of three generations of his family in the South dating from the days of slavery.

Returning from Europe in 1958, Baldwin looked in upon a revolution about to happen. He accurately read the signs of the times and then proceeded to devote his craftsmanship to the task of reflecting the bitterness and the hang-ups of a new generation of young blacks. In his third novel, *Another Country,* Baldwin rendered the judgment that integration, interracial cooperation, interracial love, and sex will lead to no millennium; that the brutal legacy of the past will be served; and that if all the material indications of injustice were removed, blacks would still retain their bitterness and whites their fear and guilt. The novel spoke almost directly to the young blacks caught up in sit-ins and the Freedom Rides of the early 1960s.

As the nonviolence crusade gave way to revolutionary black nationalism, Baldwin became more strident and more militant in his themes. In his fourth novel, *Tell Me How Long the Train's Been Gone,* he struck out savagely against the racist nature of American society. Indeed, through Black Christopher, one of the novel's major characters, Baldwin speaks the language of the black revolutionist:

> It's the spirit of the people, baby, the *spirit* of the people, they don't want us and they don't like us, and you see that spirit in the face of every cop. Them laws they keep passing, shit, they just like the treaties they signed with the Indians. Nothing but lies, they never *meant* to keep those treaties, baby, they wanted the land and they got it and now they mean to keep it, even if they have to put every black motherfucker in this country behind barbed wire, or shoot him down like a dog.[6]

As powerful a novelist as he was, Baldwin was vastly more effective, especially among blacks, with his essays. Critics generally acclaimed him to be one of the two or three greatest essayists in the history of American literature. He published three books of essays, *Notes of a Native Son* (1955), *Nobody Knows My Name* (1961), and *The Fire Next Time* (1963). Going through almost twenty editions, *The Fire Next Time* was a veritable sermon on white racism in America. Baldwin employed the rhythmic, oratorial style so characteristic of black speakers and orators. Among black students and intellectuals *The Fire Next Time* for a time ranked in popularity with the *Autobiography of Malcolm X*.

Toward the end of the decade of the 1960s Baldwin began rapidly to lose favor among blacks generally. He had never been too popular among the militants, many of whom were convinced that he was ambivalent on the question of "blackness." Eldridge Cleaver was a particularly passionate critic of Baldwin. He accused Baldwin of expressing a deep self-hatred of himself as a black and demonstrating a servile love of whites. By 1970 Baldwin had been relegated by the black avant-garde to the category of "Negro writers" of social protest literature. The charge was that protest literature was cowardly and demeaning; that it was really addressed to whites, threatening them, beseeching them, petitioning them for a redress of the race's grievances.

After 1965 the new theme for young black writers came to be the "black aesthetic." The new black literature was, of course, ideologically oriented. Weaned from Richard Wright, these writers were following guidelines for black literature set down by Frantz Fanon. In his *Wretched of the Earth* Fanon identifies three stages in the development of the black writer—assimilation, ethnic discovery, and revolution. The militant black writers considered themselves to be operating in the third or revolutionary stage. Fanon states that in this stage, the black writer must become "an awakener of the people" who now produces "a fighting literature, a revolutionary literature, and a national literature."[7]

Fanon had special instructions for the poets among the black writers. Their poetry must first of all be a "poetry of revolt," but it must also be descriptive and analytical. "The poet ought however to understand that nothing can replace the reasoned, irrevocable taking up of arms on the people's side."[8] In short the black poet must preoccupy himself with a literature of combat. LeRoi Jones, a chief disciple of Fanon, elaborated on the theme:

The Black Artist's role in America is to aid in the destruction of America as he knows it. His role is to report and reflect so precisely the nature of the society, and of himself in that society, that other men will be moved by the exactness of his rendering and, if they are black men, grow strong . . . and if they are white men, tremble, curse, and go mad, because they will be drenched with the filth of their evil.[9]

In time LeRoi Jones became known as the "high priest" of the black aesthetic. Jones was born in Newark, New Jersey, in 1934 of middle-class parents. The city's black community was not the dehumanizing slum that it was later to become. Jones moved normally through elementary and secondary schools going on to Rutgers and then to Howard University. After graduating in 1954, Jones took postgraduate courses at Columbia University and the New School of Social Research. He subsequently did two years of service in the Strategic Air Command. From his earliest childhood Jones had evidenced definite potentiality as a creative writer. After leaving the SAC, he took up residence in Greenwich Village and devoted his full time to teaching and writing poetry. Harold Cruse, who knew him and ran across him occasionally, states that Jones "was then just another addition to the black intellectual scene of Greenwich Village—and rather late at that."[10]

However, Jones was not destined to remain an undistinguished member of the "beat generation." Between 1960 and 1964 he wrote more than a score of social essays, some of which were autobiographical but most of them forceful and penetrating. They were published in 1966 under the title of *Home.* During these years Jones also published a volume of his poetry along with a novel entitled *The System of Dante's Hell.* It was as a playwright, however, that Jones was to achieve his greatest national acclaim. In 1964 he turned out three plays: *The Slave, The Toilet* (said to have been written in six hours), and *The Dutchman. The Dutchman* was a one-act play in which a young three-buttoned middle-class black turns into a Bigger Thomas when confronted with the inescapable entrapment of his kind in a cynical, racist society. The work won the *Village Voice's* Obie Award for the Best American Play of the 1963–1964 season. By 1965 Jones had become a celebrity. An acquaintance of his writes:

He [Jones] was invited to all the enchanted-circle, beautiful-people parties, literary events, show business orgies, and hip gatherings. The more he attacked white society, the more white society patronized him. . . . Whitey seemed insatiable; the masochistic vein was a source of hitherto untapped appeal, big box office stuff, and LeRoi Jones was one of the very first to exploit it.[11]

Unlike most of his running buddies from the Village, however, there was much more to Jones than the mad pursuit of the high life. At heart he was desperately in search of a cause or a movement to which he could devote his time and his not inconsiderable talent and creativity. During the summer of 1960, Jones, along with a group that included Harold Cruse, Robert Williams, Julian Mayfield, and John Henrik Clarke, accepted an invitation from the new Castro regime to visit Cuba. Cruse notes that Jones made a very formidable impression on the intelligentsia of the Castro regime.[12] On the other hand, the regime made a "believer" of Jones. He wrote enthusiastically of his Cuban impressions in the essay "Cuba Libre." During the early 1960s Jones worked first with one group known as the "Organization of Young Men" and later with another which called itself the "On Guard for Freedom Committee." Both of these groups were inter-racial. Black nationalism, however, was on the rise among all levels of blacks, and interracial organizations and activities were becoming decidedly unpopular among them. Jones was a frequent visitor to Harlem, and he found it increasingly difficult to remain outside of the new movement.

By 1965 Jones was ready to make a complete break with his interracial past. He moved uptown to Harlem, away from the hip, white, cynical, jaded jet set. He took his art with him. He withdrew from an agreement with Grove Press to publish *Black Magic,* a complete collection of his poetry, and he withdrew from an option to produce a new three-act play on Broadway. As one observer was to put it: Jones "traded in his successful writer's suit for an Afro-American costume."[13] More to the point, Jones was about ready to launch a drive for a separate black culture, with its own symbols and its own personal myths, the cultural phase of revolutionary black nationalism. In the spring of 1965, Jones along with several other young black artists announced the opening of the Black Arts Repertoire Theater and School. It was housed in a four-story brownstone townhouse in the dead center of black Harlem.

Echoing Frantz Fanon's views on the nature and function of black art, Jones now declared:

The Revolutionary Theatre, which is now peopled with victims, will soon begin to be peopled with new kinds of heroes—not the weak Hamlets debating whether or not they are ready to die . . . but men and women . . . digging out from under a thousand years of "high art" and weak-faced dalliance. We must make an art that will function so as to call down the actual wrath of world spirit. We are witch doctors and assassins. . . . This is a theatre of assault.[14]

During the late spring of 1965, Jones's "Theatre of Assault" received a grant of $44,000 from the HARYOU administration in New York City for the purpose of sponsoring cultural field demonstrations in the black community. Harlem more than welcomed the new activity. During the hot summer months Jones and his entourage presented concerts and poetry-reading sessions; they produced a number of plays including *The Dutchman, Black Mass,* and *Experimental Death Unit # One.*

From the very beginning, however, the Black Arts Theater was a controversial enterprise. It was far too militant for some of the black and white politicos on the one hand, and not militant enough for some of the local "brothers" on the other. Cruse describes this latter group as representing the "terrorist fringe" of Harlem black nationalism. They were in his opinion "dangerously irrational, misguided, negative, and disoriented." Under any circumstances, they made it impossible for Jones to obtain the broad community support without which the Black Arts Theater could not hope to survive.[15] On September 17, the HARYOU administration terminated its funding not only of the theater but also of the activities of several local militant groups such as the "Five Percenters" who were allegedly tied in with Jones's program.

Some months later Jones packed up his Black Theater and moved it across the Hudson River to Newark. Spirit House, which he set up in a three-story building in the heart of the black community, became the headquarters of revolutionary black art in America. Once back in his hometown, however, Jones became more of a political and social activist than an artist. He became personally involved in almost every cause involving blacks. During the racial strife in Newark in the summer of 1967, Jones, along with two companions, was arrested (and later convicted) for possessing two loaded revolvers and a box of ammunition. During the late 1960s Jones was evolving into something of a black ombudsman in the Newark ghetto. His work was a key factor in Kenneth Gibson's successful campaign to become Newark's first black mayor. In the meanwhile his Spirit House had served as a model for several other such centers which popped up in black communities across the nation. These included Ron Karenga's Black House in San Francisco, the New School for Afro-American Thought in Washington, D.C., the Institute for Black Studies in Los Angeles, Forum 66 in Detroit, and to some extent, Vincent Harding's Institute of the Black World in Atlanta, Georgia.

An ambitious but short-lived movement for the promotion of black art got under way in Chicago during 1967. During that summer ten young talented black men including the poet Conrad Kent Rivers and Hoyt Fuller, editor of the *Negro Digest,* established the Organization of Black American Culture. An executive council of members representing the various arts was established. Classes in writing and art were set up in the community with an eye toward encouraging as well as discovering those with talent. For the public at large and for those who were not interested in art the OBAC conducted community workshop meetings. These quickly came to be known as "rapping Black" sessions with such personages as Ron Karenga invited to conduct discourses on black consciousness. Of specific interest to the new group was the clarification and the promotion of the "Black Aesthetic." The group urged all black writers to reject the assumptions of the "Literary Establishment" and to "strive to invest their works with the same free, soulful qualities which the great jazz innovators had brought to music."[16]

Spurred by such groups as the OBAC and Forum 66 of Detroit, the concept of a black aesthetic began to take hold among an increasing number of black writers throughout the nation. However, its acceptance was far from unanimous and in order to get a reading on the state of mind of the average black writer, the *Negro Digest* in late 1967 polled some thirty-eight black writers asking them twenty-five questions, all relating to their work and attitudes as black writers.[17] Those polled covered the "whole range of creativity, from the authors highly esteemed by the 'Literary Establishment' to those who are known only to a small category of local readers."

More than half of the thirty-eight writers who responded named Richard Wright as the most important black writer of all time. The Pulitzer Prize winning poet, Miss Gwendolyn Brooks, felt that Wright was the greatest writer ever to emerge in America. The choice of Langston Hughes over James Baldwin and Ralph Ellison as the second most important black writer of all time came as a mild surprise to many. Hughes, as a main figure of the Harlem Renaissance, was on the other side of the generational gap. However, Hughes also won overwhelmingly as the most important black poet of the century. The top vote in the category, "the most important novel written by a black man since publication of *Invisible Man,*" was shared by John A. Williams' *The Man Who Cried I Am,* and John O. Killens' *And Then We Heard the Thunder.* James Baldwin's *Go Tell It on the Mountain* received what amounted to honorable mention. Baldwin was already being considered by many critics to be on the decline. Also the consensus was that he was not as great a novelist as he was an essayist, and Fuller's poll did not include the category "the greatest black essayist of all time."

LeRoi Jones, who was now calling himself Imamu Amiri Baraka, emerged clearly from the poll as the dominant black literary figure of the contemporary scene. He was described variously as the "most promising" of young black writers, the "most important " living black poet, and lastly, the most important black playwright of this century. As one of the respondents to the poll put it: "LeRoi Jones not only crafts but he also has something to say." Most of those responding to the poll agreed that black writers ought to make maximum use of the black experience, that black writers should direct their work primarily toward black audiences, and that black writers should strive to promote a black aesthetic. As might be expected, the older writers figured prominently among those who disagreed but, as Editor Fuller pointed out, there were also some young and vocal dissidents. He felt that the more removed the writer was from personal association with the black revolution, the less sympathetic he would be toward black consciousness and the black aesthetic.[18]

The fundamental problem with all discussions dealing with contemporary black culture is, of course, the absence of concrete, working guidelines for the black aesthetic. Beginning in the mid-1960s, the term became increasingly popular in black literary and artistic circles. One could simply not afford to be unaware of it. But even as Mr. Fuller's poll indicated, the majority of black writers had no real notion of what the black aesthetic was or should be. There are of course some definitions. Addison Gayle felt that the question for the black critic today is not how beautiful a piece of writing is in itself, but how much more beautiful has it made the life of a single black man? How far has the work gone in transforming an American Negro into an African-American or black man? "The Black Aesthetic, then, as conceived by this writer, is a corrective—a means of helping black people out of the polluted mainstream of Americanism. . . ."[19] Hoyt Fuller suggests that the black aesthetic is a system of evaluating the artistic work of black people which reflects the special character of the black experience.[20]

On the other hand, there is the venerable J. Saunders Redding who insists that "aesthetics has no racial, national or geographic boundaries" and that a so-called black aesthetic will not be established in America. Then there is the poet Robert Hayden who said:

> It seems to me that a "black aesthetic" would only be possible in a predominantly black culture. Yet not even black African writers subscribe to such an aesthetic. And isn't the so-called black "aesthetic" simply protest and racist propaganda in a new guise? [21]

Finally, there are some black writers who consider a black aesthetic to be a hindrance to their success and development. What interests them generally are recognition and reward for their creations; and to achieve these, they demand a greater public than that which would be provided by contemporary considerations of black consciousness. One of these young writers was to put it this way: "To write solely for a black audience is limiting and presumes too much; that they will appreciate your efforts; that they will try to understand you; that they will care enough about your work to buy your book...." And from yet another: "The Negro has enough working against him—why should he limit his output to the black experience?" [22]

For all this, however, the problem still remains. There can be no denying that a new black literature has emerged upon the contemporary scene and that some young and gifted black poets are breaking with established academic poetic usages both in form and content. Don L. Lee and Nikki Giovanni have been delving into the black consciousness and the black life-style with laudable results. LeRoi Jones, Gwendolyn Brooks, Larry Neal, and others have been working in both the old and new traditions with equally successful results. But there are in black literature the marginal and the non-poets whose sole objective is the politicization of the black masses. The output of these writers is never above the level of militant rhetoric and crude propaganda. They all claim, however, to be working for the expansion of black consciousness, and they *are* black writers.

Mel Watkins, in a book review article in the *New York Times*, addressed himself to the problem:

> Still, there are critical and evaluative distinctions to be made about the raft of contemporary black poetry that is now being published. At its best it incorporates the current positive black awareness and consciousness and, by creating new images and employing the elements of black speech, produces imaginative, relevant poetic works. At worst, it is dull, repetitive and simplistic...propagandistic. For the sake of the poets themselves, someone should begin making critical distinctions. [23]

In nonfiction literature, the fifteen-year period between 1955 and

1970 saw the publication of an unprecedented number of books by black writers. The black revolution in creating a demand for black literature put the black writer in the unique position of operating in a seller's market. A significant number of these works were general or specialized treatments of the revolution while it was in progress. However, there were about a half dozen titles that are noteworthy because of the part they played either in helping to initiate the revolution or to shape it once it got going. These would include Frantz Fanon's, *Wretched of the Earth* and the *Autobiography of Malcolm X* for ideology; Kenneth B. Clark's *Dark Ghetto* and E. Franklin Frazier's, *Black Bourgeoisie* for sociology; Lerone Bennett, Jr.'s *Before the Mayflower* for history; and William H. Grier's and Price M. Cobbs' *Black Rage* for psychology.

One of the books on the required reading list for leaders of the Black Panther party was the *Wretched of the Earth*. For Bobby Seale and especially for Huey Newton, Fanon's words came to be regarded almost as a holy writ. These two men together gave the *Wretched of the Earth* more promotion perhaps than any other individuals outside of the sales personnel of Grove Press. The book rapidly became the basic text for black revolutionary nationalism in America. The English translation of the book was issued in 1965, and by the end of 1970 its sales had exceeded 750,000 copies and were still going strong. Fanon was the product of a middle-class family of Martinique in the French West Indies. As a teenager he joined the French army and later fought with the Free French forces in North Africa during World War II. At the conclusion of the war he returned to France to study medicine. He completed training as a psychiatrist in 1953 and went immediately into practice in a hospital in war-torn Algiers.

In *Wretched of the Earth*, Fanon analyzes and draws conclusions from the operation of colonialism and imperialism in Africa. It was addressed to black Africans—those still in bondage and those who had recently emerged from it. Militant black nationalists in America, however, were quick to perceive the possibilities of the book for their cause. Indeed, *Wretched of the Earth*, which had just been translated from French into English, was quickly translated by the militants into the language of the black liberation. Thus Eldridge Cleaver states:

> The feelings and thoughts and passions that were racking us were incoherent and not connected until we read Fanon. Then many things fell together for us harmonizing our attitudes and making it possible for us to organize into a political organization.[24]

In the tenth plank of their "Platform and Programs" the Black Panthers began using Fanon. They demanded a United Nations-supervised plebiscite to be held throughout the black colony in which only black colonial subjects would be allowed to participate, for the purpose of determining the will of black people as to their national destiny. Cleaver later supplied the term "white mother country" with the result that black militants wound up demanding the liberation of American black colonial subjects from the oppression of the white mother country.

Fanon was the prime source of such other black revolutionary concepts as the need to transform the black culture into a vehicle for promoting revolution and liberation; the demand for money reparations from the colonialists for the centuries of oppression and exploitation; the viability of pitting guerrilla warfare against the vaunted military superiority of the establishment; and lastly the value of discrediting, attacking, and even killing the official representatives of the system. It was Fanon's view that the native revolutionaries who kill policemen are the "types" that "light the way for the people, form the blueprints for action and become heroes." [25] The early Black Panther confrontations with the police in the black ghettos were undoubtedly inspired by *Wretched of the Earth*. Seale indicated that the Panther leadership internalized "everything that Fanon said about violence and the spontaneity of violence, how spontaneous violence educates those who are in a position with skills to lead the people to what needs to be done." [26]

It must be emphasized, however, that Fanon, in his book, directed his advice to natives living and dying in a traditional, old-world colonial system. He evinced little interest in the condition of American blacks. And while he recognized that Afro-Americans are an oppressed minority, he warned that their problems are uniquely different from those of the Africans. Speaking of an African Cultural Society meeting in Paris in 1956, Fanon had this to say:

> . . . the American Negroes of their own accord considered their problems from the same standpoint as those of their African brothers. Cultured Africans, speaking of African civilizations, decreed that there should be a reasonable status within the state for those who had formerly been slaves. But little by little the American Negroes realized that the essential problems confronting them were not the same as those that confronted the African Negroes.[27]

The identification, therefore, of the plight of the American blacks with that of their African brethren cannot be attributed to Fanon.

Rather, it was the work of militant ideologists and amateur sociologists. If it has been a productive and useful exercise for them, it has had little or no impact on the vast majority of black Americans. They know nothing of Frantz Fanon, and they are equally oblivious of their designation as "an oppressed black colony within a white mother country."

By the time the *Autobiography of Malcolm X* was published in mid-1965, the activist black youth in the country had already concluded that nonviolence was a failure and Martin Luther King was a captive of the establishment. The *Autobiography* seemed not only to support them in their judgment of King but also to deepen their disenchantment with the man and his movement. With more than four million copies sold by the end of 1970, the *Autobiography* was very probably read by more American blacks than any book save the Bible. The book gave to a new generation of American blacks their first real introduction to Marcus Garvey and to the arguments for black mass emigration to Africa or separatism within the United States. The *Autobiography* also stimulated a new interest in the history and culture of ancient black Africa.

The book had its greatest impact in the area of revolutionary black nationalism, however. In his earlier years Malcolm had preached that the civil rights-nonviolence crusade was a fraud, a mere asking to be accepted into the system. It was time, he insisted, for blacks to be trying to overturn the system, to bring it down. In short, it was time for revolution—black revolution. The *Autobiography* created instant militants in almost every sizable black community in the nation. Black youth had found a new and ideal father figure. Almost overnight the black ghettos began to be overrun by imitation Malcolm X's. Many of these young blacks subsequently organized themselves into chapters and branches of the RAM, the RNA, and the Black Panthers. The *Autobiography* did much also to promote an interest among these youth in Third-World liberation movements. In this connection it was to become a companion work with *Wretched of the Earth*.

For young militant black readers the last two chapters of the *Autobiography* were perhaps the least interesting and least understood. These dealt with the last couple of years in Malcolm's life during which time he backed away from black violence and black revolution and in effect called upon blacks to work within the system. During the high tide of the revolution this phase of Malcolm's development was generally ignored. By 1970, however, with the movement rapidly failing, some of the more thoughtful among Malcolm's disciples began searching for the causes. There can be little doubt that many of them began reading the last chapters of the *Autobiography* with a newer and deeper interest.

Beginning with its publication in 1947, and for a decade and a half thereafter, the standard work in Afro-American history in the United States was John Hope Franklin's *From Slavery to Freedom*. By the mid-1960s, however, Franklin's book had been edged aside by a new publication, Lerone Bennett, Jr.'s *Before the Mayflower: A History of the Negro in America*. Bennett initially earned national acclaim for building *Ebony* magazine into one of the nation's great popular periodicals, black or white. Bennett is also a prolific writer, and aside from his work on black history he has written several other books including an award winning biography of Martin Luther King. First published in 1962, *Before the Mayflower* benefited from the accelerating black revolution and the resulting demand for new material dealing with the black experience. Within a half dozen years sales of the book reached 100,000; it had been translated into some six different languages, and it had been adopted by scores of school systems, colleges, and universities throughout the nation.

Lerone Bennett, Jr., is a good writer, and *Before the Mayflower* was generally agreed to be a well-written and interesting volume. But questions arose as to whether it was sound reliable history. Some critics insisted that it was good journalism but not good history; that it was poorly researched; that it was based principally upon secondary sources; and that it utterly lacked scholarship. Whatever may have been the merit of these criticisms, and they were by no means universal, they did not affect the sale of the book. Bennett did not set out to duplicate the work of John Hope Franklin or that of another well-known black historian, Benjamin Quarles. Quite the contrary, *Before the Mayflower* was in fact a revolt against traditional, standard black history. It became a "blockbuster" because of its radically new interpretation of existing material and because of its new point of view. Bennett mirrored the 350-year sojourn of blacks in America as a constant brutalizing and dehumanizing battle against racial injustice and oppression, and he depicted black leaders from Richard Allen to Martin Luther King as heroes in the struggle. Indeed, a more apt title for Bennett's book could well have been "The Struggle for Black Liberation in America." At any rate, this is how young black readers interpreted it, and this is principally why they made *Before the Mayflower* the basic history text in the new Black Studies courses which were established throughout the country.

Whenever black nationalism is in the ascendancy, in the United States a favorite target of the militants becomes the black middle class. A good deal of Marcus Garvey's popularity among the black rank and file during the early 1920s can be attributed to his scathing denunciations of W. E. B. Du Bois as a representative of the mulatto dominated black elite. During the 1960s, however, the militant assault upon the black middle class assumed more serious proportions. Essentially ideological in nature, the assault was aimed at isolating this class and labeling its members as "Toms," lackeys, and tools of the white establishment. At least one group of revolutionary nationalists, the RAM, marked this class out for liquidation. The writings of both Malcolm X and Fanon provided ammunition for the attack on this class.

However, E. Franklin Frazier's *Black Bourgeoisie* became a basic source for the militants. Bobby Seale tells of students at Merritt College getting into an argument with Newton and how "Huey whipped out a copy of *Black Bourgeoisie* by E. Franklin Frazier and showed him what page, what paragraph, and corrected the person." [28] Paradoxically, Frazier himself was a bona fide member of the black elite. He was also a renowned scholar and teacher. *The Black Bourgeoisie* was first published in France in 1955, and a year later it was selected for the McIver Lectureship Award by the American Sociological Society. The first English edition was published in the United States in 1957. The book begins with a very familiar and popular account of the social and economic history of blacks in America. Frazier then deals with what he calls the "world of make-believe" which he claims the black middle class has created in order to compensate for its feeling of inferiority and its lack of identification with either the black masses or the whites.

The black middle class as a whole was thoroughly familiar with Frazier's material and his main thesis. They had long been part of black folk tales and legends. What they did object to were Frazier's conclusions and generalizations, as for instance:

> In attempting to escape identification with the black masses, they [black bourgeoisie] have developed a self-hatred that reveals itself in their depreciation of the physical and social characteristics of Negroes. Likewise, their feelings of inferiority and insecurity are revealed in their pathological struggle for status within the isolated Negro world and craving for recognition in the white world. [29]

Frazier's book was widely read and his comments had material results. Thus, while the black middle class is numerically larger than ever, new recruits are reluctant to identify openly with it. On the other hand, there appears to have occurred within the class a superficial reorientation of values. Slavish imitation of whites has been abandoned in favor of lip service to black consciousness and the black experience. In short, the mink coat and the Brooks Brothers suit are acceptable as long as they are topped off by an Afro hairdo.

On June 12, 1962, Mayor Robert F. Wagner of New York City announced plans for the inauguration of a program to improve employment as well as economic and social opportunities for youths of the city's black community. The program was placed under the direction of a group of local citizens known as Harlem Youth Opportunities Limited (HARYOU). Dr. Kenneth B. Clark was named chief project consultant and chairman of the board of directors. Under Clark's direction, the new agency undertook an intensive investigation of the conditions of youth in central Harlem. Some eighteen months later the results of the study were published in a 620-page report entitled *Youth in the Ghetto: A Study of the Consequences of Powerlessness and a Blueprint for a Change*. The demand for copies of the document was so great Dr. Clark made the decision to publish it in book form. *Dark Ghetto,* with a few charts and tables and more articulate exposition than the report, was the result.

Dr. Clark was himself of Harlem. Because of his more than forty years of residence in the community, he called himself an "involved observer." He was in fact not only an expert on Harlem but on black ghetto life everywhere in the United States. Beyond this, he was recognized as one of the nation's leading social psychologists. He had a major hand in shaping the NAACP's brief in the *Brown* v. *Board of Education* case. He was, however, neither an activist nor a militant. Malcolm X, who knew him and personally liked him, referred to him as "a black man with brains gone to bed."

Dark Ghetto became a starting point for studies and analyses of the long hot summers which ran from 1963 to 1968. It was a chief source for the Kerner Commission and similar investigative groups. The book probes into the conditions of the unfortunates who are confined to ghetto areas and whose free access to the "normal channels" of economic mobility and economic opportunity are cut off. Specifically, it inquires into the personal and social consequences of the ghetto, the consequences of the victims' lack of power to change their status, and finally the consequences of the "inability or unwillingness of those with power" to employ them for constructive social change. Clark concluded: "The ghetto is institutionalized pathology; it is chronic, self-perpetuating pathology; and it is the futile attempt by those with power to confine that pathology so as to prevent the spread of the contagion to the larger community."[30] For black militants everywhere, *Dark Ghetto* became required reading.

Black Rage by William H. Grier and Price M. Cobbs is a continuation of the inquiry into the psychological effects of racial oppression and injustice. Where Clark limited his research to the black ghetto, and Fanon spoke specifically of the black African colonials, Grier and Cobbs dealt with black paranoia on the national level in the United States. They diagnosed the listlessness, the depression, and the apathy which they found to be characteristic of blacks generally, and they insisted that white America by its systematic and thoroughgoing repression has reduced the black American to half a man. If the mood of the book is, as the authors admit, "mournful, painful, desolate," they explain: "This dismal tone has been deliberate. It has been an attempt to evoke a certain quality of depression and hopelessness in the reader and to stir these feelings. These are the most common feelings tasted by black people in America."[31]

To a number of psychologists and psychiatrists throughout the country, however, *Black Rage* was a gross overstatement of the problem. Dr. Clark, for instance, insisted that in stirring these feelings in their readers Grier and Cobbs had

> joined the present fashionable cult of literate black and white flagellants who now believe that America's racial problem can be clarified and racial justice obtained through a sadomasochistic orgy of black rage and white guilt—or through conscious or unconscious black and white guile.[32]

All the same, *Black Rage* was a tremendously popular book. It became another standard reference work for the Black Liberation movement.

Grier and Cobbs not only employed revolutionary rhetoric, but like the black revolutionaries who made up their most devoted readers they were also caught up in the vision of an impending apocalypse. Thus:

> The time seems near . . . for the full range of the black masses to put down the broom and buckle on the sword. And it grows nearer day by day. Now we see skirmishes,

sputtering erratically, evidence if you will that the young men are in a warlike mood. But evidence as well that the elders are watching and may soon join the battle.[33]

The major appeal of *Black Rage* turned out to be its main drawback. It sold like "hot cakes" during the rhetorical crescendo of the black revolution, but it quickly lost credibility (and sales) when the cataclysm it predicted, "black rage, apocalyptic and final," was not forthcoming.

CHAPTER 13

Postscript

During the early years of the decade of the "seventies" there was a growing tendency among blacks generally to shrug off the black revolution, to question whether it brought about any positive, measurable improvement in the condition of black people in the United States. Among other things, black persons point to the disproportionately high percentage of blacks on public welfare, the high unemployment rate of black males, the apparent impregnability of de facto segregation in the cities, and the widespread white hysteria against busing to achieve public school desegregation. They insist that the distance between the levels of black and white life in the United States has increased rather than decreased during the 1960s and that while white racism now wears a new mask, it is nonetheless ubiquitous. While these contentions are essentially sound, whether they constitute a fair and proper judgment of the black revolution is open to question. One could, of course, quibble about the use of the term "revolution" as a designation of black activism during the decade, but the problem here is not one of semantics.

Essentially the so-called black revolution was a social movement that began spontaneously in the Deep South during the mid-1950s. Over the next fifteen years the movement divided into two distinct phases, each with its own goals, its own leadership, and its own ideology. Each also made its individual impact upon American society. The first phase of the movement, which is sometimes characterized as the "Era of Nonviolence," or the Age of Martin Luther King, spanned the ten-year period between 1955 and 1965. Originating out of the bus boycott in Montgomery, Alabama, it later encompassed the sit-in crusade of 1960 and the Freedom Rides of 1961. In 1962 the movement took on the dangerous and difficult task of reenfranchising the millions of voteless blacks in the Southern states. In all of these campaigns the movement was successful. In something less than eighteen months black college students changed the face of the South. Challenging age-old traditions, customs, and entrenched racism, they managed to bring about the desegregation of public accommodations at a time and in a place where it was thought impossible. They had brought about a major social change. When the federal government enacted the Civil Rights Act of 1964, it was belatedly endorsing an institutional change brought about by the movement some three years earlier.

Of equal importance was the movement's success in restoring political rights to Southern blacks. Although the funding and some of the supervision came from sources outside of the movement, the hard, dangerous work of voter education and voter registration was undertaken by virtually the same young blacks who had served on the sit-ins and the Freedom Rides. In the two-year period between 1962 and 1964, these youngsters were instrumental in adding more than 700,000 new black voters to the registration rolls in the states of the "Old Confederacy." They thus laid the foundation for the federal Voting Rights Act of 1965. During the next five years, the black vote in the region became a patent political force. It placed hundreds of blacks into political office for the first time since Reconstruction and brought an end to much of the "red neck" demagoguery for which the region was so well known. In short, after the lapse of more than one hundred years the promises of the Fifteenth Amendment were finally being fulfilled.

There were several specific reasons behind the success of the first phase of the black revolution. For one thing, all of its goals were unmistakenly system oriented. Invoking the American creed itself, there were demands that the age-old disparity between the expressed ideals and the actual performance of American democracy be ended. Beyond this, there was an effective appeal to the conscience of white America. Perhaps the most vital accomplishment of Martin Luther King was his success in getting the so-called "Negro question" recognized and accepted as the basic moral issue before the country. King was thus able to isolate the white South while providing the rest of the nation's whites with an opportunity to expiate their collective guilt. This was the prime reason for the white Northern support of the Civil Rights Act of 1964 and the Voting Rights Act of 1965.

Of equal importance with the goals of the first phase of the movement were the means it employed to achieve them. As modes of social protest, nonviolence and "love" were new and confusing on the

American scene. Nevertheless, they were inherent in the Judeo-Christian tradition that undergirded the American ethos. Morally, the American people could not openly invoke retaliation and repression. Skeptical at first, white America was moved ultimately to give unprecedented support to nonviolence and the goals to which it was directed. Nonviolence won for Dr. King, at least, the qualified support of two national administrations, that of President Kennedy and President Johnson. And beyond this it won almost universal approval abroad. Indeed, it was because of his philosophy and his ability to implement it that Dr. King won the Nobel Peace Prize.

If there was one indispensable reason for the success of the first ten years of the black revolution, it was the leadership provided by Dr. King. More than any other black leader in the history of the country, he knew his people, understood their fears and anxieties, their hopes and their aspirations. Dr. King was an activist, but his activism was rooted deeply in religious and moral commitments. He maintained an abiding faith in the American system and at the same time strived to correct its sins and omissions. He realized, as some of his younger and more impetuous critics did not, that black Americans had few if any options outside of the system.

Black protest movements in the United States, beginning even with the first one (1795–1815), appear to follow a common developmental pattern. The movement begins usually with low-keyed demands or protestations against specific ills or conditions. As it gathers momentum, it is expanded to include a broader range of grievances. The point will be reached where pragmatic or conventional approaches will be rejected and demands will be made for decisive, radical, or even apocalyptic solutions of the black man's problems. As extremists and/or militants begin to assume command, the movement begins to take on nationalistic overtones. Calls for black separation or emigration to Africa will become more and more persistent, and the effort will be made to convert the movement into a black nationalist crusade. In the modern black revolution this phase (the second phase) had definitely developed by 1965. It lasted through 1971.

Because of the excitement, the agitation, and the tumult associated with it, the black nationalist phase of the movement has managed to obscure the period from 1955 to 1965. Indeed, in the minds of a growing number of Americans the "black revolution" is associated only with militant black nationalism and the images of Stokely

Carmichael, Huey P. Newton, and LeRoi Jones. However, in terms of its material impact upon American institutions black nationalism was far less revolutionary than nonviolence. Over a five-year period the goals of black nationalism were broadcast first as "Black Power" and then as "Black Liberation." At no time was there ever any consensus on what either of the terms really envisioned. As its chief apostle, Carmichael gave one definition of Black Power: "It is a call for black people to begin to define their own goals, to lead their own organizations and to support those organizations. It is a call to reject the racist institutions and values of this society."[1] Before the phrase was to lose its popular appeal, it had been given almost as many definitions as there were black groups in the nation.

The term "Black Liberation" hardly fared much better. To the old-line black nationalists it meant mass black emigration to Africa and the establishment of a powerful black nation. To other groups, such as the Black Muslims, the Revolutionary Action Movement, and the Republic of New Africa, black liberation meant separatism rather than emigration. Specifically, these groups called for the acquisition by black people of six to twelve Southern states and the building thereon of a separate, sovereign, independent "nation within a nation." As the chief ideologist of the Black Panther party, Eldridge Cleaver defined black liberation as the liberation of the black colony from the oppression of the white mother country. This was to be brought about by black participation in a socialist revolution to overthrow the imperialistic capitalistic American system. To the large number of unattached young black militants, black liberation came generally to denote a nebulous kind of autonomy for the black community which would enable it to pursue its own goals, social, cultural, or political—in short, "to do its own thing."

Equally as nebulous and visionary were the black militant projections of black armed uprisings and mass slaughter of whites. None of this activity ever moved beyond the talking stage. On the other hand, there was evidence of some serious study of the possibilities of adopting the guerrilla warfare theories of Ché Guevara, Vo-Nguyen-Giap and Mao Tse-tung for black ghetto use. The RAM and RNA probably went further with this work than any other group. In this, as in other things, however, the activities of the militants received far more notoriety than they merited. The nation's press invariably magnified and spread any rumor it received of black urban guerrilla activity. There is almost a certainty that no sizable group of black militants ever received all of the training and know-how necessary to mount successful guerrilla activity in urban America. Even if one group had, the community support necessary to sustain such a campaign would not have been forthcoming. Urban blacks are not given to that kind of violence. Black militant confrontations with the local police, however, were another matter. They fascinated the black community, especially the "block boys," and they were acceptable substitutes for the mass slaughter of whites that was forever being promised. Essentially, the confrontation was a public display of *machismo*, that is, virility, courage, and bravado. These were the qualities historically denied the black male by American society.

If there was one common tie among all black militants, college boy and block boy, it was their special brand of speech or "rhetoric." Almost a new language, it consisted of words, phrases, and even metaphors culled from "black English," the writings of Fanon, Malcolm X, and socialist revolutionary literature. The rhetoric also employed a good deal of profanity and obscenity, the purpose of which was to shock and distress listeners. Name-calling, especially as a confrontation tactic, was also heavily relied upon. In his *Seize the Time*, Bobby Seale devotes an entire chapter to a discussion of the origins and usages of such Black Panther terminology as "Pigs," "Off the Pigs," "Jacknape," and "Motherfucker." All things considered, their rhetoric was perhaps the most effective thing the militants had going for them. While it did not produce the revolution, it did have a discernible effect upon the minds of the ghetto youth. Such admonitions as "Kill the pig upon the hill" and "get the honkey" were bound to be taken literally by some ghetto juveniles. In effect, they were indoctrination for crime disguised as revolutionary catechisms.

By mid-1970, revolutionary black nationalism was definitely beginning to lose its aura for an increasing number of black youth. They had been led to expect what in effect was a second coming, a final apocalypse. They had given of their hopes, their enthusiasm, and their labor, and still there was no deliverance, or any sign of deliverance. There were only promises and interminable rhetoric. The result for many of these youths was moodiness and despair, even despondency. Some of the college militants accepted the proffered embrace of the Black Muslims; others, reluctantly, made peace with the establishment. For the block boys the result was far more critical.

The aggression and hostility which only recently had been directed toward whites were once again turned on the black community and produced a crime rate unprecedented in the history of the nation. Moreover, the need to escape from utter hopelessness was perhaps not unrelated to the alarming rise of narcotic addiction in the black communities.

For all this, however, militant black nationalism did have a positive discernible impact upon blacks and especially upon Afro-American culture. The Black Studies crusade which it launched during the mid-1960s was initially a political movement, but others were to recognize its intrinsic worth and develop it into a legitimate academic pursuit. The more than six hundred colleges and universities that were offering Black Studies courses in 1972 all owed a debt to the movement. Less concrete but far more pervasive was the movement's influence on the growth of black consciousness within the race. The obsequious, docile, and apologetic "Uncle Tom" had vanished from the scene and the young blacks who were reaching maturity in 1970 were evidencing a greater pride in their blackness than had any generation before them.

In the arts and letters, the dominant theme for Afro-American craftsmen was also the black awakening. The struggle to produce a new black poetry was meeting with success, and black playwrights were winning their battle for recognition of the black theater. In the motion picture area, however, the movement had its most dramatic impact. Gone from the scene were such slack-mouthed versions of Uncle Tom as Stepin Fetchit, Manton Moreland, and Eddie "Rochester" Anderson. The so-called black film made its debut, and it presented black audiences with such new characters as "Shaft," "Nigger Charlie," and "Superfly." The new films were popular enough, but they did not meet universal approval. They tended to make heroes of black narcotic pushers, pimps, and miscellaneous hustlers. In the view of many observers they were producing new black stereotypes. From others, mostly of the motion picture industry, the rebuttal was that the films were producing unprecedented opportunities for black directors, black producers, black technicians, and black actors. As the controversy continued, there was the growing demand for the establishment of a Black Review Board.

As with any new cause, the singular pursuit of black consciousness began to produce excesses. There was the growing tendency to apply the "black perspective" to all social problems regardless of their nature. Thus, by 1970, there had come into existence upwards of a score of black professional groups almost all of which had achieved "liberation" by separating themselves from the predominantly white national organizations. Calling this a "new tribalism," Bayard Rustin observed: "Their various manifestos and agendas reflect a narrow vision of society in which racial awareness replaces political organization and life-style is a substitute for economic and social progress."[2]

The black revolution, specifically its activist phase, lasted for about fifteen years. This was about average for previous such movements among black Americans. Just when the next black revolution will occur would be difficult to predict. But given the tendency of white America never to deal with the problems of race until it has been jolted by a black uprising, there ought to be no doubt about the inevitability of another one. Whether it will be nonviolent or not is another question. The loyalties and constraints that have historically kept blacks to the path of peaceful protests were sorely tested during the decade of the "sixties." In the next black revolution they may very well be trampled under.

Bibliography

COLLECTIONS AND ARCHIVAL SOURCES

Civil Rights Documentation Project, Howard University, Washington, D.C.: "Transcript of a Recorded Interview of John Lewis, Third Chairman of S.N.C.C.," by Katherine M. Shannon.

Files of the Student Nonviolent Coordinating Committee on deposit at the Martin Luther King, Jr., Center for Social Change, Atlanta, Ga.

The Martin Luther King, Jr., Collection, Mugar Library, Boston University, Boston, Mass.

The Negro History Collection, Trevor Arnett Library, Atlanta University, Atlanta, Ga.

White House Central Files. Subject: Human Rights. The Lyndon Baines Johnson Library, Austin, Texas.

UNPUBLISHED SOURCES

Romaine Anne Cooke, "The Mississippi Freedom Democratic Party Through August, 1964," *Unpublished Master's Thesis,* University of Virginia.

ARTICLES, MONOGRAPHS, AND PAMPHLETS

"An Approach to Black Studies," *Statement of the Planning Staff Institute of the Black World,* Martin Luther King, Jr., Memorial Center, Atlanta, Ga., May, 1969.

"Black over White." *Commonweal,* May 30, 1969.

"Black Studies: Perspective 1970." *Danforth News and Notes,* March 1, 1970. Danforth Foundation, St. Louis, Mo.

Brimmer, Andrew F., "Income and Welfare in the Black Community." *Ebony,* October, 1972.

Bunzel, John H., "Black Studies at San Francisco State." *The Public Interest,* Fall, 1968.

"Civil Rights: Year-end Summary." *Southern Regional Council,* December 31, 1963.

Clark, Kenneth B., "Letter of Resignation from Board of Directors of Antioch College." *Black Studies: Myths and Realities.* A. Philip Randolph Educational Fund, September, 1969.

Clarke, Kenneth B.; Bond, Julian; and Hatcher, Richard G., "The Black Man in American Politics." *Metropolitan Applied Center and Institute for Black Elected Officials,* December, 1969.

Clarke, John Henrik, "The New Afro-American Nationalism." *Freedomways,* Fall, 1961.

Cohen, Michael, *Guns on Campus: Student Protest at Cornell.* Chicago: Urban Research Corporation, 1970.

Fischer, Roger A., "Ghetto and Gown: The Birth of Black Studies." *Current History,* November, 1969.

Goldman, Ralph F., "Confrontation at S. F. State." *Dissent,* March–April, 1969.

Good, Paul, "The Meridith March." *New South,* Summer, 1966.

Hadden, Jeffrey K.; Masotti, Lewis B.; and Thiessen, Victor, "The Making of Negro Mayors, 1967." Shank, Alan, *Political Power and The Urban Crisis.* Boston: Holbrook Press, 1969.

Johnson, Tobe, "Black Studies: Their Origin, Present State and Prospects." A paper presented at the American Conference of Academic Deans, Pittsburgh, Penn., January 13, 1969.

————, "Metropolitan Government: A Black Analytical Perspective." Joint Center for Political Studies, Washington, D.C., 1972.

Lythcott, Stephen, "The Case for Black Studies." *The Antioch Review,* Summer, 1969.

Piven, Francis F., and Cloward, Richard A., "Black Control of Cities." Shank, Alan, *Political Power and the Urban Crisis.* Boston: Holbrook Press, 1969.

"A Reparations Jubilee." *World's Work,* June, 1969.

"The Republic of New Africa: Short Official Basic Documents." *Republic of New Africa,* New Orleans, La.

Roberts, Gene, "The Story of Snick: From 'Freedom High' to 'Black Power.'" *The New York Times Magazine,* September 25, 1966.

Rooks, Charles S., *The Atlanta Elections of 1969.* Atlanta: The Voter Education Project, June, 1970.

Rosovsky, Henry, "Black Studies at Harvard." *The American Scholar,* Autumn, 1969.

Rowan, Carl T., "Martin Luther King's Tragic Decision." *Reader's Digest,* September, 1967.

Rustin, Bayard, "'Black Power' and Coalition Politics." *Commentary,* September, 1966.

Sindler, Allan P., "A Case Study of a University's Pattern of Error." A paper presented at the Annual Meeting of the American Political Science Association, September, 1969.

"The Student Protest Movement: A Recapitulation, September, 1969." *Southern Regional Council,* September 29, 1961.

Tate, Charles, "Brimmer and Black Capitalism: An Analysis." *The Review of Black Political Economy,* Spring/Summer, 1970.

"What Happened in the South." Voter Education Project, Inc., December 15, 1970.

"Will the Black Manifesto Help Blacks?" *Christian Century,* May 21, 1969.

Woodward, C. Vann, "Clio with Soul." *Black Studies: Myths and Realities.* A. Philip Randolph Educational Fund, September, 1969.

Zinn, Howard, "Registration in Alabama." *The New Republic,* October 26, 1963.

GOVERNMENT PUBLICATIONS

United States Congress, *Congressional Record,* 89th Congress, 1st Session, vol. 111, part 1, January 4, 1965.

United States Congress, *Congressional Record*, 90th Congress, 1st Session, vol. 113, part 4, March 1, 1967.

United States Congress, *Congressional Record*, 91st Congress, 1st Session, vol. 115, part 1, January 3, 1969.

United States Congress, "Gun-Barrel Politics: The Black Panther Party, 1966-1971." *Report by the Committee on Internal Security, House of Representatives, Ninety-Second Congress, First Session,* August 18, 1971.

United States Congress, "Investigation Activities of the Department of Justice," 66th Congress, 1st Session, 1919, *Senate Documents,* vol. 12, pp. 161-167.

"Political Participation." *A Report of the United States Commission on Civil Rights.* Washington, D.C.: United States Government Printing Office, May, 1968.

Report of the National Advisory Commission on Civil Disorders. Washington, D.C.: United States Government Printing Office, 1968.

BOOKS

Anthony, Earl, *Picking Up the Gun.* New York: The Dial Press, 1970.

Aptheker, Herbert, ed., *A Documentary History of the Negro People in the United States.* New York: Citadel Press, Inc., 1951.

Baraka, Imamu Amiri (LeRoi Jones), *Raise Race Rays Raze: Essays Since 1965.* New York: Random House, Inc., 1969.

Barbour, Floyd B., ed., *The Black Power Revolt: A Collection of Essays.* Boston: Extending Horizons Books, 1968.

Bennett, Lerone, Jr., *What Manner of Man: A Biography of Martin Luther King, Jr.* Chicago: Johnson Publishing Company, Inc., 1964.

Bishop, Jim, *The Days of Martin Luther King, Jr.* New York: G.P. Putnam's Sons, 1971.

Bracey, John H.; Meier, August; and Rudwick, Elliott, *Black Nationalism in America.* Indianapolis: The Bobbs-Merrill Co., Inc., 1970.

Breitman, George, ed., *Malcolm X Speaks: Selected Speeches and Statements.* New York: Grove Press, Inc., 1965.

Breitman, George, *The Last Year of Malcolm X: The Evolution of a Revolutionary.* New York: Merit Publishers, 1967.

Brisbane, Robert H., *The Black Vanguard: Origins of the Negro Social Revolution.* Valley Forge: Judson Press, 1970.

Camus, Albert, *The Rebel: An Essay on Man in Revolt.* New York: Alfred A. Knopf, 1954.

Cantor, Norman F., *The Age of Protest: Dissent and Rebellion in the Twentieth Century.* New York: Hawthorn Books, Inc., 1969.

Carmichael, Stokely, and Hamilton, Charles, *Black Power: The Politics of Liberation in America.* New York: Random House, Inc., 1967.

Carmichael, Stokely, *Stokely Speaks: Black Power Back to Pan-Africanism.* New York: Vintage Books, division of Random House, Inc., 1971.

Clark, Kenneth B., *Dark Ghetto: Dilemmas of Social Change.* New York: Harper & Row, Publishers, 1965.

Clark, Ramsey, *Crime in America.* New York: Simon & Schuster, Inc., 1970.

Clarke, John Henrick, *Harlem, U.S.A.* New York: The Macmillan Company, 1964.

_____, *Malcolm X: The Man and His Times.* New York: Collier Books, 1969.

Cleaver, Eldridge, *Soul on Ice.* New York: McGraw-Hill Book Company, 1968.

Cruse, Harold, *The Crisis of the Negro Intellectual: From Its Origins to the Present.* New York: William Morrow & Co., Inc., 1967.

Douglass, Frederick, *The Life and Times of Frederick Douglass.* New York: The Macmillan Company, 1962.

Draper, Theodore, *The Rediscovery of Black Nationalism.* New York: The Viking Press, 1969.

Eckman, Fern Marja, *The Furious Passage of James Baldwin.* New York: M. Evans and Company, 1966.

Eichel, Lawrence E.; Jost, Kenneth; Luskin, Robert D.; and Neustadt, Richard M., *The Harvard Strike.* Boston: Houghton-Mifflin Company, 1970.

Fanon, Frantz, *The Wretched of the Earth.* New York: Grove Press, Inc., 1963.

Farmer, James, *Freedom—When?* New York: Random House, Inc., 1965.

Foner, Philip, ed., *The Black Panthers Speak.* Philadelphia: J. B. Lippincott Company, 1970.

Forman, James, *The Making of Black Revolutionaries.* New York: The Macmillan Company, 1972.

Gayle, Addison, *Black Expression: Essays by and About Americans in Creative Arts.* New York: Weybright & Talley, Inc., 1969.

Gibson, Donald, B., ed., *Five Black Writers: Essays on Wright, Ellison, Baldwin, Hughes, and LeRoi Jones.* New York: New York University Press, 1970.

Gitlow, Benjamin, *I Confess: The Truth About American Communism.* New York: E. P. Dutton and Company, 1939.

Goldman, Eric F., *The Tragedy of Lyndon Johnson.* New York: Alfred A. Knopf, Inc., 1969.

Graham, Hugh Davis, and Gurr, Ted Robert, *A History of Violence in America: A Report to the Commission on the Causes and Prevention of Violence.* New York: Praeger Publishers, Inc., 1969.

Grimshaw, Allen D., ed., *Racial Violence in the United States.* Chicago: Aldine-Atherton, Inc., 1969.

Gross, Bella, *Clarion Call: The History and Development of the Negro People's Convention Movement in the U.S. from 1817 to 1840.* New York: Bella Gross, 1947.

Jones, LeRoi, *Home: Social Essays.* New York: William Morrow & Co., Inc., 1966.

King, Coretta Scott, *My Life with Martin Luther King, Jr.* New York: Holt, Rinehart and Winston, Inc., 1969.

King, Martin Luther, Jr., *Stride Toward Freedom: The Montgomery Story.* New York: Harper & Row, Publishers, 1958.

King, Martin Luther, Jr., *Where Do We Go from Here—Chaos or Community?* Boston: Beacon Press, 1968.

King, Martin Luther, Jr., *Why We Can't Wait.* New York: Harper & Row, Publishers, 1963.

Lecky, Robert S., and Wright, H. Elliott, *Black Manifesto: Religion, Racism, and Reparations.* New York: Sheed & Ward, Inc., 1969.

Lester, Julius, *Revolutionary Notes.* New York: Richard W. Baron Publishing Co., 1969.

Lewis, David L., *King: A Critical Biography.* New York: Praeger Publishers, Inc., 1970.

Lincoln, C. Eric, *The Black Muslims in America.* Boston: Beacon Press, 1961.

Litwack, Leon F., *North of Slavery: The Negro in the Free States, 1790-1860.*

Chicago: University of Chicago Press, 1961.

Lomax, Louis E., *The Negro Revolt*. New York: Harper & Row, Publishers, 1962.

_____, *To Kill a Black Man*. Los Angeles: Holloway House Publishing Co., 1968.

_____, *When the Word Is Given: A Report on Elijah Muhammad, Malcolm X and the Black Muslim World*. Cleveland: The World Publishing Company, 1963.

Lubell, Samuel, *The Hidden Crisis in American Politics*. New York: W. W. Norton & Company, Inc., 1970.

McMillen, Neil R., *The Citizens' Councils: Organized Resistance to the Second Reconstruction, 1954-64*. Urbana: University of Illinois Press, 1961.

Major, Reginald, *Panther Is a Black Cat*. New York: William Morrow & Co., Inc., 1971.

Malcolm X (Assisted by Alex Haley), *The Autobiography of Malcolm X*. New York: Grove Press, Inc., 1964.

Marine, Gene, *The Black Panthers*. New York: Signet Books, 1969.

Mays, Benjamin E., *Born to Rebel*. New York: Charles Scribner's Sons, 1971.

Meier, August, and Rudwick, Elliott, *CORE: A Study of the Civil Rights Movement, 1942-1968*. New York: Oxford University Press, 1973.

Miller, William Robert, *Martin Luther King, Jr*. New York: Avon Books, 1968.

Moore, Chuck, *I Was a Black Panther*. New York: Doubleday & Company, Inc., 1970.

Muse, Benjamin, *The American Negro Revolution: From Nonviolence to Black Power, 1963-1967*. Bloomington: Indiana University Press, 1968.

_____, *Virginia's Massive Resistance*. Bloomington: Indiana University Press, 1961.

Neary, John, *Julian Bond: Black Rebel*. New York: William Morrow & Co., Inc., 1971.

Newton, Huey P., and Blake, Herman, *Revolutionary Suicide*. New York: Harcourt Brace Jovanovich, Inc., 1973.

Oppenheimer, Martin, *The Urban Guerrilla*. Chicago: Quadrangle Books, 1969.

Quarles, Benjamin, *Negro in the Making of America*. New York: The Macmillan Company, 1964.

Reddick, Lawrence, *Crusader Without Violence*. New York: Harper & Row, Publishers, 1959.

Redkey, Edwin S., *Black Exodus: Black Nationalist and Back-to-Africa Movements, 1890-1910*. New Haven: Yale University Press, 1969.

Robinson, Armstead L.; Foster, Craig C.; and Ogilvie, Donald H.; eds., *Black Studies in the University: A Symposium*. New Haven: Yale University Press, 1969.

Rowan, Carl T., *Go South to Sorrow*. New York: Random House, Inc., 1957.

Schanche, Don A., *The Panther Paradox: A Liberal's Dilemma*. New York: David McKay Co., Inc., 1970.

Scheer, Robert, ed., *Eldridge Cleaver: Post-Prison Writings and Speeches*. New York: Random House, Inc., 1967.

Schlesinger, Arthur M., Jr., *A Thousand Days: John F. Kennedy in the White House*. Boston: Houghton Mifflin Company, 1965.

Seale, Bobby, *Seize the Time: The Story of the Black Panther Party and Huey P. Newton*. New York: Vintage Books, 1970.

Sellers, Cleveland, and Terrell, Robert, *The Autobiography of a Black Militant and the Life and Death of S.N.C.C.* New York: William Morrow & Co., Inc., 1973.

Shank, Alan, ed., *Political Power and the Urban Crisis*. Boston: Holbrook Press, Inc., 1969.

Shapiro, Fred C., and Sullivan, James W., *Race Riots: New York 1964*. New York: Thomas Y. Crowell Company, 1964.

Shoemaker, Don, *With All Deliberate Speed*. New York: Harper and Row, Publishers, 1957.

Silver, James W., *Mississippi: The Closed Society*. New York: Harcourt Brace Jovanovich, Inc., 1966.

Sullivan, Leon H., *Build Brother Build*. Philadelphia: Macrae Smith Company, 1969.

Tindall, George Brown, *South Carolina Negroes, 1877–1900*. Columbia: University of South Carolina Press, 1952.

Warren, Robert Penn, *Who Speaks for the Negro?* New York: Random House, Inc., 1965.

Waskow, Arthur I., *From Race Riot to Sit-in, 1919 and the 1960's: A Study in the Connections Between Conflict and Violence*. Garden City, N.Y.: Doubleday & Company, Inc., 1966.

Watters, Pat, and Cleghorn, Reese, *Climbing Jacob's Ladder: The Arrival of Negroes in Southern Politics*. New York: Harcourt Brace Jovanovich, Inc., 1967.

White, Theodore H., *The Making of the President, 1964*. New York: Atheneum Publishers, 1965.

White, Walter F., *How Far the Promised Land?* New York: The Viking Press, Inc., 1955.

Wolff, Miles, *Lunch at the Five and Ten*. New York: Stein & Day Publishers, 1970.

Wright, Richard, *Native Son*. New York: Harper & Row, Publishers, 1940.

Zinn, Howard, *SNCC: The New Abolitionists*. Boston: Beacon Press, 1964.

Notes

CHAPTER 1

[1] Herbert Aptheker, ed., *A Documentary History of the Negro People in the United States* (New York: Citadel Press, Inc., 1951), p. 32.

[2] See Leon F. Litwack, *North of Slavery: The Negro in the Free States, 1790–1860* (Chicago: University of Chicago Press, 1961), pp. 69-74.

[3] Bella Gross, *Clarion Call: The History and Development of the Negro Peoples Convention Movement in the United States from 1817 to 1840* (New York: Bella Gross, 1947), pp. 5-8.

[4] *Ibid.*, pp. 8-20.

[5] Litwack, *op. cit.*, p. 244.

[6] *Ibid.*, p. 265.

[7] Theodore Draper, *The Rediscovery of Black Nationalism* (New York: The Viking Press, Inc., 1969), p. 27.

[8] Frederick Douglass, *Life and Times of Frederick Douglass* (Boston: De Wolfe, Fiske and Co., 1893), p. 355.

[9] For an exhaustive treatment of this movement see: Edwin S. Redkey, *Black Exodus: Black Nationalist and Back-to-Africa Movements, 1890–1910* (New Haven, Conn.: Yale University Press, 1969).

[10] *Ibid.*, pp. 100-101.

[11] John H. Bracey, Jr., August Meier, and Elliott Rudwick, eds., *Black Nationalism in America* (Indianapolis: The Bobbs-Merrill Co., Inc., 1970), pp. 172-173.

[12] Redkey, *op. cit.*, pp. 22, 102-126. See also George Brown Tindall, *South Carolina Negroes, 1877–1900* (Columbia, S.C.: University of South Carolina Press, 1952), pp. 153-168.

[13] Redkey, *op. cit.*, pp. 219-240.

[14] Quoted in Louis E. Lomax, *The Negro Revolt* (New York: Signet Books, 1962), p. 52.

CHAPTER 2

[1] Walter F. White, *How Far the Promised Land?* (New York: The Viking Press, Inc., 1955), pp. 222, 228.

[2] *Montgomery Advertiser*, May 12, 1957.

[3] Weldon James, *With All Deliberate Speed*, p. 18, quoted in Neil R. McMillen, *The Citizens' Council: Organized Resistance to the Second Reconstruction, 1954-64* (Urbana, Ill.: University of Illinois Press, 1971), p. 117.

[4] *Congressional Record*, 84th Congress, 2nd Session, vol. 102, part 4, April 12, 1956, pp. 4459-4461.

[5] Benjamin Muse, *Virginia's Massive Resistance* (Bloomington: Indiana University Press, 1961), p. 20.

[6] *Ibid.*, pp. 148-154.

[7] Carl T. Rowan, *Go South to Sorrow* (New York: Random House, Inc., 1957), p. 20.

[8] *Ibid.*, pp. 21-23.

[9] *Ibid.*, p. 101.

[10] Louis E. Lomax, *The Negro Revolt* (New York: Signet Books, 1962), p. 85.

[11] Langston Hughes, *Fight for Freedom, The Story of the NAACP* (New York: W. W. Norton & Company, Inc., 1962), pp. 145-146.

[12] William Robert Miller, *Martin Luther King, Jr.* (New York: Avon Books, 1968), p. 47. Copyright © 1968 by William Robert Miller. Published by Weybright and Talley, Inc. Reprinted by permission of the David McKay Co., Inc.

[13] Rowan, *op. cit.*, pp. 118-119.

[14] Martin Luther King, Jr., *Stride Toward Freedom: The Montgomery Story* (New York: Harper & Row, Publishers, Perennial Library Edition, 1958), p. 48.

[15] Rowan, *op. cit.*, p. 119.

[16] King, *op. cit.*, p. 66.

[17] David L. Lewis, *King: A Critical Biography* (New York: Praeger Publishers, Inc., 1970), p. 70.

[18] Miller, *op. cit.*, p. 59.

[19] Rowan, *op. cit.*, pp. 132-133.

[20] Jim Bishop, *The Days of Martin Luther King, Jr.* (New York: G. P. Putnam's Sons, 1971), p. 172.

[21] *Ibid.*, p. 173.

[22] *Ibid.*, p. 174.

[23] King, *op. cit.*, p. 139.

[24] *Ibid.*, pp. 139-140.

[25] *Ibid.*, p. 140.

[26] Lerone Bennett, Jr., *What Manner of Man: A Biography of Martin Luther King, Jr.* (Chicago: Johnson Publishing Company, Inc., 1964), p. 77.

[27] King, *op. cit.*, p. 150.

CHAPTER 3

[1] "The Student Protest Movement: A Recapitulation, September, 1961," *Southern Regional Council* (September 29, 1961).

[2] James Farmer, *Freedom—When?* (New York: Random House, Inc., 1965), p. 64. See also August Meier and Elliott Rudwick, *CORE: A Study in the Civil Rights Movement, 1942-1968* (New York: Oxford University Press, 1973), p. 33.

[3] William Robert Miller, *Martin Luther King, Jr.* (New York: Avon Books, 1968), pp. 98-99.

[4] Miles Wolff, *Lunch at the Five and Ten* (New York: Stein and Day, Publishers, 1970), pp. 11-12.

[5] "Transcript of a Recorded Interview of John Lewis, Third Chairman of SNCC," by Katherine M. Shannon for *The Civil Rights Documentation Project*, Washington, D.C., 1967. Lewis to Shannon, p. 18. Used by permission.

[6] Howard Zinn, *SNCC: The New Abolitionists* (Boston: Beacon Press, 1964), pp. 23-24. Copyright © 1964, 1965 by Howard Zinn. Reprinted by permission of Beacon Press.

[7] John Neary, *Julian Bond: Black Rebel* (New York: William Morrow & Co., Inc., 1971), pp. 57ff.

[8] Benjamin E. Mays, *Born to Rebel* (New York: Charles Scribner's Sons, 1971), p. 288.

[9] Mays, *op. cit.*, p. 289.

[10] Quoted in Zinn, *op. cit.*, p. 27.

[11] Miller, *op. cit.*, p. 100.

[12] Lewis to Shannon, p. 50.

[13] *New York Times*, April 17, 1960.

[14] *Ibid.* See also Cleveland Sellers and Robert Terrell, *The River of No Return: The Autobiography of a Black Militant and the Life and Death of SNCC* (New York: William Morrow & Co., Inc., 1973), p. 35.

[15] Mays, *op. cit.,* pp. 287-299.

[16] Jim Bishop, *The Days of Martin Luther King, Jr.* (New York: G. P. Putnam's Sons, 1971), p. 239.

[17] *Ibid.,* pp. 239-240.

[18] *Ibid.,* p. 240.

[19] Farmer, *op. cit.,* pp. 78-81. See also Meier and Rudwick, *op. cit.,* pp. 135-136.

[20] Louis E. Lomax, *The Negro Revolt* (New York: Harper & Row, Publishers, 1962), p. 134.

[21] Lewis to Shannon, pp. 61-62.

[22] *Ibid.,* p. 64.

[23] Howard Zinn, *op. cit.,* pp. 42-44. See also Meier and Rudwick, *op. cit.,* p. 138.

[24] Lewis to Shannon, p. 67. See also Meier and Rudwick, *op. cit.,* pp. 138-139.

[25] *New York Times,* May 21, 1961, p. 79.

[26] Zinn, *op. cit.,* p. 47.

[27] Lewis to Shannon, p. 80.

[28] Farmer, *op. cit.,* p. 73.

[29] Lerone Bennett, Jr., *What Manner of Man* (Chicago: Johnson Publishing Company, Inc., 1964), p. 127.

[30] Martin Luther King, Jr., Collection, Mugar Memorial Library, Boston University, Boston, Mass., File #VII 51B. Used by permission.

[31] Arthur M. Schlesinger, Jr., *A Thousand Days: John F. Kennedy in the White House* (Boston: Houghton Mifflin Company, 1965), p. 935.

[32] Miller, *op. cit.,* p. 122.

[33] Zinn, *op. cit.,* pp. 58-61.

[34] Lomax, *op. cit.,* p. 97.

[35] *Ibid.,* p. 98.

[36] *Ibid.*

[37] David L. Lewis, *King: A Critical Biography* (New York: Praeger Publishers, Inc., 1970), p. 149.

[38] *Ibid.,* p. 151.

[39] *Ibid.*

[40] *Time,* January 3, 1964, p. 15.

[41] Miller, *op. cit.,* p. 128.

[42] Bennett, *op. cit.,* p. 130.

[43] Martin Luther King, Jr., *Why We Can't Wait* (New York: Harper & Row, Publishers, 1963), p. 37.

[44] *Ibid.,* p. 72.

[45] Coretta Scott King, *My Life with Martin Luther King, Jr.* (New York: Holt, Rinehart and Winston, Inc., 1969), p. 227.

[46] Bishop, *op. cit.,* p. 290.

[47] King, *Why We Can't Wait,* pp. 77-100.

[48] Bishop, *op. cit.,* p. 304.

[49] Schlesinger, *op. cit.,* p. 959.

[50] *Ibid.,* p. 963.

[51] *Ibid.*

[52] *New York Times,* June 12, 1963.

[53] Schlesinger, *op. cit.,* p. 966.

[54] John Henrik Clarke, ed., *Malcolm X: The Man and His Times* (New York: The Macmillan Company, 1969), pp. 176-177.

[55] Schlesinger, *op. cit.,* p. 969.

[56] *New York Times,* July 18, 1963, p. 10.

[57] Lewis to Shannon, pp. 127-128.
[58] Lewis, *King*, p. 229.
[59] Malcolm X, *The Autobiography of Malcolm X* (New York: Grove Press, Inc., 1964), p. 284. Reprinted by permission of Grove Press, Inc. Copyright © 1964 by Alex Haley and Malcolm X. Copyright © 1965 by Alex Haley and Betty Shabazz. Introduction © 1965 by M. S. Handler. "On Malcolm X" by Ossie Davis © 1965 by Roger Price.

CHAPTER 4

[1] Pat Watters and Reese Cleghorn, *Climbing Jacob's Ladder: The Arrival of Negroes in Southern Politics* (New York: Harcourt Brace Jovanovich, Inc., 1967), Appendix II.
[2] "What Happened in the South, 1970," *Voter Education Project* (December 15, 1970).
[3] David L. Lewis, *King: A Critical Biography* (New York: Praeger Publishers, Inc., 1970), p. 93.
[4] William R. Miller, *Martin Luther King, Jr.* (New York: Avon Books, 1968), p. 122.
[5] Robert P. Moses to Anne Cooke Romaine in Anne Cooke Romaine, "The Mississippi Freedom Democratic Party Through August, 1964," Master's Thesis, University of Virginia (Based on interviews of members of the MFDP), on deposit in the Martin Luther King, Jr., Center for Social Change, Atlanta, Ga.
[6] Moses to Romaine.
[7] *Ibid.*
[8] Howard Zinn, *SNCC: The New Abolitionists* (Boston: Beacon Press, 1964), p. 67.
[9] "What Happened in the South, 1970," *op. cit.*
[10] "News Release," *Voter Education Project* (March 31, 1963), p. 3.
[11] Zinn, *op. cit.*, p. 79.
[12] Watters and Cleghorn, *op. cit.*, p. 49.
[13] Dr. Aaron Henry to Romaine.
[14] Watters and Cleghorn, *op. cit.*, p. 64.
[15] Zinn, *op. cit.*, pp. 93-94.
[16] Watters and Cleghorn, *op. cit.*, pp. 132-133.
[17] "News Release," *op. cit.*, p. 14.
[18] Watters and Cleghorn, *op. cit.*, p. 60.
[19] Zinn, *op. cit.*, pp. 91-92.
[20] *New York Times*, March 31, 1963.
[21] Watters and Cleghorn, *op. cit.*, p. 65.
[22] *Ibid.*, pp. 66-67.
[23] *Ibid.*
[24] *Ibid.*, pp. 64-65.
[25] Moses to Romaine.
[26] *Ibid.*
[27] *New York Times*, June 21, 1964.
[28] James W. Silver, *Mississippi: The Closed Society* (New York: Harcourt Brace Jovanovich, Inc., 1966), p. 247.
[29] *New York Times*, June 21, 1964, p. 64.
[30] William McCord, *Mississippi, The Long Hot Summer* (New York: W. W. Norton & Company, Inc., 1965), p. 48.
[31] Silver, *op. cit.*, p. 255.
[32] Stokely Carmichael and Charles V. Hamilton, *Black Power: The Politics of Liberation in America* (New York: Random House, Inc., 1967), p. 93.
[33] McCord, *op. cit.*, pp. 114-115. See also Cleveland Sellers and Robert Terrell, *The River of No Return: The Autobiography of a Black Militant and the Life and Death of SNCC* (New York: William Morrow & Co., Inc., 1973), pp. 108-110.

[34] Rauh to Romaine.

[35] Letter from Walter Adams to Walter Jenkins, Special Assistant to the President, Executive File PL/FT/ Box 23, Lyndon B. Johnson Library.

[36] *New York Times*, August 22, 1964.

[37] Jack Minnis, "The Mississippi Freedom Democratic Party," *Freedomways*, Spring, 1965, p. 269.

[38] Watters and Cleghorn, *op. cit.*, p. 290.

[39] Telegram from Dr. Martin Luther King to the President, August 24, 1964. Executive File PL/FT/ Box 24, Lyndon B. Johnson Library.

[40] Theodore H. White, *The Making of the President, 1964* (New York: Atheneum Publishers, 1965), pp. 293-294.

[41] Rauh to Romaine.

[42] *Ibid.*

[43] Bill Higgs to Romaine.

[44] Minnis, *op. cit.*, p. 271.

[45] Higgs to Romaine.

[46] *Ibid.*

[47] *New York Times*, August 26, 1964.

[48] Silver, *op. cit.*, p. 344.

[49] Moses to Romaine.

[50] *Congressional Record*, 89th Congress, 1st Session, vol. 3, part 1, January 4, 1965, pp. 19, 50.

[51] Benjamin Muse, *The American Negro Revolution: From Nonviolence to Black Power, 1963-1967* (Bloomington: Indiana University Press, 1968), p. 182.

[52] *New York Times*, December 11, 1964.

[53] *Ibid.*, October 15, 1964.

[54] Lewis, *op. cit.*, p. 255.

[55] Benjamin E. Mays, *Born to Rebel* (New York: Charles Scribner's Sons, 1969), p. 272.

[56] Watters and Cleghorn, *op. cit.*, p. 251.

[57] *Ibid.*

[58] Coretta Scott King, *My Life with Martin Luther King, Jr.* (New York: Holt, Rinehart and Winston, Inc., 1969), p. 256.

[59] *New York Times*, February 11, 1965.

[60] *Ibid.*, March 7, 1965.

[61] *Ibid.*

[62] *Ibid.*

[63] *Ibid.*, March 8, 1965.

[64] Lewis, *op. cit.*, p. 275.

[65] *New York Times*, March 9, 1965.

[66] Lewis to Shannon, p. 143.

[67] Lewis, *King*, p. 279.

[68] Jim Bishop, *The Days of Martin Luther King, Jr.* (New York: G. P. Putnam's Sons, 1971), p. 388.

[69] Eldridge Cleaver, *Soul on Ice* (New York: Dell Books, imprint of Dell Publishing Co., Inc., 1968), p. 74. Used with permission of McGraw Hill Book Company.

[70] *New York Times*, March 12, 1965.

[71] Eric F. Goldman, *The Tragedy of Lyndon Johnson* (New York: Alfred A. Knopf, Inc., 1969), p. 314. See also background papers for the President's meeting and press conference with Governor Wallace, Executive File HU2/ST1/ Box 25, Lyndon B. Johnson Library.

[72] *Ibid.*, p. 315.

[73] *New York Times*, March 16, 1965, p. 30.

[74] *Ibid.*, March 19, 1965. See also telegram from the Lieutenant Governor of Alabama,

James B. Allen, to the President, Executive File HU2/ST1/ Box 25, Lyndon B. Johnson Library.
[75] Muse, *The American Negro Revolution,* p. 170.
[76] *New York Times,* March 26, 1965.
[77] Watters and Cleghorn, *op. cit.,* pp. 257-258.

CHAPTER 5

[1] Louis E. Lomax, *To Kill a Black Man* (Los Angeles: Holloway House Publishing Co., 1968), pp. 246-248. See also *Autobiography of Malcolm X* (New York: Grove Press, Inc., 1964), pp. 434-437.
[2] Robert Penn Warren, *Who Speaks for the Negro?* (New York: Random House, Inc., 1965), p. 266.
[3] Malcolm X, *Autobiography of Malcolm X* (New York: Grove Press, Inc., 1964), p. 400.
[4] *Ibid.,* p. 6.
[5] *Ibid.,* p. 396.
[6] *Ibid.,* p. 162.
[7] Louis E. Lomax, *When the Word Is Given . . . A Report on Elijah Muhammad, Malcolm X, and the Black Muslim World* (New York: World Publishing Company, 1963), pp. 17-18.
[8] Lomax, *To Kill a Black Man,* p. 67.
[9] Malcolm X, *op. cit.,* p. 242.
[10] *Ibid.,* p. 250.
[11] *Ibid.,* p. 399.
[12] Lomax, *To Kill a Black Man,* p. 79.
[13] C. Eric Lincoln, *The Black Muslims in America* (Boston: Beacon Press, 1961), p. 154.
[14] Lomax, *When the Word Is Given,* p. 203.
[15] *New York Times,* November 8, 1964.
[16] Lomax, *When the Word Is Given,* p. 91.
[17] Malcolm X, *op. cit.,* p. 299.
[18] *Ibid.,* p. 300.
[19] *Ibid.*
[20] *Ibid.,* p. 302.
[21] *Ibid.,* p. 303.
[22] Malcolm X., *op. cit.,* p. 306.
[23] *Ibid.,* p. 413.
[24] Lomax, *To Kill a Black Man,* p. 102.
[25] Eldridge Cleaver, *Soul on Ice* (New York: A Delta Book, 1968), p. 54.
[26] Malcolm X, *op. cit.,* p. 317.
[27] George Breitman, *The Last Year of Malcolm X: The Evolution of a Revolutionary* (New York: Merit Publishers, 1967), p. 60.
[28] *Ibid.,* p. 76.
[29] Malcolm X, *op. cit.,* pp. 345-346.
[30] Breitman, *op. cit.,* p. 65.
[31] Malcolm X, *op. cit.,* p. 415.
[32] Cleaver, *op. cit.,* p. 56.
[33] Breitman, *op. cit.,* p. 77.
[34] Robert H. Brisbane, *The Black Vanguard: Origins of the Negro Social Revolution, 1900–1960* (Valley Forge: Judson Press, 1970), p. 74.
[35] *Ibid.,* p. 197.
[36] *Ibid.,* pp. 197-199.
[37] George Breitman, ed., *Malcolm X Speaks: Selected Speeches and Statements* (New

York: Grove Press, Inc., 1965), pp. 75-77. Copyright © 1965 by Merit Publishers and Mrs. Betty Shabazz.

[38] *Ibid.*, p. 84.

[39] Malcolm X, *op. cit.*, p. 37.

[40] *Ibid.*, p. 421.

[41] *Ibid.*, p. 374.

[42] *Ibid.*, p. 382.

[43] Lewis to Shannon, p. 138.

[44] Malcolm X., *op. cit.*, p. 313.

[45] *Ibid.*, p. 430.

[46] Allan Morrison, "Who Killed Malcolm X?" *Ebony*, October 5, 1965, p. 138.

[47] *Ibid.*, p. 139.

CHAPTER 6

[1] *Atlanta Daily World*, p. 1.

[2] Lewis to Shannon, pp. 153-155. For other discussions of this meeting, see John Neary, *Julian Bond: Black Rebel* (New York: William Morrow & Co., Inc., 1971), pp. 143-145; and James Forman, *The Making of Black Revolutionaries* (New York: The Macmillan Company, 1972), pp. 447, 454.

[3] Lewis to Shannon, p. 158, and Forman, *op. cit.*, pp. 454-455.

[4] Gene Roberts, "The Story of Snick: From 'Freedom High' to 'Black Power,'" *New York Times Magazine*, September 25, 1966, p. 126.

[5] Lewis to Shannon, p. 116.

[6] Robert Penn Warren, *Who Speaks for the Negro?* (New York: Random House, Inc., 1965), p. 95.

[7] Howard Zinn, *SNCC: The New Abolitionists* (Boston: Beacon Press, 1964), p. 17.

[8] Neary, *op. cit.*, pp. 89-91.

[9] *Ibid.*, p. 94.

[10] *Ibid.*, p. 124.

[11] Forman, *op. cit.*, pp. 101ff.

[12] Warren, *op. cit.*, p. 184.

[13] *Ibid.*

[14] Lewis to Shannon, p. 52.

[15] Zinn, *op. cit.*, p. 80.

[16] *Ibid.*, pp. 123ff.

[17] Lewis to Shannon, p. 7.

[18] *Ibid.*, p. 170.

[19] *Ibid.*, p. 150.

[20] Zinn, *op. cit.*, p. 40.

[21] Stokely Carmichael and Charles V. Hamilton, *Black Power: The Politics of Liberation in America* (New York: Random House, Inc., 1967), p. 96.

[22] *Ibid.*, p. 100.

[23] *Ibid.*, pp. 103-104.

[24] *Ibid.*, p. 104. See also Cleveland Sellers and Robert Terrell, *The River of No Return: The Autobiography of a Black Militant and the Life and Death of SNCC* (New York: William Morrow & Co., Inc., 1973), pp. 151-154.

[25] *Ibid.*, p. 106.

[26] *Ibid.*, p. 98.

[27] *Ibid.*, p. 120.

[28] Lewis to Shannon, p. 138.

[29] Albert Camus, *The Rebel* (New York: Alfred A. Knopf, 1954), p. 258.

[30] Roberts, *op. cit.*, p. 29.

[31] Lewis to Shannon, p. 141.

[32] Frantz Fanon, *The Wretched of the Earth* (New York: Grove Press, Inc., 1963), p. 215. Reprinted by permission of Grove Press, Inc. Copyright © 1963 by Presence Africaine.

[33] *Ibid.*, p. 61.

[34] *Ibid.*, p. 94.

[35] Lewis to Shannon, p. 138.

[36] Roberts, *op. cit.*, p. 27.

[37] Quoted in Floyd B. Barbour, ed., *The Black Power Revolt: A Collection of Essays* (Boston: Extending Horizons Books, imprint of Porter Sargent, Publishers, 1968), p. 189.

[38] Conversation—author with John Lewis.

[39] Paul Good, "The Meridith March," *New South* (Summer, 1966), p. 8.

[40] *New York Times*, June 6, 1966.

[41] Martin Luther King, Jr., *Where Do We Go from Here: Chaos or Community?* (Boston: Beacon Press, 1968), pp. 23-25. Used with permission of Harper & Row, Publishers, Inc. See also Sellers and Terrell, *op. cit.*, pp. 160, 162.

[42] *Ibid.*, p. 25.

[43] *Ibid.*, p. 26.

[44] *Ibid.*, p. 27.

[45] David L. Lewis, *King: A Critical Biography* (New York: Praeger Publishers, Inc., 1970), p. 322.

[46] *Ibid.*, p. 323.

[47] *Ibid.*

[48] Good, *op cit.*, p. 8.

[49] *New York Times*, June 17, 1966.

[50] *Ibid.*

[51] *Ibid.* See also King, *Where Do We Go from Here . . . ?* p. 29.

[52] King, *Where Do We Go from Here . . . ?* p. 30.

[53] *Ibid.*, p. 31.

[54] *Ibid.*

[55] *Ibid.*

[56] *New York Times*, June 27, 1966.

[57] *Ibid.*, July 5, 1966. See also August Meier and Elliott Rudwick, *CORE: A Study in the Civil Rights Movement, 1942-1968* (New York: Oxford University Press, 1973), p. 407.

[58] *Ibid.*, July 6, 1966. See also Meier and Rudwick, *op. cit.*, pp. 412-414.

[59] *Ibid.*, July 8, 1966. See also Meier and Rudwick, *op. cit.*, pp. 416-417.

[60] *Ibid.*, August 6, 1966.

[61] *Ibid.*, August 5, 1966.

[62] *Ibid.*, July 6, 1966.

[63] Bayard Rustin, "'Black Power' and Coalition Politics," *Commentary* (September, 1966), p. 35.

[64] Benjamin Muse, *The American Negro Revolution: From Nonviolence to Black Power, 1963-1967* (Bloomington: Indiana University Press, 1968), p. 243.

[65] *New York Times*, July 31, 1966.

[66] *Where Do We Go from Here . . . ?* Chapter 2, pp. 23-66.

[67] See Letters and Correspondence of Stokely Carmichael on deposit in the archives of the Martin Luther King, Jr., Center for Social Change, Atlanta, Ga. The following letters are identified by dates and initials. Used by permission of the Student Nonviolent Coordinating Committee.

[68] R. C.—November 22, 1966.

[69] S. F. C.—November 23, 1966.

[70] S. E. K.—November 8, 1966.

[71] Unsigned—November 14, 1966.

[72] The term was given extensive discussion in Carmichael and Hamilton's book *Black Power,* published in 1967.

[73] *New York Times,* August 5, 1966, p. 10.

CHAPTER 7

[1] Edward C. Banfield, *The Unheavenly City* (Boston: Little, Brown and Company, 1970), pp. 69-70.

[2] *Ibid.,* pp. 197-198.

[3] Kenneth B. Clark, *Dark Ghetto: Dilemmas of Social Power* (New York: Harper & Row, Publishers, 1965), p. 81.

[4] Hugh Davis Graham and Ted Robert Gurr, *The History of Violence in America: A Report Submitted to the National Commission on the Causes and Prevention of Violence* (New York: Praeger Publishers, Inc., 1969), pp. 412ff.

[5] Robert Brisbane, *The Black Vanguard* (Valley Forge: Judson Press, 1970), p. 60.

[6] See Arthur I. Waskow, *From Race Riot to Sit-In, 1919 and the 1960s: A Study in the Connections Between Conflict and Violence* (Garden City, N.Y.: Doubleday & Company, Inc., 1966; Anchor Books Edition, 1967), pp. 70-104.

[7] Brisbane, *op. cit.,* p. 165.

[8] *Ibid.,* pp. 142-143, and p. 165.

[9] William Robert Miller, *Martin Luther King, Jr.* (New York: Avon Books, 1968), p. 159.

[10] "Civil Rights: Year-End Summary," *Southern Regional Council* (December 31, 1963).

[11] Theodore H. White, *The Making of the President, 1964* (New York: Atheneum Publishers, 1965), p. 242.

[12] *New York Times,* April 11, 1964. See also August Meier and Elliott Rudwick, *CORE: A Study in the Civil Rights Movement, 1942-1968* (New York: Oxford University Press, 1973), p. 322.

[13] *Report of the National Advisory Commission on Civil Disorders* (Washington, D.C.: United States Government Printing Office, 1968), p. 20.

[14] Fred C. Shapiro and James W. Sullivan, *Race Riots: New York 1964* (New York: Thomas Y. Crowell Company, 1964), pp. 43ff.

[15] *Ibid.,* pp. 127ff. See also Meier and Rudwick, *op. cit.,* pp. 301-302.

[16] *Ibid.,* p. 130.

[17] David L. Lewis, *King: A Critical Biography* (New York: Praeger Publishers, Inc., 1970), pp. 245-246.

[18] *Report of the Nat. Adv. Comm.,* p. 20.

[19] *Ibid.*

[20] White, *op. cit.,* p. 248.

[21] *New York Times,* July 30, 1964.

[22] See *Report of the Nat. Adv. Comm.,* p. 20.

[23] Allen D. Grimshaw, ed., *Racial Violence in the United States* (Chicago: Aldine Publishing Company, 1969), pp. 226-228.

[24] *New York Times,* August 18, 1965.

[25] Martin Luther King, Jr., *Where Do We Go from Here . . . ?* (Boston: Beacon Press, 1968), p. 112.

[26] *New York Times,* August 19, 1965.

[27] King, *Where Do We Go from Here . . . ?,* p. 112.

[28] Quoted in Miller, *Martin Luther King, Jr.,* p. 247.

[29] *Ibid.,* pp. 247-248.

[30] Lewis, *op. cit.,* p. 320.

[31] *Ibid.,* p. 332.

[32] *Ibid.,* p. 333.

[33] *Report of the Nat. Adv. Comm.,* p. 21.

[34] *Ibid.*

[35] *Ibid.*, pp. 65-67.

[36] *Ramparts*, September, 1967, p. 27.

[37] *Ibid.*, p. 26.

[38] Benjamin Muse, *The American Negro Revolution: From Nonviolence to Black Power, 1963-1967* (Bloomington: Indiana University Press, 1968), pp. 310-311.

[39] Imamu Amiri Baraka (LeRoi Jones), *Raise Race Rays Raze: Essays Since 1965* (New York: Random House, Inc., 1969), p. 68.

[40] *Report of the Nat. Adv. Comm.*, pp. 30-38.

[41] *Life*, July 28, 1967, pp. 27-28.

[42] *New York Times*, July 26, 1967.

[43] *Report of the Nat. Adv. Comm.*, pp. 47-61.

[44] *Ibid.*, p. 50.

[45] John Hershey, *The Algiers Motel Incident* (New York: Alfred A. Knopf, 1968).

[46] *Report of the Nat. Adv. Comm.*, p. 89.

[47] *Ibid.*

[48] *Ibid.*, p. 91.

[49] Floyd B. Barbour, ed., *The Black Power Revolt: A Collection of Essays* (Boston: Extending Horizons Books, 1968), p. 174.

[50] Benjamin Muse, *The American Negro Revolution*, p. 299.

[51] Baraka, *op. cit.*, p. 52.

[52] Barbour, *op. cit.*, pp. 189-190.

[53] *Ibid.*, p. 195.

[54] *New York Times*, July 24, 1967, p. 16.

[55] Barbour, *op. cit.*, p. 198.

CHAPTER 8

[1] Carl T. Rowan, "Martin Luther King's Tragic Decision," *Reader's Digest*, September, 1967, p. 42.

[2] David Halberstam, "The Second Coming of Martin Luther King," *Harper's*, August, 1967, p. 49.

[3] David L. Lewis, *King: A Critical Biography* (New York: Praeger Publishers, Inc., 1970), p. 357.

[4] Martin Luther King, Jr., "Showdown for Non-Violence," *Look*, April 16, 1968, p. 25.

[5] William Robert Miller, *Martin Luther King, Jr.* (New York: Avon Books, 1968), pp. 287-288.

[6] *Ibid.*

[7] Jim Bishop, *The Days of Martin Luther King, Jr.* (New York: G. P. Putnam's Sons, 1971), pp. 54-62.

[8] *U.S. News and World Report*, April 22, 1968, p. 49.

[9] *Ibid.*, p. 50.

[10] John Henrik Clarke, "The New Afro-American Nationalism," *Freedomways*, Fall, 1961, pp. 285ff.

[11] *New York Times*, February 16, 1961.

[12] *Ibid.*, February 26, 1961.

[13] *Ibid.*, February 17, 1961.

[14] George Breitman, *The Last Year of Malcolm X: The Evolution of a Revolutionary* (New York: Merit Publishers, 1967), p. 57.

[15] Quoted in John Henrik Clarke, *Harlem, U.S.A.* (Berlin: Seven Seas Publishers, 1964), p. 85.

[16] Breitman, *Last Year of Malcolm X*, p. 59.

[17] LeRoi Jones, *Home: Social Essays* (New York: William Morrow & Co., Inc., 1966), p. 239.

[18]*Ibid.,* p. 244.

[19] James Forman, *The Making of Black Revolutionaries* (New York: The Macmillan Company, 1972), p. 451.

[20] Floyd McKissick, *Three-Fifths of a Man* (New York: The Macmillan Company, 1969), p. 145.

[21]*Ibid.,* p. 164.

[22] Clarke, "The New Afro-American Nationalism," *op. cit.,* pp. 290-291. Reprinted by permission of *Freedomways* magazine, vol. 1, no. 3 (1961). Published at 799 Broadway, New York City.

[23] Harold Cruse, *The Crisis of the Negro Intellectual: From Its Origins to the Present* (New York: William Morrow & Co., Inc., 1967), p. 556.

[24]*Life,* May 28; 1971, p. 63.

[25] Martin Oppenheimer, *The Urban Guerrilla* (Chicago: Quadrangle Books, 1969), p. 111.

[26] George Breitman, ed., *Malcolm X Speaks: Selected Speeches and Statements* (New York: Grove Press, Inc., 1965), p. 50.

[27] Frantz Fanon, *The Wretched of the Earth* (New York: Grove Press, Inc., 1963), p. 94.

[28] Cruse, *op. cit.,* pp. 351-353.

[29]*Ibid.,* p. 382.

[30]*Ibid.,* pp. 386-387.

[31] John Bracey *et al.,* eds., *Black Nationalism in America* (New York: The Bobbs-Merrill Co., Inc., 1970), pp. 508ff.

[32]*New York Times,* June 22, 1967.

[33]*Ibid.,* September 28, 1967.

[34] See "The Republic of New Africa: Short Official Basic Documents," *Republic of New Africa,* New Orleans, La.

[35]*New York Times,* August 24, 1969.

[36]*Esquire,* January, 1969, p. 75.

[37]*Ibid.*

[38]*Ibid.,* p. 74.

[39]*New York Times,* December 4, 1969.

[40]*Atlanta Journal,* August 19, 1971.

[41]*New York Times,* August 24, 1971.

[42] Robert S. Lecky and H. Elliott Wright, *Black Manifesto: Religion, Racism, and Reparations* (New York: Sheed & Ward, Inc., 1969), p. 7.

[43] Foreman, *op. cit.,* p. 545.

[44] Lecky and Wright, *op. cit.,* pp. 114-126.

[45]*Ibid.,* p. 116.

[46]*Ibid.,* p. 118.

[47]*Ibid.*

[48]*Ibid.*

[49]*Ibid.,* pp. 119-120.

[50]*New York Times,* May 5, 1969. See also Lecky and Wright, *op. cit,,* p. 127, footnote.

[51] Lecky and Wright, *op. cit.,* p. 128.

[52]*New York Times,* May 6, 1969.

[53]*Ibid.,* May 5, 1969.

[54] Lecky and Wright, *op. cit.,* pp. 157-162.

[55] Quoted in *ibid.,* p. 151.

[56]*The Christian Century,* May 21, 1969, p. 701.

[57]*Commonweal,* May 30, 1969, p. 308.

[58] Lecky and Wright, *op. cit.,* p. 141.

[59]*Ibid.,* p. 22.

[60] Forman, *op. cit.,* p. 548.

[61] Lecky and Wright, *op. cit.*, p. 13.
[62] Forman, *op. cit.*, p. 549.

CHAPTER 9

[1] "Gun-Barrel Politics: The Black Panther Party, 1966–1971," *Report by the Committee on Internal Security, House of Representatives, Ninety-Second Congress, First Session* (August 18, 1971), p. 143.

[2] *Ibid.*

[3] *Ibid.*, p. 135.

[4] Gene Marine, *The Black Panthers* (New York: Signet Books, 1969), pp. 12-17. See also Huey P. Newton, *Revolutionary Suicide* (New York: Harcourt Brace Jovanovich, Inc., 1973), p. 78.

[5] Bobby Seale, *Seize the Time: The Story of the Black Panther Party and Huey P. Newton* (New York: Vintage Books, 1970), p. 12. Used with permission of Random House, Inc.

[6] *Ibid.*, p. 20.

[7] *Ibid.*, pp. 30-31.

[8] *Ibid.*, pp. 33.

[9] *Ibid.*

[10] *Ibid.*, p. 59. See also Newton, *op. cit.*, pp. 114-115.

[11] *Ibid.*, pp. 66-68.

[12] *Ibid.*, pp. 63-64.

[13] Earl Anthony, *Picking Up the Gun* (New York: The Dial Press, 1970), p. 4. Copyright ©1970 by Earl Anthony. Reprinted by permission of The Dial Press, Inc. See also Newton, *op. cit.*, p. 113.

[14] *New York Times*, September 13, 1966.

[15] Seale, *op. cit.*, p. 65.

[16] *Ibid.*, pp. 73-76.

[17] *Ibid.*, p. 64.

[18] *Ibid.*, p. 80.

[19] Marine, *op. cit.*, pp. 45-46.

[20] Seale, *op. cit.*, pp. 85-93. See also Newton, *op. cit.*, p. 123.

[21] Don A. Schanche, *The Panther Paradox: A Liberal's Dilemma* (New York: David McKay Co., Inc., 1970), p. 34.

[22] Robert Scheer, ed., *Eldridge Cleaver: Post-Prison Writings and Speeches* (New York: Random House, Inc., 1967), p. 27.

[23] *Ibid.*, pp. 29-30.

[24] *Ibid.*, pp. 35-36. See also Seale, *op. cit.*, p. 128; and Newton, *op. cit.*, pp. 131-132.

[25] *Report by the Committee on Internal Security, House of Representatives* (hereafter H.C.I.S.), p. 25.

[26] Marine, *op. cit.*, pp. 62-63. See also Newton, *op. cit.*, p. 145.

[27] Seale, *op. cit.*, pp. 153-163.

[28] Anthony, *op. cit.*, p. 95.

[29] *Ibid.*, p. 24.

[30] Scheer, *op. cit.*, p. 27.

[31] Seale, *op. cit.*, p. 132.

[32] Scheer, *op. cit.*, pp. 57-72.

[33] *Ibid.*, pp. 172-173.

[34] Anthony, *op. cit.*, pp. 24-25.

[35] *Ibid.*, pp. 33-34.

[36] Marine, *op. cit.*, pp. 77ff. See also Newton, *op. cit.*, p. 174.

[37] Anthony, *op. cit.*, p. 44.

[38] *Ibid.*, p. 45.

[39] *Ibid.*, p. 58.
[40] James Forman, *The Making of Black Revolutionaries* (New York: The Macmillan Company, 1972), p. 530.
[41] *Ibid.*, p. 534.
[42] Marine, *op. cit.*, p. 123.
[43] Julius Lester, *Revolutionary Notes* (New York: Richard W. Baron Publishing Co., 1969), p. 144.
[44] Forman, *op. cit.*, p. 539.
[45] Chuck Moore, *I Was a Black Panther* (Garden City, N.Y.: Doubleday & Company, Inc., 1970), p. 101.
[46] Anthony, *op. cit.*, p. 104.
[47] Schanche, *op. cit.*, pp. 57-58.
[48] *Ibid.*, pp. 15-16.
[49] *New York Times Magazine*, October 27, 1968.
[50] Anthony, *op. cit.*, p. 97.
[51] Seale, *op. cit.*, pp. 412-422.
[52] *H.C.I.S.*, pp. 61-62.
[53] Seale, *op. cit.*, p. 417.
[54] *H.C.I.S.*, pp. 60-61.
[55] *Ibid.*, p. 60.
[56] *The Black Panther*, November 8, 1969.
[57] Stokely Carmichael, *Stokely Speaks: Black Power Back to Pan-Africanism* (New York: Random House, Inc., 1971), pp. 121-122.
[58] Anthony, *op. cit.*, p. 147.
[59] Philip S. Foner, ed., *The Black Panthers Speak* (Philadelphia: J. B. Lippincott Company, 1970), p. 229.
[60] *The Black Panther*, August 30, 1969.
[61] Schanche, *op. cit.*, p. 208.
[62] *The Black Panther*, August 29 and September 5, 1970.
[63] *Washington Post*, November 30, 1970.
[64] *H.C.I.S.*, p. 69.
[65] *The Black Panther*, January 4, 1969. See also Seale, *op. cit.*, pp. 389-391.
[66] *H.C.I.S.*, p. 86.
[67] Foner, *op. cit.*, p. xxvi.
[68] Party members Fred Hampton and Mark Clark were shot to death in this raid.
[69] *New York Times*, May 18, 1970.
[70] *H.C.I.S.*, p. 118.
[71] *The Black Panther*, February 27, 1971.
[72] Seale, *op. cit.*, p. 68.
[73] *Ibid.*, p. 349.
[74] *The Black Panther*, February 13, 1971. See also Newton, *op. cit.*, 302.
[75] *Liberated Guardian*, New York, February 25, 1971.
[76] *The Black Panther*, March 20, 1971. See also Newton, *op. cit.*, pp. 330-331.
[77] *The Black Panther*, April 17, 1971. Supplement.
[78] *Washington Post*, May 21, 1971.

CHAPTER 10

[1] John H. Bunzel, "Black Studies at San Francisco State," *The Public Interest*, Fall, 1968, pp. 25-27.
[2] *Ibid.*, pp. 27-28.
[3] Ralph F. Goldman, "Confrontation at S. F. State," *Dissent*, March-April, 1969, p. 169.
[4] *Ibid.*, p. 170.

[5] For a discussion of Dr. Hare's program, see Bunzel, *op. cit.*, pp. 28ff.

[6] *Ibid.*, p. 32.

[7] Goldman, *op. cit.*, p. 170.

[8] *Ibid.*, p. 172.

[9] Roger A. Fischer, "Ghetto and Gown: The Birth of Black Studies," *Current History*, November, 1969, p. 291.

[10] Notes from a conversation with Gordon Joyner, a senior at Morehouse College, Spring, 1971.

[11] Armstead L. Robinson, Craig C. Foster, and Donald H. Ogilvie, eds., *Black Studies in the University: A Symposium* (New Haven: Yale University Press, 1969), p. 219.

[12] *Ibid.*, p. vii.

[13] For the total program, see *ibid.*, Appendix.

[14] From notes prepared for this work by Clarence L. James, a black student at Harvard during this period.

[15] For Rosovsky's account of his work, see his "Black Studies at Harvard," *The American Scholar,* Autumn, 1969, pp. 562-572.

[16] Lawrence E. Eichel, Kenneth W. Jost, Robert D. Luskin, and Richard M. Neustadt, *The Harvard Strike* (Boston: Houghton Mifflin Company, 1970), pp. 268-269.

[17] *Ibid.*, p. 279 (footnote).

[18] *New York Times*, April 23, 1969.

[19] Eichel, Jost, Luskin, and Neustadt, *op. cit.*, p. 285.

[20] *New York Times*, April 27, 1969.

[21] Professor Richard A. Musgrave, *New York Times*, April 24, 1969.

[22] Michael Cohen, *Guns on Campus: Student Protest at Cornell* (Chicago: Urban Research Corporation, 1970), p. 4.

[23] *Ibid.*

[24] Allan P. Sindler, "A Case Study of a University's Pattern of Error," a paper presented at the annual meeting of the American Political Science Association, September, 1969, New York City, p. 8.

[25] Cohen, *op. cit.*, p. 7.

[26] Sindler, *op. cit.*, p. 10.

[27] Cohen, *op. cit.*, pp. 10-13.

[28] Sindler, *op. cit.*, p. 17, and *New York Times*, April 21, 1969.

[29] Cohen, *op. cit.*, p. 15.

[30] *Ibid.*, p. 18.

[31] *Ibid.*

[32] Sindler, *op. cit.*, pp. 19-20.

[33] Gene Marine, *The Black Panthers* (New York: Signet Books, 1969), pp. 208-210.

[34] Tobe Johnson, "Black Studies: Their Origin, Present State, and Prospects," a paper presented at the American Conference of Academic Deans in Pittsburgh, Pennsylvania, January 13, 1969.

[35] "Black Studies: Perspective 1970," *Danforth News and Notes*, March 1, 1970, Danforth Foundation, St. Louis, Missouri.

[36] "An Approach to Black Studies," a statement of the Planning Staff Institute of the Black World, Martin Luther King, Jr., Memorial Center, May, 1969.

[37] Johnson, *op. cit.*

[38] Stephen Lythcott, "The Case for Black Studies," *The Antioch Review*, Summer, 1969, p. 153.

[39] *New York Times*, May 3, 1969.

[40] *Ibid.*, May 7, 1969.

[41] *New York Times*, February 1, 1970.

[42] *Danforth News and Notes, op. cit.*

[43] Robinson, Foster, and Ogilvie, *op. cit.*, p. 177.

CHAPTER 11

[1] Stokely Carmichael and Charles V. Hamilton, *Black Power: The Politics of Liberation in America* (New York: Random House, Inc., 1967), p. 104.

[2] *Ibid.*

[3] "Political Participation," *A Report of the United States Commission on Civil Rights* (Washington, D.C., May, 1968), p. 41.

[4] *Ibid.*, p. 58.

[5] *Ibid.*, pp. 21ff.

[6] *Ibid.*, p. 164.

[7] Pat Watters and Reese Cleghorn, *Climbing Jacob's Ladder: The Arrival of Negroes in Southern Politics* (New York: Harcourt Brace Jovanovich, Inc., 1967), p. 266.

[8] *Jackson Daily News*, November 4, 1971.

[9] See Charles S. Rooks, *The Atlanta Elections of 1969* (Atlanta: The Voter Education Project, Inc., June, 1970).

[10] *The Atlanta Constitution*, February 24, 1972.

[11] Kenneth B. Clark, Julian Bond, and Richard G. Hatcher, *The Black Man in American Politics*, Metropolitan Applied Research Center and Institute for Black Elected Officials, December, 1969, pp. 133-134.

[12] Alan Shank, *Political Power and the Urban Crisis* (Boston: Holbrook Press, 1969), pp. 88-94.

[13] Samuel Lubell, *The Hidden Crisis in American Politics* (New York: W. W. Norton & Company, Inc., 1970), p. 105.

[14] *Ibid.*, pp. 97-98.

[15] *Ibid.*, p. 40.

[16] Carmichael, *Black Power*, p. 80.

[17] Jeffrey K. Hadden, Lewis B. Masotti, and Victor Thiessen, "The Making of Negro Mayors, 1967," in Shank, *op. cit.*, pp. 225-226.

[18] *Ibid.*, p. 227.

[19] *Ibid.*, p. 231.

[20] *Ibid.*, p. 230.

[21] *New York Times*, November 8, 1967.

[22] *Ibid.*

[23] Imamu Amiri Baraka (LeRoi Jones), *Raise Race Rays Raze: Essays Since 1965* (New York: Random House, Inc., 1969), p. 65.

[24] *New York Times*, December 18, 1969.

[25] *Ibid.*, June 17, 1970.

[26] *Ibid.*

[27] See Tobe Johnson, "Metropolitan Government: A Black Analytical Perspective," Joint Center for Political Studies, Washington, D.C., 1972.

[28] *New York Times*, September 11, 1969.

[29] *Ibid.*

[30] *JCPS, Newsletter*, Joint Center for Political Studies, Washington, D.C., December, 1971.

[31] *New York Times*, April 5, 1972.

[32] *Congressional Record*, 90th Congress, 1st Session, vol. 113, part 4, March 1, 1967, pp. 5020-5037.

[33] *Ibid.*, 91st Congress, 1st Session, vol. 115, part 1, January 3, 1969, pp. 30-34.

[34] *Newsweek*, June 7, 1971, pp. 30-31.

[35] *New York Times*, January 22, 1971.

[36] *Ibid.*, February 16, 1971.

[37] *Ibid.*, March 27, 1971.

[38] *Ibid.*, March 29, 1971.

[39] *Ibid.*, June 20, 1971.

[40] *Ibid.*, November 23, 1971.

[41] *Ibid.*, June 20, 1971.

[42] John Bracey, Jr., August Meier, and Elliott Rudwick, eds., *Black Nationalism in America* (New York: The Bobbs-Merrill Company, Inc., 1970), p. 503.

[43] Andrew F. Brimmer, "Income and Welfare in the Black Community," *Ebony*, October, 1972, pp. 65-66.

[44] Charles Tate, "Brimmer and Black Capitalism: An Analysis," *The Review of Black Political Economy*, Spring Summer, 1970, p. 85.

[45] *Newsweek*, January 12, 1970, p. 59.

[46] Leon H. Sullivan, *Build Brother Build* (Philadelphia: Macrae Smith Company, 1969), pp. 69, 76, 77.

[47] *Ibid.*, p. 112.

[48] *Ibid.*, pp. 132-134.

[49] *Ibid.*, pp. 166-170. See also Leon Sullivan, *Alternatives to Despair* (Valley Forge: Judson Press, 1972), pp. 92-97.

[50] *Ibid.*, pp. 169-173.

CHAPTER 12

[1] Donald Gibson, *Five Black Writers: Essays on Wright, Ellison, Baldwin, Hughes, and LeRoi Jones* (New York: New York University Press, 1970), p. 256. Reprinted by permission of New York University Press.

[2] Richard Wright, *Native Son* (New York: Harper & Row, Publishers, 1940), p. 364.

[3] *Ibid.*, p. 392.

[4] *Ibid.*, pp. 361-362.

[5] Fern Marja Eckman, *The Furious Passage of James Baldwin* (New York: M. Evans & Co., Inc., 1966), p. 104.

[6] James Baldwin, *Tell Me How Long the Train's Been Gone* (New York: The Dial Press, Inc., 1968), p. 479.

[7] Frantz Fanon, *The Wretched of the Earth* (New York: Grove Press, Inc., 1963), pp. 222-223.

[8] *Ibid.*, p. 226.

[9] LeRoi Jones, *Home: Social Essays* (New York: William Morrow & Co., Inc., 1966), p. 251.

[10] Harold Cruse, *The Crisis of the Negro Intellectual* (New York: William Morrow & Co., Inc., 1967), p. 355.

[11] Gibson, *op. cit.*, p. 194.

[12] Cruse, *op. cit.*, p. 356.

[13] Gibson, *op. cit.*, p. 194.

[14] Jones, *op. cit.*, pp. 214-215.

[15] Cruse, *op. cit.*, p. 541.

[16] "OBAC—A Year Later," *Negro Digest*, vol. 17, no. 9 (July, 1968), pp. 92-93.

[17] *Negro Digest*, January, 1968, p. 13.

[18] *Ibid.*

[19] Addison Gayle, *The Black Aesthetic* (Garden City, N.Y.: Anchor Books, 1972), p. xxii.

[20] Addison Gayle, *Black Expression: Essays by and About Americans in the Creative Arts* (New York: Weybright and Talley, Inc., 1969), p. 268.

[21] *Negro Digest*, January, 1968, p. 12.

[22] *Ibid.*, p. 28.

[23] *New York Times Book Review*, August 13, 1972.

[24] *Saturday Review*, July 17, 1971, p. 16.

[25] Fanon, *op. cit.*, p. 69.

[26] Bobby Seale, *Seize the Time: The Story of the Black Panther . . .* (New York: Vintage Books, 1970), p. 34.

[27] Fanon, *op. cit.*, pp. 215-216.

[28] Seale, *op. cit.*, p. 13.

[29] E. Franklin Frazier, *Black Bourgeoisie: The Rise of a New Middle Class in the United States* (Glencoe, Ill.: The Free Press, 1957), p. 213.

[30] Kenneth Clark, *Dark Ghetto* (New York: Harper & Row, Publishers, 1965), p. 81.

[31] William H. Grier and Price M. Cobbs, *Black Rage* (New York: Bantam Books, Inc., 1969), p. 174.

[32] *New York Times Book Review*, September 22, 1968.

[33] Grier and Cobbs, *op. cit.*, p. 177.

CHAPTER 13

[1] Stokely Carmichael and Charles Hamilton, *Black Power: The Politics of Liberation in America* (New York: Random House, Inc., 1967), p. 44.

[2] *Newsweek*, November 13, 1972, p. 18.

Index